SERVICE
MANAGEMENT

SERVICE MANAGEMENT

AN INTEGRATED APPROACH TO SUPPLY CHAIN MANAGEMENT AND OPERATIONS

Cengiz Haksever

Barry Render

Vice President, Publisher: Tim Moore
Associate Publisher and Director of Marketing: Amy Neidlinger
Executive Editor: Jeanne Glasser
Editorial Assistant: Pamela Boland
Operations Specialist: Jodi Kemper
Marketing Manager: Megan Graue
Cover Designer: Alan Clements
Managing Editor: Kristy Hart
Project Editor: Betsy Gratner
Copy Editor: Apostrophe Editing Services
Proofreader: Debbie Williams
Indexer: Erika Millen
Senior Compositor: Gloria Schurick
Manufacturing Buyer: Dan Uhrig

© 2013 by Cengiz Haksever and Barry Render
Published by Pearson Education, Inc.
Publishing as FT Press
Upper Saddle River, New Jersey 07458

FT Press offers excellent discounts on this book when ordered in quantity for bulk purchases or special sales. For more information, please contact U.S. Corporate and Government Sales, 1-800-382-3419, corpsales@pearsontechgroup.com. For sales outside the U.S., please contact International Sales at international@pearsoned.com.

Company and product names mentioned herein are the trademarks or registered trademarks of their respective owners.

Printed in the United States of America

First Printing June 2013

ISBN-10: 0-13-308877-4
ISBN-13: 978-0-13-308877-9

Pearson Education LTD.
Pearson Education Australia PTY, Limited.
Pearson Education Singapore, Pte. Ltd.
Pearson Education Asia, Ltd.
Pearson Education Canada, Ltd.
Pearson Educación de Mexico, S.A. de C.V.
Pearson Education—Japan
Pearson Education Malaysia, Pte. Ltd.

Library of Congress Cataloging-in-Publication Data

Haksever, Cengiz.
Service management : an integrated approach to supply chain management and operations / Cengiz Haksever, Barry Render. — 1 Edition.
      pages cm
  ISBN-13: 978-0-13-308877-9 (hardcover : alk. paper)
  ISBN-10: 0-13-308877-4
  1. Service industries—Management. 2. Business logistics. I. Render, Barry. II. Title.
  HD9980.5.H345 2013
  658—dc23
                                              2013001438

This book is dedicated to
Fulya—CH
and to
Donna, Charlie, and Jesse—BR

CONTENTS

3
CUSTOMERS: THE FOCUS OF SERVICE MANAGEMENT 39

4
GLOBALIZATION OF SERVICES 55

Part II: Building the Service System

7

TECHNOLOGY AND ITS IMPACT ON SERVICES AND THEIR MANAGEMENT   109

8

DESIGN AND DEVELOPMENT OF SERVICES AND SERVICE DELIVERY SYSTEMS   129

9

SUPPLY CHAINS IN SERVICES AND THEIR MANAGEMENT 161

10

LOCATING FACILITIES AND DESIGNING THEIR LAYOUT 181

Part III: Operating the Service System

12
SERVICE QUALITY AND CONTINUOUS IMPROVEMENT 247

12 SUPPLEMENT
TOOLS AND TECHNIQUES OF TOTAL QUALITY MANAGEMENT 269

13

SERVICE PRODUCTIVITY AND MEASUREMENT OF PERFORMANCE 291

14

MANAGEMENT OF PUBLIC AND PRIVATE NONPROFIT SERVICE ORGANIZATIONS 321

Part IV: Tools and Techniques for Managing Service Operations

15
FORECASTING DEMAND FOR SERVICES   341

16
VEHICLE ROUTING AND SCHEDULING   365

17

PROJECT MANAGEMENT 387

18

LINEAR AND GOAL PROGRAMMING APPLICATIONS FOR SERVICES 409

19
SERVICE INVENTORY
SYSTEMS 435

Appendix
AREAS UNDER THE STANDARD
NORMAL CURVE 455

Index
459

ABOUT THE AUTHORS

Cengiz Haksever is a Professor of Management Sciences at the College of Business Administration of Rider University. He received his B.S. and M.S. degrees in Industrial Engineering from Middle East Technical University in Ankara, Turkey, his M.B.A. from Texas A & M University in College Station, Texas, and his Ph.D. in Operations Research from the University of Texas in Austin.

His research interests include service management, supply chain management, operations research, operations management, quality and continuous improvement, and data envelopment analysis. Dr. Haksever's work appeared in *European Journal of Operational Research*, *Journal of the Operational Research Society*, *Computers & Operations Research*, *Computers & Industrial Engineering*, *Journal of Construction Engineering and Management*, *International Journal of Production Economics*, *Journal of Small Business Strategy*, *Journal of Business Ethics*, *Education Economics*, *International Journal of Production Economics*, *International Journal of Information and Management Sciences*, and *Business Horizons*.

He has taught courses in operations management, supply chain management, service operations management, management science, quality assurance, statistics, and regression in undergraduate and M.B.A. programs. He served as examiner and senior examiner for the New Jersey Governor's Award for Performance Excellence. During the 1993–1994 academic year, he was a Fulbright Senior Lecturer at Marmara University in Istanbul, Turkey. At Rider University, he was awarded the Jessie H. Harper Professorship for the academic year of 2000–2001. Dr. Haksever served on the Editorial Advisory Board of *Computers & Operations Research* and was a guest editor of a special issue of the journal *Data Envelopment Analysis*.

Barry Render is Professor Emeritus, the Charles Harwood Professor of Operations Management, Crummer Graduate School of Business, Rollins College, Winter Park, Florida. He received his B.S. in Mathematics and Physics at Roosevelt University and his M.S. in Operations Research and Ph.D. in Quantitative Analysis at the University of Cincinnati. He previously taught at George Washington University, University of New Orleans, Boston University, and George Mason University, where he held the Mason Foundation Professorship in Decision Sciences and was Chair of the Decision Sciences Department. Dr. Render has also worked in the aerospace industry for General Electric, McDonnell Douglas, and NASA.

Professor Render has coauthored 10 textbooks for Prentice Hall, including *Managerial Decision Modeling with Spreadsheets*, *Quantitative Analysis for Management*, *Service Management*, *Introduction to Management Science*, and *Cases and Readings in Management Science*. *Quantitative Analysis for Management*, now in its eleventh edition, is a leading text in that discipline in the United States and globally. Dr. Render's more than 100 articles on a variety of management topics have appeared in *Decision Sciences, Production and Operations Management, Interfaces, Information and Management, Journal of Management Information Systems, Socio-Economic Planning Sciences, IIE Solutions,* and *Operations Management Review,* among others.

Dr. Render has been honored as an AACSB Fellow and was twice named a Senior Fulbright Scholar. He was Vice President of the Decision Science Institute Southeast Region and served as Software Review Editor for *Decision Line* for six years and as Editor of *The New York Times* Operations Management special issues for five years. From 1984 to 1993, Dr. Render was President of Management Service Associates of Virginia, Inc., whose technology clients included the FBI, the U.S. Navy, Fairfax County, Virginia, and C&P Telephone. He is currently Consulting Editor to *Financial Times Press.*

Dr. Render has taught operations management courses in Rollins College's M.B.A. and Executive M.B.A. programs. He has received that school's Welsh Award as leading professor and was selected by Roosevelt University as the 1996 recipient of the St. Claire Drake Award for Outstanding Scholarship. In 2005, Dr. Render received the Rollins College M.B.A. Student Award for Best Overall Course and in 2009 was named Professor of the Year by full-time M.B.A. students.

PREFACE

This book has been written to serve as a resource and reference book for professionals in service organizations. This text has been written from a multidisciplinary perspective. Discussions of topics blend concepts, theory, and practice from fields such as operations, marketing, international management, economics, strategy, psychology, human resources, and management science. The authors believe a multidisciplinary approach is best for efficient and effective management of service organizations and their operations.

The book can also be used as a textbook for college-level courses such as Service Management or Service Operations Management with its companion textbook. Although Parts I and II present nonquantitative material, Parts III and IV present both quantitative and nonquantitative material that can be used for efficient and effective management of service operations. Because of this, it is suitable for a service management course with or without quantitative orientation. It is also suitable for a traditional operations management course with special emphasis on services.

Part I, "Understanding Services," consists of Chapters 1 through 6 and focuses on *understanding services*. It introduces the reader to the service concept and provides background material in several important areas. Chapter 1, "The Important Role Services Play in an Economy," addresses the role of services in our society. Chapter 2, "The Nature of Services and Service Encounters," discusses characteristics of services and examines the importance of the service encounter. Chapter 3, "Customers: The Focus of Service Management," focuses on customers as consumers of services and their needs and motives as they impact service purchase decisions. Chapter 4, "Globalization of Services," provides an international perspective on services and discusses the challenges of globalization. Chapter 5, "Service Strategy and Competitiveness," prepares the groundwork for the three themes of quality, customer satisfaction, and value creation, and focuses on the impact of strategy on competitiveness. Chapter 6, "Ethical Challenges in Service Management," explores ethical issues and challenges managers, in general, and service managers in particular, face.

The emphasis of Part II, "Building the Service System," is on *building the system to create customer value and satisfaction* with superior quality services. Chapter 7, "Technology and Its Impact on Services and Their Management," focuses on the role technology plays in service management. Chapter 8, "Design and Development of Services and Service Delivery Systems," lays out the principles of service design and discusses the application of techniques that have been successfully used in manufacturing to build quality and value into services. Chapter 9, "Supply Chains in Services and Their Management," focuses on supply chains of service organizations. This section concludes with Chapter 10, "Locating Facilities and Designing Their Layout," which discusses two other important topics in building and operating the system: facility location and layout design.

Part III, "Operating the Service System," is concerned with issues related to *operating the service system* and challenges managers of service organizations face. One of the major challenges, managing the demand for and supply of services, is the topic of Chapter 11, "Managing Demand and Supply in Services." A supplement to this chapter, "Queuing and Simulation," covers two important topics: queuing and simulation. Chapter 12, "Service Quality and Continuous Improvement," provides the basic concepts of quality in general and service quality in particular. Technical aspects of quality assurance are presented in a supplement, "Tools and Techniques of Total Quality Management." One of the biggest challenges service managers face is increasing the productivity of service employees. This important topic and approaches to increasing productivity in service organizations are discussed in Chapter 13, "Service Productivity and Measurement of Performance." Also presented is a brief discussion of Data Envelopment Analysis as a powerful tool in measuring the efficiency of service organizations. Part III concludes with Chapter 14, "Management of Public and Private Nonprofit Service Organizations," with a discussion of an important segment of the service industry: public and nonprofit service organizations. The nature of these organizations as well as the challenges their managers face is discussed.

Part IV, "Tools and Techniques for Managing Service Operations," presents the *tools and techniques for managing service operations.* Chapter 15, "Forecasting Demand for Services," Chapter 16, "Vehicle Routing and Scheduling," Chapter 17, "Project Management," Chapter 18, "Linear and Goal Programming Applications for Services," and Chapter 19, "Service Inventory Systems," are included in this section.

We would like to thank our editor Jeanne Glasser Levine for envisioning this project and her encouragement for its completion. We also thank our project editor Betsy Gratner and the professional staff of FT Press for their help with the preparation of the book for publication. Last but not the least, we hope this text helps you achieve your professional and educational objectives as a successful manager and decision maker in any service organization.

1

THE IMPORTANT ROLE SERVICES PLAY IN AN ECONOMY

1.1 Introduction

There has been a surge of interest in all aspects of service management in recent times. Many books, articles, and research papers on services and service management have appeared in popular and academic business literature starting in the 1980s and continue to be published today. The impetus for this phenomenon can be traced back to two major developments in recent history. First, the quality movement that started in the 1980s had brought most consumers, news media, and academicians to the realization that the overall quality of services in the United States was not ideal, acceptable, or competitive in the international markets. Second, the fact that services no longer formed the least important (tertiary) sector of the economy became obvious. Contrary to the once widely held view among economists, services in the second half of the twentieth century had increasingly played a significant role in the economic life in the United States and in all industrialized countries.

Growing attention paid to service quality and customer satisfaction had stirred managers of many service organizations into action. Even the executives and managers of one service conglomerate almost everyone loved to criticize, the federal government, were not immune to the mounting pressure. A lot has been done to improve quality and customer satisfaction in most service industries during the 1980s and in the twenty-first century. As a result, there have been marked improvements in the quality of many services. Nevertheless, mediocre service quality is still a fact of life in the United States and around the world. Exhibit 1-1 confirms this fact.

Exhibit 1-1 American Customer Satisfaction Index (ACSI)

	Baseline 1994	1995	2000	2005	2010	2012
Manufacturing						
Durable goods	79.2	79.8	79.4	78.9	81.3	83.0
Nondurable goods	81.6	81.2	80.8	81.8	81.3	81.9
Services						
Accommodation & food services	73.2	71.6	71.2	74.2	77.3	79.4
Transportation	70.3	71.1	70.0	72.4	73.3	73.6
Information	78.5	78.3	69.4	65.8	72.8	71.9
Finance and insurance	78.5	74.1	74.4	73.9	76.1	75.4
E-Commerce	NA	NA	75.2	79.6	79.3	80.1
E-Business	NA	NA	63.0	75.9	73.5	74.2
Energy, utilities	75.0	74.0	75.0	73.1	74.1	76.7
Retail trade	75.7	74.6	72.9	72.4	75.0	76.1[†]
Health care & social assistance	74.0	74.0	69.0	70.8	77.0	78.5
Public administration/government	64.3	61.9	67.0	67.1	66.9	67.0[†]

NA: Not Available

[†] 2011 survey

Source: Adapted from American Customer Satisfaction Index 1994–2012 (http://www.theacsi.org/acsi-results/acsi-results)

Exhibit 1-1 presents a summary of American Customer Satisfaction Index (ACSI) numbers for select years between 1994 and 2012. The ACSI is designed to measure the quality of goods and services as evaluated by customers. The index is based on surveys of the customers of more than 200 organizations in more than 40 industries in seven major consumption areas.[1] It measures satisfaction by asking consumers to compare their expectations of a good or service with their actual experience with it. It is clear from the data that overall customer satisfaction with goods and services has fluctuated over the years but has not changed much. Referring to Exhibit 1-1 it can be seen that customer satisfaction with accommodation and food services, transportation, e-Commerce, and e-Business have increased over the years while satisfaction with other services had ups-and-downs. Actually, Information, Finance and Insurance, and Utilities declined from their baseline levels. Over the years, satisfaction with government services has been consistently the lowest of all services.

Perhaps the most important revelation of the ACSI data is that no service in the recent past has had a customer satisfaction index equal to those for goods. It is not certain if an index of 100 percent satisfaction will ever be achieved, or if that is even possible, in any industry. However, it is clear that both private and public service organizations have a long way to go, and managers of these organizations face a tremendous challenge. Will they rise to the challenge and raise customer satisfaction with services to the same levels attained by manufacturers, or possibly surpass them? We certainly hope so! This book is written with the hope that it can help managers of service organizations develop strategies and practices to do so. Chapter 1 begins by defining services and exploring the role of services in our society.

1.2 What Are Services?

The material gains of a society are achieved by adding value to natural resources. In advanced societies, there are many organizations that extract raw materials, add value through processing them, and transform intermediate materials and components into finished products. There are, however, other organizations that facilitate the production and distribution of goods, and organizations that add value to lives through a variety of intangibles they provide. Outputs of this latter group are called **services**.

Services can be defined as economic activities that produce time, place, form, or psychological utilities. Services are acts, deeds, or performances; they are intangible. A maid service saves the consumer **time** from doing household chores. Department stores and grocery stores provide many commodities for sale in one convenient **place**. A database service puts together information in a **form** more usable for the manager. A "night out" at a restaurant or movie provides **psychological** refreshment in the middle of a busy workweek.

Services also can be defined in contrast to goods. A **good** is a tangible object that can be created and sold or used later. A **service** is intangible and perishable. It is created and consumed simultaneously (or nearly simultaneously). Although these definitions may seem straightforward, the distinction between goods and services is not always clear-cut. For example, when we purchase a car, are we purchasing a good or the service of transportation? A television set is a manufactured good, but what use is it without the service of television broadcasting? When we go to a fast-food restaurant, are we buying the service of having our food prepared for us or are we buying goods that happen to be ready-to-eat food items?

In reality, almost all purchases of goods are accompanied by **facilitating services**, and almost every service purchase is accompanied by **facilitating goods**. Thus the key to understanding the difference between goods and services lies in the realization that these items are not completely distinct, but rather are two poles on a continuum. Exhibit 1-2 shows such a continuum.

Exhibit 1-2   A Comparison of Various Goods and Services

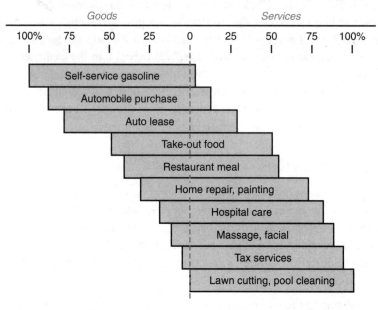

Source: Based on Earl W. Sasser, Jr., R.P. Olsen, and D. Daryl Wyckoff, *Management of Service Operations* (Boston, Allyn and Bacon, 1978), p.11.

Referring to Exhibit 1-2, one would probably classify the first three items as "goods" because of their high-material content. There is little service in purchasing self-service gasoline; an automobile is mostly a physical item; and although its lease does require some service, a leased car is a good. Take-out food can be considered as consisting of half good and half service. One would probably classify the remaining items as "services" because of their high-service content; although, some physical materials may be received. For instance, restaurants not only give the customer a meal of physical food and drink, but also a place to eat it, chefs to prepare it, waiters to serve it, and an atmosphere in which to dine. Tax preparation is almost pure service, with little material goods (most tax returns are now filed electronically) received by the consumer.

1.3 The Service Sector of the U.S. Economy

From a macro viewpoint, an economy may be divided into three different sectors for study: the extractive sector, which includes mining and agriculture; the goods producing sector, which includes manufacturing and construction; and the service sector. The service sector has a tremendous impact on the U.S. economy. The next five headings discuss this impact.

Employment—The role services play in terms of employment is the easiest to illustrate. The U.S. economy today is characterized as a "service economy." This is because the majority of the working population is employed in the service sector. Trend analyst John Naisbitt made the following observation: "In 1956, for the first time in American history, white-collar workers in technical, managerial, and clerical positions outnumbered blue-collar workers. Industrial America was giving way to a new society, where, for the first time in history, most of us worked with information rather than producing goods."[2] The share of the service jobs grew steadily to 76 percent by the mid-1990s, and as indicated in Exhibit 1-3, it had reached 84 percent by 2010. In other words, anyone who is planning to enter the workforce today has about an 84 percent chance that she'll be working in a service organization. Exhibit 1-4 illustrates the dramatic increase in service jobs since 1970.

Exhibit 1-3 U.S. Employment by Industry (Millions)

	1970		1980		1990		2000		2010	
Extraction	*4.14*	*6%*	*4.44*	*5%*	*3.99*	*4%*	*4.35*	*3%*	*4.17*	*3%*
Agriculture	3.46		3.36		3.22		3.75		3.42	
Mining and logging	0.68		1.08		0.77		0.6		0.75	
Goods producing	*21.5*	*30%*	*23.18*	*25%*	*22.96*	*20%*	*24.06*	*18%*	*17.04*	*13%*
Construction	3.65		4.45		5.26		6.79		5.52	
Durable goods	10.76		11.68		10.74		10.88		7.06	
Nondurable goods	7.09		7.05		6.96		6.39		4.46	
Service providing	*46.1*	*64%*	*66.26*	*70%*	*85.77*	*76%*	*107.1*	*79%*	*112.12*	*84%*
Wholesale trade	3.42		4.56		5.27		5.93		5.45	
Retail trade	7.46		10.24		13.18		15.28		14.44	
Utilities	0.54		0.65		0.74		0.6		0.55	
Transportation and warehousing	NA		2.96		3.48		4.41		4.19	
Information	2.04		2.36		2.69		3.63		2.71	
Financial activities	3.53		5.03		6.61		7.69		7.65	
Professional and business services	5.27		7.54		10.85		16.67		16.73	
Education and health services	4.58		7.07		10.98		15.11		19.53	
Leisure and hospitality	4.79		6.72		9.29		11.86		13.05	
Other services	1.79		2.75		4.26		5.17		5.33	
Government (Federal, state, and local)	12.69		16.38		18.42		20.79		22.49	
Total employed	**71.74**	**100%**	**93.88**	**100%**	**112.7**	**100%**	**135.6**	**100%**	**133.33**	**100%**

Source: Bureau of Labor Statistics, Employment, Hours, and Earnings from the Current Employment Statistics survey (National), http://data.bls.gov/cgi-bin/surveymost?ce (Accessed on 07/5/12).

Gross domestic product—Gross domestic product (GDP) is the total output of goods and services produced in the United States, valued at market prices. In other words, GDP represents the total value of goods and services attributable to labor and resources located in the United States. Services will be producing more than 82 percent of GDP in the years ahead. Exhibit 1-5 presents data on the breakdown of GDP and change in its composition since 1970. It is clear from this exhibit that service sector produces most of the value in our economy. This does not imply that manufacturing will eventually disappear or become unimportant, but it does indicate that more of the economic activity will be in the service sector. As shown in Exhibits 1-5 and 1-6, the share of GDP in extraction industries has been hovering above an average of approximately 2.5 percent in the last three decades. The share of goods production, however, has steadily declined to 15 percent in 2010 from a high of 27 percent in 1970.

Exhibit 1-4   How Jobs in the Service Sector Have Soared

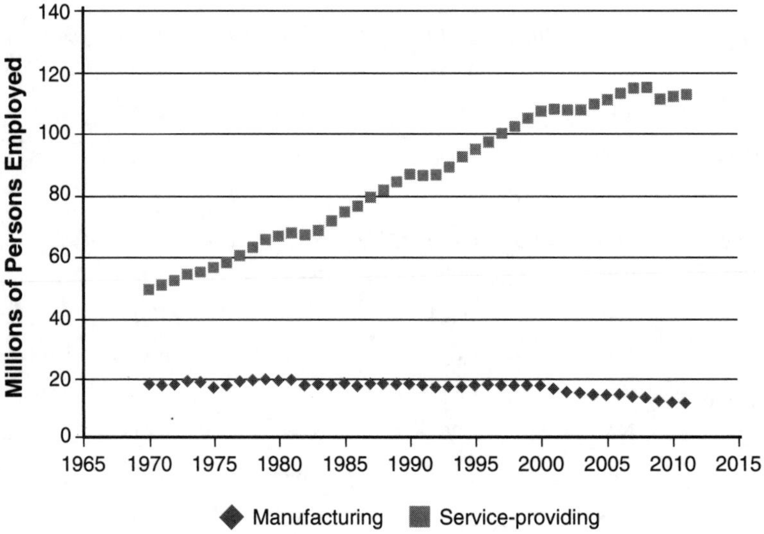

Source: Bureau of Labor Statistics, Employment, Hours, and Earnings from the Current Employment Statistics survey (National), http://data.bls.gov/cgi-bin/surveymost?ce (Accessed on 07/5/12).

Exhibit 1-5   U.S. Gross Domestic Product by Industry (in Billions of Dollars)

	1970		1980		1990		2000		2010	
Extraction	*42.4*	*4%*	*152.9*	*5%*	*184.1*	*3%*	*204.5*	*2%*	*396.5*	*3%*
Agriculture, forestry, fishing, and hunting	27.3		62.1		95.7		95.6		157	
Mining	15.1		90.8		88.4		108.9		239.5	
Goods producing	*285.1*	*27%*	*689.8*	*25%*	*1212.5*	*21%*	*1882.9*	*19%*	*2213.5*	*15%*
Construction	49.5		131.5		243.6		467.3		511.6	
Manufacturing	235.6		558.3		968.9		1415.6		1701.9	
Service producing	*711.0*	*69%*	*1945.3*	*70%*	*4404.1*	*76%*	*7864.1*	*79%*	*11916.5*	*82%*
Wholesale trade	67.7		186.3		347.7		617.7		797.3	
Retail trade	83		198.3		400.4		686.2		884.9	
Utilities	21.7		61		145.5		173.9		264.9	
Transportation and warehousing	40.2		102.6		172.8		301.4		402.5	
Information	37.4		108.3		235.6		417.8		623.5	
Finance, insurance, real estate, rental, and leasing	152.8		446.8		1049.2		1997.7		3007.2	
Professional and business services	52		173.1		516.5		1116.8		1782.8	
Educational services, health care, and social assistance	40.3		134.1		376.7		678		1272.3	
Arts, entertainment, recreation, accommodation, and food services	29.8		83		199.6		381.6		555.8	
Other services, except government	27.8		68.5		153.9		277.6		356.8	
Government	158.3		383.3		806.2		1215.4		1968.5	
Total Gross domestic product (*)	**1038.3**	**100%**	**2788.1**	**100%**	**5800.5**	**100%**	**9951.5**	**100%**	**14526.5**	**100%**

*Sum of extraction, goods producing, and service producing may not be equal to totals due to rounding.

Source: Bureau of Economic Analysis, "GDP by Industry." http://bea.gov/iTable/iTable.cfm?ReqID=5&step=1 (07-06-2012)

Number of business starts—Some of the new jobs are created in the existing organizations as they grow, but others are created when new companies are established. The service sector is where most new companies are formed. About 73 percent of all new private businesses are service companies. In other words, the service sector is "where the action is" and where entrepreneurial spirit is most vigorous.

Exhibit 1-6   Changes in Major Components of GDP over the Years 1970–2011

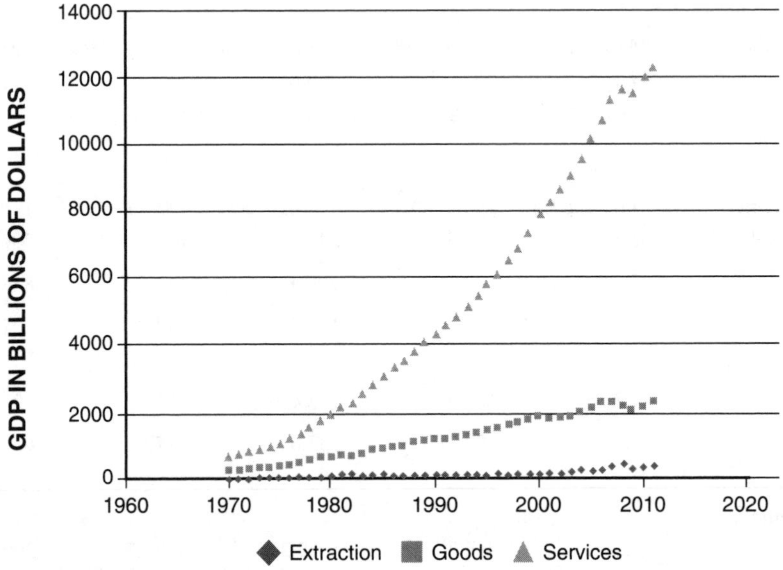

Source: Bureau of Economic Analysis, "GDP by Industry."
http://bea.gov/iTable/iTable.cfm?ReqID=5&step=1 (07-06-2012)

International trade—Services also play an important role in the U.S. international trade. During the 1960s and 1970s, service exports constituted approximately 22 percent of the U.S. exports. However, in the 2000s the service exports have reached approximately 30 percent of the total exports. The United States also imports services from abroad; currently, approximately 20 percent of the imports are services. The most important fact, however, is that the service exports consistently exceeded service imports since 1971. In other words, services exported bring more revenue than what is paid to other nations for their services. The U.S. has had a negative trade balance every year since 1976. That is, what we paid to other countries for goods and services we bought from them exceeded what we received from them for the goods and services we sold to them. Exhibit 1-7 provides international trade balance data from the recent past. As can be seen from this exhibit, the trade deficit would have been much bigger if it weren't for the surplus in service trade.

Exhibit 1-7   U.S. Trade Balance (Billions of Dollars)

Year	Total	Goods	Services
1960	3.51	4.89	−1.38
1970	3.90	2.58	−0.35
1980	−19.41	−25.50	6.09
1990	−80.87	−111.04	30.17
2000	−376.75	−445.79	69.04
2010	−516.90	−645.12	150.39

Source: Bureau of Economic Analysis, Table 1 U.S. International Transactions, http://www.bea.gov/international/xls/table1.xls (07/10/2012).

Contributions to manufacturing—Although we customarily divide the economy into three sectors, these sectors are not wholly independent of each other. The relationship between manufacturing and services is the strongest; one cannot exist without the other. Some services would not exist if not for goods. For example, automobile repair service would not exist without cars. Similarly, some goods would not exist without the existence of services. For example, stadiums would not be built if there were no football, baseball, or soccer to be played in them; or there would be no drugs to cure illnesses without research and development services.

The relationship between manufacturing and services goes much beyond this simple relationship in which one uses the output of the other. Most manufacturing companies would not produce goods without the support of numerous services. Some of these services are commonly provided internally, such as accounting, design, advertising, and legal services. Other services are provided by outside vendors in areas such as banking, telecommunication, transportation, and police and fire protection.

1.4 Theories Explaining the Growth of Services

Economists have been studying the reasons for the growth of services for many years. An early contribution to this line of inquiry was by A.G.B. Fisher who introduced the concept of primary, secondary, and tertiary industries.[3] Primary production was defined as agriculture, pastoral production, fishing, forestry, hunting, and mining. Secondary production consisted of manufacturing and construction. Some authors included mining in this category. Finally, tertiary production was composed of transportation, communications, trade, government, and personal services. Fisher suggested that an economy can be characterized with respect to the proportion of its labor force employed in these sectors. He also argued that as income rises demand shifts from the primary to secondary and then to tertiary sectors. Sociologist Daniel Bell described the development of human societies in three general stages.[4]

Preindustrial society—The dominant characteristic of economic activity in pre-industrial society is extractive, that is, agriculture, fishing, forestry, and mining. Life is primarily a game against nature. The level of technology is low or nonexistent; people are dependent on raw muscle power to survive, and therefore the productivity is low. Their success is largely dependent on the elements: the seasons, the rain, and the nature of the soil. The social life is organized around the family and extended household. Because of low productivity and large population, there is significant underemployment, which is resident in both the agricultural and domestic-service sectors. Because most people in this society struggle not to starve, they often seek only enough to feed themselves. Thus there is a large number of people employed or available to be employed in personal or household services (see Exhibit 1-8).

Exhibit 1-8   Preindustrial Society

Economic Sector	Occupational Scope	Technology	Design	Methodology	Time Perspective	Axial Principle
PRIMARY: EXTRACTIVE ■ Agriculture ■ Mining ■ Fishing ■ Timber	■ Farmer ■ Miner ■ Fisherman ■ Unskilled	■ Primitive ■ Raw materials	■ Game against nature	■ Common sense and experience	■ Orientation to the past ■ Ad hoc responses	■ Traditional ■ Limited resources

Source: Adapted from Daniel Bell, *The Coming of Post-Industrial Society: A Venture in Social Forecasting* (New York, Basic Books, 1973), p. 117.

Industrial society—The dominant characteristic of economic activity in industrial society is goods production. Life is a game against fabricated nature. Economic and social life has become mechanized and more efficient. Machines and the energy that powers them dominate production; they have replaced muscle power. Productivity has increased tremendously; the art of making more with less is valued. The economic watchwords are maximization and optimization. Division of labor is further extended. Technological advancements lead to new, faster, and more specialized machines that constantly improve productivity and replace more workers. The workplace is where men, women, materials, and machines are organized for efficient production and distribution of goods. It is a world of planning and scheduling in which components for production are brought together at the right time and in the right proportions to speed the flow of goods. The workplace is also a world of organization based on bureaucracy and hierarchy. People are treated as "things" because it is easier to coordinate things than people. The unit of social life is the individual in a free market society. Quantity of goods possessed by an individual is an indicator of his standard of living (see Exhibit 1-9).

Exhibit 1-9   Industrial Society

Economic Sector	Occupational Scope	Technology	Design	Methodology	Time Perspective	Axial Principle
SECONDARY: ■ Goods producing ■ Manufacturing	■ Semiskilled worker ■ Engineer	■ Energy	■ Game against fabricated nature	■ Empiricism ■ Experimentation	■ Ad hoc adaptiveness ■ Projections	■ Economic growth: State or private control of investment decisions

Source: Adapted from Daniel Bell, *The Coming of Post-Industrial Society: A Venture in Social Forecasting* (New York, Basic Books, 1973), p. 117.

Postindustrial society—The dominant characteristic of economic activity in postindustrial society is service production. Life is now a game between persons. What matters now is not muscle or machine power or energy, but information and knowledge. The central character of economic life is the professional. She possesses the kinds of skills and knowledge increasingly demanded in this society. This demand for increased technical knowledge and skills in the workplace makes higher education a prerequisite to entry into postindustrial society and good life. The quantity and quality of services such as health, education, and recreation that an individual can afford are indicators of his standard of living. Citizens' demand for more services such as healthcare, education, arts, and so on and the inadequacy of the market mechanism in meeting these demands lead to the growth of government, especially at the state and local level (see Exhibit 1-10).

Exhibit 1-10 Postindustrial Society

Economic Sector	Occupational Scope	Technology	Design	Methodology	Time Perspective	Axial Principle
TERTIARY: ■ Transportation ■ Recreation						
QUATERNARY: ■ Trade ■ Finance ■ Insurance ■ Real estate	■ Professional and technical ■ Scientists	■ Information	■ Game between persons	■ Abstract theory: models, simulation, decision theory, systems analysis	■ Future orientation ■ Forecasting	■ Centrality of and codification of theoretical knowledge
QUINARY: ■ Health ■ Education ■ Research ■ Government						

Source: Adapted from Daniel Bell, *The Coming of Post-Industrial Society: A Venture in Social Forecasting* (New York, Basic Books, 1973), p. 117.

Several substages are involved in the transition from an industrial to a postindustrial society. First, an expansion of services such as transportation and public utilities is needed for the development of industry and distribution of goods. Second, mass consumption of goods and population growth require an expansion of wholesale and retail services, as well as services such as finance, real estate, and insurance. Finally, as personal incomes rise, the percentage of money devoted to food declines. Increments in income are first spent for durable consumer goods, such as housing, automobiles, and appliances. Further increases in income are spent on services such as education, healthcare, vacations, travel, restaurants, entertainment, and sports. This tendency in consumption behavior leads to the growth of the personal services sector.

There are many other reasons given to explain the growth of services; some inspired by the theories previously discussed, and some are independently developed by various researchers. Some of these are summarized as follows.[5]

■ The increase in efficiency of agriculture and manufacturing that releases labor to services

■ The flow of workers from agriculture and other extraction to manufacturing and then to services

- The application of comparative advantage in international trade

- A decrease in investment as a percentage of gross domestic product (GDP) in high-income industrialized countries or an increase in the percentage of the GDP in low-income countries

- A rise in per capita income

- An increase in urbanization

- Deregulation

- Demographic shifts

- An increase in international trade

- Joint symbiotic growth of services with manufacturing

- Advances in information and telecommunication technologies

1.5 Overview of the Book

This book covers a wide range of issues in managing service organizations and their operations. It focuses on creating value and customer satisfaction. Therefore, the book is designed to provide a comprehensive coverage of topics relevant to that end. Its content is quite different from traditional operations management textbooks; although we have also included some of the topics covered in those books. The discussions draw upon the knowledge and experience of various areas of business as well as on disciplines other than business. For example, discussions frequently rely on the theory and practice of strategy, marketing, international management, human resources, management science, economics, psychology, and sociology. Hopefully, this multidisciplinary and cross-functional approach helps managers and future managers develop a well-rounded and solid understanding of the complexities of services and their management.

The book is organized in four parts. Part I, Chapters 1–6, begins with this introduction and focuses on developing an in-depth understanding of services. Chapter 2 discusses the nature of services and service encounters. Chapter 3 examines customers and their needs, and factors that influence their decisions in services purchasing. Chapter 4 discusses the globalization of services and forms of globalization. Chapter 5 deals with the issues concerning value creation and service strategy. Finally, Chapter 6 contains a discussion of ethical issues in service management and ethical challenges managers face.

Part II covers topics relevant to developing service systems. Building a competitive service system that creates value and customer satisfaction requires the effective use of certain inputs. These inputs are technology (Chapter 7), service design and development (Chapter 8), service supply chains (Chapter 9), the selection of an appropriate site for a service facility, and the design of its layout (Chapter 10).

Part III is devoted to topics that are crucial to managers for operating a service system effectively and efficiently. Topics covered in this part include managing demand and supply (Chapter 11), service quality and continuous improvement (Chapter 12), and service productivity and measurement of performance (Chapter 13). Chapter 14 includes a brief study of the management of public and nonprofit service organizations because these organizations play an increasingly important role in our economic and social life.

Part IV presents various quantitative tools and techniques for managing service operations. This part contains chapters discussing some of the most powerful and widely used quantitative techniques in managing operations of both manufacturing and service organizations. Chapter 15 discusses forecasting. Chapter 16 focuses on techniques to optimize decisions in routing vehicles. Project management is discussed in Chapter 17, and linear and goal programming is discussed in Chapter 18. Chapter 19, the final chapter of this part, covers inventory systems for service operations.

1.6 Summary

This chapter examined the concept of services from a macro viewpoint. Definitions of service and service economies were presented, as well as the importance of services in our society. It discussed the important role services play in the U.S. economy for employment, gross domestic product, number of business starts, international trade, and contributions to manufacturing. We then considered the theories explaining why services grew so much in the economies of industrial nations in the second half of the twentieth century. Theories concerning the three types of production, primary, secondary, and tertiary industries and how societies may migrate from one dominant form of production to the next also were discussed.

Endnotes

1. Claes Fornell, Michael D. Johnson, Eugene W. Anderson, Jaesung Cha, and Barbara E. Bryant, "The American Customer Satisfaction Index: Nature, Purpose, and Findings," *Journal of Marketing*, Vol. 60 (October 1996), pp. 7–18.

2. John Naisbitt, *Megatrends: Ten New Directions Transforming Our Lives* (New York, Warner Books, 1982), p. 12.

3. A. G. B. Fisher, "Economic Implications of Material Progress," *International Labour Review* (July 1935), pp. 5–18; and "Primary, Secondary and Tertiary Production," *Economic Record* (June 1939), pp. 24–38.

4. The discussion of preindustrial, industrial, and postindustrial societies has been adopted from Daniel Bell, *The Coming of Post-Industrial Society: A Venture in Social Forecasting* (New York, Basic Books, 1973), pp. 123–129.

5. For a more detailed discussion of the various theories explaining the growth of services, see P. W. Daniels, *Service Industries in the World Economy* (Oxford, UK, Blackwell Publishers, 1993), Chapter 1, pp. 1–24; Steven M. Shugan "Explanations for the Growth of Services," in Roland T. Rust and Richard L. Oliver (Eds.), *Service Quality: New Directions in Theory and Practice* (Thousand Oaks, London, Sage Publications, 1994), pp. 223–240; and J. N. Marshall and P. A. Wood, *Services and Space: Key Aspects of Urban and Regional Development* (Essex, England, Longman Scientific and Technical, 1995), Chapter 2, pp. 9–37.

2

THE NATURE OF SERVICES AND SERVICE ENCOUNTERS

2.1 Introduction

The definition of a service business or service organization has been a continuing problem for students of productive systems. Manufacturing is often taken as the point of departure, and service organizations are distinguished in terms of differences from manufacturing organizations. This approach tries to identify services by some criteria for the output, the process, or the consumption of the output that contrasts with manufacturing organizations.

This chapter examines the general concepts of a productive system and the characteristics that make services unique. Also discussed are service encounters that play a crucial role in the relationship between a customer and a service organization and significantly impact perceptions of service quality, customer satisfaction, and repeat purchase decisions.

2.2 General Concept of a Productive System

A **system** is, simply, a set of elements that works toward a common goal by acting on inputs to produce outputs. A productive system is one that adds value, economic or otherwise, in the conversion of inputs to outputs. A general representation of a productive system is shown in Exhibit 2-1.

Exhibit 2-1   A General Productive System

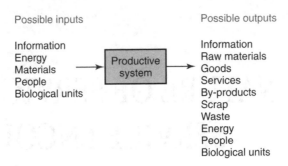

Possible inputs

Information
Energy
Materials
People
Biological units

Productive
system

Possible outputs

Information
Raw materials
Goods
Services
By-products
Scrap
Waste
Energy
People
Biological units

A productive system consists of physical elements related to each other. There are five types of productive systems:

1. Extraction of materials or energy from the environment

2. Biological growth and change

3. Tangible output conversion systems

4. Intangible output conversion systems

5. Hybrid conversion systems

Examples of each of these are shown in Exhibit 2-2. **Services**, as usually defined, fall into either of the last two groups. For example, a restaurant is generally considered to be a service, but its output consists of both tangible and intangible components. For example, although the food consumed by the customer is tangible, the pleasant dining experience is an intangible component of the service. Manufacturing organizations also fall within two groups, the third and the fifth. The sole output of a manufacturing organization cannot be intangible (the fourth group). However most "manufacturing" firms provide a *combination* of tangible and intangible outputs. Consider a custom automobile "manufacturer" that works in contact with a customer throughout the process. Is this firm actually a manufacturer or is it primarily a "service" firm?

Exhibit 2-2   Types of Productive Systems

Extraction

Mining the earth (or moon) surface

Mining under the ocean

Processing oceans or other bodies of water
(such as salt lakes)

Extracting gases from the atmosphere

Biological

Agriculture
Animal and fish husbandry

Biological growth and genetic changing
of microorganisms

Tangible-Output Conversion Systems

Unit, or custom

Batch

Continuous (long runs of identifiable units)

Process (identity of individual units is lost
as in chemical, textile, rubber, and electrical
power production)

Intangible-Output Conversion System

Consulting

Movies

Radio broadcasting
Physical examinations

Day-care centers

Public administration

Hybrid Conversion Systems

Restaurants

Book publishing
Barber shop
Automobile repair
Surgery

From the preceding, we see that the dichotomy of "service" versus "manufacturing" is not easily maintained. Rather, there is a continuous spectrum of organizations with varying amounts of tangible and intangible outputs (see Exhibit 2-3). Intangibility is an important characteristic of services. The next section presents a discussion of intangibility and some other important characteristics that distinguish services.

Exhibit 2-3   Tangibility-Intangibility Spectrum

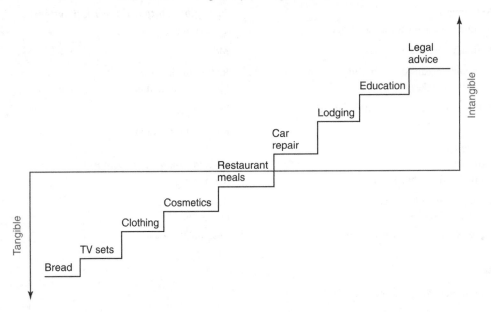

Source: Adapted from G. Lynn Shostack, "Breaking Free from Product Marketing," *Journal of Marketing* (April 1987).

2.3 Characteristics of Services

Through the years, researchers and analysts have used one or more criteria to characterize services. They have identified various characteristics[1] that are common to most services. The following five are the most often mentioned characteristics that differentiate them from manufactured goods—the primary characteristics of services:

1. Intangibility

2. Lack of ownership

3. Inseparability

4. Perishability

5. Variability

Although not all services possess all these characteristics, they do exhibit most of them and some others that are the consequences of them. These characteristics are now discussed in more detail. The discussion also provides hints of some of the unique problems managers of service operations encounter.

Intangibility

Most services are intangible. This characteristic can be understood easily when one thinks about the tangible nature of goods. A **good** is a physical object; it can be touched, felt, sometimes smelled, and if it is a food item, it can be tasted. **Services** are not physical objects. They may utilize physical objects or be embodied in physical objects, but they are not physical. For example, software consists of instructions for a computer to perform. It is written in a computer language, and its instructions can be executed only by a computer. These instructions are usually recorded on a CD or can be downloaded to a hard disk from the Internet. Consequently, the service provided by a software developer is embodied in a physical object (CD or hard disk) and cannot be used without the aid of another physical object (computer).

Most services are performances. A service such as legal advising usually involves the act of giving advice and representation of a client in a courtroom. Such services usually have no tangible output. When there is a tangible output, it is not the service itself but a medium through which the service output is delivered to the customer. For example, a report that proposes solutions to a client's business problem is not the real output of a consulting service; the real output is the ideas expressed in the report to solve the problem. Other services combine an intangible output with a physical output, as in the case of restaurants, gasoline stations, or interior decorating. Although it is true that manufacturing output also can include intangibles (such as warranties, technical information, and prestige of ownership), the primary output of manufacturing is always a physical product. Intangibility describes the uniqueness of services more succinctly than any other characteristic.

Lack of Ownership

An important consequence of intangibility is that for most services, purchasing the service does not result in ownership. Purchasing a good implies ownership. For example, a customer who buys a stereo music set becomes the owner of the set and can do a number of things with it: enjoy music, give it to someone as a gift, trade it for a TV set, or sell it. Purchasers of most services do not have such options. For example, if you buy a ticket to a Broadway show, you obtain the right to be in the audience at a particular date and time. If you watch the show, you have exercised that right and it is gone; you cannot claim a right to watch the show again, unless you buy another ticket. In other words, you don't have the ownership of anything valuable after the show. Does the expired ticket you hold have any value? An exception to this limitation is when the service is embedded in a physical product. For example, if you buy the video of the Broadway show, you will have the same options a good provides.

Inseparability

Provision and consumption of most services are inseparable; they can be consumed only when they are produced. For most goods these two processes can be and usually are separate locationally and temporally. TV sets can be produced in a factory in one geographical location and shipped to wholesalers and retailers all over the world and consumed in many different places. Someone who buys a TV set does not have to use it right away; it can stay in its box indefinitely. A physician's advice to a patient, however, is consumed as it is given.

A second form of inseparability is the inseparability of the customer from the service delivery process. In other words, most services cannot be stored for future use; the customer must be present when the service is created. A customer's presence is not required when a TV set is produced, but a physical examination in a doctor's office cannot be performed unless the patient is there. A lecture in a classroom, a football game, a rock concert, a train ride are just a few additional examples in which both forms of inseparability can be seen; the performance and consumption of these services are simultaneous and inseparable, and customers must be present to enjoy the benefits of these services. Of course, exceptions may be cited, such as a football fan watching a game on TV from a recording device long after the game was played.

Joint consumption of some services is a third form of inseparability. Some services are provided for a large group of customers. For example, a theatrical production, a concert, a cruise ship vacation are services produced for and experienced by a group of people. Although each person's experience may be different in these services, the entire group may suffer from the behavior of an intoxicated and unruly patron. Consequently, in some services what one customer experiences cannot be separated from the entire group's experience.

Perishability

Most services, because they are simultaneously produced and consumed, are considered perishable, noninventoriable commodities. The person who phones in to a time service to find the correct time uses up the service at the time it is provided. Hotel rooms, seats on an airplane or in a theater, and an hour of a lawyer's day cannot be stored and retrieved for later use.

However, perishability may be different from a consumer's point of view. Although a customer cannot carry home a service after it is produced, she can enjoy the "effects" of the service long after it has been purchased. For example, the surgeon who performs a heart transplant is providing not just a single operation, but also a benefit that is enjoyed over the patient's life. Even a movie may be enjoyed in retrospect or provide educational benefits that extend beyond the time that the movie is presented.

The perishability of services, coupled with the highly varying demand patterns that most services experience, requires that managers allocate service capacity carefully and attempt to actively manage service demand.

Variability

Most services are provided by humans for other humans. Service providers may be performing a service on a customer's body, mind, or property. In any case, however, the customer and service provider(s) must interact. The outcome of the service depends on the outcome of this interaction and on the customer's perception of it. When humans interact, results usually exhibit great variability and are not easily predictable. The beauty shop, the custom dress design firm, and the executive recruiting firm provide services that vary with the individual client.

On one level this means that even if the same person provides a service to several customers in exactly the same way, different customers may have different perceptions of what they have received and therefore experience different levels of satisfaction. On another level, the same person performing the same service may not deliver the exact same service at every performance. His physical and psychological condition play an important role in service delivery, and these conditions may not always be the same every day.

The variability in the performance of service providers and the variability in the perception of customers create significant challenges for managers in services. An important consequence of this is that most services defy attempts at standardization. It is difficult, if not impossible, to standardize the output because each client varies in terms of needs and desires before and during the performance of the service. In many services, the design of the service is determined by the person who actually provides the service, such as the consultant, the real estate agent, or the physician. The individual service provider must match the service to the client's needs and desires. Variability in service outcomes also makes control and assurance of quality difficult. Finally, variability makes measurement of productivity a challenging task for managers of service organizations.

2.4 The Service Organization as a System

This chapter began with a description of the general concept of a productive system. We now apply that concept to service organizations in more detail. In Chapter 1, "The Important Role Services Play in an Economy," services were defined as "economic activities that produce time, place, form, and psychological utilities." In other words, services are deeds, acts, or performances that are created through one or more processes. For many services, the process and the output of the system are the same or closely related. These processes are designed and applied as a result of a concerted effort by various components of the service organization. For our purposes, the most important components of this system are represented in Exhibit 2-4. Take a closer look at a service organization as a system.

Exhibit 2-4   The Service System

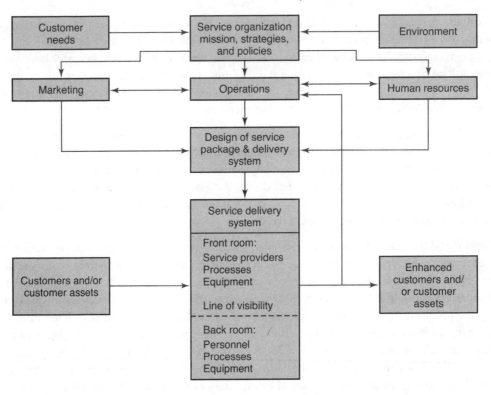

The service organization exists to provide a service (or set of services) to its customers. It is defined and shaped by its mission, strategies, and policies. The **operations** system designs the service package and the delivery system in cooperation with marketing, finance, and human resources. Other functions of the operations system include day-to-day running of the system, deploying the resources to produce the service(s), and providing input for personnel training. The **marketing system** manages the organization's contact with customers including advertising, sales, promotion, distribution, and market research. Operations and marketing functions overlap in many cases. For example, in some cases operations personnel, while providing a service, may also sell other services of the company and act as marketers. In general these two functions have to work closely and cooperate for success. Probably the most important area of cooperation is the design of the **service** and the **delivery system**.

The marketing system collects data and provides information to operations concerning the customer needs and requirements. This is the main input to the design process. Service design should also consider the organization's mission, strategies, competencies, and resources. Other inputs to service design include environmental factors, such as laws and government regulations, customs, and norms. The objective of the design process is to determine what benefits to provide to the customer. Design of the delivery system aims at determining where, when, and how these benefits should be provided. A service delivery system consists of equipment and physical facilities, processes, and personnel. Service personnel play a crucial role in service delivery and success of the organization. Selection, hiring, and training of service providers are facilitated by the **human resources** function. Chapter 8, "Design and Development of Services and Service Delivery Systems," discusses the design of services and delivery systems in more detail.

The service delivery system can be considered in two parts: front room and back room. The front room, also known as front stage, is part of the delivery system that is visible to the customer. This is where the customer interacts with service providers and comes into contact with facilities and processes. The back room, or backstage, is usually invisible to the customer and consists of all the personnel, facilities, equipment, and processes that support the front-line personnel and processes. An imaginary "line of visibility" separates the two parts of the delivery system. What goes on below this line is usually of no concern to the customer; however, failures in the backroom may seriously affect the front-room activities and customer satisfaction. J. W. "Bill" Marriott, Jr., the chairman and CEO of Marriott International Inc., describes the back room in a large hotel as follows:

> In every large hotel—hidden from the eyes and ears of guests—exists an invisible city. Behind doors, below ground, a maze of corridors connects kitchens to loading docks, housekeeping to the laundry, accounting to the communications center. An around-the-clock army of cooks, housekeepers, engineers, waiters, dishwashers, electricians, and other specialists bustles along these hallways, each member responsible for making his or her part of hotel operations run smoothly. The lodging industry has a special term to describe this hidden world. We call it the "heart of the house."[2]

Finally, in the model in Exhibit 2-4, customers, and/or their assets, enter into the service process as inputs. The service may consist of tangible actions applied to a customer's body (such as dental services), tangible actions applied to their goods or physical possession(s) (such as car repair), intangible actions directed at their minds (such as entertainment programs), or intangible actions directed at their intangible assets (such as investment banking). Examples of these are shown in Exhibit 2-5 and discussed in more detail.[3]

1. **People processing: tangible actions directed at the customer's body**—These services require the physical presence of the customer during the service process. Services such as a heart transplant operation or air travel require the presence of the customer. In these cases, the customer will have close contact with the service organization, its employees, and facilities, usually for a significant length of time.

Exhibit 2-5 Services and Service Processes

Inputs	Tangible	Intangible
Customer	PEOPLE PROCESSING Passenger transportation Heart transplant Immunization Physical therapy Criminal justice system	MENTAL STIMULUS PROCESSING Entertainment Education Art exhibit Concerts TV programs
Assets	POSSESSION PROCESSING Repair and maintenance Dry cleaning Housecleaning services Landscaping Package delivery	INFORMATION PROCESSING Internet services Banking Financial services Insurance Software development

Source: Adapted from Christopher Lovelock & Jochen Wirtz, *Services Marketing: People, Technology, Strategy,* 7th Edition, Prentice Hall (NJ, Upper Saddle River, 2011), p. 19.

2. **Possession processing: tangible actions directed at goods and other physical posses-sions of the customer**—These services require the presence of the object but not neces-sarily the customer. In many cases, the customer drops off the object, or the service provider comes to it; he gives the necessary information and instructions for the service and is no longer needed until the service is completed. Car repair and landscaping/lawn care are two examples. In both cases, the length of the encounter is usually short, unless the customer chooses to be present during the service.

3. **Mental stimulus processing: intangible actions directed at the customer's mind**— When these services are delivered, the customer must be mentally but not necessarily physically present. For some of these services, such as TV or radio broadcast, the mes-sage is the only contact the customer has with the service organization. In others, such as traditional educational institutions, concerts, and counseling, the customer's presence is required. Therefore, in the latter case, a service provider's performance as well as her behavior determines the customer's perception of the service he has received. In addi-tion, physical environment, policies of the organization, and other customers may play an important role in forming this perception if the customer is in the facility.

4. **Information processing: intangible actions directed at the customer's intangible assets**—These are services that process the customer's money, records, data, and the like. After the customer contacts the service organization and requests the service, her presence or involvement is not necessary. The nature of these services and the current

level of technology make physical contact with the service organization almost unnecessary. Many banking services, for example, can be obtained over the Internet, phone, by mail, or through automated teller machines. However, there are still some services many people prefer to receive in person such as opening a savings account or applying for a home mortgage loan.

The outputs of the service system are enhanced customers or assets that have increased in value. The role of the service operations manager is to monitor and control the service process based on feedback from the system to ensure that the needs of the customers and service personnel are being met. In other words, feedback from the customers and employees make quality assurance possible.

2.5 Service Encounters

Leonard L. Berry describes a service as "a deed, a performance, an effort."[4] Although some services may result in physical goods, such as a consultant's report, what is invariably important in all services is the transformation of the customer's body, mind, assets, or information. These transformations are achieved by a series of purposeful acts, that is, through a **process**. A customer comes into contact with the service organization when her body, mind, assets, or information is processed. This is generally known as a "service encounter." Whether or not the customer is satisfied with the service experience depends on the outcome of the service encounter. A service encounter involves not only the customer and service employees, but also other customers, the service delivery system and physical evidence.

A **service encounter**, also known as a "moment of truth" can be defined as

> Any episode in which the customer comes into contact with any aspect of the organization and gets an impression of the quality of its service.[5]

The term "moment of truth" comes from the language of bullfighting and refers to the moment when the matador faces the bull before he takes his final action that ends the fight. The term was introduced to service management literature by Richard Normann[6] to dramatize the importance of the encounter of a customer with a service organization. Jan Carlzon, the former president of Scandinavian Airlines System (SAS), popularized the term in his effort to turn the money-losing company into one of the best-run airlines. He expressed the importance of service encounters as follows:

> Last year, each of our 10 million customers came in contact with approximately five SAS employees, and this contact lasted an average of 15 seconds each time. Thus SAS is 'created' in the minds of our customers 50 million times a year, 15 seconds at a time. These 50 million 'moments of truth' are the moments that ultimately determine whether SAS will succeed or fail as a company. They are the moments when we must prove to our customers that SAS is their best alternative.[7]

It must be emphasized that a service encounter may occur practically at any time and any place. Some obvious service encounters are as follows: A customer enters a service facility, asks directions from a service employee, is given forms to fill out, or is in contact with the service provider during the service performance. A customer also experiences a service encounter when he sees a billboard advertisement or a TV commercial by the service organization, or a vehicle in the street that belongs to the organization, reads a news item in a newspaper or hears someone talk about the service or the organization, and when he receives a bill for the service. Probably the most important thing for managers to remember is that for a customer in a service encounter, whatever or whomever she is in contact with she perceives it/him as *the* organization. In other words, when a customer is treated badly by an employee, the customer does not think that he came into contact with a rude person working for the company, but he thinks he is dealing with a rude company. When a customer sits in a waiting area that is not kept clean, she sees a dirty company not failed custodial services. When a technician fails to show up for a scheduled cable service, the customer concludes that the cable company is unreliable. In short, most customers equate service failures or quality problems with the organization that is responsible for the service. Therefore, Carlzon was right when he said his company is "created" in the minds of customers during service encounters.

Most customers don't think about a service or the organization outside the encounters, and when they do it is usually for a limited length of time. A service organization, therefore, has a few brief opportunities to make a good impression on the customer. There are, however, many opportunities to make mistakes and lose customers. It is clear that a service organization cannot leave these service encounters to chance if it wants to keep its customers satisfied and keep them coming back. Therefore, service encounters must be carefully designed and managed. Naturally, we need to understand these events well before we can discuss their design and management.

The Nature of Service Encounters

Service encounters may be simple or complex processes. Usually they consist not of a single, but a series of episodes, with multiple facets of an organization. For instance, consider the hypothetical example of a music lover going to a rock concert (Exhibit 2-6). Obviously, this example may have included many more encounters, but the rock music fan had 14 service encounters. Most of these encounters were with the rock group, but there were other organizations associated with the concert. For example, the arena where the concert was held most likely is not owned but rented by the group or the organizer. In addition to providing a place for the concert, the arena's management may have also provided ticket, parking, and security services. Similarly, the vendor who sells the group's T-shirts is probably a different organization that paid royalties to the group for the use of its name. The concession stand is probably run by still another organization. Clearly, performances of other service organizations may have an effect on the overall experience of the customer. If the customer experiences a problem with any of them, she may not distinguish it from the rock group's organizational performance and hence may conclude that "the concert was good but the organization was terrible." However, if everything goes well, she probably would not even be aware of most of these encounters.

The encounters in the previous example are fairly simple. More complex encounters include a lawyer interacting with a client or a physician trying to diagnose a patient's illness. The complexity originates from the knowledge and skills needed for these services as well as the presence of risk and customer emotions.

Exhibit 2-6   Service Encounters: Going to a Rock Concert

1. A music lover has seen in a newspaper an advertisement of an upcoming concert by a popular rock group at the local arena.

2. She calls the arena for schedule, prices, and directions, getting the information she needs from a recording.

3. She calls another number to reserve her ticket with her credit card.

4. On a local TV news program, she views a report about the rock group's arrival in town.

5. On the day of the concert, she drives to the arena; at the entrance, she sees banners of the group.

6. Security personnel direct her to the entrance of the parking lot.

7. She pays for parking and parks her car.

8. She arrives at the ticket window, gives her name, and receives her ticket.

9. She approaches the entrance and sees the crowd and security personnel.

10. She presents her ticket to an attendant and goes in.

11. She buys a T-shirt commemorating the concert.

12. She goes to a concession stand and buys a soda.

13. She receives help from an usher to locate her seat.

14. She enjoys the concert.

For most organizations, the "make-or-break" service encounters are those between customers and service providers. We can view these encounters as human interactions with the following characteristics:[8]

1. **Service encounters are purposeful**—Regardless of who initiates it, most service encounters are goal-oriented. A sick patient walks into a hospital to get a diagnosis and medical treatment for his ailment. A commercial on TV is aimed at current or potential customers. The UPS symbol on a brown delivery truck has a purpose—to advertise and tell everyone that United Parcel Service is making a delivery.

2. **Service providers are not altruistic**—Most service encounters are part of daily work life at least for the service provider. The primary purpose of the service provider is to perform duties for which she is paid. Therefore, for her the service encounter is "work." It is possible that the customer is also at work during the service encounter. For example, a secretary may call a service technician to have the copy machine in her office repaired. In this case both are at work when they interact in an encounter. There are, of course, many exceptions, such as a lawyer doing pro bono work or a volunteer working in a soup kitchen.

3. **Prior acquaintance is not required**—In most cases the customer and the service provider are strangers who would not normally interact outside the service setting. However, they usually feel comfortable interacting, in many cases, even without introducing themselves to each other. Examples include buying a ticket at a theater box office, a passenger asking directions from a bus driver on a public transit system, or buying a sandwich at a fast food restaurant. These encounters usually have no long-term consequences. However, others not only require formal introduction, they also require a lot more information to be given, usually by the customer. For example, a patient visiting a dentist for the first time has to be known not only by name, but also by other important data such as address, telephone number, age, allergies, medication, insurance company, records of previous dental work, and so on. Consequently, the patient and the dentist are no longer strangers.

4. **Service encounters are limited in scope**—Although greetings, courtesies, and small talk may be part of some service encounters, the time spent on nontask issues is usually short. The scope of interaction between the customer and service provider is limited by the nature of the service task. A physician normally would not discuss with a patient how he can repair his car, and a car mechanic normally would not offer medical advice during a service encounter.

5. **Task-related information exchange dominates**—Most service encounters with a service provider require information exchange. Although some informal settings may involve nontask related information exchange, task-related information is indispensable and has the priority. For example, in a beauty salon most of the conversation between a customer and the beautician may be on weather and the latest fashion. However, task-related information such as how short the customer wants her hair, style, and whether she needs a shampoo must be provided first. At the other extreme, a telephone encounter between a financial advisor and his client, for example, will probably move to the point and focus entirely on the requirements of the customer. In some cases, it may be difficult to separate the two. Consider, for example, a travel agent scheduling a vacation package for a couple. In addition to the relevant information about the vacation package, the agent may recount her own vacation at some of the locations the couple is going to visit. Such conversation may be considered as "small talk" but may also provide useful information to the customers.

6. **Client and provider roles are well defined**—The interaction between a customer and service provider in an encounter requires rules of behavior for effective and efficient service performance. The relevant rules are usually learned from experience; otherwise, a service provider may guide the customer to conform with the rules. For a landscaping project, the customer tells the contractor how he wants his lawn and garden to look, what types of flowers to plant, and the like, and the contractor is expected to follow these instructions. In an encounter between a physician and a patient, however, roles are different; in this case, the patient answers questions and is expected to follow the doctor's instructions.

7. **A temporary status differential may occur**—An important characteristic of some service encounters is that they involve a temporary suspension of "normal" social status enjoyed by each party. For example, a lawyer, who is considered to have a high social status, may work for a criminal whose status is much lower. Or a judge who is stopped by a police officer for a traffic violation has to follow the instructions of the officer.

Service Encounters from Various Perspectives

Service encounters may be depicted in various ways depending on one's orientation during the exchange. Obviously, an encounter involving human interactions has a social component, but it can also be viewed from economic, productive, contractual, and employment perspectives.[9]

- **Social encounter**—Service encounters may be seen as social encounters in which customers come into contact with service providers and interact as human beings. Participants in the encounter are expected to follow certain rules of the society that apply to similar interactions between people. A proper greeting, courtesy, treatment as a human being are minimum standards expected of both sides in many countries. Some encounters may involve small talk, such as weather and recent sporting events, but most exchanges between the parties are task-related. Another understanding is that customers will be treated equally, and the same or equal level of service will be provided to all customers.

- **Economic exchange**—Some service encounters may also be characterized as economic exchanges in which resources are exchanged between a customer and a service organization. More specifically, a service organization gives up its resources in the form of labor, skill, technology, or information to satisfy some need of a customer or provide a benefit. In return, the customer sacrifices some of her resources, such as money, time, and labor.

- **Production process**—Customers come to a service organization to satisfy some need, such as food, or to obtain a benefit, such as education. The service organization has to deploy its resources for this purpose. Resources may include labor, technology, information, facilities; their proper use will create the desired result. Therefore, a service encounter is a production process in which resources are converted to satisfactions and benefits for the customer. Although most resources will be supplied by the organization, sometimes customer's resources will also be used.

- **Contract**—Another way to view a service encounter is as a contractual relationship between a service organization and a customer. The customer hires the service organization to perform a service on his behalf. Through this contract, the customer delegates some authority to the organization or the service provider to make decisions about himself or his property. Therefore both sides operate within the implicit contractual agreement. A surgeon, for example operates on a patient with the patient's permission. During the surgery the patient is most likely to be unconscious, but the surgeon has to make many decisions. She makes all the necessary decisions due to the authority delegated to her by the patient and is expected to keep the patient's best interests in mind.

- **Partial employment**—Some services require active participation of the customer in the creation of the service, such as a patron preparing a salad at the salad bar in a restaurant. In these cases the customer provides the necessary labor, and hence, in a sense, is employed by the service organization. Clearly, this is not employment in the regular sense; nevertheless, it is usually beneficial to both sides; the restaurant saves money on labor and passes part of the savings on to the customer in the form of lower cost of meals. Therefore, we may say, the customer is "paid" by the restaurant for his labor.

Elements of a Service Encounter

A service encounter is comprised of four elements: the customer, the service provider, the delivery system, and the physical evidence.

- **Customer**—The customer is the most important element of a service encounter. The ultimate objective of an encounter must be the satisfaction of the customer. The customer's perception of service quality, her overall satisfaction with the service, and repeat purchase decision all depend to a large extent on her perception of the service encounter. Therefore, the service and its delivery system must be designed to meet the customer's needs in the most effective and efficient manner. Various characterizations of a service encounter previously given remind us that first of all a customer is a human being and expects to be treated with courtesy and respect. She also expects to be treated equally as other customers and given the same or equal service. These are the basic, minimum requirements for a service encounter regardless of the nature of the service.

  However, in many cases the organization has to go beyond that minimum for successful encounters, especially if the service consists of tangible actions directed at a customer's body. Encounters in "people processing services" need to be designed and managed with utmost care. The major reason for this is that the customer is physically present in the service facility, probably for an extended period of time. This gives the customer an opportunity to observe the service performance and make a judgment about its quality. Consequently, a customer's comfort, safety, and overall well-being should be a major concern for the service organization. If it is the customer's possession that is being processed, and he is not required to be present during the service, the focus of the service organization will be on efficient operations that optimizes convenience for the customer, as well as minimize time and effort he needs to spend for the service.

When a customer is expected to supply her labor for the service, she would probably like to have some benefit from her contribution to the service production. In these cases the service organization must provide clear instructions as to what is expected from the customer and make sure that the equipment she has to use is in working order and easy to operate. Failure to educate customers in proper procedures may lead to inefficient operations and unsatisfactory encounters. On the other hand, a customer may also have a significant impact on the outcome of a service encounter by her behavior. If a customer fails to provide the necessary information, follow instructions, or conform to her expected role, or in general, if she is a difficult person, she may make the service provider's job difficult and the experience unsatisfactory for both parties and even for other customers.

- **Service provider**—The service provider or employee is the other crucial human element in service encounters. As a human being he expects courtesy from customers and fellow employees, and would like to be appreciated by customers and management. He must have the requisite knowledge and proper training to perform his tasks. However, this is usually not sufficient for successful encounters.

A service employee represents the organization and is the force that keeps the delivery system going. Her words and actions are seen by the customer as those of the organization. As indicated earlier, she is expected to act on behalf of the customer and in his best interest because the customer has entrusted himself or his property to her care. This dual role may sometimes be problematic for the service employee, especially when the customer's best interests conflict with company policies or when she is bound by strict rules as to what she can and cannot do. There may be many other stressful situations for the employee as well as the customer. For example, when the service involves some risk to the customer, as in surgery, or to his property, as in dry cleaning, the employee has to demonstrate more than technical competence; she must have the skills and ability to ease customer's concerns about the process. This means that she must have interpersonal skills.

Another important thing to remember is that a service encounter may be a first, or one of very few, for a customer, but for the provider it is one of hundreds of encounters during a workday or week. Years of performing the same tasks may condition employees to look at the encounter only in terms of its efficiency and effectiveness rather than the entire process experienced by the customer. Understanding the customer's inexperience, anxiety, or concerns about the service, and at times showing empathy go a long way in making the encounter a satisfactory one for the customer. It is largely management's responsibility to help a service employee to develop interpersonal skills such as friendliness, warmth, concern, and empathy. Sometimes they have to suppress their own feelings and interact with customers with the organization's goals and customers' interests in mind. In short, service providers must look at service encounters and processes from the customer's viewpoint. Therefore, the employee must be trained to develop these behavior patterns. Obviously, these are not easy traits to acquire, and training alone does not guarantee the desired result. Management must also exercise great care in selecting employees who will be interacting with customers.

Simultaneous production and consumption of some services and the intangible nature of most services make quality control difficult. Unlike manufacturing goods, services cannot be inspected before they are produced or delivered. Even after delivery, most services present a challenge in quality assessment. "Did your lawyer present your case in the most effective way? Did your tax preparer find all the tax deductions you are entitled to? Did your doctor diagnose your illness correctly or your symptoms disappeared by themselves?" These and similar questions may never be answered. A common way for managers to ensure quality in service delivery is to control inputs, that is, choose who to serve, and carefully select the right people for the job, check their competency and credentials, give them proper training, and provide them with clear guidelines as to what is expected of them.

Although satisfying customers may be the most important issue for a service organization, a related and an important matter is to satisfy service providers. Some companies go even further. Herb Kelleher, former CEO of Southwest Airlines, one of the most successful airlines in the United States, explains

"It used to be a business conundrum: 'Who comes first?: The employees, customers, or shareholders?' (…) That's never been an issue to me. The employees come first. If they're happy, satisfied, dedicated, and energetic, they'll take real good care of the customers. When the customers are happy, they come back. And that makes the shareholders happy."[10]

- **Delivery system**—A delivery system consists of equipment, supplies, processes, programs, and procedures, as well as the rules, regulations, and organizational culture. Many service organizations assume that if its departments or functions are organized to operate in the most effective and efficient way according to well-established principles of the relevant field, this will also ensure customer satisfaction. For example, a service organization may believe that if its processes are designed to collect and keep the most accurate accounting records, the customers will be best served by such a system. Or a hospital administration may assume that if its facilities and procedures are designed and followed carefully so that a test lab can operate in the most efficient manner, this will ensure that patients receive the best possible medical care. Unfortunately, this approach usually ends up frustrating customers and may lead them to competitors.

This, of course, refers to the part of the system that is above the line of visibility, the part with which customers come into direct contact (refer to Exhibit 2-4). This part has to be designed and operated with the customer and his needs in mind. And the backroom, or backstage, operations should be designed to support the operations above the line of visibility. When these premises have been established, there is no harm in focusing on the efficiency of backstage operations.

Another important issue in delivery system design is the core service. Many services consist of a core service and several supplementary services. A prerequisite for customer satisfaction is the flawless delivery of the core service. Excellence in supplementary services will not mean much to the customer if the organization fails in the core service. Therefore, it is critical that the delivery system is designed and managed for perfection in the delivery of the core service. Supplementary services may then be added to support and enhance the core service. These issues will be covered in more detail in Chapter 8.

- **Physical evidence**—Physical evidence includes all the tangible aspects of a service or service organization a customer experiences. Backstage facilities, or facilities below the line of visibility, are not considered part of physical evidence because they are not directly experienced by the customer. A subset of physical evidence, called "servicescape,"[11] is the physical facility in which the service is delivered and consumed. For example, the exterior design of the building where the service organization is located, parking, landscape, as well as all the furniture and fixtures in the building, equipment, signage, lighting, temperature, and noise level within the facility, tidiness, and cleanliness of the facility constitute the "servicescape." Other tangibles such as forms and supplies used in service processes, brochures, and employee dresses and uniforms, make the rest of the physical evidence.

Physical evidence is important for the success of service encounters especially in "people processing" services. First, because most services are produced and consumed at the same time, in general, customer satisfaction may be enhanced or diminished by the servicescape. If the customer's body is the recipient of tangible actions, then customer comfort and safety must be the primary focus in the design of physical evidence. In general, the longer the customer is in the facility, the greater the importance of the physical evidence.

In addition, physical evidence may affect the behavior of both customers and employees; consumer research has shown that servicescape can influence customer behavior and purchase decisions. For example, Barnes & Noble, which owns and operates a chain of bookstores, has adopted a revolutionary concept in store design. Its superstores have sofas, lounge chairs, and tables for customers to sit and read books, as well as a cafe within the store where customers can have gourmet coffee and pastries. An executive of the bookstore industry made the following observation on this approach: "Barnes & Noble understood the social implications of a bookstore. They understood the role of coffee, high ceiling heights, the sofas, the chairs. They understood the stores could be an extension of my living room."[12]

Service providers spend most of their working hours within the service facility; hence their job satisfaction as well as motivation and performance may also be affected by the physical evidence. Servicescape should be designed to help employees perform their tasks with minimum hindrance and facilitate flow of customers and work through the system. For example, proper signage in large facilities such as a full-service hospital, a metropolitan airport, a subway system, or an amusement park can help reduce the number of disoriented people, avoid congestion, and relieve service employees from the time-consuming task of giving directions.

Role of Other Customers in Service Encounters

Many services are produced for and consumed by a large group of people. Some of these can be enjoyed by the customer in the privacy of her home without any contact with other consumers, such as Internet services, recorded music, and radio and TV broadcasts. However, some others, such as air and rail travel, vacation on a cruise ship, live entertainment, sporting events, and traditional education require the physical presence of the customer and proximity to other customers. In these cases behavior of one customer or a group of customers may have an impact on the outcome of service encounter for others. A drunken passenger on an airliner may make the trip an unpleasant experience for other passengers and service providers. On the other hand, a group of cruise ship vacationers with similar interests and social background may have an enjoyable experience because of the mix of the group. It is largely management's responsibility to make sure that the encounter is a pleasant one for everyone. This can be accomplished by the following:[13]

1. **Selecting the right customers**—A service organization may use formal and informal rules to limit the service offering only to those who would enhance each other's positive experience. Formal criteria may include age limits, such as adults-only resorts; dress codes, such as formal-attire requirement at some restaurants; or membership requirement at some clubs. Informal criteria include limited targeted advertising, pricing, and design of servicescape. For example, for many years suburban malls have been a favorite hangout place for teenagers, but the congregation of teenagers sometimes leads to unsavory incidents, which adult shoppers don't appreciate, such as loud talk, food-court fights, and even shooting. As a result, mall developers and management companies try to control their customer mix by selecting more exclusive stores that don't attract teenagers, offering few places for them to congregate, and creating opulent interiors meant to evoke a luxury hotel.[14]

2. **Establishing rules of behavior expected from customers**—Management can establish and communicate clear rules of behavior in service facilities to ensure a satisfactory encounter for all customers. No smoking signs on public transportation and no running, no diving, no horse play signs at swimming pools are some examples that may prevent undesirable behavior before it happens.

3. **Facilitating positive customer-customer interaction**—Interaction with others may increase the enjoyment of some services such as a vacation at a resort or on a cruise ship. Management can organize gatherings or activities for customers to mix and socialize and create shared enjoyment. In a completely different environment such as a hospital, interaction among patients who suffer from the same ailment may help reduce their anxiety and risk perception. Toronto's Shouldice Hospital performs only external

type abdominal hernia operations on healthy patients. From the moment patients arrive, Shouldice creates many opportunities and organizes activities for patients to meet, socialize, and share their experiences. One of these activities is an evening tea-and-cookies gathering where preoperative patients talk to patients whose operations have been completed earlier that same day.

2.6 Summary

A productive system is defined as a set of elements that works together toward the common goal of creating value through conversion of inputs into outputs. There are five kinds of productive systems: extraction, biological growth, tangible output conversion, intangible output conversion, and hybrid conversion systems. Services fall into the last two categories. Services exhibit some important characteristics that differentiate them from goods: Services are intangible and perishable. Service output exhibits much variability due to the involvement of humans and their varied needs, perceptions, and expectations. Service production and consumption are inseparable for most services. Another distinguishing characteristic of services is customer involvement, and sometimes participation, in service delivery. Due to these characteristics, service quality and productivity are difficult to measure, and measures of effectiveness are usually subjective.

The service organization as a system consists of three main subsystems: operations, marketing, and human resources. The operations system, which produces and delivers the service, consists of a front room and back room with an imaginary line of visibility separating the two. Services and their delivery systems can be classified into four categories: (1) people processing: tangible actions directed at the customer's body; (2) possession processing: tangible actions directed at goods and other physical possessions of the customer; (3) mental stimulus processing: intangible actions directed at the customer's mind; and (4) information processing: intangible actions directed at the customer's intangible assets.

A service encounter is defined as "any episode in which the customer comes into contact with any aspect of the organization and gets an impression of the quality of its service." These encounters are events of utmost importance to a service organization because they have a significant influence on customer satisfaction. That is why they are also called "moments of truth." It is important that service managers understand the nature and dynamics of service encounters. Most service encounters are purposeful interactions between a customer and service provider. In these interactions service providers are not necessarily altruistic. Interactions are also "work" to service employees. Prior acquaintance is not required for service encounters and is limited in scope. Task-related information exchange dominates most encounters. Client and provider roles are well defined, and sometimes a temporary status differential occurs between a customer and service provider.

A service encounter may be perceived in different ways, depending on the interest of the observer. It can be seen as a social encounter or an economic exchange. It is also possible to view a service encounter as a production process, or as a contract between the service organization and a customer. Finally, because some services require customers to perform some of the tasks of service production, service encounters can be seen as partial employment for the customer.

Service encounters have four basic elements: (1) the customer, (2) the service provider, (3) the delivery system, and (4) the physical evidence. "Other customers" in the service system can be added as a fifth element because they sometimes influence a customer's service experience. These elements and their interrelationships must be kept in mind when designing effective service systems that create value for the customer.

Endnotes

1. W. Earl Sasser, R. Paul Olsen, and D. Daryl Wycoff, *Management of Service Operations: Text, Cases, and Readings* (Boston, MA, Allyn and Bacon, 1978), pp. 15–18; Roland T. Rust, Anthony J. Zahorik, and Timothy L. Keiningham, *Service Marketing* (New York, NY, Harper Collins, 1996), pp. 7–10.

2. J. W. Marriott, Jr. & Kathi Ann Brown, *The Spirit to Serve: Marriott's Way* (New York, NY, Harper Business, 1997), pp. xvii-xviii.

3. Christopher Lovelock and Jochen Wirtz, *Services Marketing: People, Technology, Strategy,* 7th Edition, Prentice Hall (NJ, Upper Saddle River, 2011), pp. 18–20.

4. Leonard L. Berry, "Services Marketing is Different," *Business* (May–June, 1980).

5. Karl Albrecht, *At America's Service* (New York, NY, Warner Books, 1988), p. 26.

6. Richard Normann, *Service Management* (Chichester, John Wiley & Sons, 1984).

7. Jan Carlzon, *Moments of Truth* (Ballinger, 1987).

8. J. A. Czepiel, M. R. Solomon, C.F. Surprenant, and E.G. Gutman, "Service Encounters: An Overview," in J. A. Czepiel, M.R. Solomon & C.F. Surprenant, (Eds.), *The Service Encounter: Managing Employee/Customer Interaction in Service Businesses* (Lexington, MA, Lexington Books, 1985), 3–15.

9. P. K. Mills, *Managing Service Industries: Organizational Practices in a Postindustrial Economy* (Cambridge, MA, Ballinger Publishing Company, 1986), pp. 22–24.

10. Kristin Dunlap Godsey, "Slow Climb to New Heights," *Success* (October 20, 1996).

11. Mary Jo Bitner, "Servicescapes: The Impact of Physical Surroundings on Customers and Employees," *Journal of Marketing*, Vol. 56 (April 1992), pp. 57–71.

12. Patrick M. Reilly, "Street Fighters: Where Borders Group and Barnes & Noble Compete, It's a War," *The Wall Street Journal* (September 3, 1996).

13. Adrian Palmer & Catherine Cole, *Services Marketing, Principles and Practice* (Upper Saddle River, NJ, Prentice Hall, 1995), pp. 110–111.

14. Louise Lee, "To Keep Teens Away, Malls Turn Snooty," *The Wall Street Journal* (October 17, 1996).

3

CUSTOMERS: THE FOCUS OF SERVICE MANAGEMENT

3.1 Introduction

There is a keen awareness today among the successful manufacturing and service companies that customers are the most valuable assets a company has. Several years ago, this fact was expressed most convincingly by an executive who achieved one of the most amazing turnarounds in Europe, former CEO of Scandinavian Airlines System (SAS) Jan Carlzon:

> Look at our balance sheet. On the asset side, you can still see so-and-so many aircraft worth so-and-so many billions. But it's wrong; we are fooling ourselves. What we should put on the asset side is, last year SAS carried so-and-so many happy passengers. Because that is the only asset we've got—people who are happy with our service and are willing to come back and pay for it once again.[1]

Karl Albrecht, the co-author of the best-selling book *Service America*, takes this assertion a step further and characterizes customers as an *appreciating asset*. "An appreciating asset is one that grows over time, and that is exactly what happens if customer satisfaction and customer loyalty are increasing over time."[2] There is also research evidence to support these claims. Frederick F. Reichheld and W. Earl Sasser, Jr.,[3] estimated that service companies can increase profits by almost 100 percent by retaining just 5 percent more of their customers. They also estimated the value of loyal customers for specific services. For example, if a credit card company reduces the defection rate of its customers from 20 percent to 10 percent, the average life of a customer account doubles from 5 to 10 years, and the value of that customer increases from $130 to $300. Another 5 percent reduction in defection rate boosts profits to $500, a 75 percent increase. Exhibit 3-1 shows how L. L. Bean, a legendary service company, defines its customers.

Exhibit 3-1   L.L. Bean's Notion of a Customer[4]

What Is a Customer?

A customer is the most important person ever in this company—in person or by mail.

A customer is not dependent on us, we are dependent on him.

A customer is not an interruption of our work, he is the purpose of it.

We are not doing a favor by serving him, he is doing us a favor by giving us the opportunity to do so.

A customer is not someone to argue or match wits with. Nobody ever won an argument with a customer.

A customer is a person who brings us his wants. It is our job to handle them profitably to him and to ourselves.

The importance of the customer cannot be more evident in any management theory than in the quality and continuous improvement movement that started in the 1980s in the United States. This movement indisputably has the "customer" as its focus. The quality and continuous improvement movement had achieved a significant level of development when the Malcolm Baldrige National Quality Award (MBNQA) was established in 1987 as a result of a collaborative effort between the Federal Government and private sector. "Customer driven quality" is one of the core values of MBNQA. Customer satisfaction is a major criterion by which companies that apply for the award are evaluated.

Whether they are manufacturers or service providers, excellent companies know their customers; they know customers' needs and requirements. Each company may have a different way of knowing or discovering its customers' needs, but usually they go to great lengths to gather this information. It is true that sometimes customers cannot articulate their needs and requirements, but this does not mean an organization should not pursue this goal. Chapter 2, "The Nature of Services and Service Encounters," discusses service encounters, or "moments of truth." Recall that many service encounters involve face-to-face interaction with a customer. This is different from manufacturing a good, say a TV set, in a plant, and shipping it to a retailer who then sells it to a nameless, faceless customer in a far away place. Almost all service providers are in contact with customers; either verbal or physical contact is necessary. Consequently, service customers are neither nameless nor faceless. They may show emotions; they may be happy or they may be angry. Whatever the situation, they cannot and should not be easily ignored. Hence, knowing your customer takes on a different meaning in services. Creating a successful service encounter every time is not the only reason for understanding customers and their needs. Service providers need this information to design effective and efficient services and delivery systems that satisfy customers, to position and market services effectively, and to forecast and manage demand.

Learning about customers, their needs, and requirements may take many forms, such as surveys, interviews, focus groups, and test marketing. Discussion of these instruments is beyond the scope of this book, however. This chapter provides a general framework for understanding customers, their needs, and requirements based on consumer behavior theories and demographics. Although organizations constitute an important segment of customers for services, the main focus in this chapter is on individuals (single individuals or a group of individuals, such as a family) as service customers.

3.2 Customers and Their Needs

Customers purchase goods and services to satisfy their needs. Dr. Maslow,[5] a clinical psychologist, developed a theory of hierarchy of human needs to help explain human motivation. Maslow identified five categories of needs that he ranked in decreasing order of priority: physiological, safety, social, egoistic, and self-actualization needs. Humans try to satisfy the lower-level needs before attempting to satisfy needs that are at a higher level. This does not imply that a lower need must be completely satisfied before a higher need comes into play. For most people no need is 100 percent satisfied; rather they are satisfied at decreasing percentages as one goes up the hierarchy. Theory suggests that human behavior is influenced by these needs; unsatisfied needs motivate behavior. It must be pointed out, however, that human behavior is not usually determined entirely by a single need, and not all behavior is motivated by the basic needs. The hierarchy of needs is represented in Exhibit 3-2. Although these needs are represented in the exhibit as mutually exclusive categories for convenience, Maslow's theory does make it clear that there is some overlap between levels; satisfaction of some needs may serve as a channel for the satisfaction of other needs. For example, a person who thinks he is hungry may actually be seeking comfort or companionship rather than nutrients.

Physiological needs are those that are essential to maintain human life, such as food, air, water, sex, clothing, and shelter. These constitute the most basic category of needs; they dominate other needs when they are chronically unsatisfied. If the physiological needs are relatively satisfied, **safety needs** emerge and dominate other needs until they are fairly satisfied. These needs include personal physical safety and security from wild animals, criminals, extremes of temperatures, and natural forces. Also included are desire for health, order, stability, routine, familiar surroundings, and people. Maslow labeled the third category as **love needs**. However, **social needs** is probably a more appropriate title because it includes not only the need for love, but also needs such as affection, belongingness, friendship, and affiliation. Most human beings have a desire for "high evaluation of themselves, for self-respect, or self-esteem, and for the esteem of others." These needs are called **esteem needs** and include desire for strength, achievement, adequacy, confidence, independence, and freedom as well as desires for esteem from other people such as desire for good reputation or prestige, recognition, attention, importance, and appreciation. The need to be what one *can* be is called the **self-actualization need**. The need to achieve self-fulfillment, to achieve one's potential, to become everything one is capable of becoming, emerges only after the physiological, safety, social, and esteem needs are satisfied. According to Maslow, most people cannot satisfy the first four levels to reach the fifth level.

Exhibit 3-2   Maslow's Hierarchy of Needs

Maslow's theory provides a useful framework for managers for understanding human behavior in general, and consumption behavior in particular. Many services exist to satisfy various needs at every level of the hierarchy. For example, a fitness center may appeal to the human desire for a long and healthy life; health or homeowner's insurance helps consumers meet their safety needs; a dating service, as well as a fitness center, may help a single person achieve his social needs by creating opportunities for meeting other singles; and learning a skill or getting a college education may help one achieve esteem, as well as self-actualization needs.

3.3 Consumer Behavior and a Consumer Decision Model

Despite its usefulness and wide acceptance, Maslow's theory is not nearly sufficient to explain the purchase behavior of contemporary consumers. Modern consumers differ in their lifestyles, tastes, expectations, and requirements. It is not possible to categorize them in a few well-defined groups; they may have some common characteristics, but they also exhibit a great deal of variety. Furthermore, consumer characteristics change through time; consumers' lifestyles, tastes, expectations, and requirements change constantly and diversify. These challenges, together with other factors that emerged mostly after World War II, such as the fast pace of product introduction, shorter product life cycles, environmental concerns, increased interest in consumer protection, public policy concerns, growth of services and nonprofit organizations, and international markets, created a need for the development of consumer behavior as a separate field of study. Consumer behaviorists study how individuals make purchasing decisions. They also investigate what consumers buy, why they buy it, how often, where, and when they buy it.[6] The field of consumer behavior borrows from concepts and theory developed in other fields of study, such as psychology, sociology, social psychology, cultural anthropology, and economics.

Marketing scholars who study consumer behavior have developed various models of consumer decision making. In this section we review one of these models by Hawking, Best, and Coney[7] based on a generic consumer decision model. It is a descriptive model that portrays consumer decision making as a process to satisfy various needs that emanate from consumer's lifestyle.

Consumer lifestyle plays a central role in the formation of needs and attitudes. Lifestyle is how a person lives. It includes goods and services a consumer buys, how she views them, as well as how she views herself. A person's, or a family's, lifestyle is the result of many influences, as shown in Exhibit 3-3. These influences may be organized in two subgroups: external and internal influences.

Exhibit 3-3   A Consumer Behavior Model

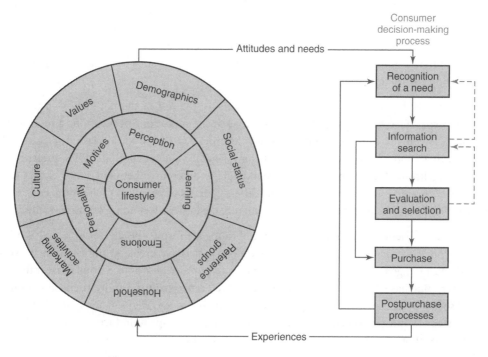

Source: Adapted from Del I. Hawkins, Roger J. Best, and Kenneth A. Coney, *Consumer Behavior*, 5th ed. (Homewood, IL, Irwin, 1992), p.22.

External Influences

External influences are forces outside an individual's sphere of influence that nevertheless form the environment in which he operates. Consequently, these forces influence the way the individual lives, perceives the world around him, thinks, and makes decisions, including purchase decisions.

Culture is the personality of a society, and for that reason influences almost anything we do or how we think. Culture is learned and is not static; it changes over time, usually slowly. However, culture is not a set of prescriptions for behavior; it rather defines the boundaries within which most people think and act. Clearly, culture provides guidance and direction in our thinking and behavior and therefore has a significant influence on our consumption decisions.

Values are part of our culture learned from parents, family, religious organizations, school, and the environment in which we live. Cultural values are widely held beliefs that identify what is desirable or right. Values may be self-oriented, other-oriented, or environment-oriented. Self-oriented values concern the individual—they reflect his objectives and approach to life in general. Other-oriented values reflect the society's desires concerning the relationships between individuals and groups. Environment-oriented values represent a society's view of desired relationship with its economic and natural environment.

Statistical characteristics such as age, sex, education, income, occupation, distribution, and density of population make the **demographics** of a society. Demographic information is widely used by marketing professionals and managers to provide objective assessment of potential customers and reveal trends in important characteristics of the population, such as age and income distribution and geographic shifts of population.

Social status is the position of an individual relative to the rest of the population in terms of some measurable demographic characteristics, such as education, occupation, and income. Individuals with the same or similar position are identified as a social class. It is generally assumed that people in the same social class have similar values, beliefs, lifestyles, preferences, and buying habits. Identifying and understanding the differences between social classes help companies develop different services to meet differing needs of people in each group. For example, banks offer different levels of service to different customers depending on their wealth.

A group is a collection of two or more people. Groups are formed because people with similar interests, objectives, values, or beliefs want to relate to each other, exchange information, or work toward common goals. Most people belong to a large number of groups. Groups that influence consumers' purchase decisions are called consumer **reference groups**. Family, friendship groups, formal social groups, and work groups are some of the reference groups. Companies that advertise their goods and services by appealing to a certain group hope to induce members to buy as a requirement for conformance to group norms and values.

Households with two or more people are important both as reference groups and as consumption units. They influence the purchase behavior of its members and they, as a unit, buy and consume many goods and services. Services such as telephone, cable TV, electricity, refuse collection, security, police, and fire protection are provided to households. Therefore, changes in household demographics and consumption patterns are usually more important than changes in general population characteristics for the provision of these services.

Marketing activities[8] focus on building and maintaining relationships with customers that will benefit both sides. They interact with both external and internal factors. Marketers must also have a good understanding of internal factors that play a significant role in consumers' purchase decisions. This is especially important because of the intangibility of services. You may have noticed that service organizations appeal to some or all the internal elements by making an intangible product tangible through promotions such as "Reach out and touch someone."

Internal Influences

Influences that originate within an individual's body, or mind, are called internal influences. Clearly, they may be in response to the external environment, but they are unique to the individual, that is, the same events will elicit different responses from different individuals.

Emotions are strong and uncontrollable feelings that are generally triggered by outside events. Fear, anger, joy, sadness, acceptance, disgust, expectancy, and surprise are considered basic emotions.[9] Physiological changes such as increased heart beat, increased perspiration, and rapid breathing are believed to *precede* emotion. Emotions may be positive or negative. Most often, consumers seek products and services that lead to the arousal of positive emotions. However, a movie or a book that makes us sad is not necessarily considered as a bad consumption experience. Adventure travel packages, movies, books, music, and in general all types of entertainment services appeal to the emotions.

Personality is the whole set of psychological characteristics that distinguishes an individual. It is believed that personality plays an important role in an individual's purchase decisions and the way she responds to advertising messages. This influence, however, is believed to be operational only in broad product categories not in brand preferences.

A **motive** is an inner force, created by a need or desire that stimulates and compels a person to act. This inner force usually emerges as a result of an unsatisfied need; consequently, the individual engages in behavior to reduce the tension created by the unfulfilled need. Recalling Maslow's hierarchy of needs, some motives are physiological in origin; others are created by social and psychological needs. It is important for managers to understand the motives their goods and services encourage. For example, an increase in burglaries in a neighborhood may appeal to an individual's safety need, which motivates the purchase of a house security system and service.

Humans learn many things to maintain their lives and function in a society. **Learning** can be defined as the process through which humans acquire knowledge, which leads to a change in the long-term **memory**. We learn when acquired information becomes part of the long-term memory. Most of our values, attitudes, preferences, tastes, and behavior are learned. Knowledge of goods and services that can satisfy our needs must also be acquired. Consumers have to know something about existing alternatives, prices, product characteristics, quality, and so on before they can make a purchase decision. Sources of information for consumption purposes are many and include family, friends, mass media, advertising, institutions, and personal experiences.

Perception is how we see the world around us. It is a process through which we select, organize, and make sense of stimuli from our environment. Stimuli are inputs, such as sound, light, image, odor, and so forth, which affect our sense organs, eyes, ears, nose, mouth, and skin. Perception is subjective and personal; a set of stimuli may lead to different perceptions in different individuals. Because consumers make purchase decisions based on their perceptions, marketers try hard to create positive perceptions of their goods and services in consumer minds.

Attitudes and Needs

Attitudes represent our orientation, favorably or unfavorably, toward an object in our environment, such as a good, service, retail outlet, or an advertisement. Attitudes are learned from the environment and formed as a result of the internal and external factors previously discussed. On the other hand, some needs are learned, and some are innate, such as food and water. Attitudes and needs are both influenced by an individual's lifestyle and a reflection of lifestyle.

Consumer Decision-Making Process

The Hawkins, Best, and Coney model depicts **consumer lifestyle** as a function of internal and external influences. Consumer lifestyle, in turn, influences attitudes and needs that trigger the decision-making process (refer to Exhibit 3-3). It must be emphasized that the influence is usually indirect and subtle. The need to understand this relationship and operationalize it for marketing purposes led to the development of a strand of research known as **psychographics**. Psychographics attempts to describe and segment consumers based on psychological dimensions. Originally it focused on activities, interests, and opinions, but more recently psychographic studies also include attitudes, values, demographics, media patterns, and usage rates.[10]

Need recognition and information search—When a consumer realizes that a need exists, the satisfaction of that need becomes the consumer's problem. If the problem can be solved with the purchase of a good and/or service, the consumer decision process begins. First, the consumer searches for relevant information. Two types of information are needed; information for developing criteria for an effective decision and information on the existing brands. The time spent by the consumer in this stage varies and depends on the nature of the need. For example, high school seniors spend a considerable amount of time choosing a college or university. However, a consumer who needs his suits cleaned would not spend nearly as much time choosing a dry cleaner.

Evaluation and selection—Consumers need criteria to select the good or service that will satisfy their needs. They also need to narrow the choices down to a manageable size. This is necessary because most consumers have limited time, energy, and capacity to process information. The resulting set of alternatives, or brands, is known as the **evoked set**. The criteria developed to select a good or service are called **evaluative criteria**. Evaluative criteria are the criteria customers use to assess the merits of competing products or services.[11] Consumers may actually start working on both of these during the information search and will probably continue after sufficient information has been collected. The nature, number, and importance of criteria depend on the consumer and the nature of the need. Some examples of criteria that are commonly used in selecting services include price, quality, convenience, ease of access, friendliness of servers, and reputation of the company.

Choice of service outlet and purchase—In many cases, selection of the service and the service organization are concurrent decisions. In other cases the consumer has to select where to buy the selected brand. Clearly, service dimensions such as availability of sales personnel to help with the purchase, their attitude, size and layout of the store, and its atmosphere all play a role in this decision.

Postpurchase processes—After the purchase and use of the good or service, one of the following possible outcomes will occur: (1) the performance confirms the expectations of the consumer, leading to a neutral feeling of satisfaction; (2) the performance exceeds expectations and the customer is delighted, which is known as **positive disconfirmation**; or (3) the performance is below the expectations, the customer is not satisfied, which is known as **negative disconfirmation**. Repeat purchase is most likely when positive disconfirmation or a neutral feeling is the result. Consumers engage in more postpurchase evaluation and information seeking with services than with goods. They also engage in more postpurchase evaluation than prepurchase evaluation when selecting and consuming services. This is because many qualities of a service cannot be evaluated until after the service is experienced. Consumer experience with a good or service becomes an input to lifestyle and future decisions (refer to Exhibit 3-3). Information on the use and postpurchase evaluation is important to operations and marketing managers because this information influences product strategies and design decisions.

3.4 Unique Aspects of Service Purchases

The model we have just reviewed is a fairly general model that is applicable to most goods and services. However, the consumer decision-making process in purchasing services exhibits some important differences that are worth considering.

Different Criteria

Consumers evaluate services differently from goods. This difference originates from the intangibility of services and the human involvement, which lead to variability in results and can be understood with reference to the following three properties (Exhibit 3-4) consumers use in evaluation.[12]

1. **Search qualities**—These attributes can be determined before a purchase decision is made. Most goods are high in search qualities and therefore are relatively easy to evaluate. Search qualities that are frequently used as evaluative criteria for goods include price, style, color, available sizes, fit, feel, and smell. For services this list is usually short and may include price, location, options and levels of service, and availability (for example, hours of operation).

2. **Experience qualities**—Experience qualities are those attributes that can be judged only during or after consumption, such as taste, wearability, and satisfaction with the performance of a service provider.

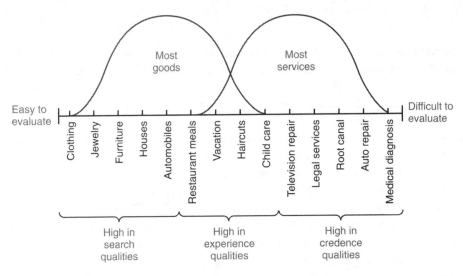

Exhibit 3-4   Continuum of Consumer Evaluation of Goods and Services

Source: Valarie A. Zeithaml, "How Consumer Evaluation Processes Differ Between Goods and Services," in N.H. Donnelly and W.R. George (eds.), *Marketing of Services*, Proceedings of the 1981 Conference on Services Marketing (Chicago: American Marketing Association, 1981), p.186. Used with permission.

3. **Credence qualities**—Attributes that the consumer may be unaware of or lack the technical knowledge to evaluate, even during or after consumption, are known as credence qualities. Services that are performed by professionals, such as medical, financial, and legal services, and services that require special technical knowledge and skills, such as auto repair, are high in credence qualities. Typical consumers of these services have neither the technical expertise nor all the relevant information for evaluation, and frequently cannot assess the quality or the necessity of the service even after the service is performed.

Exhibit 3-4 views consumer evaluation of goods and services on a continuum from high in search qualities to high in credence qualities.

Different Sources of Information

There are five basic sources of information:[13] **memory** (personal experiences), **personal sources** (friends and family), **independent sources** (consumer groups), **marketing sources** (sales personnel and advertising), and **experiential sources** (inspection or trial use). When buying services, consumers rely mostly on memory and personal sources. This is true because mass media sources provide information about search qualities but little about experience qualities. Friends and experts who are familiar with the service can provide reliable information on experience qualities. Also nonpersonal sources may not be available because some service organizations are small local companies that do not have the funds or expertise to advertise.

A Smaller Evoked Set

Earlier we mentioned that the limited number of alternatives a consumer considers for purchase is called an evoked set. This set tends to be smaller for services than for goods. The major reason for this is that although a certain brand of good can be purchased at many different retail outlets, service companies almost always sell only one "brand"—theirs. Consequently, for most services after a brand decision has been made, there is only one place to buy the selected brand. Some service companies, such as banks, may have branches at various locations. In such a case after the bank has been selected, the problem may simply be determining the branch that has the most convenient location. Another reason for the limited evoked set is that demand in a given geographic location can support only a small number of service companies, and therefore a consumer is not likely to find an extensive set of alternative companies offering the wanted service.

Brand Switching and Repeat Purchase Behavior

Brand switching in services is less frequent. Consumers make some service purchase decisions few times in their lives and do not consider them again until a major event or a problem occurs. For example, after a consumer selects a bank for his checking and/or savings accounts, he tends to stay with it until he moves to another town or becomes unhappy with the bank's service. For some services the decision is whether to buy it because the company offering the service is the only alternative. This is the case for most utilities, such as gas, electric, water, and telephone services. Another reason for seldom brand-switching behavior in services is the switching costs and perceived risk. The costs involved in switching brands may be greater in services than in goods. Switching costs may be monetary, such as installation and membership fees, or nonmonetary, such as the disruption it may cause in one's lifestyle, and time spent in information gathering, evaluation of alternatives, decision making, and learning the new system and its requirements.

Risk Perception

Research indicates that consumers usually perceive greater risk in service consumption than purchase and use of goods.[14] Perceived risks that consumers find to be higher in services than in goods include time, performance, financial, social, and psychological. Also, some research indicates that consumers perceive no difference between goods and services in terms of physical risk. The major reason for this is the intangibility of services and their simultaneous production and consumption. If the customer is unfamiliar with the service or not a frequent user, she faces many unknowns, and unknowns usually imply risk. Another reason for risk perception is the nonstandardized nature of many services. Even if the same company and the same server provide the service, there may be variations in the performance and the outcome. A third reason for the perceived risk is that some services do not come with guarantees or warranties, or they are not meaningful; a money back guarantee is not much use if your dentist pulls the wrong tooth. For these reasons some service purchases are "habitual" (same barber for a hair cut) or automatic (telephone service).

3.5 A Cultural Profile of American Customers

The previous section focused on consumers at a micro level, that is, we looked at the individual customer and how he is influenced by internal and external factors in shaping a lifestyle, which in turn influences his purchase decisions. This, of course, is essential for understanding customers and designing appropriate service systems. But we also need to understand consumers as a group, how they behave as a group, and how they change their consumption behavior. In this section, we review cultural characteristics of the residents of the United States (Americans, for short).

The United States is usually characterized as a country built by immigrants who came from many countries of the world; hence Americans have a rich and varied cultural and ethnic background. This leads to the obvious question: "Can the character of such a large population of people with a mosaic of ethnic origins be accurately described with a few cultural traits?" The answer seems to be "yes" according to recent studies. Following are eleven cultural values that characterize Americans:[15]

1. **Achievement and success**—Achievement and success are related but different concepts. Achievement is its own direct reward; finishing college and getting an advanced degree are achievements. Historical roots of this core value can be traced back to the Protestant work ethic, which considers hard work good and spiritually rewarding. Success, however, implies extrinsic rewards, such as achieving wealth and prosperity, and usually results from achievement. Both of them have consumption implications; they act as justification for acquisition of goods and services. ("You deserve it.")

2. **Activity**—Americans attach an extraordinary amount of importance to being active. Keeping busy is considered as a healthy and necessary part of American life. This view stimulates interest in and purchase of services and goods that are time-savers.

3. **Efficiency and practicality**—Efficiency is valued by Americans because it leads to saving time and effort. Americans also value practicality because of their admiration of things that solve problems and save time. Because of these they are interested in goods and services that are easy to use.

4. **Progress**—This is another favorite watchword for Americans because of the central belief that people can improve themselves and tomorrow should be better than today. This value seems to be closely related to the previous three. It can explain why many Americans desire new goods and services that meet their needs and desires better than the old. This is probably the main reason why advertisers use the terms "new" and "improved" for so many products and services.

5. **Material comfort**—Although owning material goods does not necessarily mean happiness, possession of many goods and purchase of services make life easier and more comfortable. For many Americans material comfort signifies the attainment of "the good life."

6. **Individualism**—Self-reliance, self-interest, self-confidence, self-esteem, and self-fulfillment are all popular desires of Americans that reflect the value they place on individualism. It leads consumers to seek goods and services that enable them to live with less dependence on others.

7. **Freedom**—Freedom of speech, freedom of worship, freedom of choice, and freedom to live a life one desires are all deeply held values in the American society. For example, freedom of choice is the most likely reason why companies offer a wide variety of goods and services.

8. **External conformity**—Although this seems to be a value contrary to individualism and freedom of choice, it is nevertheless necessary for individuals to adapt to society. While individualism leads people to buy goods and services that their friends do not have, conformity leads them to be like others in their social group.

9. **Humanitarianism**—Americans are often generous to those less fortunate than they are or to people who have been the victims of tragic events. Outpouring of sympathy for and aid to people who suffered from hurricane Sandy and to the families of the victims of the Sandy Hook massacre in Newtown, Connecticut, in 2012 are just the most-recent examples.

10. **Youthfulness**—Expressions such as "young at heart," and "young in spirit," are reflections of Americans' obsession with looking and acting young, regardless of their chronological age. The desire for looking and acting young stimulated the development and marketing of many goods and services for fitness and health.

11. **Fitness and health**—As previously mentioned, Americans' obsession with youthfulness led many of them to exercise, eat right, take vitamins and health supplements. Fitness and health have become lifestyle choices for many Americans. Consequently, the desire for a healthy and fit body stimulated companies to offer a large variety of products and services, such as exercise equipment and fitness centers.

3.6 A Look into the Future

As we look into the early part of the twenty-first century, there are several trends relevant to the consumption of goods and services.[16]

Age Distribution

Probably the most important trend is the "graying" or "maturing" of the American population. The size of the age group "65 and over" was less than 20 million in 1970, but this group is expected to more than quadruple to 88.5 million by 2050, constituting 20.2 percent of the population. In other words, by that time, one in five Americans will be 65 or over. This change in the age distribution is expected to have a significant impact on social, economic, and political life.

In addition to healthcare, elderly will demand many other services. It must be pointed out that the 65-and-over age group is not homogenous; depending on the status of their health, their needs will be quite different. They will be experienced, mature, and well-educated consumers. Many people in this group will think younger and lead active lifestyles; they will travel, eat out, and vacation a lot. This will create growth opportunities in entertainment, air travel, hospitality, resort, and cruise industries. Elderly will also be purchasing many other services they used to perform themselves, such as lawn care, cooking, home maintenance, snow removal, repairs of all types. As they age further and become less mobile, their demand for some of these services as well as health-related services will increase, and some additional services will be demanded, such as transportation services for shopping and doctor visits, home delivery of groceries, and home shopping of all types of goods. They will also have an increased demand for physical and psychological security.

Households

Household is an important consumption unit; demand for some goods and services depends on the nature and size of the household and the ages of the members. According to some projections, the number of households will be almost 129 million in the year 2015, and 143 million in 2025.[17] An increase in households will create more demand for household-related goods and services. Some of the services that are affected by these increases include lawn mowing, snow removal, landscaping, telephone, water, waste removal, electricity, cable and satellite broadcast, and package and newspaper delivery services. Related to these, demand for services that are provided by governments at different levels, such as mail, police, fire protection, parks, and recreational services will also increase.

Education, Occupation, and Income

American consumers will be more educated and better informed. As the economy becomes more and more a knowledge-based economy, the best paying and most exciting jobs will go to those with advanced education and skills. It is also clear that current and future technologies will change the delivery, and perhaps the nature, of education. Distance learning, Internet, videos, satellite link-ups are some examples of technology used at all levels of the educational system. Learning and education will become a lifelong effort as knowledge and skills become obsolete faster. These trends will lead to an increase in demand for new, more efficient and effective tools and methods of learning and updating and upgrading skills and knowledge.

3.7 Summary

This chapter provided basic concepts of consumer behavior and a cultural and demographic profile of American consumers. Maslow's hierarchy of needs has been presented to explain some of the consumer needs. Maslow's theory asserts that human needs have a hierarchy: Physiological needs or innate needs such as hunger and thirst have the first priority. Safety needs, social needs, esteem needs, and self-actualization needs have decreasing degrees of priority. Humans try to satisfy these needs in the given order of priority; however, a higher level need may emerge even if lower-level needs have not been completely satisfied.

The Hawking, Best, and Coney consumer behavior model explains how consumers' lifestyles are formed by a set of external and internal influences. External influences include values, demographics, social status, reference groups, household, and marketing activities. Internal influences are emotions, personality, motives, learning and memory, and perception. The model depicts lifestyle as a determining factor for consumer attitudes and needs and then explains what steps are usually taken by consumers before a purchase decision is made to satisfy those needs. The decision process begins with need recognition, followed by information search, evaluation, and selection of a brand and purchase outlet. The final step is postpurchase evaluation to assess the value of the product and satisfaction level.

The purchase decision for services is significantly different than the purchase decision for goods. Consumers tend to reduce the alternatives to a small set of choices, called the evoked set. The evoked set is usually smaller for services than for goods. Services are high in experience and credence qualities; goods are high on search qualities. Consumers perceive higher risks with service purchases and do not switch brands as readily.

This chapter also presented a cultural profile of Americans and developing trends. The most important demographic change in the future is the aging of the American population.

Endnotes

1. Jan Carlzon, *Moments of Truth* (Ballinger, 1987).

2. Karl Albrecht, *At America's Service* (New York, NY, Warner Books, 1988), p. 24.

3. Frederick F Reichheld and W. Earl Sasser, Jr., "Zero Defections: Quality Comes to Services," *Harvard Business Review*, September-October 1990, pp. 105–111.

4. L.L. Bean Website, http://www.llbean.com/customerService/aboutLLBean/company_values.html?nav=s1-ln (08/10/2012).

5. Abraham H. Maslow, "A Theory of Human Motivation," *Psychological Review*, Vol. 50, 1943, pp. 370–396.

6. Leon G. Schiffman and Leslie L. Kanuk, *Consumer Behavior*, Tenth Edition (Upper Saddle River, NJ, Prentice-Hall, 2010), p. 5.

7. Del I. Hawkins, Roger J Best, and Kenneth A. Coney, *Consumer Behavior*, Fifth Edition (Homewood, Illinois, Irwin, 1992), pp. 16–23.

8. For more information on marketing of services, see Christopher H. Lovelock and Jochen Wirtz, *Services Marketing*, 7/E (Upper Saddle River, NJ, Prentice Hall, 2011).

9. R. Plutchik, *Emotion: A Psychoevolutionary Synthesis* (New York, NY, Harper & Row, 1980).

10. Hawkins, Best, and Coney, pp. 327–328.

11. Michael R. Solomon, *Consumer Behavior: Buying, Having, and Being*, Ninth Edition (Upper Saddle River, NJ, Prentice Hall, 2011), p. 325.

12. Valarie A. Zeithaml, "How Consumer Evaluation Processes Differ Between Goods and Services" in Donnelly, J. H. and George, W. R. (Eds.), Marketing of Services, Proceedings of the 1981 Conference on Services Marketing (Chicago: American Marketing Association, 1981), pp. 186–190.

13. Hawkins, Best, and Coney, p. 471.

14. For a review of research findings, see for example, William R. George, Marc G. Weinberger, and J. Patrick Kelly, "Consumer Risk Perceptions: Managerial Tool for the Service Encounter," in J. A. Czepiel, M. R. Solomon, and C. F. Surprenant (Eds.), *The Service Encounter: Managing Employee/Customer Interaction in Service Businesses* (Lexington, Ma, Lexington Books, 1985), pp. 83–100.

15. Adopted from Leon G. Schiffman and Leslie L. Kanuk, in collaboration with Joseph Wisenblit, *Consumer Behavior*, Tenth Edition (Upper Saddle River, NJ, Prentice-Hall, 2010), pp. 361–367.

16. U.S. Census Bureau, Statistical Abstract of the United States (Washington, DC, U.S. Department of Commerce, 2012).

17. George S. Masnick and Eric S. Belsky, "Household Projections in Retrospect and Prospect: Lessons Learned and Applied to New 2005–2025 Projections," (Joint Center for Housing Studies, Harvard University, 2009). (http://www.jchs.harvard.edu/sites/jchs.harvard.edu/files/w09-5_masnick_and_belsky.pdf).

4

GLOBALIZATION OF SERVICES

4.1 Introduction

Foreign trade has been in existence since states, cities, and even villages identified themselves as separate entities from others and traded with them. As early as 4,000 years ago, there was active trade in the Middle East and Asia Minor (current Turkey); Egyptians were trading with peoples of this region; and the Sumerians, who inhabited the region of present-day Iraq, traded with Asia Minor and Syria.[1] Today international trade is alive, well, and growing stronger every year. International trade in services existed alongside the trade in goods for all these years, for without services, international trade in goods would not be possible.

This chapter focuses on the globalization of services, which includes not only international trade, but also investments made in other countries to produce and sell services to the residents of those countries. Unlike international trade, foreign direct investment in services has only recently become a significant phenomenon in the world economy.[2]

Globalization of services plays an important role in the U.S. economy as well. In 1960, United States exported $19.7 billion worth of goods and $6.3 billion of services, while importing $14.8 billion worth of goods and $7.7 billion of services.[3]

By the end of 2011, these numbers had grown tremendously (see Exhibit 4-1): exports of goods to $1.50 trillion and services to $606 billion. Similarly, imports of goods grew to $2.24 trillion and services to $427 billion. Also, from the detailed international trade data we can see that in 2011 there was a trade deficit of approximately $738 billion in goods, but a surplus of $178.5 billion in services. The U.S. international trade balance has been negative between 1971 and 2011 (except in 1973 and 1975) but service trade has been consistently positive during this period. In other words, the trade deficit many people have been concerned about would have been much larger had it not been for services. Consequently, in addition to constituting more than 82 percent of gross domestic product, services also play a significant role in foreign trade, and hence in the overall U.S. economy.

Exhibit 4-1   Growth of the U.S. International Trade in Goods and Services

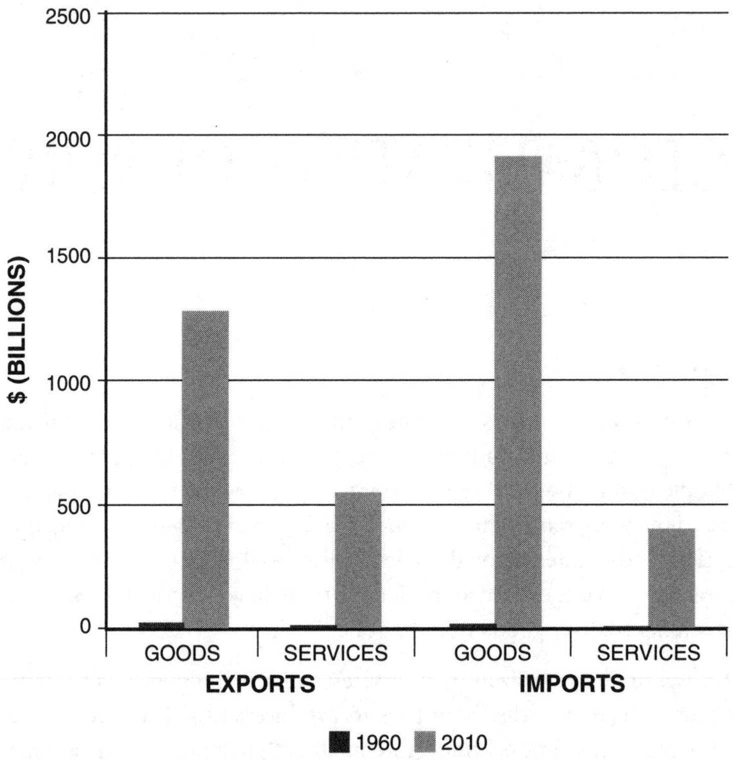

Source: Bureau of Economic Analysis, Table 1 U.S. International Transactions, http://www.bea.gov/
international/xls/table1.xls (07/10/2012).

This chapter explores international trade and foreign direct investment in services, the environment in which global service companies operate, different forms of going global, and recent trends in service globalization.

4.2 International Trade in Services

International trade would not be possible without services. This is true for services provided both domestically and in the international arena. Some of the essential services for international exchange of goods and services include transportation, the Internet, telecommunication, insurance, legal, and banking services. When these services are used by a domestic company in exporting goods or services to another country, or by a foreign company importing goods or services to the United States, they are being traded internationally. For example, if an American shipping company transports machine tools sold to Russia by an American manufacturer, it is exporting transportation services to Russia. Or if a Russian shipping company transports these machine tools, then the Russian company is exporting shipping services to the United States. Similarly, companies that insure the shipment, provide credit for the purchase, transfer funds, and carry communications between the trading companies are all involved in international trade. Clearly, then, international trade would not exist without these and other services.

In these examples, services are involved in international trade indirectly. It is, of course, possible for services to be exported or imported directly. For example, an American movie producer who sells the European rights of her movie to a movie distributor in England is exporting a service. An American automobile manufacturer who hires an Italian designer for his next model is importing a service from Italy. In short, when services are bought from or sold to foreigners, a service is being traded internationally.

The dollar volume of international trade in services has been increasing for the past several decades. There are two basic reasons for this increase: a general increase in the demand for services in many countries and an increase in world merchandise trade.

General Increase in Demand for Services

The economic role services play has been increasing steadily for decades in many countries. In industrialized countries the share of services in the gross domestic product (GDP) reached or exceeded 65 percent in the early 1990s, and it has been significant in other countries. Households and firms have been demanding more and better quality services. This increase in demand can be explained by four developments:[4] a growing underlying need for service functions, deintegration of service activities formerly performed in-house to specialized outside service vendors, the privatization of public services, and advances in computer and telecommunication technologies.

A growing need for services—Many countries around the world are enjoying a higher standard of living, which leads to many changes in lifestyles, such as urbanization; a higher demand for travel, education, vacation, and entertainment; demand for higher quality healthcare services; and a higher demand for domestic services. Businesses are also demanding more of a variety of services. As competition intensifies, the demand for advertising, consulting, and legal and investment services increases creating new opportunities for American companies in those countries. For example, countries of the former Soviet block and developing countries do not have much experience or well-established organizations in advertising, accounting/consulting, or investment banking. Consequently, experienced international service organizations may find an untapped market in these countries. Also, as the complexity and technological sophistication of goods increase, the demand for design, training, and maintenance services increases. Regulatory changes and advances in technology also lead to the creation of new services, such as hazardous waste disposal and testing services.

Deintegration of service activities—Many households in developed as well as developing countries are dual-career households. This, together with increased prosperity, creates both the necessity and ability to purchase some services previously performed by household members. For example these households may use more of take out or delivered food services. This is one of the reasons for the expansion of American fast food outlets in many countries. For example, Domino's currently has more than 3,500 stores outside of the United States in more than 60 international markets; Starbucks has more than 17,000 stores in 56 countries; and another American icon, Kentucky Fried Chicken, has more than 1,500 restaurants in 109 countries. Similarly, many businesses are outsourcing some of the noncritical services previously performed internally, such as payroll processing, security, and custodial and maintenance services for their office buildings. In many cases the main reason for the deintegration is the cost-savings offered by the specialized service companies, which can achieve economies of scale in some aspects of their service operations through standardization of equipment, procedures, and methods, and in purchasing equipment and supplies because of larger volume of business they can obtain. When large companies outsource, foreign companies specializing in these services find an attractive market.

Privatization of public services—A third reason for the increased demand for services is the privatization of some government services in both industrialized and developing countries. For example, many developing as well as former Soviet block countries are privatizing telecommunications, healthcare, and education services.

Advances in computer and telecommunication technologies—Advances in computers and voice and data transmission capabilities of telecommunication networks and the Internet amaze many people daily. They also have a significant impact on the service trade; these developments have made the trade easier for many services, increased the speed of information exchange, and created opportunities for new services. The impact is most visible in services that rely on data and information exchange and processing, such as collection and dissemination of the news and financial data, and distribution of databases and software.

These developments lead not only to an increase in trade, but also to an increase in foreign direct investments in services. Whether through changes in incomes and lifestyles or through deintegration, as the demand for various services in each country increases, these markets become more attractive to international service companies. Before privatization, many service markets, such as telecommunications, education, and healthcare, were not open to competition. They were mainly government monopolies. Now that these monopolies are disappearing, their markets are not only becoming more competitive, but they are also opening up for international firms.

Increase in International Trade of Goods

As the international trade volume increases, so does the demand for certain services. Transportation, communication, insurance, banking, and legal services are the most essential services needed for international trade. Internationally traded goods must be transported by ship, train, truck, or planes between countries. Sometimes it is necessary for people involved in the trade to travel to other countries, and they may have to use travel services, such as airlines, car rentals, and hotels for this purpose. Communication is essential for trading partners to initiate and complete a transaction; companies that provide telephone or Internet services, carry mail or packages, or provide courier services make the communication possible. Goods shipped from one country to another must be insured against damage and theft in transition; hence the services of insurance companies are needed. Transfer of goods or services in one direction requires transfer of money in the other direction, and banks make this possible. Services of lawyers are needed to prepare the necessary documents for trade between two parties and deal with many issues relating to laws and regulations of the countries involved. In addition to these, many other service providers, such as advertising professionals, accountants, customs experts, translators, and the like, will be needed for international trade to take place. It is also clear that experienced operations managers who are well versed in international management are needed to run these services effectively and efficiently.

4.3 Why Service Companies Go Global

This section reviews the reasons for service companies to go global through international trade or foreign direct investment. First, for clarification, brief definitions of some important terms are presented in Exhibit 4-2. As can be seen from these definitions, the most important differences among various types of companies are in their competitive strategies and the way they are organized. With these differences in mind, the terms **globalization** and **internationalization** are used interchangeably to refer to the process of entering the international stage in one form or another, assuming that such a company may eventually evolve into a "global" corporation or even a "transnational" one.

Exhibit 4-2   A Classification of Firms from an International Perspective

Domestic Enterprise: Operates within the boundaries of its own country; buys mostly from domestic suppliers and sells to domestic customers.	**Exporter/Importer:** Exporter sells its goods and services in other countries, usually through independent distributors. Importer sells products of foreign companies in its own country.
International Enterprise: Has sales, distribution, and/or production organizations and facilities in other countries. Units in other countries operate independently of each other and compete against local companies. However, strategy, technology, and resource allocation are centralized. Technology transfer constitutes the key relationship between headquarters and country units.	**Multinational (Multidomestic) Enterprise:** A replica of the company is created in different countries, and each is run by local managers. A multinational company hopes to be seen as a national company and thus gain a competitive advantage. Domestic operations are supplemented by globally sourced resources, skills, and technology.
Global Enterprise: Sees the whole world as a single market and its operations in this market as a single operation. It has standardized global products. Its products can be produced anywhere and can be sold anywhere in the world. It has one coordinated and centralized strategy for its worldwide operations and competition.	**Transnational Corporation:** A transnational corporation combines the advantages of international, multinational, and global corporations: it has the technology transfer capability of international, local responsiveness of multinational, and the efficiency of global enterprises. In other words, a transnational corporation tries to excel in all three forms at once.

Source: Adapted from Stephen H. Rhinesmith, *A Manager's Guide to Globalization*, 2nd ed. (Chicago, Irwin Professional Publishing, 1996), pp. 5–11; and Christopher A. Bartlett and Sumantra Ghoshal, *Managing Across Borders: The Transnational Solution* (Cambridge, MA, Harvard Business School, 1989).

Companies invest in other countries to reduce costs, expand markets, or as a strategic move. As domestic markets become saturated, many service companies look abroad for new business opportunities. Many service companies believe that the success they achieved in their home market can be replicated in foreign markets after some modification to the service concept and/or delivery system. This is not necessarily a correct assumption as many international companies discover that considerable challenges exist in going global. Lovelock and Yip[5] identify eight reasons service firms go global; these reasons are discussed next.

Common Customer Needs

Theodore Levitt was probably the first to identify the trend for the homogenization of consumer tastes around the world when he wrote, "Everywhere everything gets more and more like everything else as the world's preference structure is relentlessly homogenized."[6]

Consumer services that are good candidates for standardization across countries are limited to those services that do not involve customers, or when customers' involvement can be closely controlled, and when customization can be limited by the service company. Fast food and airline services are two examples for global services; in both cases customers' involvement is closely controlled and choices are limited for customization. Some service companies have the opportunity to offer a standard core service around the world and nationally customize it with the addition of a carefully selected set of supplementary services. For example, Club Med can use local entertainers to supplement its global core service, Club Med Vacation.

Global Customers

When a global company sets up shop in a foreign country, some service companies follow them to the same market. That was what the accounting firm Coopers & Lybrand did when Ford Motor Company established a venture in Hungary.[7] It quickly moved to open a branch office in this new market because of the concern that one of its competitors, already established in Hungary, may begin to build a relationship with its client. The uniformity of service is sought also by clients in other fields, for example, by airlines in aircraft maintenance and global manufacturers in factory and machinery maintenance and repair.

In addition, many American travelers feel more comfortable going into a McDonald's restaurant in a foreign country rather than a local restaurant. Similarly, they may prefer renting a car from an American company they are familiar with.

Global Channels

The Internet created a global channel for the sale and distribution of many services. Almost any good and many information processing services, such as banking, entertainment, software, and travel services, can be purchased through this electronic channel. Hence, even small service companies may offer their services through the Internet without establishing a presence in other countries.

Global Economies of Scale

Services provide few opportunities for economies of scale. The main reason for this is that for most services the demand is geographically dispersed; hence building large service facilities to exploit economies of scale in operations is usually not possible. In many cases the service capacity and workforce employed exceed average demand. Consequently, idle capacity is not uncommon in service facilities. When economy of scale is possible, it creates an incentive for a service organization to go global.

Favorable Logistics

Costs of travel and transportation have been declining for many years. This has made some previously inaccessible services economically feasible for people in other countries. Lower air travel costs increased tourism all around the world. Also, some specialized services, such as healthcare and higher education in developed countries, have become affordable for newly emerging middle class in many developing countries. For example, London hospitals attract many patients from the Middle East. Similarly, American hospitals and doctors attract patients and American universities attract students from all around the world.

Advances in Technology

For many services that generate, process, or use information, the developments in computer and telecommunications technologies have not only eliminated some barriers for internationalization of services, but they also created opportunities for new services and new forms of service production and delivery. They also contribute to foreign direct investment in service industries, for example

> A flourishing computer-software industry has grown up around Bangalore, India, following initial investments in the area by Texas Instruments Inc., and later by Digital Equipment Co. (DEC), Hewlett-Packard, Siemens, and Motorola, drawn by low-cost high-quality English-speaking Indian software engineers. (...) Similarly, some of Hong Kong's paging services are manned from China. In Perth, in Western Australia, EMS Control Systems monitors the air-conditioning, lighting, lifts and security in office blocks in Singapore, Malaysia, Sri Lanka, Indonesia and Taiwan....[8]

Government Policies and Regulations

Governments can and do restrict trade and foreign direct investments in their countries. Many instruments exist for this purpose, such as tariffs and import quotas, export subsidies for domestic companies, local content requirements, currency and capital flow restrictions, and ownership restrictions. In most cases the main objectives of these restrictions are to protect the domestic firms against foreign companies and improve trade balance and foreign exchange reserves. Imposition of such restrictions and barriers may reduce both the trade and foreign direct investment. Conversely, the elimination or reduction of these restrictions would stimulate globalization of services. The current worldwide trend seems to be in that direction.

Transferable Competitive Advantage

An important reason for many service companies to go global is the ability to replicate their domestically successful service concept and delivery system in other countries. When service companies develop a new service or a delivery system, they do not have the patent protection some manufacturers enjoy. Their advantage lies in the network they own and in the management know-how; otherwise, practically any service or delivery system can be imitated. For example, any bank or financial company can offer a credit card, but if the card does not belong to one of the existing networks (that is, Visa, MasterCard, American Express, or Discovery) it doesn't have much chance for success. Establishing such a network would be very costly and a challenging undertaking. On the other hand, an established company, such as American Express, can introduce new services and establish itself in a foreign country with relative ease because of its existing network, managerial experience, and know-how accumulated through many years of operations in international markets.

4.4 Global Environment for Service Businesses

Any company entering the international business arena, whether in the form of exporting, importing, or foreign direct investment, must be aware of the different conditions under which it will operate, such as political conditions; the role of governments; economic, social and cultural environments; and technological conditions. In most cases, international companies cannot change these conditions; therefore they have to accept them as given and learn to reduce their risks when operating in these environments. Frequently, their success in global markets depends on these conditions and how well they adjust to them. A service company that has global aspirations has to think, act, and behave globally. A global company has to remember that it is not dealing with a single culture, single religion, or single set of rules and regulations anymore and therefore must abandon its nationalistic approach to service. Robert Ayling, former CEO of British Airways, who was trying to transform his company to a global airline, emphasized the importance of this when he said, "We don't want to ram our Britishness down people's throats."9 The following paragraphs discuss these environmental factors.

Political conditions—Political stability is one of the most important conditions all international companies seek before setting up operations and investing in a country. Political instability, such as civil war or a government with an uncertain future, increases risks for an international company.

The role of governments—Governments may bring many restrictions to trade and foreign direct investment. A major objective of many governments in dealing with international companies is to maximize the benefits from the international company while minimizing the risks (for example, national security risks). Governments frequently require foreign companies to acquire local partners when they set up operations in their countries. Another common requirement is that the international company hire a specified proportion of its employees from among locals and set up training programs for these employees. Governments may also impose licensing requirements in many professional services such as engineering, accounting, and financial services.

The economic environment—The demand for services in general increases as the level of income increases. International service companies look at such statistics as gross domestic product (GDP) when they assess the attractiveness of a new market. Also important are the current level of economic development and predictions for the future performance of the economy in the candidate country. Finally, the intensity of competition in an industry is another important factor to consider before investing in a foreign country.

The social and cultural environments—Understanding the cultural and the social environment in a country is important for service operations managers because of the customer contact involved. If the encounter is not designed carefully with the host country's social and cultural norms in mind, it may turn into a clash of cultures and the service company loses.

The technological environment—Delivery of high-quality reliable service depends on the existence of a reliable and modern communications infrastructure, as well as the availability of the necessary equipment for the service delivery and services to maintain the equipment. A well-developed financial services system, such as a banking system, is also crucial for international service companies to operate successfully in a foreign country.

4.5 Forms of Globalization

Like manufacturers, service companies may enter the international business world in several forms. In general we can group these as trade and foreign direct investment. This section reviews these forms and which services are likely to use each different form.

International Trade

Exports/imports—When a domestic service company sells to a resident of a foreign country, it is a service export. Similarly, when a resident individual of your country buys a service from a foreign company, it is a service import. The nature of services (specifically, intangibility, inseparability, perishability, and customer contact and involvement) puts limits on the number of opportunities for import/export of services. Information and knowledge-based services or services that can be delivered from a distance are most likely to be traded. Some of these services are embodied in physical products, such as music on CDs, movies on DVDs, and software on disks or CD-ROM. For example, software engineers in Bangalore, India, are exporting their services to clients located in different parts of the world. There are other forms of service trade. Tourists traveling to other countries are importing a service from the country they are visiting. Another form of exports/imports is when the service provider travels to the country of the customer, for example when a consultant goes to another country to deliver a seminar or perform consulting services.

Licensing/franchising—Licensing is an agreement between two companies that gives one (licensee) the right to produce and sell a good or service using the patents, technology, or trademarks that belong to the other company (licensor). Licensor receives money, called a royalty, for granting these rights. Franchising is an additional form of international service trade.

Management contracting—Management contracting is another form of exporting by a company that has special expertise in managing a particular service system. The service company supplies the managerial know-how as well as the management team to run the service facility for a fee. Management contracting has been observed in hotel management, aviation, and retailing.

Foreign Direct Investment

When the nature of a service makes its export difficult or impossible, a service company has no choice but to set up facilities in foreign countries for marketing its services. As services grow in importance for most economies, foreign direct investments in services have also been growing for the past 20 years.

The main difference between international trade in services and foreign direct investment is that sales revenues, commissions, fees, or interest charges are collected when services are sold to foreigners, whereas in foreign direct investment, profits are sought from foreign-based equity.[10] There are a few, but interesting, exceptions to this purpose. For example, New York Life, an insurance company, ships health insurance claims overnight to Ireland.[11] Claims are processed and returned via dedicated telecommunication lines to the data processing center of the company in New York, where a check or a reply is mailed to the customer. The facilities in foreign countries have been established to reduce labor costs rather than obtain profits from overseas investments. Whatever the purpose may be, foreign direct investment implies establishment and staffing of a service facility in another country and consequently taking more risks than exporting.

Foreign direct investment may take one of several forms. One form of direct investment is when a company has minority ownership of a foreign company; the investor may have some say in the management of the company but does not control the enterprise. A second form may be equal ownership, and a third is majority ownership in which the international firm has more control. In all these forms, the ownership, management, and risks are shared by two or more companies. Finally, whole ownership of a company in a foreign country is the fourth form of direct investment; this is the form in which the investor has full control of the company and assumes all the risks of the business venture.

Alliances

An important development in the 1990s in the services sector was the growth of alliances between various companies including competitors. Most of these alliances do not involve any equity exchanges but focus on sharing networks and resources. In many cases partners supplement each other's competencies and resources. Microsoft's alliance with NBC in creating the MSNBC news channel is well known.

Alliances seem to have much more significance in the airline industry. For example, Star Alliance, the world's first and largest global airline alliance, was formed in 1997 by five major airlines. Star Alliance has since grown considerably; it now has 27 member airlines with more than 21,100 daily departures combined. These flights reach 1,356 airports in 193 countries.[12] Many alliances were formed among airlines during the 1990s. These alliances give each partner access to the other's network of routes, make it possible to share passengers and revenues, and enable them to coordinate their schedules, fares, travel packages, discounts, frequent-flier programs, even some of the ground operations.[13] For passengers these alliances may mean easy connections to many destinations around the world, including baggage transfers between flights.

Trends in Service Globalization

The discussion of the globalization of services has indicated that some services can be traded more easily than others, and some services can be created for the residents of another country only by the presence of service facilities in that country. In this section, current trends in the globalization of particular groups of services will be identified, which group of services tend to globalize through international trade, and which group through foreign direct investment.

Vandermerwe and Chadwick[14] identified six groups of services in terms of their globalization potential and the form of globalization they tend to use. They used two dimensions to organize services for the purpose: relative involvement of goods and degree of consumer/producer interaction (see Exhibit 4-3). The first dimension represents the degree to which a good is essential for service delivery, and the second dimension represents the degree to which interaction between the service provider and consumer is essential for service delivery.

Exhibit 4-3   Clustering of Services and Internationalization Modes

Degree of Consumer/Service Provider Interaction	Pure Service	Service with Some Goods or Delivered Through Goods	Services Embodied in Goods
HIGHER	**Sector 4** Engineering Consulting Advertising Education Insurance	**Sector 5** Personal air travel Maintenance Banking	**Sector 6** Electronic mail Internet shopping
LOWER	**Sector 1** Mail delivery House painting Knife sharpening	**Sector 2** Retailing Couriers Fast food Shipping Hotels Air freight	**Sector 3** On-line news service Music/compact discs, DVDs, books, magazines

LOWER ← Relative Involvement of Goods → **HIGHER**

Source: Adapted from Sandra Vandermerwe and Michael Chadwick, "The Internationalization of Services." *The Service Industries Journal* (January 1989), pp.79-93.

Sector 1: Low goods/lower interaction—The first group consists of "pure" services for which consumer/producer interaction is minimal, and the role goods play in their delivery is not significant. These services have limited globalization potential because they may exist in any country, and there is little profit potential for an international company in this market.

Sector 2: Medium goods/lower interaction—In this group are services that require some interaction, and goods play a more significant role. This group has a higher potential for globalization because of the ease with which the facilitating goods can be taken to foreign countries.

Sector 3: High goods/lower interaction—Services in this sector are either embodied goods or can be transmitted through a telecommunications network or the Internet, and they require little, if any, interaction between the consumer and the producer. They are the easiest services to export.

Sector 4: Low goods/higher interaction—Most of the services in this group are professional services and characterized by high interaction between the provider and the client, but goods do not play a prominent role in their delivery. Globalization of these services requires the movement of people; usually the service provider travels to the client's country, or it requires an institutional presence in the client's country, usually in the form of a branch or subsidiary of the service company.

Sector 5: Medium goods/higher interaction—Customer/producer interaction is important in this group of services, and goods play a relatively significant role. Also important in the delivery of these services are telecommunications facilities and technology. Globalization may be in various forms such as foreign direct investment, franchising, licensing, or management contracting.

Sector 6: High goods/higher interaction—Both dimensions are at their highest levels in this group of services, and telecommunications networks and technology in general play a significant role in delivery. Globalization potential for this group is increasing with advances in technology.

At first glance services tend to converge to one of three forms of globalization (see Exhibit 4-3). The first cluster is "exportable" services consisting of services embodied in goods. This form requires little investment or presence in the country of destination; it also involves little control of the distribution and use of the service. The second cluster consists of services that can go global with relative ease through franchising, licensing, or management contracts. This form requires some presence; usually managers from the service company are stationed in the foreign country to deliver the service, and it may require some investment. Foreign direct investment seems to be the most appropriate form for the third cluster of services.

4.6 Summary

This chapter focused on the globalization of services and related issues. The globalization of services may occur as international trade or as foreign direct investments. This chapter reviewed reasons for globalization, the environment in which global service companies have to operate, the different forms of going global, and recent trends in service globalization. The general increase in demand for services and increase in international trade of goods are the major reasons for the increase in international service trade. Service companies go global to take advantage of common customer needs, global customers, global channels, economies of scale, favorable logistics, favorable policies and regulations of the government of the host country, advances in technology, and competitive advantages that can be transferable to markets in other countries.

The conditions and factors in the international arena that a service organization must be aware of before deciding whether to go global or set up operations in other countries were also discussed, as well as the three different forms of globalization for service companies: international service trade, foreign direct investment, and foreign alliances. The chapter concluded with a look at trends in service globalization.

Endnotes

1. R. Vernon, L. T. Wells, and S. Rangan, *The Manager in the International Economy*, Seventh Edition (Upper Saddle River, NJ, Prentice Hall, 1996), pp. 3–4.

2. K. P. Sauvant, "The Tradability of Services," in P. A. Messerlin and K. P. Sauvant (Eds.), *The Uruguay Round, Services in the World Economy* (Washington, D.C., The World Bank, 1990), pp. 114–122.

3. The data in this section is from Bureau of Economic Analysis, Table 1 U.S. International Transactions, http://www.bea.gov/international/xls/table1.xls (07/10/2012).

4. The first three of these developments have been suggested by Michael E. Porter, *Competitive Advantage of Nations* (New York, The Free Press, 1990) p. 242.

5. Christopher H. Lovelock and George S. Yip, "Developing Global Strategies for Service Businesses," *California Management Review*, Vol. 38, No. 2 (Winter 1996), pp. 64–86.

6. Theodore Levitt, "The Globalization of Markets," *Harvard Business Review*, May–June 1983.

7. Gary W. Loveman, op. cit.

8. *The Economist*, September 30, 1995.

9. R. B. Lieber, "Flying High, Going Global," *Fortune*, July 7, 1997.

10. J. J. Boddewyn, M. B. Halbrich, and A. C. Perry, "Service Multinationals: Conceptualization, Measurement, and Theory," *Journal of International Business Studies* (Fall 1986), pp. 41–57.

11. B. M. Hoekman and P. Sauvé, *Liberalizing Trade in Services* (Washington, D.C. The World Bank, 1994), p. 6.

12. From Wikipedia, the free encyclopedia (http://en.wikipedia.org/wiki/Star_Alliance) (07/11/2012).

13. S. McCartney, "Airline Alliances to Alter Overseas Travel," *The Wall Street Journal*, June 11, 1996; S. McCartney, "AMR and British Air to Share Profits, As Well as Passengers, From Alliance," *The Wall Street Journal*, June 12, 1996; and A. Q. Nomani, "Airline Pacts' Antitrust Question Sparks Controversy," *The Wall Street Journal*, January 3, 1997.

14. This section is largely based on the following paper: Sandra Vandermerwe and Michael Chadwick, "The Internationalization of Services," *The Service Industries Journal*, January 1989, pp. 79–93.

5

SERVICE STRATEGY AND COMPETITIVENESS

5.1 Introduction

A firm survives and prospers if it can create value for its stakeholders on a continual basis. A firm's stakeholders include customers, employees, shareholders, suppliers, and community at large. A firm that provides value equally well as its rivals, or better than its rivals, will be a competitive firm. Why is creating value so important? A customer who believes that he has received good, or better yet, exceptional service will be a satisfied customer. A satisfied customer will be a loyal customer, and a loyal customer means repeat business for the firm in the months and years to come. A satisfied customer also helps recruit new customers for the firm. Satisfied customers are more likely to buy other services from the firm. Consequently, satisfied customers are not only a long-term source of revenues for the firm, but they also provide free advertising and free marketing services for the firm by word-of-mouth. In general, the higher the value a customer sees in the service, the higher the price she is willing to pay. As long as the firm keeps its customers satisfied, its revenues will continue to grow.

To be competitive, a service firm must also provide value to its other stakeholders. For example, a service firm can create value for its shareholders in the form of profits and/or higher share value. Satisfied customers generate the revenues for the service firm, but managers must control costs without jeopardizing the value generation ability of the firm.

The realities of public service organizations are different. A public service organization has no shareholders, but it has many stakeholders such as taxpayers, public officials, unions, or anyone who uses its services. Most of the stakeholders are also customers. Stakeholders, of course, do not receive any income as a result of the public service organization's operations. However, they do receive value through a higher quality service, lower tax burden (as a result of efficient operations), or increased variety and scope of services. Many public service organizations generate either little or no revenue and hence depend on public funds for their existence. Police, firefighters, and K-12 school system are some examples. Public service organizations, such as the U.S. Postal Service, generate significant amounts of revenue but may still rely on public funds for their operations. In either case, satisfied stakeholders are the best assurance for a public organization's continued existence.

Finally, value will be created for employees when they are satisfied as internal customers of the organization. Employees will be satisfied if they like their work and the environment they work in, have job security, and if they perceive the income and benefits they receive as fair and adequate. Satisfied external customers provide the revenues for a company to offer attractive salaries and greater job security to satisfy the employees. Satisfied employees are much more likely to make both internal and external customers happy and keep them satisfied. Hence the cycle is complete.

5.2 Value

Brief Historical Background on Value

The concept of economic value has been a subject of study and debate among philosophers and economists for more than 2,000 years.[1] Adam Smith (1723–1790) identified two different types of value: value in use and value in exchange. In his well-known work, *The Wealth of Nations*, he wrote

> The things which have the greatest value in use have frequently little or no value in exchange; and on the contrary, those which have the greatest value in exchange have frequently no value in use. Nothing is more useful than water, but it will purchase scarce anything: scarce anything can be had in exchange for it. A diamond, on the contrary, has scarcely any value in use: but very great quantity of other goods may frequently be had in exchange for it.[2]

Another well-known economist, Alfred Marshall (1842–1924) defined value in microeconomic terms of marginal utility and marginal cost. Marshall defined value as the equilibrium price formed when the marginal cost equaled the marginal utility.[3] Hence the marginal analysis indicates that the exchange value is determined not by the total usefulness of a good but the last unit of it that is consumed. And price of a good formed in the marketplace reflects not only the marginal use of it for a consumer, but also the marginal cost of producing the last unit of that good.

More recently, scholars in various fields of management and engineering have paid increased attention to the concept and measurement of value and inevitably have come up with different definitions. These range from value being simply equal to "price" to more elaborate definitions. For example, Michael Porter defines value as

> …what buyers are willing to pay,…superior value stems from offering lower prices than competitors for equivalent benefits or providing unique benefits that more than offset a higher price.[4]

De Marle, on the other hand, uses quite a different approach to defining value. His approach is rooted in science and engineering and focuses on the design of goods:

> Value is the primary force that motivates human actions. It is dichotomous, centered in people and the objects they desire. Value is a potential energy field between us and objects we need. It draws us to items in our environment that we find appealing. When this attraction is large, we expend our energy to acquire, possess, use, and exchange objects that are rewarding.[5]

Definition of Value

For the purposes of this book the following definition is proposed:

Value is the capability of a good or service to satisfy a need or provide a benefit to a customer.

According to this definition, a good or service has value only if it satisfies a need or provides a benefit to a customer (a person or organization). Value is subjective; its existence depends on the perception and particular needs of the customer. A car may be valuable for a person who needs transportation. However, the same car has little or no value for someone who lives on a small island with no paved roads.

More important, value in a good or service either exists for a customer or it doesn't; if something has no value for a customer, improving its components (for example, increasing its quality or lowering its price) does not make it valuable. A choice steak may be just what a hungry person needs and therefore is valuable to her. However, the same steak has no value for a vegetarian, no matter how high a quality it may have in the eyes of nonvegetarians, how tastefully it is prepared and served, or how inexpensive (or free) it may be. A daycare center in the neighborhood may be a valuable service for a single parent or a couple with young children. However, the same daycare center has no value for a single person, or a couple with no children or with adult children.

A Model of Service Value[6]

The service value model used in this book is a modified version of the Zeithaml model focusing on customer value.[7] The model includes perceived quality, intrinsic attributes, extrinsic attributes, monetary price, and nonmonetary price as the components of perceived value. We expand this model by adding "time" as the sixth component of service value (see Exhibit 5-1).

Exhibit 5-1   The Service Value Model

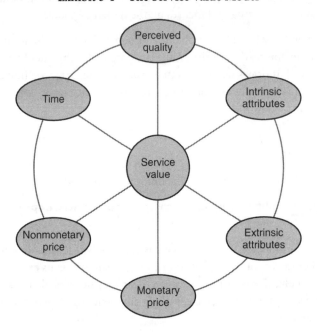

Perceived quality—Quality is frequently defined as "fitness for use." This definition applies to both manufactured goods and services. However, a more appropriate definition of quality for services may be "customer satisfaction" or "external and internal customer satisfaction."[8] This definition captures the essence of quality for services by emphasizing the important fact that quality exists in the eyes of the customer. The customer is the final arbiter of quality; quality exists as the customer perceives it. Customers' expectations are formed through word-of-mouth communication, personal needs, past experience, and external communications from the service organization.

It is clear that if customers' perceptions of what they received matches or exceeds their expectations of the service, they will be satisfied, and hence value has been created for the customer. The higher the perceived quality, the higher the perceived value of the service.

Intrinsic attributes—Intrinsic attributes of a service are the benefits provided to customers. Intrinsic attributes may be considered in two groups: core service and supplementary services. Core service is the basic, or minimum, benefit a customer expects from the service. For example, in passenger air transport the core service may be defined as "transporting customers on an airplane from one airport to another safely and comfortably." Supplementary services include pre-assigned seats, food and beverages, newspapers, movies, pillows and blankets, and connecting flight information by airline representatives at the gate.

Some supplementary services are needed for delivery of the core service. Without them the service will be impossible. Yet others enhance the value for a customer. The relative importance of supplementary services depends on the nature of the service. Clearly, a service organization that fails to deliver the core service will not survive long; hence, providing the core service without failure and as expected by customers is the first and the fundamental step in creating value for customers. However, that is usually not enough to be competitive. Consequently, a service organization can create more value for its customers by both increasing the variety of supplementary services that are appreciated by its customers and performing them at least as well as customers expect.

Extrinsic attributes—Extrinsic service attributes are related to the service, but they exist outside the service package. The reputation of a university as being the "best" in a certain discipline provides extrinsic value to a degree obtained from that school in that particular discipline. Locating a service facility in a fashionable neighborhood may provide added value to customers in addition to the core and supplementary services. In short, all the psychological benefits associated with the service constitute extrinsic attributes. A service organization normally has no direct and immediate influence or control over these attributes. It may, however, create these attributes, and hence create value for its customers in the long run.

Monetary price—The sum of the expenses incurred by a customer to obtain a service is the monetary price. This includes the price charged by the service organization, as well as other expenses a customer has to incur to access the service. A heart patient who needs a by-pass operation may have to travel to a distant city to have access to an expert surgeon. In addition to hospital charges and surgeon's fees, this patient has to consider other expenses, such as airfare and lodging for himself and perhaps for a companion. Monetary price is sometimes the most important factor for customers in making purchase decisions. It is not uncommon to hear consumers define *value* as "low price." A service organization, therefore, can create significant value for its customers if it can lower its prices without causing deterioration in the other attributes of the service.

Nonmonetary price—Any perceived sacrifice, other than financial, that a customer has to make to access and receive a service is defined as nonmonetary price. Nonmonetary sacrifice includes time spent searching for the right service or provider, inconvenience for the customer to access the service provider, time spent traveling to and from the service location, and time spent waiting for and during the service performance. Nonmonetary price also includes psychological costs such as perception of risk, and anxiety felt before, during, and after the service. For example, it is natural for a patient to feel considerable anxiety before surgery. Stress experienced before or during the service, such as waiting in line that feels like forever, and pain experienced in a dentist's chair, can also be part of nonmonetary price customers perceive they are paying.

Time—Time plays an important role in value creation in services in three ways:

1. *Time needed to use the service*—Some services require minimal involvement by a customer; therefore, the time spent by the customer is usually not significant. Establishing phone service at a new address, for example, usually takes a phone call to the local phone company and consumes only a few minutes. Yet some services require considerable expenditure of time. College education, for instance, normally takes at least 4 years to complete. Time spent in accessing, waiting for, and receiving a service may mean a significant sacrifice in terms of other activities, or earnings lost. In general, the less the required time to use a service, the higher the value of the service for the customer.

   There is also an important connection between time and service quality. For example, service quality dimension "responsiveness" is defined as "willingness to help customers and provide prompt service."[9] Time becomes a critical factor in many service failures. When a service failure occurs, even if the service company takes necessary measures to correct the problem, the customer usually ends up losing time, and no corrective measure can restore the lost time. For example, a canceled flight due to a mechanical problem means loss of time for passengers until the airline solves the problem or finds alternative flights. This loss may be significant for some customers, especially if it means missing an important business appointment or missing an important event such as a wedding.

   As discussed earlier, time is also an important element in perceived nonmonetary price. Customers consider the amount of time they have to spend for a service in making purchase decisions. For example, amusement parks are usually crowded on weekends; therefore, the wait is longer for rides. This means that either a customer has to spend much more time in the park than is normally necessary during the week or forego the enjoyment of some rides. Consequently, some customers may prefer to schedule their trip to the amusement park during the week. Reducing the service time usually adds value to service for many customers; sometimes benefit to customers is so significant that they may even be willing to pay a premium price for the time-savings. For example, a flight from New York to Paris on a regular jetliner takes about 7 hours; the same flight on a supersonic Concorde jet, when it was in service, required about 3 1/2 hours; and the cost was three times as much. Obviously, for some customers the reduction in flight time was so valuable that they were willing to pay extra for it.

2. *Service as a time-saving alternative to another service*—Many services are offered as alternatives to existing services; they create value in an important way; and they provide the same service faster and save time for the customer. Many of these services have been enthusiastically embraced by customers. Federal Express provides an alternative to regular mail; letters or small packs are delivered overnight rather than in several days with the U. S. Postal Service's regular service. Fax machines provide an even faster alternative over the phone lines. Also, sending documents over the Internet, if appropriate, is instantaneous and free. When first introduced, air travel provided a new alternative and

a huge advantage over land transportation. Millions of people still use airlines every day for domestic travel as the preferred alternative to travel by train, bus, or car because of the time-savings achieved. For transoceanic travel, of course, airlines provide the only sensible alternative for time-conscious passengers.

3. *The time horizon within which the service provides benefits*—Benefits provided by services create value to customers for different lengths of time periods. Four possibilities may be identified:

   a. *Value now and for a short period of time*—Some services provide immediate benefits to customers that last for a limited length of time. A haircut, for example, has immediate benefits for the customer that last for a few weeks, the benefits however decrease by time. A stay in a hotel provides shelter and an opportunity to rest immediately, and the benefits continue as long as the customer does not check-out.

   b. *Value now and for an indefinite period of time*—Services such as telephone, TV broadcast, police protection, mail delivery, nutrition counseling, and inoculations for various diseases are examples of services that provide benefits immediately and continuously for an indefinite period of time.

   c. *Value in the future for a limited period of time*—Some services provide value for customers or potential customers in a future time period and for a limited time. A new elementary school to be built in the neighborhood may mean an increase in the property taxes for all the residents of a town; however, the new school will provide value for some families only in the future. A couple with no school-aged children will benefit from this service in the future if the couple has preschool-aged children or are planning to have children later. When the benefits accrue, they last for a limited time—until the kids finish school.

   d. *Value in the future for an indefinite period of time*—Services such as college education or a dentist's service to straighten the teeth of a youngster take a long time to complete but provide benefits for the rest of the recipient's life. Major benefits usually do not accrue to the recipient until the service is completed. For example, a college student normally will not find a full-time job in the field she has chosen until graduation. There may, of course, be occasional visits back to the service provider for updates (for example, courses to bring graduates up to date on new techniques) but most services continue to provide benefits even without these updates.

In summary, a service organization can create value for customers by improving the quality of service. It can create value by designing a core service that meets customers' needs and supplementary services that are valued by customers. A service organization can also create value for customers indirectly by creating perceived intrinsic attributes. This is usually accomplished through many years of delivering consistently high-quality, reliable service. It can also be accomplished through advertising and creating a high-value service image. When the monetary price of a service is reduced, customers usually perceive an increase in value. Finally, if access, waiting, and delivery times for service can be reduced, and benefits can be made available sooner and last longer, additional value is created for the customer. For example, the Motor Vehicle Commission in New Jersey increases access time by conducting inspections on Saturdays, in addition to regular weekdays, from 7:00 a.m. until noon so that motorists can have their cars inspected without losing time from work. Shouldice hospital in Toronto, Canada, performs hernia operations so well that its patients return to work in one-half the time it takes patients of other hospitals. Also, the recurrence rate of all operations at Shouldice is 0.8 percent, whereas recurrence rate for hernias performed in U.S. hospitals is 10 percent. This means that benefits Shouldice patients receive from their operations on average last for a much longer period of time.

The service value model presented provides a framework for crafting strategies to create value for customers through the design, development, and delivery of services. Chapter 8, "Design and Development of Services and Service Delivery Systems," discusses the design and development of services and the design of service delivery systems. The remainder of this chapter focuses on strategy and related issues.

5.3 Strategy

Customers buy goods and services when they perceive value in them. They will continue to purchase goods and services as long as they are satisfied—or better yet, delighted—with what they have received. The survival and prosperity of a service organization is closely linked with this outcome. So how should a service organization approach this most important task? What should be their strategy? Clearly, not in a haphazard or random way; successful service companies do not happen by accident; they are created as a result of determined efforts by their employees and managers that are aimed at customer satisfaction. Just having a strategy, of course, is no guarantee for success. This section reviews basic concepts of competitive strategy and discusses how a successful service strategy can be developed for creating value for the customer. First, here are some basic concepts and definitions.

Definition of Strategy

Bruce D. Henderson offers the following definition and perspective on strategy:

> Strategy is a deliberate search for a plan of action that will develop a business's competitive advantage and compound it. For any company, the search is an iterative process that begins with a recognition of where you are and what you have now.... The differences between you and your competitors are the basis of your advantage.[10]

It is clear from this definition that an organization needs a good understanding of its environment to develop an effective strategy. Then it can embark upon designing plans to respond and shape this environment to its advantage. The issue of developing effective strategies will be discussed later in this chapter; however, it is important to note that not all firms follow a well-organized, step-by-step procedure in developing a competitive strategy. Strategy may appear in many different forms:[11]

- **Strategy as plan**—Strategy may be developed as a plan that is designed before an action takes place to achieve certain goals. It is a way for executives to steer the organization in the desired direction.

- **Strategy as ploy**—Strategy may sometimes be a ploy, "just a specific 'maneuver' to outwit an opponent or competitor."

- **Strategy as pattern.** Consistent behavior, or a theme, in a series of activities may be identified as evidence of strategy whether or not the pattern was planned.

- **Strategy as position**—This definition implies positioning of an organization in its environment, or carving itself a niche in this environment. It indicates how an organization is trying to cope with its competitors and survive.

- **Strategy as perspective**—Strategy may also be defined as an organization's "personality," that is, "an ingrained way of perceiving the world."

Strategy may appear in one or more of these forms at any one time. Together, they provide a more comprehensive description of strategy than a single definition might convey. Following are a few more definitions of terms that will be used in discussing strategy.

- **Strategic goals (or objectives)**—Goals emanate from strategy and specify targets for the organization's efforts. In other words, strategic goals define what is to be achieved for survival and competitiveness.

- **Tactics**—Tactics are action-oriented plans with shorter time horizons than strategy. Their main function is to focus an organization's efforts on specific tasks that when accomplished will help achieve the objectives of a strategy. The distinction between a strategy and tactic may depend on the level of organization where it resides, the scale of action, or the perspective of the leader. For example, what a chief executive officer considers a tactic may be a strategy to a lower-level manager.[12]

- **Policies**—Policies define the limits within which the organization will operate, conduct business, and resolve conflicts when there is disagreement among various objectives.

Why an Organization Needs Strategy

Mintzberg identified four main reasons for an organization's need for a strategy:[13]

First, an organization needs strategy to draw a route to desired outcomes, that is, to defend itself against competitors, to remain competitive, and to prosper. In this sense, strategy provides a sense of direction, a destination to aim for. Second, strategy helps an organization focus its activities and energies on certain ends and promote the coordination of these activities. It provides a sense of purpose and direction. In other words, a strategy may help the whole organization pull together in one direction. Third, strategy helps define an organization as character or personality defines an individual. In this sense, strategy provides meaning for the members of an organization as well as outsiders.

Finally, Mintzberg argues that "providing consistency" may be the clearest reason for strategies. A properly designed strategy helps reduce uncertainty for an organization and its members. It helps them organize, interpret, and deal with experiences and incoming information in a consistent way. Reducing uncertainty helps members function more efficiently and feel less stress. In this sense, strategy also simplifies various tasks for the members of the organization. For example, it reduces the need to learn to deal with every new situation; it provides them with a standard way of responding to most situations.

The previous arguments explain why organizations need strategies, but they also provide implicit guidelines for service organizations for designing their competitive strategies as well as designing services and service delivery systems.

Understanding the Competitive Environment

A profound understanding of the environment an organization operates in is a prerequisite to developing an effective strategy. An organization that does not know its rivals or understand its industry and the rules of competition cannot develop an effective competitive strategy. Porter[14] identifies five forces in any industry that define the competitive environment: the entry of new competitors, the threat of substitutes, the bargaining power of buyers, the bargaining power of suppliers, and the intensity of rivalry among the existing competitors. An organization develops a strategy to determine how to respond to competitors and, better yet, how to change the environment and the rules of competition to its advantage.

New entrants—New entrants into an industry usually means new competitive challenges for the existing firms. A new entrant may bring additional capacity to an industry if it brings facilities and a workforce that were not previously in that industry. A new entrant means new challenges or possibly increased competition because a new entrant may be bringing new ideas, new technology, and new services to an industry in addition to increased capacity. For the existing firms this may mean loss of customers, loss of market share, and a reduction in profits.

The seriousness of this type of threat for an organization depends on the barriers to entry as well as the competitive strength and determination of the organization to meet the challenge. Porter identified the following barriers to entry:[15]

- **Economies of scale**—Unit costs decline as the volume of production increases when accompanied with increased capacity (that is, a larger factory). This phenomenon may be observed not only in the manufacture of goods, but also production of services. The major reason for this is that fixed costs will be divided among a larger number of customers served.

- **Product differentiation**—If the existing companies in an industry have brand identification, loyal customers, and product differentiation, a potential entrant may face a difficult barrier to overcome. Many banks entering the credit card market offer Visa or MasterCard with no annual fee and reduced interest rates for a limited time to attract customers from other card issuers.

- **Capital requirements**—Some industries require substantial upfront investment to be a player. Investment may be required not only for equipment and facilities, but also for advertising, research and development, and setting up an order taking and processing system. Clearly, large investment requirements make many service industries, such as airline and healthcare industries, inaccessible for all but companies with substantial financial resources.

- **Switching costs**—Another barrier new entrants may face is the reluctance or unwillingness of customers in an industry to switch to another company due to the costs involved. Customers may be unwilling to switch for other reasons, such as to not give up the comfort of familiar routine or change well-entrenched habits.

- **Access to distribution channels**—Finding a distribution channel or establishing a new one may be a significant barrier for new entrants. Existing competitors in an industry may have exclusive arrangements with distributors that prevent them from accepting business from new or existing competitors. For example, until 2004, rules of Visa and MasterCard prevented their member banks in the United States from issuing American Express cards.

- **Cost disadvantages independent of scale**—Another barrier for new entrants may be the cost advantages existing firms have achieved independent of their size or scale of operations. Some of these advantages originate from the learning curve effect a company enjoys for being in business longer than its competitors.

- **Government policy**—Federal, state, or local governments may create barriers to entry in many industries. For example, licensing requirements exist in industries such as healthcare, law, and education.

- **Expected retaliation**—Another important deterrent to entry may be the expected behavior of the existing competitors. If companies in an industry have a history of meeting a newcomer by fierce competition, a potential entrant may have to think twice before drawing such a hostile reaction from well-established competitors.

Intensity of rivalry among existing competitors—Rivalry among competitors may occur in various forms, including price wars, advertising, new product introduction, and increased customer service or guarantees. Several reasons can be listed for the intensity of rivalry among the existing competitors:[16]

- **Equally balanced competitors**—When firms in an industry are about equal in size and resources, their fight may be fierce and last a long time.

- **Slow industry growth**—Competition in a slow-growing industry means someone's market share gain is someone else's share loss.

- **High fixed costs**—High fixed costs create pressures to use the capacity of a firm at full capacity, which may lead to intense price competition.

- **Lack of differentiation or switching costs**—If the service is considered a commodity, price competition may result.

- **Capacity augmented in large increments**—If increment is big enough to disrupt the balance of industry supply and demand, it may lead to overcapacity, which in turn may lead to price wars.

- **Diverse competitors**—When the strategies, goals, or personalities of competitors differ significantly from each other, they usually cannot read each other's intentions and end up in direct clashes.

- **High strategic stakes**—Some diversified firms may place a high priority on success in a particular industry as part of their overall corporate strategy.

- **High exit barriers**—Specialized assets, labor contracts, government, and social restrictions may create barriers to exit.

Substitutes—A substitute for a service is another service that performs the same basic function or functions. Which function is expected from a service or which function is valuable depends on the customer's needs. A frozen dinner from a supermarket or a sandwich from a deli may be a substitute for a meal in a restaurant if the function is to provide nourishment. However, frozen dinners or sandwiches are not substitutes for someone who wants a dining experience in a pleasant atmosphere with a companion. Substitute products reduce the profit potential of an industry.

Buyers (customers)—Customers create competitive pressures on the organizations in an industry by their search and demand for lower prices, higher quality, or more services, and by playing them against each other. The impact of such behavior on a competitor will be significant if the customer's purchases from the company constitute a major portion of the company's sales.

Suppliers—Similarly, suppliers may create pressures over the members of an industry by their demands for higher prices, or by lowering the quality of products they supply. An important supplier group in service industries is labor (blue and white collar workers or professional athletes). Organized labor may play an important role in an industry as football players' and basketball players' strikes in recent years have shown.

Generic Competitive Strategies

Formulation of a strategy should include an appraisal of all five forces and their interrelationships. Specifically, an organization developing a strategy should assess its own strengths and weaknesses, including its competencies and resources, as well as opportunities and threats that exist in its industry.[17] Also relevant are the values an organization shares, especially of those who implement strategy, and societal impact of such factors as government policy, social concerns, and evolving mores.[18] Consequently, each organization's strategy is unique. However, it is possible to identify patterns in strategy selection. Porter identified three such generic strategies, which are distinctly different in their approach to achieving competitive advantage.[19] This section is based on his classification and description of these generic strategies.

Cost leadership—An organization would be following a cost leadership strategy if it is striving to be the low-cost producer in its industry. Typically, a low-cost producer offers a set of standard, no-frills products (goods and/or services). This approach covers *many segments* of an industry; it is not limited to one particular segment of the market. Cost advantage of a low-cost producer may originate from various sources, including economies of scale, learning-curve effects, innovative or proprietary technology, and preferential access to raw materials. The focus on costs, however, does not mean a cost leader can ignore the differentiation aspects of competition; to remain competitive, it must be equal, or close, to its competitors in the bases of differentiation. If the cost leader does not have parity in differentiation, it should be close enough so that the price reduction it has to offer to gain and maintain market share does not eliminate its cost advantage. An organization following the cost leadership strategy must pay close attention to cost control and overhead minimization and work hard to exploit the learning-curve effect when it exists.

Cost leadership provides protection for the organization against the five forces of its industry in various ways. Customers cannot put too much pressure to reduce its prices—they are already at the lowest levels. Suppliers will not have much power against a low-cost producer if it has economies of scale and hence is a significant customer for the supplier. Cost leadership also provides protection against new entries and substitutes.

An example provided at the end of this chapter discusses Southwest Airlines and its operations. As will be clear from the example, cost leadership is a part of Southwest's strategy; it provides low-cost air transportation on all routes it flies.

Differentiation—Differentiation strategy requires that an organization be unique in a way that is valued by its customers. Uniqueness is *industrywide* and may include product attributes, delivery system, or marketing that meet specific needs of a group of customers. Differentiation strategy is based on the assumption that customers are willing to pay a premium price for the uniqueness the firm offers. Usually, differentiation is obtained through activities that increase costs for the organization. However, the organization cannot completely ignore costs; if its prices are too high, competitors' low cost may overcome the attraction of uniqueness for customers.

This strategy also helps protect an organization against the five forces of its industry. If the organization is successful in creating differentiation of its goods or services in customers' minds, it may achieve loyalty among them and thus reduce customers' bargaining power, at the same time create a barrier for potential entrants and provide a defensible position against competitors and substitutes. In general, this strategy leads to higher profit margins but low market share.

Focus—This strategy is built on the concept of serving a limited segment of the potential market well. By focusing on a limited segment of the market, an organization may tailor its products, operations, and all the relevant activities to serve the selected segment effectively and efficiently. It has two forms: **cost focus** and **differentiation focus**. The difference between these and the previous two generic strategies is that the latter encompasses the entire industry or wide industry segments; cost focus and differentiation focus, however, are limited in scope. They are designed to achieve competitive advantage in costs or differentiation in the selected segment.

For any of the focus strategies to be successful, the selected segment must be somehow neglected by competitors who are trying to serve an entire industry or broad segments of it. Cost focus may be successful if, for example, an organization can identify customers that are inexpensive to serve. Shouldice Hospital in Toronto, Canada, for example, performs only inguinal hernia operations and accepts only healthy patients; consequently, it selects patients that are less expensive to serve. Because of this, it can charge a price that is about one-third of what its competitors charge.

Differentiation focus in services may be achieved if a segment of the market with special needs can be identified and served to meet those special needs. Jiffy Lube, Midas Muffler, and AAMCO each focus on meeting a particular need of car owners. It is, of course, possible to follow both cost and differentiation focus for a limited segment and be successful at it as demonstrated by Shouldice Hospital.

Fragmented industries—A phenomenon that is particularly relevant to services is a fragmented industry. An industry in which no firm has a dominant position or a significant market share is said to be fragmented. These industries usually have a large number of small and medium size firms, none of which can influence industry practices. This is a common phenomenon in many services such as dry cleaning and auto repair. Some of the reasons for industry fragmentation are low entry barriers, absence of economies of scale or learning curve effects, high inventory costs, lack of power in dealing with buyers or suppliers, high product differentiation, exit barriers, and government rules and regulations.

5.4 Formulating a Competitive Service Strategy

Value is created for a customer when a service satisfies a customer's need(s) or provides some benefit to the customer. The higher the value a customer sees in a service, the higher the price he is willing to pay. A customer who perceives value in the service will be a satisfied customer, and a satisfied customer is like an insurance policy for the future of the service organization. Consequently, the purpose of a service strategy must be to create value for its customers. This section focuses on formulating and developing a service strategy to create value for the customer. Strategic service vision is discussed and Southwest Airlines is presented as an example of its application.

James L. Heskett developed the concept of "strategic service vision" in his book *Managing in the Service Economy*.[20] Strategic service vision consists of four basic and three integrative elements.

Basic Elements of the Strategic Service Vision

Target market segment—Like most goods, most services are valuable only to some people; a service organization cannot satisfy everybody. Consequently it should carefully select and identify customers it is able and willing to serve. This is called segmentation. **Segmentation** tries to identify a group of customers with common characteristics, needs, purchasing behavior, or consumption patterns. Effective segmentation results in a grouping of customers that are similar to these or other relevant dimensions but at the same time different from other segments. Segmentation may be based on geographical, demographic, psychographic, or any other relevant basis.

Service concept—A service concept describes the service for customers, employees, and other stakeholders. A service must be defined in terms of outcomes or benefits it provides to customers. The service concept flows from the definition of an organization's business. In other words, the answer to the question "What business are we in?" defines the service concept. The definition of business an organization is in should be broad enough not to eliminate future extensions that may arise because of advances in technology, change in consumption patterns, or other opportunities. Also, a narrow definition may expose the organization to surprise attacks from organizations in related industries. On the other hand, it should not be too broad to lead to businesses outside the organization's abilities and competencies.

Operating strategy—Operating strategy is a set of strategies, plans, and policies concerning an organization's operations, financing, marketing, human resources, and control so that it can bring its service concept to life. It includes hiring, organization policies, control of quality and costs, and ways of leveraging value over cost.

Service delivery system—A service delivery system is how an organization prepares for and conducts itself in service encounters. It includes facilities and their layout, technology and equipment used, processes for delivering the service, job descriptions for employees, and the roles they and customers play during a service encounter. A service delivery system must be designed to achieve maximum customer satisfaction. Most service concepts can be copied by competitors, but a well-designed service delivery system may not be easily duplicated, and hence may serve as a barrier to potential competitors.

Integrative Elements of Strategic Service Vision

Integrative elements help the basic elements fit together for a consistent service strategy. They provide guidelines for planning actions to implement the service vision and include positioning, leveraging value over cost, and strategy/system integration.

Positioning—How an organization differentiates itself from its competitors is called positioning. It requires profound knowledge and understanding of customers' needs, organization's capabilities, competitors' service offerings and capabilities, as well as the ability of the service concept to meet customers' needs. When these elements are understood, the organization seeks a unique set of attributes to match the service concept with the selected segment's characteristics. Uniqueness may be achieved in terms of costs, service features, advertising and promotion, distribution channels, and delivery system.

Value/cost leveraging—A well-designed and positioned service concept provides unique benefits to customers and hence creates value or more value than competitors provide. In general, such uniqueness justifies premium prices for the service, but it also costs more to create. If an organization manages to deliver such high perceived value without driving its costs too high, it is said to leverage value over cost and enjoys higher margins than its competitors. In other words, value is leveraged over cost when the perceived additional value in dollar terms far exceeds the costs of creating it. Clearly, this requires great skill. Various tactics may be used in leveraging value over cost, including customizing certain features that are highly valued by customers, and standardizing others, carefully managing quality at critical points in the service process, managing demand and supply, and involving the customer in service creation.

Strategy/system integration—In addition to consistency between target segment and service concept, and between service concept and operating strategy, operating strategy must be consistent with the delivery system for this collection to become a whole. An excellent service organization achieves consistency between its operating strategy and service delivery system by carefully designing its hiring policies, service processes, and facilities. It also pays close attention to its employee compensation, promotion, and reward policies. Excellent service companies know that without satisfied employees they cannot have satisfied customers.

An Example: Southwest Airlines

This chapter closes with an example of how an excellent service organization achieves success through its strategy. Although there is no evidence to suggest that Southwest Airlines consciously applied the strategic service vision, its practices fit the model.[21] Southwest's practices are summarized in Exhibit 5-2, in which the elements of strategic service vision and their relationships are represented.

Exhibit 5-2   Strategic Service Vision as Applied to Southwest Airlines

Target Market Segment	Positioning	Service Concept	Value-Cost Leveraging	Operating Strategy	Strategy-System Integration	Service Delivery System
Cost-conscious traveler (business, individuals, and families).	Short, point-to-point (rather than hub-and-spoke system) flights. A large number of flights between targeted cities. "Fun-loving rebel airline" image. Keep the corporate culture at the heart of every campaign.	Safe, no-frills, low-cost air travel: "mass transportation." Convenient schedules. Save time for passengers with point-to-point flights and on-time arrivals. Make flying fun.	Despite the "no-frills" image, passengers are provided with a standard meal that has their choice of soft drink and a small bag of peanuts labeled "frills." Point-to-point flights save time for passengers in addition to their savings in ticket price. Flight attendants with a sense of humor entertain and amuse passengers. Attractive uniforms (earlier hot pants, now shorts).	Load and unload planes quickly for on-time arrivals and save time for passengers to increase aircraft utilization. Keep (training, record keeping, parts inventory, maintenance, crew scheduling) costs down by using one type of plane. Make employees the first priority: Profit-sharing plan for employees. Job security. Airline as a "family." Hire people who have a sense of humor and "who know how to have fun." Train employees for necessary skills; create a sense of responsibility and ownership. Encourage trying new ideas as long as safety is not compromised. Disciplined, fiscally prudent growth keeps financial costs down. Encourage employees to think like entrepreneurs.	Free advertising and promotion through off-the-wall events. No tickets; passengers with a reservation show a picture ID at the gate. No assigned seats for quick loading of planes and low cost. Plastic cards with numbers determine boarding order. Board 30 passengers at a time for quick loading. Planes are unloaded and loaded in 20 minutes. Language of the airline: "love potions" (drinks), "love bites" (peanuts), "love machines" (ticketing machines), "Luv Lines" (employee newsletter). Create a strong company culture: Deliver on "We Care About You" promise. Employees own about 13% of the company and receive a share of profits.	An efficient system for maintenance, loading, and unloading planes. Single type of aircraft—Boeing 737—ultimate in delivery system standardization. Employees deliver service with a sense of humor.

Air Southwest Co. (later Southwest Airline Co.) was founded by Rollin W. King and was granted permission to fly between the three largest cities of Texas: Dallas, Houston, and San Antonio. Southwest chose Dallas's Love Field as its headquarters. Southwest purchased three new Boeing 737s and started flying on June 18, 1971, between the three major Texas cities at low prices: $20 each way on all its routes versus competitors' $27 and $28, and with a different image than its competitors.

By 1975, the airline expanded its flight schedule to eight more cities. By 1978, it was one of the country's most profitable airlines. As of the end of 2011, Southwest has been profitable for 39 consecutive years, has never had layoffs, and never had a fatal accident. The airline started with 195 employees in 1971; the number of employees reached 37,000 in 2012; 82 percent of which is unionized. The regional carrier with three planes and three routes became a major airline in 1989 when its revenues exceeded the billion dollar mark. As of 2012, Southwest flies more than 550 Boeing 737 aircraft among 73 cities, operating more than 3,200 flights daily. It is the largest U.S. carrier based on domestic passengers boarded as of March 31, 2011, as measured by the U.S. Department of Transportation.

Southwest's mission is *"dedication to the highest quality of Customer Service delivered with a sense of warmth, friendliness, individual pride, and Company Spirit."* Howard Putnam, a consultant, and early CEO of the airline, described the company as follows: "We weren't an airline. We were mass transportation."[22] Southwest achieves high levels of profit by keeping its costs down and controlling growth. Costs are kept low by an efficient system of operations including ticketing, maintenance, baggage handling, training, and servicing planes. For example, after a plane pulls into a gate, Southwest could turn it around and fly again in 20 minutes. The industry average is 45 minutes.

Southwest uses only Boeing 737 planes, making it possible to switch crews from one flight to another when need arises. Using only one type of plane keeps its training, record keeping, maintenance, and inventory costs low. Most of Southwest's flights are about 1 hour; this implies that it doesn't have to serve meals. Its ticketing system is also kept simple. Passengers are given reservations, and they can get their boarding passes online 24 hours before their flight or at self-service kiosks at the airport. There are no assigned seats on Southwest flights. A letter and number on the boarding pass represent a place in the boarding group. When a boarding group is called, passengers board the plane in numerical order. This strategy keeps costs down and operations simple; the airline does not have to print boarding passes, passes may be used many times, and fewer employees are needed at the gate.

Major airlines use a hub-and-spoke system, where passengers are flown to a central airport from outlying areas, and then they make connections to their destinations. Most of Southwest's flights are short, point-to-point flights; that is, passengers are flown to their destinations directly. Together with a 20-minute plane turnaround, this saves time and money for both the airline and its customers by keeping planes in the air longer resulting in higher efficiency. Passengers save time because they don't have to wait at hub airports for their connecting flights. Southwest has achieved a competitive cost position in its industry. For example, excluding fuel and special items, its cost per available passenger mile in 2011 was 7.61 cents, whereas all other major airlines have higher costs. It also has extremely high labor efficiency in terms of passengers per employee and employees per aircraft. In addition, Southwest's distribution system helps keep its costs down. Most major airlines use computerized reservations system through which travel agents make reservations for passengers. Southwest does not use that system; reservations are made at Southwest's website.

Another important result of the efficient operations system is Southwest's on-time performance. According to the 2011 yearend U.S. Department of Transportation Air Travel Consumer Report issued February 2012, Southwest placed first in the industry Customer Satisfaction ranking. Also in 2012, it was named one of J.D. Power and Associates' 2012 Customer Service Champions.

Southwest has a distinct company culture and hiring policy. Herb Kelleher, the former president and CEO, made this clear by putting employees first. He reasons, if they are happy, satisfied, and dedicated, they will make customers happy and satisfied; satisfied customers come back and that makes shareholders happy.[23]

Southwest's hiring policy requires that employees have a sense of humor; recruiting brochures and employment ads stress that it seeks employees who are comfortable with themselves and know how to have fun. Southwest has a profit-sharing plan; each year Southwest rewards employees with a portion of the company's profit to Employee Profit Sharing accounts. When hired, employees go through training for skills and teamwork. The airline tries to create a sense of responsibility and ownership. Employees are encouraged to try new ideas without compromising safety. The informality of corporate culture and fun-loving attitude does not mean Southwest is run haphazardly. Growth is carefully managed, fast growth is avoided.

Other airlines tried to imitate Southwest's successful strategies without much success. For example United Airlines launched "Shuttle by United" in California in 1994 hoping to duplicate the low costs and quick turnaround times of Southwest. After 16 months of operations, United could achieve only an 8 cents a mile per available seat mile, well above Southwest's 7.1 cents.[24] As a result, United has withdrawn from many routes in California, and Southwest increased its California business. Kelleher had this to say about competition:

> They can imitate the airplanes. They can imitate our ticket counters and all the other hardware. But they can't duplicate the people of Southwest and their attitudes.[25]

5.5 Summary

A service organization's survival and prosperity depends on its capability to create value for its customers, employees, suppliers, and shareholders. Satisfied employees lead to satisfied customers; satisfied customers mean repeat business for the organization and prosperity. Prosperity of the service organization keeps suppliers in business and makes shareholders happy. Consequently, value creation should be the main strategy of a service organization.

Value was defined as the capability of a good or service to satisfy a need or provide a benefit to a customer. A model of service value was presented to provide an insight into how a service organization may create value for its customers. The model has six components: perceived quality, intrinsic attributes, extrinsic attributes, monetary price, nonmonetary price, and time. Customers will be satisfied and hence value will be created for them if their perception of what they received matches or exceeds their expectations of the service. The higher the **perceived quality**, the higher the perceived value of the service. **Intrinsic attributes** of a service are the benefits provided to customers. To create value for customers, a service organization must deliver the core service flawlessly and reliably. **Extrinsic attributes** are related to the service, but they exist outside the service package; that is, all the psychological benefits associated with the service.

The sum of the expenses incurred by a customer to obtain a service is the **monetary price**. Extra value is created for the customer if the organization can deliver the same service at lower monetary cost with no deterioration of quality. Any perceived sacrifice, other than financial, that a customer has to make to access and receive a service is defined as the **nonmonetary price**.

Time plays an important role in value creation in services. A service organization can create value for its customers by reducing the time needed to use the service, offer a service as a time-saving alternative to another service, or by extending the time horizon within which the service provides benefits.

The survival and prosperity of a service organization is closely linked with the outcome of the value creation process. To achieve this end an organization must have a strategy. Strategy is a deliberate search for a plan of action that develops a business's competitive advantage and compounds it. Strategy can also be seen as a plan, a ploy, a pattern, a position, or as a perspective.

The competitive environment in any industry is defined by five forces: the entry of new competitors, the threat of substitutes, the bargaining power of buyers, the bargaining power of suppliers, and the intensity of rivalry among the existing competitors.

In this chapter three generic strategies were discussed as a possible starting point for developing strategy: cost leadership, differentiation, and focus. Then, the "strategic service vision" was discussed as a specific approach to developing strategy for a service organization. This model has four basic elements (target market segment, service concept, operating strategy, and service delivery system) and the integrative elements (positioning, value/cost leveraging, and strategy/system integration) that tie the basic elements together. Finally, Southwest Airlines was used as an example of how this model can be applied in a service organization.

Endnotes

1. See, for example, Hannah R. Sewall, *The Theory of Value Before Adam Smith* (New York, NY: Augustus M. Kelley Publishers, 1968) and Jeffrey T. Young, *Classical Theories of Value: From Smith to Sraffa* (Boulder, Colorado: Westview Press, 1978).

2. Adam Smith, *An Inquiry into the Nature and Causes of the Wealth of Nations* (New York, NY: The Modern Library, 1937), p. 28.

3. Phyllis Deane, *The Evolution of Economic Ideas* (London: Cambridge University Press, 1978), p. 118.

4. Michael E. Porter, *Competitive Advantage: Creating and Sustaining Superior Performance* (New York, NY: The Free Press, 1985), p. 3.

5. David J. De Marle, "The Value Force," in M. Larry Shillito and David J. De Marle, *Value: Its Measurement, Design, and Management* (New York, NY: John Wiley & Sons, 1992), pp. 3–4.

6. For a broader discussion of value creation see Cengiz Haksever, Radha Chaganti, and Ronald G. Cook, "A Model of Value Creation: Strategic View," *Journal of Business Ethics*, Vol. 49, No. 3 (February 2004), pp. 291–305.

7. Valarie A. Zeithaml, "Consumer Perceptions of Price, Quality, and Value: A Means-End Model and Synthesis of Evidence," *Journal of Marketing*, Vol. 52 (July 1988), pp. 2–22.

8. J. M. Juran and Frank M. Gryna, *Quality Planning and Analysis* (New York, NY: McGraw-Hill, 1993), p. 5.

9. Valarie A. Zeithaml, A. Parasuraman, and Leonard L. Berry, *Delivering Quality Service: Balancing Customer Perceptions and Expectations* (New York, The Free Press, 1990), p. 26.

10. Bruce D. Henderson, "The Origin of Strategy," *Harvard Business Review*, (November–December 1989).

11. Henry Mintzberg, "Five Ps for Strategy," *California Management Review* (Fall, 1987).

12. James B. Quinn, *Strategies for Change: Logical Incrementalism* (Homewood, IL, Richard D. Irwin, 1980).

13. Henry Mintzberg, "The Strategy Concept II: Another Look at Why Organizations Need Strategies," *California Management Review* (Fall, 1987), pp. 25–32.

14. Michael E. Porter, *Competitive Advantage*, pp. 4–5.

15. Michael E. Porter, *Competitive Strategy: Techniques for Analyzing Industries and Competitors* (New York, The Free Press, 1980), pp. 7–14.

16. Michael E. Porter, *Competitive Strategy*, pp. 17–21.

17. See for example Chapter 3, in Kenneth R. Andrews, *The Concept of Corporate Strategy* (Homewood, Illinois: Irwin, 1987).

18. Michael E. Porter, *Competitive Strategy*, pp. xvii–xvii.

19. Michael E. Porter, *Competitive Advantage*, pp. 12–20, and *Competitive Strategy*, pp. 34–46.

20. James L. Heskett, *Managing in the Service Economy* (Boston, MA: Harvard Business School Press, 1986).

21. Information for this example, unless otherwise indicated, has been gathered from the following sources: Southwest Airlines homepage: www.southwest.com/ (accessed on 07/12/2012); Kristin Dunlap Godsey, "Slow Climb to New Heights," *Success* (October 20, 1996); Kenneth Labich, "Is Kelleher America's Best CEO?," *Fortune* (May 2, 1994); "Southwest Airlines (A)," Harvard Business School Case 575-060 Rev. 2/85.

22. Scott McCartney, "Turbulence Ahead: Competitors Quake as Southwest Air Is Set to Invade Northeast," *The Wall Street Journal* (October 23, 1996).

23. Kristin Dunlap Godsey, "Slow Climb to New Heights."

24. Scott McCartney and Michael J. McCarthy, "Southwest Flies Circles Around United's Shuttle," *The Wall Street Journal* (February 20, 1996).

25. Kristin Dunlap Godsey, "Slow Climb to New Heights."

6

ETHICAL CHALLENGES IN SERVICE MANAGEMENT

6.1 Introduction

It seems that not a day passes without newspapers, television news programs, or other news organizations reporting a scandal in the United States or around the world. The number and variety of these events is truly astounding. We may be reading or hearing stories such as these:

- n Marital infidelity by a member of the Congress or a high ranking government official

- n A financial executive defrauding investors

- n A financial executive giving insider information to his friends

- n A pharmaceutical company hiding information about the inefficacy of one of its drugs or its harmful side effects

- n A government official or a member of the Congress accepting bribes for preferential treatment of a person or company

- n Athletes using performance enhancing drugs

- n A contractor falsifying test results of equipment it is supposed to supply to military

- n An advertiser making false claims about the benefits of a product or service

- n Human organ trade

- n Extensive use of child labor by suppliers in some countries

This list is just a small sample, and it can be extended with many more unpleasant and shocking events. Most of the acts in these events are obviously illegal, but they are all unethical. They violate one or more ethical norms most people believe.

Managers and employees of most organizations, manufacturing or service, private or public, face decision-making situations that may involve ethical dilemmas. Some of these situations may have choices that are clearly illegal and/or unethical, but some pose great challenge because some may not be clearly identifiable as one or the other. This chapter focuses on some of the ethical challenges managers and employees of private and public organizations face.

6.2 What Is Ethics?

The definition of ethics can be found in dictionaries and encyclopedias; *Merriam Webster's Collegiate Dictionary*[1] has the following definitions: "**1:** the discipline dealing with what is good and bad and with moral duty and obligation **2 a:** a set of moral principles or values **b:** a theory or system of moral values **c:** the principles of conduct governing an individual or group **d:** guiding philosophy."

Philosophers and ethics scholars provide detailed explanation of ethics. Ethics has two meanings: first, it is a field of philosophical study of morality; it is "the search for principles that justify the moral standards that we seek to apply."[2] In other words, ethics is an academic discipline that examines the moral standards of people or society and how these standards may apply to people or society. It also examines moral standards, whether they are reasonable or unreasonable.[3]

The second meaning of ethics is relevant to the practice of moral philosophy in an area of human activity, such as marketing ethics, legal ethics, medical ethics, and so forth. In this sense, it is the collection of moral standards appropriate to a particular area and their application by the people working in that area. Because unethical behavior can harm people physically, financially, or psychologically, or it can harm the environment, ethics in practice can be defined as avoidance of harm or potential harm to people and/or the environment.[4]

It is clear that morality and moral standards is the core of ethics in both meanings. Moral standards include norms that are general rules about behavior such as "stealing is wrong," or "you must always tell the truth." Most people start to learn moral standards at an early age from their parents, school, religious institutions, and social environment. As people mature and gain more life experience, they may revise some of these standards, abandon some, and/or acquire new ones. The moral standards people hold influence their life-style and guide their behavior.

We should also mention the relationship between ethics and the law. Laws are enacted to set limits to people's or organizations' activities. Hence, everyone must obey the laws of the country they live in or visit; it is also the ethical thing to do. Many laws are made after seeing the harmful effects of some unethical acts on people, such as Sarbanes-Oxley federal law, and the environment. However, given the vast number of situations in which potential exists for unethical behavior, laws do not cover all possibilities. Furthermore, some laws may be downright unethical and inhuman, such as laws that permitted owning slaves in the early history of the United States, or laws, or lack of, permitting child labor in some countries.

6.3 Is There an Ethics Problem in Private and Public Sectors?

An *Economist* article in 2010 started with the following observation:

> It is 15 years since Moisés Naím coined the memorable phrase 'corruption eruption.' But there is no sign of the eruption dying down. Indeed, there is so much molten lava and sulphurous ash around that some of the world's biggest companies have been covered in it.[5]

A recent report of National Business Ethics Survey (NBES) by Ethics Resource Center (ERC) seems to confirm this observation.[6] Based on 4,683 responses from employees in the for-profit sector, the report's findings are crystallized in its foreword as follows:

> On the one hand, misconduct has reached an historic low and observers of wrongdoing are more willing to report than ever. But with this good news we also see some very ominous signs—ethics cultures are eroding and employees' perceptions of their leaders' ethics are slipping. Additionally, pressure from employers to compromise standards is at an all-time high and retaliation has reached an alarming rate.

NBES has observed some positive developments in business ethics compared to previous surveys:

- "The percentage of employees who witnessed misconduct at work fell to a new low of 45 percent. That compares to 49 percent in 2009 and is well down from the record high of 55 percent in 2007.

- Those who reported the bad behavior they saw reached a record high of 65 percent, up from 63 percent two years earlier and 12 percentage points higher than the record low of 53 percent in 2005."

These encouraging signs are explained as due to the U.S. economic crisis that started in 2008. Historical patterns indicate that when the economy is in recession companies and their leaders seem to behave more ethically. As the economy starts to recover misconduct tends to rise and reporting of unethical behavior seems to decline. A new trend NBES detected was the influence of employees who spend a significant time on social networks. They seem to report a large number of negative ethical experiences in their workplace compared to employees who do not participate in social networks. Also, social networkers are much more likely to experience pressure to compromise ethical standards and become the target of retaliation (Exhibit 6-1).

Exhibit 6-1   Major Findings of National Business Ethics Survey

> n Retaliation against employee whistleblowers increased significantly. More than one in five employees (22 percent) who reported misconduct say they experienced some form of retaliation in return.
>
> n The percentage of employees who perceived pressure to compromise standards to do their jobs increased to 13 percent, almost reaching the all-time high of 14 percent in 2000.
>
> n The percent of companies with weak ethics cultures also increased to a near-record level at 42 percent.
>
> n By 32 percentage points, active social networkers are much more likely to feel pressure than less-active networkers and non-networkers.
>
> n Most of the active networkers who reported misconduct say they experienced retaliation as a result: 56 percent compared to just 18 percent of less-active social networkers and non-networkers.
>
> Survey authors believe that the following were observed because of the times of economic hardship:
>
> n About one-third (34 percent) of employees say management now watches them more closely.
>
> n More than 4 in 10 employees (42 percent) say their company has increased efforts to raise awareness about ethics.
>
> n Thirty percent of employees agree that bad actors in their company are laying low because of fears about the recession.

Source: *2011 National Business Ethics Survey: Workplace Ethics in Transition* (Ethics Resource Center, Arlington, VA, 2012).

One of the alarming findings of the NBES was an increase in retaliation to whistleblowers; compared to the 2009 survey, retaliation has increased in 2011 in every category (Exhibit 6-2). Another disturbing trend is an increase of pressure on employees to compromise ethical rules or even break the law; 13 percent of employees felt this pressure, highest since the 2000 survey. Probably because of the increased pressure, significant increases were observed in the percentage of employees witnessing unethical and illegal behavior in certain categories. For example, the percentage of employees who observed insider trading increased to 4 percent in 2011 from 1 percent in 2009. Similarly, incidence of sexual harassment in 2011 increased to 11 percent from 7 percent in 2009 (Exhibit 6-3).

Exhibit 6-2 Top Six Forms of Workplace Retaliation Against Whistleblowers: Percent of Employees Who Experienced Some Form of Retaliation

	Survey Year	
Type of Retaliation	2009	2011
Excluded from decision making work activity	62	64
Given a cold shoulder by co-workers	60	62
Verbal abuse by supervisor/manager	55	62
Almost lost job	48	56
Did not receive promotion or raise	43	55
Verbal abuse by coworkers	42	51

Source: Adapted from *2011 National Business Ethics Survey: Workplace Ethics in Transition* (Ethics Resource Center, Arlington, VA, 2012).

As in many other things, such as embracing a new idea, implementing a new business process, or striving to reach some business goals, leadership plays an important role in instilling ethical behavior in employees. Not surprisingly, earlier surveys indicated that the two major drivers of ethics culture are senior executives and supervisors. Unfortunately, NBES has found that employees are losing confidence in top executives and supervisors. Confidence in senior leadership was at 62 percent, the lowest level since 2009; 34 percent of employees think that their leaders do not exhibit ethical behavior (Exhibit 6-4).

Exhibit 6-3 Increases in Workplace Misconduct: Percent of Employees Who Observed Some Form of Misconduct

	Survey Year	
Type of Misconduct	2009	2011
Sexual harassment	7	11
Substance abuse	7	11
Insider trading	1	4
Illegal political contributions	1	4
Stealing	9	12
Environmental violations	4	7
Improper contracts	3	6
Contract violations	3	6
Improper use of competitor's information	2	5
Anticompetitive practices	2	4
Health/safety violations	11	13

Source: Adapted from *2011 National Business Ethics Survey: Workplace Ethics in Transition* (Ethics Resource Center, Arlington, VA, 2012).

NBES has also looked into critical aspects of ethics culture in organizations, including management's trustworthiness, whether managers at all levels talk about ethics and model appropriate behavior, the extent to which employees value and support ethical conduct, accountability, and transparency. Lack of confidence in top managers was likely the major reason that NBES has found that 42 percent of employees believe that their organization has a weak ethics culture (Exhibit 6-5).

Exhibit 6-4   Employees' View of Their Supervisors' Ethics: Percent of Employees Who Perceive That Their Supervisors Do Not Display Ethical Behavior

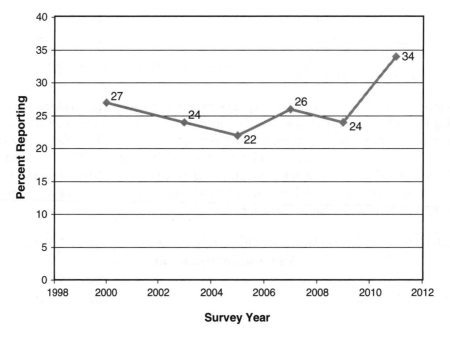

Source: Adapted from *2011 National Business Ethics Survey: Workplace Ethics in Transition* (Ethics Resource Center, Arlington, VA, 2012).

NBES observations inevitably lead to the following ominous warning:

Traditional Pattern Likely to Re-emerge as Recovery Occurs:

History teaches a bittersweet lesson that goes with the good omens: when economic recovery takes place, some companies lose their focus on ethics, some employees will return to risky behavior, and misconduct is likely to rise. Indeed, the rise in retaliation, increased pressure to break rules, and the decline in ethics cultures suggests that—at least at the corporate level—some slippage has occurred already. The stage is set for a larger jump in misconduct once a strong economy reduces companies' ethics focus and eases employees' worry about job security.

Exhibit 6-5   Strength of Organizational Ethics Culture Since 2000:
Employees' View of Their Organization (Percent)

Culture Strength	Survey Year					
	2000	2003	2005	2007	2009	2011
Weak	9	9	9	11	9	11
Weak Leaning	34	30	29	28	26	31
Strong Leaning	48	52	48	44	44	40
Strong	9	9	14	17	21	18
Total	100	100	100	100	100	100

Source: Adapted from *2011 National Business Ethics Survey: Workplace Ethics in Transition* (Ethics Resource Center, Arlington, VA, 2012).

It should be emphasized that most major corporations, public organizations, as well as nonprofits, have ethical standards. Most professional organizations such as American Medical Association, American Bar Association, Certified Financial Planners, American Nurses Association, International Federation of Social Workers, American Institute of Certified Public Accountants, and all American engineering societies have developed ethical standards relevant to the practice of their professions. In 2012, the U.S. Department of Justice published *A Resource Guide to the U.S. Foreign Corrupt Practices Act* (FCPA). Although nonbinding, informal, and summary in nature, the document "...*endeavors to provide helpful information to enterprises of all shapes and sizes—from small businesses doing their first transactions abroad to multi-national corporations with subsidiaries around the world.*"[7] Even most international organizations such as United Nations (UN) and Organization for Economic Co-operation and Development (OECD) have codes of ethics.

Unfortunately, the existence of codes, standards, or training programs for ethical behavior does not prevent bad behavior in all types of organizations. For example, energy company Enron had a 64-page ethics policy, but that did not stop its top executives, as well as its consulting and auditing company Arthur Anderson, from committing fraud and devastating the lives of many people. Shareholders lost almost $11 billion, and employees not only lost their jobs, but also their retirement savings invested in the company stock. Even nonprofits, such as the charitable organization United Way, suffered from fraud and misuse of their funds. The late William Aramony, CEO of United Way in the 1990s, was convicted of fraud and several other charges, lived a lavish lifestyle, and was estimated to have misused between $600,000 and $1.2 million of the organization's funds during a decade of his tenure.

"What leads people to behave unethically or even break the law?" is a natural question you may ask. It is not difficult to guess some answers, but a survey conducted by Human Resource Institute for American Management Association provides a long list of possible reasons.[8] Not surprisingly, "Pressure to meet unrealistic business objectives/deadlines" is by far the most mentioned reason. Desire to advance in one's career and protecting one's livelihood are also most frequently mentioned drivers to unethical behavior (Exhibit 6-6).

Exhibit 6-6   Top Ten Drivers of Unethical Behavior

What are the top factors that are most likely to cause people to compromise an organization's ethical standards?

1.	69.7%	Pressure to meet unrealistic business objectives/deadlines
2.	38.5%	Desire to further one's career
3.	33.8%	Desire to protect one's livelihood
4.	31.1%	Working in environment with cynicism or diminished morale
5.	27.7%	Improper training/ignorance that the act was unethical
6.	24.3%	Lack of consequence if caught
7.	23.5%	Need to follow boss's orders
8.	14.9%	Peer pressure/desire to be a team player
9.	9.5%	Desire to steal from or harm the organization
10.	8.7%	Wanting to help the organization survive

Source: Adapted from *The Ethical Enterprise: A Global Study of Business Ethics 2005–2015* (American Management Association/Human Resource Institute, 2006).

6.4 Challenges for Service Employees and Managers

Ethical issues discussed in this chapter are relevant to managers and employees of all organizations; private or public, for-profit or nonprofit, manufacturing or service. It is clear that some managers and employees encounter situations that have ethical consequences more frequently than others due to the nature of their work. For example, managers of companies that have a presence in other countries may have to deal with corrupt public officials that expect or demand bribes. In addition to ethical challenges manufacturing employees and managers face, those who work in services have some additional challenges their counterparts in manufacturing may not have to deal with.

The major difference between manufacturing and service is what is processed in each line of work. Manufacturing mainly processes material to produce goods; in other words they deal mostly with inanimate objects. Of course, there is a great deal of human-to-human interaction in manufacturing, such as between a manager and her subordinates, other managers, and superiors. Ethical issues may arise in these interactions, as well as in dealing with suppliers, customers, or other stakeholders.

Service organizations on the other hand almost exclusively process people, their possessions, or information; if any material is involved, it is incidental and is used to make performance of a service possible. As discussed in Chapter 2, "The Nature of Services and Service Encounters," outcomes of service encounters depend on the interactions between customers and service providers. Service providers must treat customers with respect, fairness, and equity. They also must keep customers' best interest in mind; any behavior or decision to the contrary would be unethical as well as poor service.

Obviously, the primary concern should be customers' health and well-being, if these could be adversely affected by the performance of the service. Service providers also must take good care of customers' possessions; these could be products, such as a car or a customer's money. Another item of extreme importance is the customer's information, such as Social Security number, credit card number, and password; if the service provider has access to these pieces of information, it should be protected with utmost care. Especially, the development and widespread use of electronic devices such as smartphones and tablets creates a potential for ethical violations. It is well known that some apps for cell phones collect information on customers' Internet searches and their physical movements, such as stores or addresses they visit, without informing them or obtaining their consent. Selling this type of customer information or benefiting from it would clearly be unethical.

6.5 Philosophical Theories of Ethics

This section presents a brief review of some of the well-known theories of ethics.

Virtue Theory

Virtue can be defined as a particular moral excellence. All three great religions (Judaism, Christianity, and Islam) propose many virtues their believers must have. "The idea behind the virtue ethics is that we should determine what characteristics are desirable and then try to promote those characteristics in people."[9]

Virtue ethics can be traced back to the teachings of Confucius, whose idea of "golden mean" can be expressed as "Moral virtue is the appropriate location between two extremes."[10] According to Confucius the virtuous person "is benevolent, kind, generous, and above all balanced, observing mean in all things."[11] In other words, a virtuous person avoids behaving at extremes, but rather at a reasonable middle. However, it should be emphasized that the "middle" should not be interpreted as the halfway point between two extremes but a point that balances the two.

The Greek philosopher Aristotle proposed similar ideas but he emphasized character rather than behavior. Before Aristotle, another Greek philosopher, Plato, proposed four cardinal virtues: temperance, justice, courage, and wisdom.[12] Aristotle suggested that temperance, or moderation, is the primary virtue from which others follow. For example, courage is the reasonable mean between cowardliness and recklessness; temperance between self-deprivation and self-indulgence; and good temper between apathy and irascibility.

Subjectivism or Subjective Relativism

Those who subscribe to this theory claim that there are no universal truths and no universal norms of right and wrong. It follows that different individuals may have completely opposite views of a moral problem, and both can be right. In defense of this philosophy, it can be said that well-meaning people may have conflicting views, and some moral issues may never be settled or agreed upon. For example, abortion has been a contentious issue in the United States for many decades, and there is no general agreement between the two sides. The major objection to subjective relativism is that it provides an ideal last line of defense, or escape route, for someone whose conduct is seen by many people as unethical. By allowing each person to decide right or wrong for herself, subjective relativism makes no moral distinction between good and evil. "Suppose both Adolph Hitler and Mother Teresa spent their entire lives doing what they though[t] was the right thing to do. Do you want to give both of them credit for living good lives?"[13]

Cultural Relativism

This theory holds that what is "right" and "wrong" depends on a society's moral guidelines. That is, what is ethical is decided by the culture of a given society. Bribing public officials, domestic or foreign, for preferential treatment is against the U.S. law. However, in some countries bribing government officials is commonplace and is accepted as one of the facts of life, despite the fact that the practice may be illegal. Some executives doing business in these countries argue that because the practice is culturally accepted, it is a necessary part of doing business in these countries. However, it is clear that acknowledging that bribery is commonplace doesn't mean that people in those countries consider it as ethical. Consequently, bribing government officials is not "right" and not fair to the people of those countries.

Psychological Egoism

Developed by Thomas Hobbes, this theory, also known as ethical egoism, is based on the belief that people are inherently selfish, and they will always behave to advance their self-interests. Hobbes described a time before the existence of government as "solitary, poor, nasty, brutish, and short." He explained the formation of government as "a social contract" in which people agreed to give up some of their natural freedoms in exchange for security. "In the short term we may lose something, but it is worth it for the long-term gains that can be achieved in an atmosphere which fosters cooperation. Thus, the major premise is to structure social institutions and rules in such a way as to maximize the overall welfare by using each individual's self-interest."14 One major criticism of this theory is that humans are complex beings, and it is difficult to determine what motivates them; hence someone behaving in a certain way may not be following her self-interest but may have other motives. Another problem is that this theory may be confusing self-interest with selfishness; not every act to advance one's self-interest is a selfish act. For example, learning a new skill, such as how to read and write, would be in a person's self-interest but not a selfish act.

Utilitarian Theory or Theological Ethics

Basic tenets of this theory were developed by Jeremy Bentham and John Stuart Mill. "This theory holds that acts are judged to be morally right or wrong not in and of themselves, but rather by the results that follow from the acts. Therefore, no act is in and of itself right or wrong."15 The theory is based on the "greatest happiness" principle or principle of "utility," which assumes the maximization of net utility for all people is the moral good. According to this theory, no motive is good or bad; it is the effect(s) it creates that makes it ethical or unethical. Consequently, lying is not morally wrong if it creates good results. Although the original utilitarian theory is called "act utilitarianism," a modified version of this theory is "rule utilitarianism," which is based on the premise that patterns or commonalities can be identified for most decision-making situations. Then you can develop moral rules from these commonalities that will maximize utility, or happiness, over the long run. "Hence, a rule utilitarian applies the Principle of Utility to moral rules, while an act utilitarian applies the Principle of Utility to individual moral actions."16 One of the criticisms of utilitarian theory is that consequences of acts cannot be determined with any certainty. Another objection to this theory is that it uses a single measure to evaluate different types of consequences.

Deontological or Duty Ethics

This theory was developed by the German philosopher Immanuel Kant and is based on a moral principle that he called **categorical imperative**, that there exists certain moral rights and duties for all human beings. Categorical imperatives are rules or principles that must be obeyed by everybody in all situations. Contrary to the Utilitarian theory, Kant believed that there are moral requirements that do not have to create good results; they must be used regardless of their consequences. He believed people should be treated as an end and not as a means to an end. According to this theory the test whether or not an act or decision is ethical can be determined by asking ourselves if we would be willing to have the same act applied to ourselves: "Act only on that maxim whereby you can at the same time will that it should become a universal law."17 One of the major criticisms of Kant's categorical imperative is that it does not allow any exceptions; however, they may be rare but usually exceptions exist to most rules. Another objection to this theory is that it is not clear what we should do when rules conflict.18

6.6 Guidelines for Ethical Business Behavior

After reviewing some of the most well-known theories of ethics, we may naturally wonder how these theories can help managers and employees of service organizations decide the morally right thing to do in an almost infinite variety of situations they find themselves. In other words "What are the policies or principles of ethical behavior in business settings?" Unfortunately, none of the theories reviewed provides what is needed. Nor is there any unified set of specific practical policies or principles that apply in every business. On the other hand, however, ethical theories are all useful to give you an idea how human thought about ethics has developed through thousands of years, and, more important, they provide a rich background of useful ideas that may help develop some suggestions.

The focus is on "What is ethical behavior in business settings in a free-market society?" In Chapter 5, "Service Strategy and Competitiveness," it was indicated that all organizations, private or public, have stakeholders. Stakeholders of an organization are individuals or groups that are impacted by the activities of an organization, or can impact the organization by their activities. A private company's stakeholders include shareholders/owners, employees, customers, suppliers, governmental organizations, competitors, and the public in general.

The main mission of a private firm is to create value for its shareholders/owners in the form of profits and increased share value. Hence, it is natural to expect a company and its managers and employees to make decisions consistent with this mission. However, a private company cannot completely ignore its other stakeholders. A decision or action by a private company that may hurt a group of stakeholders financially or physically may cause a backlash against the company. As a result, the company may lose customers, market share, and profits, which does not help with its mission. A simple example of a backlash is the maelstrom of customer anger in 2011 that caused Bank of America to reverse its decision to charge a $5 monthly debit card fee. Unethical or corrupt behavior may have a negative impact on a much wider scale than on a single group of stakeholders. For example, the damage a culture of bribery may cause to business firms and society in general is succinctly explained in the foreword of *A Resource Guide to the U.S. Foreign Corrupt Practices Act* as follows:

> Corruption has corrosive effects on democratic institutions, undermining public accountability and diverting public resources from important priorities such as health, education, and infrastructure. When business is won or lost based on how much a company is willing to pay in bribes rather than on the quality of its products and services, law-abiding companies are placed at a competitive disadvantage—and consumers lose.[19]

Thus, the assumed mission of business...is the mission of capitalistic firms. The question for business ethics then becomes how to make the practice of capitalism more ethical (i.e. less potentially harmful to its stakeholders).[20]

Public organizations' stakeholders include taxpayers, employees, law-makers, business firms, suppliers, anyone who uses their services, and the public in general. The main mission of public organizations is to create value for their stakeholders by providing services they were established to provide and follow the laws and regulations that apply to them. In performing their duties, managers and employees of these organizations must avoid harm to stakeholders, treat everyone equally, fairly, and with respect, be transparent in decision making, and not waste taxpayer funds.

One element that creates potential for unethical behavior in business settings is the power differential between the managers and employees of an organization and its stakeholders. The power differential may arise from various sources. However, the major reason is that stakeholders usually do not have access to the same knowledge and/or information an organization may possess. Although the Internet and World Wide Web diminished some of this differential for those who actively seek information, specific information about a firm's costs, for example, or potentially harmful effects of a product or service in development is usually not available to the public. Another source of power difference is the resources an organization may have. A giant corporation may exert tremendous pressure on a small supplier for lowering the price of material or service the supplier provides, which may lead to deterioration of quality and cause harm to customers. For example, an airline executive may pressure a company responsible for maintenance and repair of its airplanes to cut costs, or falsify reports of safety inspections, which may have disastrous results.

As mentioned, ethical behavior can be defined as avoiding harm to people and/or the environment. This can be considered as the mission of ethics. It is clear that stakeholders are the most likely groups to be harmed by an organization's decisions or practices; they are also the groups to benefit most. "Thus the mission of ethics is to ameliorate the abusive use of power and reduce the negative impact of chance in the everyday lives of humans. Realistically, improving the human condition of stakeholders within the naturally occurring 'human jungle' provides an appropriate test for business ethics."[21]

It was mentioned earlier that most professional organizations and most major organizations have codes of ethics specifically developed for their members and employees. Consequently, for those who want to stay within the law and behave ethically, it is not difficult to do so; just follow the law and codes of ethics of your profession as well as your organization. If you find yourself in a situation that is not covered by law or the codes, or if your organization has not developed such edicts, we offer the following general principles:

1. Avoid behavior or decision making that would harm people (physically, financially, psychologically, or in any other way) or the environment.

2. Treat people with respect.

3. Be fair.

6.7 Summary

This chapter discussed the topic of ethics in business and pointed out that ethical violations occur in all types of organizations with undesirable effects on society and economic life. It started with a list of some well-known examples of unethical behavior by people from all segments of the society. Two meanings of ethics are given: 1.) as a field of philosophical study of morality; and 2.) the practice of moral philosophy in an area of human activity. We adopted a definition of ethics as "avoidance of doing any harm to people or the environment."

In section 6.3 some compelling evidence from a National Business Ethics Survey (NBES) was presented. NBES indicated that widespread unethical behavior exists in for-profit business organizations. Particularly troubling findings include: 1.) Retaliation against employee whistleblowers rose sharply since 2009; 2.) The percentage of employees who experienced pressure to compromise standards reached the highest level since 2000; 3.) The share of companies with weak ethics cultures climbed to near record levels at 42 percent; 4.) Confidence in senior leadership decreased to its lowest level since 2009, more than one-third of employees think that their leaders do not exhibit ethical behavior; and 5.) 42 percent of employees believe that their organization has a weak ethics culture. NBES also has a dire prediction of the future of ethics in corporate America; a significant increase in unethical behavior is expected when the economy recovers. Historical evidence indicates that a strong economy reduces companies' ethics focus and eases employees' worry about job security.

Section 6.4 discussed special challenges employees and managers of service organizations face that are different from what their counterparts face in manufacturing. It was pointed out that the major difference is due to what is processed in each line of work. Manufacturing firms process material; that is, inanimate objects, whereas service organizations process people, their possessions, or information. Consequently, there is potential for unethical behavior by service providers and harm to service customers.

A brief review of some of the most well-known philosophical ethical theories was presented to provide a background of important ethical concepts. Then some ideas were discussed that may help develop ethical guidelines any manager or employee of any organization can use. It was pointed out that most major organizations and professional societies have developed codes of ethics specific for their line of work and for their members to follow. In case a manager's or employee's organization does not have written codes, or when they find themselves in a situation not covered by relevant codes, we suggested three basic principles to guide behavior and decision making: 1.) Avoid behavior or decision making that would harm people or the environment; 2.) Treat people with respect; and 3.) Be fair.

Endnotes

1. *Merriam Webster's Collegiate Dictionary*, 10th Ed., Merriam Webster, Inc. Springfield, MA, 1996.

2. Jeffrey Reiman, "Criminal Justice Ethics," in Paul Leighton and Jeffrey Reiman, Eds. *Criminal Justice Ethics* (Prentice-Hall, Upper Saddle River, NJ, 2001), p. 2.

3. Manuel G. Velasquez, *Business Ethics: Concepts and Cases*, 7th Ed. (Pearson Education, Inc. Upper Saddle River, NJ, 2012), p. 13.

4. D. Robin, "Toward an Applied Meaning for Ethics in Business," *Journal of Business Ethics*, Vol. 89 (2009), pp. 139–150.

5. Schumpeter, "The Corruption Eruption," *The Economist*, April 20, 2010.

6. Michael G. Oxley and Patricia J. Harned, *2011 National Business Ethics Survey: Workplace Ethics in Transition* (Ethics Resource Center, Arlington, VA, 2012).

7. *A Resource Guide to the U.S. Foreign Corrupt Practices Act* (U.S. Department of Justice and U.S. Securities and Exchange Commission, Washington DC, November 12, 2012).

8. *The Ethical Enterprise: A Global Study of Business Ethics 2005–2015* (American Management Association/Human Resource Institute, 2006), p.55.

9. Brett S. Sharp, Grant Aguirre, and Kenneth Kickham, *Managing in the Public Sector: A Casebook in Ethics and Leadership* (Longman, Pearson Education, Inc. Upper Saddle River, NJ, 2011), p. 12.

10. Clifford G. Christians, Mark Fackler, Kathy B. Richardson, Peggy J. Kreshel, and Robert H. Woods, Jr., *Media Ethics: Cases and Moral Reasoning*, 9th Ed. (Allyn & Bacon, Pearson Education, Inc. Upper Saddle River, NJ, 2012), p. 11.

11. Daniel Bonevac, William Boone, and Stephen Williams, Eds. *Beyond the Western Tradition: Readings in Moral and Political Philosophy*, (Mountain View, CA, Mayfield Publishing, 1992), pp. 264–269.

12. Clifford G. Christians et. al. *Media Ethics: Cases and Moral Reasoning*, p. 10.

13. Michael J. Quinn, *Ethics for the Information Age*, 5th Ed. (Addison-Wesley, Pearson Education, Inc., Upper Saddle River, NJ, 2013), p. 59.

14. Sharp, Aguirre, and Kickham, *Managing in the Public Sector: A Casebook in Ethics and Leadership*, p.5.

15. Sharp, Aguirre, and Kickham, *Managing in the Public Sector: A Casebook in Ethics and Leadership*, p.6.

16. Michael J. Quinn, *Ethics for the Information Age*, p. 80.

17. Immanuel Kant, *Groundwork of the Metaphysic of Morals*, trans. by H.J. Patton (Harper Torchbooks, New York, 1964), p.70.

18. Sharp, Aguirre, and Kickham, *Managing in the Public Sector: A Casebook in Ethics and Leadership*, p.12.

19. *A Resource Guide to the U.S. Foreign Corrupt Practices Act* (U.S. Department of Justice and U.S. Securities and Exchange Commission, Washington DC. November 12, 2012).

20. Robin, "Toward an Applied Meaning for Ethics in Business."

21. Robin, "Toward an Applied Meaning for Ethics in Business."

TECHNOLOGY AND ITS IMPACT ON SERVICES AND THEIR MANAGEMENT

7.1 Introduction

Every day we watch on TV and read in your newspapers news about advances in technology such as

Artificial organs	Automated language translation
Cloning	Digital, wireless communications, smartphones, tablets
Software as a Service	Space travel
Distance learning	Telecommuting
Smart Cards	Genetic engineering
3-D Printers	Geographical positioning systems (GPS)
Cloud computing	Social networking (Facebook, LinkedIn, and Twitter)

Technology is the practical application of science to any human endeavor. Technology includes the resources and knowledge needed to achieve an objective. Hence, when early humans used flint to make fire, or bows and arrows to kill animals for food, they were using technology. We use the word technology in this broadest sense. Clearly, we try to achieve many objectives through our activities and try to solve numerous problems, such as space exploration, producing goods and services for our needs, protecting the environment, finding cures to diseases, generating energy economically, communicating with others, to name just a few. When we use science for such purposes, a technology is created for that area of human activity, such as space technology, manufacturing technology, environmental technology, medical technology, and communications technology. Naturally, all these technologies influence our lives and organizations that produce goods and services. However, information technology is probably the technology that has the greatest impact on how services are created and delivered. Therefore, this chapter is devoted to a discussion of information technology and its impact on services and their management. This chapter also focuses on how technology can be turned into a competitive weapon for service organizations.

7.2 Process Technology and Information Technology

A **process** is any purposeful activity or group of activities that result in an outcome. A process requires inputs such as human intelligence, information, machines, and materials, and may produce a physical output or service. In manufacturing, many different technologies are used, such as computer-aided design (CAD) to design goods and chemical, electrical, metallurgical, or mechanical technologies to produce them. Batch, continuous, or mass production technologies are used, depending on the goods being produced or the quantity needed. Processes are also essential for the creation and delivery of services. Actually, any service is the result of a process. Service processes, however, cannot be easily classified or labeled as is done in manufacturing. Service processes are numerous and varied. The types of activities and inputs required for service processes depend on the service. For example, surgeons operating on a patient in a hospital use information about the patient and medical technology and follow well-established medical procedures. An investment banker, on the other hand, uses financial information and information technology, and follows the established principles of her profession, as well as the applicable laws. Clearly, these two groups of professionals use different process technologies; however, they both rely on information technology.

Information technology (**IT**) consists of computer and telecommunications technologies. **Computer technology** is based on hardware and software and is essential for storing and processing data and information. **Telecommunications technology** consists of both equipment and software and is needed for transmitting voice, data, and information.

7.3 Technology in Services

The stereotype of a service firm is a small-scale, labor-intensive establishment with unsophisticated processes that require little or no investment in technology. This dated view of services is not supported by evidence; there have been significant investments in information technology (IT) since the early 1980s. For example, it is estimated that U.S. health information technology (IT) investments was $27.2 billion in 2008, which is expected to grow to $32.8 billion by 2012.[1] It is also estimated that approximately 85 percent of all investments in IT hardware are in services. It is interesting to note that although investments in capital and technology usually lead to higher productivity in manufacturing,[2] there has been some controversy about the effect of IT investments on firm performance. The slow growth in service productivity despite the significant investments in IT is known as an "**information technology paradox**."[3] A report by a committee of National Academy of Sciences[4] offers several possible explanations for this so-called paradox:

1. **Wasteful and inefficient use of IT**—Although information technology provides powerful tools for service workers at all levels, there is no assurance that these tools are used competently or correctly. In many cases IT had been used to automate inefficient systems or processes without streamlining the system first.

2. **Impact of other problems**—It may be that IT has increased productivity in services, but other problems caused a slowdown in productivity growth because IT is only one of the factors that affect productivity.

3. **Outdated methods of productivity measurement**—A third possibility is that IT did have a positive impact on service productivity but these improvements have been missed by current methods of measurement. For example, existing data on productivity does not capture important elements of service quality.

4. **Lagged effect**—It is possible that IT does have a positive effect on service productivity, but it takes time for the results to emerge.

5. **Level of aggregation**—Finally, a fifth possible explanation is that we should look at the impact of IT expenditures on service productivity at lower levels (that is, firm level) of aggregation rather than macro levels.

Peter F. Drucker, probably the most influential management thinker of our time, looked at the issue from a different perspective: "…capital cannot be substituted for labor (that is, for people) in knowledge and service work. Nor does new technology by itself generate higher productivity in such work. In making and moving things, capital and technology are **factors of production**, to use the economist's term. In knowledge and service work, they are **tools of production**. Whether they help productivity or harm it depends on what people do with them, on the purpose to which they are being put, for instance, or on the skill of the user."[5] However, recent research has come up with evidence that investments in IT lead to improvements in performance with a time lag; specifically, studies have found that it took an average of approximately 3 to 4 years after the year of investment for the firms to realize the greatest performance benefits.[6]

7.4 Why Service Companies Invest in Technology

It is safe to say that all service industries use some technology. However, the level of sophistication of the technology and the degree of utilization varies across industries. This is largely due to the nature of the business. Some organizations, such as telephone companies, software developers, and Internet service providers are in the business of developing information technology. Some others, however, invest in technology for other reasons, mainly to stay competitive. For example FedEx and United Parcel Service (UPS) are both investing more than $1 billion a year into technology research.[7] Another example is banks: "…in a sense, banks are technology companies. Many have hundreds, if not thousands, of people working in huge information-technology departments.[8]

In section 7.6, applications of technology in services are reviewed, but first we review the major reasons why many service organizations invest in technology and rely on it. These are identified by a Committee of the National Academy of Sciences from the many interviews it conducted with service industry executives.[9]

1. **Preserving or expanding market share**—Although it may sometimes be an inappropriate and misleading indicator, market share is used as a key measure of performance by some companies. Market share may also be used as a basis for obtaining marketing power and favorable terms from suppliers as well as improved economies of scale or scope. Some service companies may feel compelled to invest heavily into technology to maintain their share; even though it does not necessarily increase their output or profitability.

2. **Avoiding risks or alternative costs**—Some organizations invest in technology to reduce or avoid risks. For example, hospitals may invest in the state-of-the-art technology to avoid malpractice suits in addition to the benefits from improved diagnostic and treatment capabilities provided by the new technology. Airports are installing explosives detection devices against terrorist attacks. Similarly, many airports are installing advanced radar systems to detect wind shear, which has been blamed for many airline accidents at or in the vicinity of airports.

3. **Creating flexibility for changing business environment**—A constant in today's business world seems to be change. Changes in government regulations (increases as well as deregulations), increased competition, globalization, complexity of operations, and changing consumer tastes all contribute to the uncertainty and complexity of the environment in which service organizations operate. Flexible information technology systems often help service organizations cope with the rapidly changing environment.

4. **Improving the internal environment**—Many organizations invest in technology to make their employees' jobs easier and create a happier work environment by eliminating tedious tasks and making jobs more interesting. Also, the use of IT improves data collection and processing, and forecasting abilities of the organization thereby providing greater stability to the organization's operations.

5. **Improving the quality of services and interactions with customers**—Quality and customer satisfaction are clearly the focus of many service organizations today. Some of the elements of customer satisfaction and quality service are reliability, consistency, accuracy, and speed of service. When used competently and efficiently, information technology can help a service organization deliver all these elements for long-term customer loyalty. Investments in technology also enhance the positive perception of both customers and employees about the organization and its services.

7.5 Technology as a Competitive Edge

Despite the doubts about a lack of a positive relationship between IT investments and profitability or productivity, there is no denying that technology has made and continues to make a huge impact on our daily lives through many goods and services. Think about the many conveniences of modern life, such as television, the Internet, fax machines, smartphones, tablet computers, voice mail, e-mail, ATMs, air travel, modern medicine, to name a few; they are all outcomes of technological progress. Consequently, even if IT is no guarantee for profits, it is clear that it has provided many benefits to millions of consumers. On the other hand, there are many organizations that made big investments in IT and achieved huge success. This section discusses how service companies can use technology as a competitive edge and become profitable.

By being the first to use new technology, as well as using it competently, a service organization may gain an important edge over its competitors. **Competitive edge** is what distinguishes an organization from its competitors. It is an asymmetry that appeals to prospective buyers of a service. A competitive edge may be the speed of service, increased scope of the service package, lower price for the same quality, or better "fit" to the customer; technology may help an organization achieve these objectives.

Information technology can help a service organization differentiate its service offerings from competing services. For example, customers of both FedEx and UPS can prepare and print their own shipping labels and request pickup at its website. Later, they can check the status of their shipment through the company's web page. These service organizations differentiate their services from competitors' with the aid of information technology.

Advances in IT may also lead to new business practices that were not possible earlier. A case in point is the strategic **alliances** among many large service organizations. These alliances may be between organizations within the same industry or between organizations in different industries. An example of the first kind is the alliances between airlines that have become commonplace in the airline industry. There are three passenger airline alliances: Star Alliance (28 members), Sky Team (17 members), and One World (12 members). Alliances between airlines usually involve establishing systems for code sharing. Code sharing involves linking flight schedules and helps airlines channel passengers to each other by selling tickets on each other's flights. Code sharing helps airlines expand their networks to other parts of the country, or the world, without making any new investments in new planes or routes. This type of alliance also provides benefits to airline passengers in the form of easy connections, baggage transfers, and frequent flier miles that they can use on any airline in the alliance. On the other hand, there is also evidence that some alliances may reduce the number of choices for passengers and lead to higher prices.[10] Alliances may also be formed between organizations in different service industries. For example, banks issue credit cards that earn miles on specific airlines.

Companies today aggressively seek a competitive advantage by monitoring new technical advances or conducting applied research. Leonard L. Berry[11] provides the following guidelines to increase the chances of achieving competitiveness through technology:

1. **Take a holistic approach**—Technology is not an end in itself—it should serve as a tool to help the service organization achieve its goals and objectives. In other words, the use of technology should support the overall strategy of the organization. This requires a clear vision of the destination the organization is trying to reach, as well as its strengths and weaknesses and its competencies. Top managers of the organization must be involved in the formulation of a technology strategy to make sure that it supports the organizational strategy and monitor its implementation. "Management must tell the technologists what the technology must do; management, not the technologists, must be in charge of the technology strategy."

2. **Automate efficient systems**—Technology does not make an inefficient service process or system efficient. As many organizations have learned from unsuccessful implementations of technology, automating an outdated, inefficient system does not increase output or profits significantly. Before making any investment in technology, an organization should study the existing service system and its processes for tasks and practices that do not add value for customers, create needless delays, or make employees' jobs unnecessarily difficult and boring. Special attention must be paid to processes that cross traditional organizational or departmental boundaries, or processes that involve many handoffs. Systems and/or processes with such undesirable characteristics must be redesigned with customer and employee satisfaction in mind, and if possible, with their input, before an advanced technology is introduced.

3. **Solve a genuine problem**—To be effective, technology should be used to solve a real problem of customers, internal or external. This requires identification of customers, finding out their needs, and obtaining their input to decisions concerning the choice of technology and system design. "Investing in technology strictly to lower operating costs rarely produces optimum results. Users need to benefit, not just the investors. The technology should help service providers perform more effectively, with more authority, confidence, creativity, quickness and/or knowledge. Or the technology should offer external customers more convenience, increased reliability, greater control, lower prices, or some other value adding property."

4. **Offer more—not less—control**—The basic reason why technology is developed in the first place is to improve the benefits of the existing technology or create new benefits for users. One of the greatest benefits technology can provide to service employees and their customers is to give them more choices and more control. Customers should have more choices so that they can choose freely what they need. Service employees should have more authority and control over their actions so that they can serve their customers better, or act quickly to solve problems. In short, technology should empower service providers and their customers.

5. **Optimize basic technologies**—Every service system or process, regardless of the level of sophistication of its technology, may have some low-tech components. Failure or inefficiencies in these low-tech components may significantly reduce the capability of the

organization to serve its customers. Consequently, great attention must be paid to components of the system that are basic to the creation and delivery of the service; they must be the first to get the benefit of advanced technology. Even after the installation of advanced technology, there may remain low-tech components. Implementers of technology must make sure that high- and low-tech components are compatible and are well integrated into producing results for the customers. The following quote illustrates a failure in this integration:

"Consider my experience while checking out of a hotel. The receptionist quickly computed my bill on the monitor in front of her, transformed it into a paper copy on the adjacent printer, and asked me to sign the credit card slip; but then she walked off, papers in hand, to the far end of the long reception desk. There she remained several minutes, standing beside a couple of her colleagues. I began to fear that something horrible had happened to my credit line. Other customers behind me muttered restlessly. Finally the receptionist returned. "You're all set!" she said. "What was the problem?" I asked. She gave me a tired smile. "Oh, we've only got one stapler on the desk, so I had to wait my turn to staple your bill and credit card slip together." For want of a low-tech $3 stapler, was lost a sizable chunk of the potential gains in employee productivity and customer satisfaction to be derived from a computer system that probably cost ten thousand times as much! (Of course, assuming that a paper receipt is needed in the first place, a better solution would be to integrate bill and card receipt into a single document.)"[12]

6. **Combine high tech with high touch**—When used competently and efficiently, technology will increase the speed of service when it is desirable, and improve accuracy and consistency of outcomes. However, some customers are technology-averse; they prefer to deal with humans rather than machines and computers even if machines provide some advantages. Also, some customers may feel that the service is rather impersonal when they have to subject themselves to tests or go through processes involving machines. Technology may be seen as the culprit in these situations, but it can also be a powerful tool when the organization, or service providers, manage to add human touch to the high-tech environment. Technology may create extra time for service providers to pay personal attention to customers by reducing the service time and/or performing tedious tasks for them.

7.6 Application Areas of Technology in Services

Technology applications in service industries are plentiful, as shown in Exhibit 7-1. For example, in banking, which is just one part of financial services, such technologies as electronic funds transfer (EFT), electronic imaging, ATMs, and magnetic ink character recognition (MICR) readers for encoding checks are widely used to increase productivity. Similar advances in technology are evident in other services. In healthcare services, technologies such as CAT scanners and fetal monitors are diagnostic in nature, whereas technologies such as pacemakers and dialysis machines aid in managing existing illnesses.

Technology may create a competitive edge by improving an existing service process. Such improvements may be in the form of speed, offering more choices to customers, or increased quality. **Office automation**, for example, helps office workers become more efficient and effective by integrating information technology into their processes. Word processing software increases efficiency in document preparation by reducing the time needed to type, revise, check spelling, and print. Similarly, spreadsheets help reduce the time needed to gather, analyze, and manipulate large amounts of numerical data for decision making.

Technology may also change the entire process through **substitution**. In the first case, examples are wide-screen movie theaters, fiber optics to transmit information, or desk-top publishing services. Examples of substitution include electronic mail as a substitute for hard-copy mail, television as a substitute for radio, air travel as a replacement for train travel, teleconferencing to air travel or in-person meetings, automated car washing as a substitute for hand washing, and computer-programmed stock trading as a substitute for judgmental trading.

Exhibit 7-1 Examples of Technology Use in Services

Service Industry	Example
Banking	Check deposit, account balance check, transfer funds, paying bills with a mobile device, debit cards, electronic funds transfer, electronic imaging, and magnetic ink character recognition
Education	Distance learning, multimedia presentations, interactive smart boards in classrooms, and course management systems (for example, Blackboard), Internet
Government	National Oceanic and Atmospheric Administration (NOAA) (weather information using satellites), Federal Aviation Administration (air traffic control), and The North American Aerospace Defense Command (NORAD) (aerospace warning and aerospace control for North America, warning of attacks from air)
Restaurants and food	Optical checkout scanners, wireless orders from waiters to the kitchen, and restaurant paging systems, noise-canceling technology for restaurants
Communications	Electronic publishing, smartphones, e-mail, voice mail, and Wi-Fi
Hotels	Electronic check-in and check-out systems, electronic key/lock systems, and checking your bill on your room TV
Wholesale/retail trade	Point-of-sale electronic terminals, electronic data interchange (EDI), and bar-code readers
Transportation	Electronic toll collection system (for example, E-ZPass) and satellite-directed navigation systems
Healthcare	Magnetic resonance imaging scanners, computerized tomography (CAT scan), sonograms, patient monitoring systems, and WebMD
Airlines	Flight scheduling, computerized reservation systems, check-ins at kiosks

Technology may be applied for four different purposes in the service business:

- Processing the customer
- Processing the customer's possessions
- Processing information
- Creating new services

Processing the Customer

Processing the customer is typical of personal services such as healthcare, cosmetics, transportation, education, and entertainment. It is one of the growing challenges in services. Several factors contribute to this problem. One factor is that customers are becoming less tolerant to waiting in service systems. Another is the high cost of staffing service outlets to meet peak demand. Consequently, service organizations sometimes reduce staffing levels to lower their costs. A third factor is the nonuniform demand for service during the day. The problem seems to be particularly acute at airports mainly created by security checks of passengers and baggage. Some airlines are trying a range of high-tech innovations to process passengers through airports to their planes. The essence of the approach is to process passengers through different channels if they don't have any problems that need to be solved at the check-in counter. For example, passengers who purchased their tickets electronically on the Internet can go to a computer kiosk at the airport for self check-in, which takes about 1 minute. Some kiosks also issue bar-coded baggage tags. Another innovation airlines have implemented is roving customer-service agents with a hand-held computer and a tiny printer attached to their belts; they check in passengers on the spot and issue boarding passes.[13] These innovations help airlines reduce lines and waiting at their check-in counters and save time for customers, and are all made possible by advanced information technology.

Processing the Customer's Possessions

The second area on the list of technology applications involves processing a customer's equipment or materials. A prominent example of new technology applied to the processing of a customer's possession is the SensAware.[14] This is first-of-its-kind information service that provides access to information and near real-time visibility into the condition of a package in transit including temperature readings, shipment's exact location, and if the contents have been exposed to light. These data are accessible even during flight on FedEx aircraft and enable customers to monitor in-transit conditions during ground transportation. Obviously, this type of information is useful to the healthcare and life sciences industries whose shipments are often very high value (for example, donor organs) and/or are extremely time-sensitive. Originally, this service was designed for the healthcare and life sciences industries but now is available to organizations in all industries.

Processing Information

The third area in which technology may be applied to improving services is data and information processing. This topic is so important it is discussed in detail later in the chapter. Basically, information comes into a firm, is edited, and is converted to a standard form. Multiple copies are prepared and distributed to different work sequences where operations are performed. The copies finally end up in files, are sent to some outside agency such as a customer or vendor, or are destroyed. Some opportunities for increasing the level of technology are electronic data interchange (EDI), computer-to-copier reproduction, and the automatic generation of orders as electronically monitored needs are detected. Consider the following example.

One of the most successful organizations in the use of technology is United Services Automobile Association (USAA), a mutual insurance and financial services company providing a variety of financial services to its members who are active or retired members of the U.S. military.[15] Former CEO Robert F. McDermott took over the company in 1968 and made it one of the most successful in insurance business. USAA went from a $200 million company with 650,000 members to a net worth of $19.9 billion and 8.8 million members in 2011. McDermott had made four important decisions and implemented them: (1) automate insurance policy-writing system; (2) reduce the workforce by attrition; (3) implement an education and training program; and (4) decentralize decision making. In short, USAA "empowered" its employees through information technology (by providing them all the data and information they need to serve customers), education and training (by giving them the necessary knowledge), and decentralized decision making (by giving them the authority to make decisions and solve customer's problem).

USAA also uses electronic imaging for storing and processing all its documents. **Document imaging systems** convert documents and images into digital form and store them in a computer data environment. Most of the documents do not even leave the mailroom; they are scanned and stored on optical disks, and they instantly become available for any service representative of the company. In 2007, the organization revolutionized consumer banking with Deposit@Home, which allowed customers to deposit checks using their personal scanners at home. And more recently, it introduced Deposit@Mobile service, which enables members to deposit checks using mobile devices such as iPhone and Android by taking a photo of the check and sending it to the company.

Creating New Services

Finally, technology may create completely new services through development of new products or processes. The development of television created the services of television programming and broadcasting, and, later, cable and satellite TV. The invention of VCRs brought with it the era of video rental stores. Knowledge and information are the essence of many new services. For example software, computer games, information services such as Dow Jones News Service (business/financial), Lexis (legal), WebMD, music downloading services, and e-book readers are all products of advancements in information technology. And think of all the services and benefits created by the introduction of the World Wide Web on the Internet! You can practically buy anything on the Web; a new or used car, a car loan, mortgage loan, a home, and groceries, or find information about almost anything. You can read newspapers and magazines and retrieve information from government agencies or numerous other sources. These are just a few of the new services created by information technology.

7.7 Information Systems

Many researchers and observers of the business world agree with the characterization that the economies of the United States and other developed nations are a "knowledge and information-based service economy." Most economic activities require information as an input. However, information plays a critical role in services. Almost all services require information as an input, and almost all services generate information as part of the service, and for some services information is the output. A service cannot happen without information. Information is generated from data by an information system.

An information system can be defined as a system of "interrelated components that collect (or retrieve), process, store, and distribute information to support decision making, coordinating, and control in an organization. In addition, information systems may also help managers and workers analyze problems, visualize complex subjects and create new products."[16]

An information system performs three basic activities: input, processing, and output. Facts, numbers, words, strings of characters or symbols, or uninterpreted observations are called **data**. Data are the **input**, or the raw material, for an information system. **Information** is the **output** of an information system; it is data that have been transformed into a useful and meaningful form for human beings. Transformation of data into information is the **processing** function of an information system.

Information systems existed in all organizations before computers and telecommunications technology were developed. However, today an information system without these components would be rare, even unthinkable, in developed countries. Consequently, it must be clear that when we mention information systems in service organizations, we refer to **computer-based information systems**.

Most service organizations have multiple information systems. These systems are usually developed at different times for different purposes as they are needed. Consequently, a service organization may have separate information systems for its operations, marketing, finance, accounting, and human resources functions. It may also have different information systems serving different organizational levels: transaction processing systems (operational-level), management information systems, decision-support (middle management level) systems, and executive support systems. Exhibit 7-2 summarizes these possibilities.[17]

Exhibit 7-2 Types of Information Systems and Groups They Serve

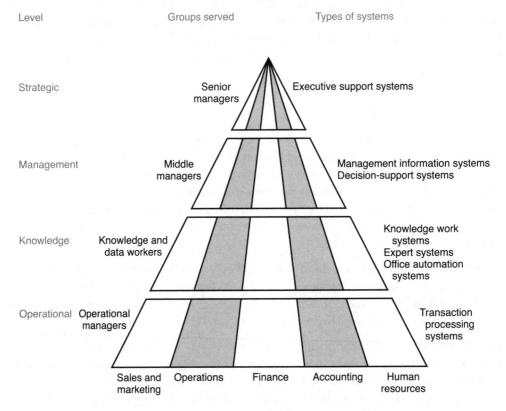

Source: Adapted from Kenneth C. Laudon and Jane P. Laudon, *Management Information Systems*, 5th ed. (Upper Saddle River, NJ, Prentice Hall, 1998), pp.37–39.

Operational-Level Systems

Operational-level systems are designed to support operational level managers by supplying them with information about day-to-day operations and transactions, such as sales, receipts, cash deposits, payroll, and material purchases. These systems are called **transaction processing systems**. They collect the necessary data and generate information needed by lower-level managers to conduct their daily activities and make routine decisions. Business processes at this level are highly structured and well defined. For example, a decision whether to grant an increase in credit limit to a credit card customer can be made by a lower-level manager by simply checking if the customer meets predetermined criteria.

Management Information Systems

Management information systems (MIS) support middle managers. MIS provide weekly, monthly, or yearly summary reports concerning a company's basic operations using the data generated by transaction processing systems. Today, most of these reports are provided online. MIS usually provide answers to prespecified routine questions.

Decision-Support Systems

These systems also serve middle managers in their duties such as planning, controlling, and nonroutine decision making. Decision-support systems (DSS) go one step further than MIS by aiding the manager in making decisions, rather than simply providing the information. These systems are interactive, user-friendly computer-based systems that utilize both internal and external data and mathematical models to help solve unstructured or semistructured problems. The ability of the user to query the DSS concerning the effect of different potential scenarios of a decision (called "what if" analysis) is an important attribute of decision-support systems.[18]

Executive Support Systems

Executive support systems (ESS) are designed for senior-level management to address strategic issues and long-term trends, such as demand patterns, cost of materials, and employment levels. Senior managers deal with problems and issues that concern the well-being of an organization in the long run. They have to deal with issues and problems that are internal to the organization as well as external. ESS address unstructured decisions, and they provide information both from within the organization and from outside. These systems use advanced graphics and communications software and are user friendly.

7.8 Enterprise Systems

As discussed in the previous section, many organizations have developed information systems for different functions at different times. A major problem with these systems is that usually they do not "talk" to each other. In other words, they are not compatible. This approach to information system design leads to inefficiencies and inaccuracies in data and information because the same type of data are collected and stored by different systems and usually information from these systems do not agree. **Enterprise applications** have been developed to solve this problem. Namely, to create an information system for the entire organization and its various functions and departments that provides seamless integration of information from different sources and functions. There are four types of enterprise applications: enterprise resource planning (ERP) systems, supply chain management (SCM) systems, customer relationship management (CRM) systems, and knowledge management systems (KMS).

ERP Systems

An ERP system consists of "a set of integrated business application programs, or modules. Each module performs a particular business function, including accounts receivable, account payable, general ledger accounting, inventory control, material requirements planning, order management, and human resources, among others."[19] An ERP system uses a common database and common set of definitions; hence its various modules can communicate with each other. ERP modules are integrated in the sense that if a transaction is processed in one area, the impact of this is reflected in all relevant areas. For example, when an order is received and processed, all the relevant areas, such as accounting, inventory, production scheduling, and purchasing are informed of the transaction and data relevant to those areas are updated.

An important characteristic of ERP systems is that they require the organization to follow a specific model of doing business. Usually, processes assumed in ERP software reflect the state of the art for the particular area and represent best industry practices. Therefore, before an ERP system can be implemented, an organization must change its business practices to conform to the model assumed by the system. Resistance to change usually creates the greatest obstacle in implementation.

Supply Chain Management Systems

These systems help a firm manage its relationships and processes with its suppliers, shippers, and customers. They help the firm share information about its orders, production schedules, inventory levels, and delivery schedules with its suppliers, distributors, and logistics companies. Sharing timely and accurate information can help all supply chain members improve their performance.

Customer Relationship Management Systems

A customer relationship management system is designed to form a strong relationship with its customers. It provides an integrated approach to a company's dealings with its customers in all aspects of its business such as sales, marketing, and support. CRM aims to optimize revenue, customer satisfaction, and customer retention.

Knowledge Management Systems

Any organization involved in research and development is essentially involved in knowledge creation. Some organizations convert the newly created knowledge into new services and products. For example, pharmaceutical companies spend billions of dollars every year for research, development, and testing of new drugs. If effective and approved by the Food and Drug Administration, new drugs represent the transformation of knowledge into products and related services. Pharmaceutical companies also have manufacturing activities to produce drugs, but, most important, they are in the knowledge creation business. There are many other ways organizations may be creating new knowledge; basically all high-tech companies such as Google, Microsoft, Apple, and Motorola, to mention a few, are all involved in creating new knowledge, and their market value is largely based on their "knowledge assets." Clearly, knowledge creation is service business.

"Knowledge management systems (KMS) are systems that enable individuals and organizations to enhance learning, improve performance, and, hopefully, produce long-term sustainable competitive advantage. Simply stated, a KMS is a system for managing organizational knowledge."[20] A KMS system collects all relevant knowledge and experience and disseminates or makes it available whenever and wherever it is needed. A number of information systems are designed to serve knowledge workers. Some of these systems are listed and organized as to their specific function in supporting knowledge workers in Exhibit 7-3. For example, a workstation and software for CAD used by an engineer at an engineering consulting firm is one of the most frequently used systems.

Exhibit 7-3   Contemporary Information Systems to Support Knowledge Workers

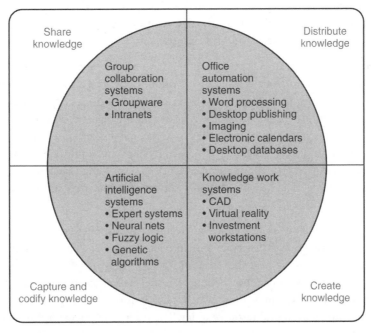

Source: Kenneth C. Laudon and Jane Laudon, *Management Information Systems: New Approaches to Organization and Technology*, 5th ed. (Upper Saddle River, NJ, Prentice Hall, 1998). Printed and electronically reproduced by permission of Pearson Education, Inc., Upper Saddle River, New Jersey.

Another knowledge-level system that is used in service organizations is an expert system. Simply put, an **expert system** (ES) is a computer program that captures the knowledge and experience of an expert in a narrow, well-defined area of knowledge. Experts can solve difficult problems, explain the result, learn from experience, restructure their own knowledge, and determine the relevance of certain data in making decisions. When used to solve a problem or to make a decision, a well-designed ES imitates the reasoning processes experts use in solving that specific problem. ES can be used as a training device or as a knowledgeable assistant by an expert.[21] Expert systems are in use in almost every industry and functional area. The significant role they play in decision making and training in services is likely to increase as these systems are improved.

7.9 Technology and the Future of Services

"The overwhelming majority of revenues we get by the end of the decade will be from services and products that have not yet been invented"[22] were the words of John C. Malone, former CEO of Tele-Communications, Inc., at the news conference in 1993 announcing the merger of his company with Bell Atlantic. Given the dizzying speed of technological developments during the last three decades, this prediction seems to have become true for many service organizations. Technological developments are the triumph and product of human intelligence, that is, brainpower. And that is what will be driving the economy in the twenty-first century. Traditional manufacturing as well as mining and agriculture will continue to exist and play a role, but manmade brainpower industries and their knowledge creation will be the driving force of the U.S. economy and economies of other developed countries.

In the nineteenth and part of the twentieth century, natural resources, such as coal, oil, minerals, and timber, gave some countries a comparative economic advantage and made them rich. Also, availability of capital was an important factor in a country's prosperity. However, this is no longer true, says economist Lester C. Thurow: "Today knowledge and skills now stand alone as the only source of comparative advantage. They have become the key ingredient in the late twentieth century's location of economic activity. Silicon valley and Route 128 are where they are simply because that is where the brainpower is. They have nothing else going for them."[23] He also adds that knowledge has become the only source of a long-run sustainable competitive advantage.

Professor Thurow is not alone in this view. Management philosopher Peter F. Drucker made the same assessment several years earlier from a microperspective: "The basic economic resource— 'the means of production,' to use the economist's term—is no longer capital, nor natural resources (the economist's 'land'), nor 'labor.' *It is and will be knowledge.* (…) Value is now created by 'productivity' and 'innovation,' both applications of knowledge to work. (…) In fact, knowledge is the only meaningful resource today. The traditional 'factors of production'…have not disappeared, but they have become secondary. They can be obtained, and obtained easily, provided there is knowledge…. These developments, whether desirable or not, are responses to an irreversible change: *knowledge is now being applied to knowledge.*"[24]

The emerging picture seems to be clear. In the future, our lives as well as our prosperity will depend more and more on the creation and use of knowledge. Manufacturing, mining, and agriculture will certainly be impacted by technological developments, but most services will exclusively depend on brainpower and knowledge. Consider, for example, service industries such as software development, telecommunications, biotechnology, pharmaceuticals, as well as computer and telecommunications hardware producers and medical equipment manufacturers, are all in the knowledge creation and application (that is, technology) business. In addition to brainpower, two of the essential ingredients in knowledge creation and application are data and information. Information technology expert Don Tapscott summarizes the situation with the following prediction:

> The new economy is all about competing for the future, the capacity to create new products or services, and the ability to transform businesses into new entities that yesterday couldn't be imagined and the day after tomorrow may be obsolete.[25]

7.10 Summary

Services have traditionally been known for low productivity and the difficulty of substituting machines for humans. This is probably the main reason for the "productivity paradox" in services. During the past three decades service organizations as well as manufacturing firms made huge investments in information technology with no apparent increase in productivity in services. The most likely explanation for this paradox seems to be that the impact technology makes on productivity and profits depends on what managers and service workers do with it. In other words, technology may not be a magic wand that can be waved over poorly designed and inefficient systems or processes. However, recent research suggests that benefits are not immediate, but rather observed after at least 3 to 4 years.

There are many service organizations (for example, USAA, FedEx, and UPS) that have been successful in the use of technology. These companies created a competitive advantage through technology and became profitable in the process.

Information technology can be used to create a competitive advantage by taking a holistic approach by automating only efficient systems and processes; solving real problems of customers, whether they are internal or external; giving more control to customers and service workers; optimizing basic technologies; and combining high touch with high tech.

Technology has many uses and application in services. Main categories of applications are processing the customer, processing the customer's equipment or material, processing information, and creating new services and products. Processing information is clearly an important application because many services create and sell information, but all services use information and they need information systems. An information system can be defined as a system of "interrelated components that collect (or retrieve), process, store, and distribute information to support decision making, coordinating, and control in an organization." Several forms of information systems that are frequently used in services have been discussed in the chapter. Information systems may be developed for operational, knowledge, managerial, or strategic levels of an organization. They include transaction processing systems, management information systems, decision-support systems, and executive support systems. Another important type of information system that has been implemented by many large organizations is enterprise systems. There are four types of enterprise applications: enterprise resource planning systems, supply chain management systems, customer relationship management systems, and knowledge management systems.

Knowledge will be the driving force of economic activity in the twenty-first century. Traditional manufacturing, mining, and agriculture will continue to exist, but our lives as well as our prosperity will depend more and more on the creation and use of knowledge. In addition to brain-power, data and information are essential raw materials for the creation of knowledge, but they are also the outcomes of knowledge creation processes. Organizations that can create new knowledge and turn them into new goods and services that consumers need will survive and prosper in the new century.

Endnotes

1. Gartner U.S. Healthcare, "Provider IT Spend Was $27.2B in 2008 Growing to $32.8B by 2012," in J.D. Lovelock, *Forecast: Healthcare Provider IT Spending, Worldwide, 2006–2012* (Stamford, Conn.: Gartner Group, 9 September 2008).

2. Productivity is simply defined as the output divided by inputs that are used to create the output. Chapter 13 discusses service productivity in more detail.

3. There have been several publications confirming this phenomenon see for example: Gregory P. Hackett, "Investment in Technology—The Service Sector Sinkhole?," *Sloan Management Review*, Winter 1990, pp. 97–103; Stephen S. Roach, "Services Under Siege—The Restructuring Imperative," *Harvard Business Review*, September–October 1991, pp. 82–91; and Paul A. Strassmann, "Will Big Spending on Computers Guarantee Profitability?" *Datamation*, February 1997, pp. 75–85.

4. *Committee to Study the Impact of Information Technology on the Performance of Service Activities, Information Technology in the Service Society* (Washington, DC, National Academy Press, 1994), pp. 27–29.

5. Peter F. Drucker, *Managing for the Future: The 1990s and Beyond* (New York, NY, Truman Talley Books/Dutton, 1992), pp. 95–96.

6. Mahmood M. Adam & Garry J. Mann, "Information Technology Investments and Organizational Productivity and Performance: An Empirical Investigation," *Journal of Organizational Computing & Electronic Commerce* (2005), Vol. 15, No. 3, pp.185–202; Matt Campbell, "What a Difference a Year Makes: Time Lag Effect of Information Technology Investment on Firm Performance," *Journal of Organizational Computing & Electronic Commerce* (2012), Vol. 22, No. 3, pp. 237–255.

7. Claudia H. Deutsch, "U.P.S. Embraces High-Tech Delivery Methods," *The New York Times*, July 12, 2007,

8. "Special Report: International Banking: Retail Renaissance," *The Economist*, May 19, 2012.

9. *Information Technology in the Service Society*, pp. 12–13.

10. Scott McCartney, "Airline Alliances Take Toll on Travelers," *The Wall Street Journal*, February 18, 1998.

11. Leonard L. Berry, *On Great Service: A Framework for Action* (New York, NY, The Free Press, 1996) pp. 147–155.

12. Christopher Lovelock, *Product Plus-How Product + Service = Competitive Advantage* (New York, McGraw-Hill, 1994), p. 181.

13. Scott McCartney, "Amid the Kiosks, Elite Treatment From a Gate Agent," *The Wall Street Journal* (Thursday, July 26, 2012).

14. From FedEx News, http://news.van.fedex.com/senseaware (07/20/2012).

15. Information on USAA, unless otherwise indicated, is based on Thomas Teal, "Service Comes First: An Interview with USAA's Robert F. McDermott," *Harvard Business Review*, September–October 1991, pp. 117–127; and www.usaa.com/ (07/20/2012).

16. Kenneth C. Laudon and Jane P. Laudon, *Essentials of Management Information Systems, Ninth Edition* (Upper Saddle River, NJ, Prentice Hall, 2011), p. 13.

17. Unless otherwise indicated, the material on information systems has been adopted from Laudon and Laudon, *Management Information Systems*, 9th edition (Upper Saddle River, NJ, Prentice Hall, 2011), pp. 47–51.

18. For more information on DSS see Efraim Turban, Ramesh Sharda, and Dursun Delen, *Decision Support and Business Intelligence Systems*, 9th edition (Upper Saddle River, NJ, Prentice Hall, 2011).

19. Carol V. Brown, Daniel W. DeHayes, Jeffrey A. Hoffer, E. Wainright Martin, and William C. Perkins, *Managing Information Technology*, 7th Edition (Upper Saddle River, NJ, Prentice Hall, 2012), p. 198.

20. Brown, et.al. p.237.

21. EfraimTurban, Ramesh Sharda, and Dursun Delen, *Decision Support and Business Intelligence Systems*, 9th edition (Upper Saddle River, NJ, Prentice Hall, 2011).

22. Edmund L. Andrews, "When We Build It, Will They Come?" *The New York Times*, October 17, 1993.

23. Lester C. Thurow, *The Future of Capitalism: How Today's Economic Forces Shape Tomorrow's World* (New York, NY, William Morrow and Company, Inc. 1996), p. 68.

24. Peter F. Drucker, *Post-Capitalist Society* (New York, NY, Harper Business, 1993), pp. 8 and 42.

25. Don Tapscott, *The Digital Economy: Promise and Peril in the Age of Networked Intelligence* (New York, McGraw-Hill, 1995), p. 43.

8

DESIGN AND DEVELOPMENT OF SERVICES AND SERVICE DELIVERY SYSTEMS

8.1 Introduction

Service design and development is an important step in creating value and satisfaction for the customer. In Chapter 2, "The Nature of Services and Service Encounters," service encounters were defined as "any episode in which the customer comes into contact with any aspect of the organization and gets an impression of the quality of its service." It was also emphasized that a service organization is made, or "created," in the minds of customers during a service encounter. The most important service encounters are those during which a service is delivered. These involve the customer, the service provider (employee), the delivery system, the physical evidence, and of course the service itself, which is an act or performance by service providers and/or equipment of the delivery system. It is clear that when so much rides on an event such as the service encounter, it cannot be left to chance; service encounters and everything associated with them must be carefully designed, planned, and executed. In other words, the service, its delivery system, and the physical evidence must be carefully designed, and service providers must be prepared for the encounter. This chapter focuses on the first three of these issues.

8.2 Why the Design Is So Important

In Chapter 5, "Service Strategy and Competitiveness," the concept of value and creation of service value for customers was discussed because this is what an organization must do to survive and prosper. Customers do not buy goods or services—they buy solutions to their problems, satisfactions for their needs, or benefits they enjoy. Consequently, a service organization creates value by creating solutions, satisfactions, or benefits for customers. The process that does all this is called **service**. To achieve its objectives, a service must be a well-thought-out and planned process. In other words it must be designed and cannot be left to chance. Design also affects the costs, quality, and image of the service as well as the company.

It is clear, then, that for success a service organization must start with a well-designed service. However, it will not end there because service design is not a one-time undertaking. An organization must create new services or improve existing ones because customers' needs are changing rapidly and new needs are emerging. Also, changes in consumers' tastes and lifestyles make some of the existing services obsolete or inadequate in meeting customers' needs. Consequently, an organization's vitality and competitiveness often depends on how well it discovers the shifts in consumers' needs and the emergence of new ones and meets them with new services or with improvements in existing services.

In addition to these reasons, other factors exist that motivate organizations to design and develop new services. These reasons will be discussed a little later in this chapter, but first an important note about what we mean by the "design and development" of services. Service design includes the development of a service concept and the design of a system through which it is delivered. Both of these are the products of an evolutionary process; that is, they evolve and change as the design progresses. When we refer to service design and development in this book, we refer to both the service concept and the delivery system because they are inseparable. We now turn our attention to another important issue: what is meant by "new" in services, or how "new" they may be.

Categories of Product Innovation

Everyone is accustomed to hearing advertisers claim that their products are "new," "all new," or "new and improved." Naturally, having some familiarity with the product, many consumers are unimpressed by these claims, or worse, confused by them because it is not at all clear what is "new" in the advertised product. Because the topic of this chapter is the design of "new" or "improved" services, it may be appropriate to shed some light on what the advertisers may mean when they make such claims or what alternatives exist for an organization contemplating designing new services.[1]

1. **Major innovations**—These are "new to the world" services for which markets are yet undefined and undimensioned. They involve a high degree of uncertainty and risk. Federal Express's overnight delivery of small packages was an example of this type of innovation.

2. **Start-up businesses**—Some new services may provide new and innovative solutions to generic needs of customers that have been served by existing services. These new services may be in the form of bundling existing services in a new package, such as health maintenance organizations that bring together general practitioners and specialists, as well as labs, X-ray facilities, and sometimes pharmacies under one roof for one-stop visit for patients.

3. **New products for the currently served market**—This category includes new services offered to the existing customers that were not previously available from the service organization. Examples include banks that introduce their Visa or MasterCard or offer

frequent flier programs for airlines with their cards, mutual funds, money-market funds, or insurance services, or museums that open gift and souvenir shops and restaurants for their patrons.

4. **Product line extensions**—Additions to the existing line-up of services that enhance the current offerings are called product line extensions. Examples include call waiting, caller ID, redial services offered in addition to regular phone service from your phone company; new routes for an airline, or new courses offered by a university.

5. **Product improvements**—Product improvements consist of changing certain features of a service to give customers better quality or increased value. These may be in the form of performing an existing service faster or may be in the form of enrichments or embellishments, that is, addition of "bells and whistles." For example, many ATMs print account balances after each deposit or withdrawal. Another example is a free car wash some automobile dealers provide with any service they perform, including oil change.

6. **Style changes**—These are the most modest but often highly visible forms of service improvements, and they include renovating and refurbishing the building where service is provided, new uniforms for employees, a new logo, and so forth.

This discussion of service design and development in this chapter assumes that the new service falls in one of the first three categories. However, what is offered in this chapter can easily be adopted for other categories.

Factors That Motivate the Design and Development of New Services

Chapter 4, "Globalization of Services," pointed out some global trends that lead not only to a general increase in demand for existing services, but also to an increase in demand for new services in many countries of the world. Earlier in this section it was stated that the main reason for the design and development of new services is to meet new and changing needs of consumers. There are other reasons that motivate organizations to design and develop new services. Some of the most important factors are reviewed in the following paragraphs.[2]

Financial goals—Management in many service organizations is under constant pressure to achieve financial goals of profit, market share, or revenue. These goals may be achieved by improving service quality and customer satisfaction with the existing services. Another way, however, is to introduce new services. As just noted, several degrees of "newness" exist for services. However, only the first three are most likely to lead to increases in market share and revenue, and help the organization achieve its financial goals.

Competitive actions—One of the strongest motivations for developing new services emerges when a competitor introduces a new service. Standing still and doing nothing usually leads to an erosion of market share and profits. Consequently, the introduction of a new service promotes similar actions from competing organizations. For example, when Merrill Lynch introduced the

Cash Management Account, which combined brokerage, debit card, and bank checking services in a single package, its competitors had to develop and offer similar services.

Globalization—The increase in global trade and foreign direct investment, establishment of European Union, and the collapse of the Soviet Union created new markets and opened up many opportunities for service firms. These developments created a need for the design and development of new services or modification of existing ones to meet the needs of different countries and cultures.

Technology—With its new products and capabilities, technology creates new needs that require new services. Chapter 7, "Technology and Its Impact on Services and Their Management," discusses how new services are motivated by technological advances. We now take an organized look at some possible ways technology may be responsible for the creation of new services or advances in existing services.

1. **New consumer goods**—When introduced, new consumer goods, such as video cassette recorders (VCRs), DVD or Blu-ray disc players, and personal computers created a need for related services, such as video rentals and services for repairing these devices. More recent products, such as portable music players (for example, the iPod) led to the creation of music downloading services; introduction of digital readers, such as Amazon.com's Kindle, or Barnes & Noble's Nook, brought with them the digital book market; and finally, tablets, such as Apple's iPad, led to the creation of services including hundreds of thousands of apps, downloading and reading newspapers and magazines on tablets, just to mention a few.

2. **New equipment**—Advances in engineering technology helped manufacturers and service organizations introduce new equipment or implement many improvements in existing equipment. These developments, in turn, led to faster delivery of existing services as well as the introduction of new services. For example, faster computers increased data storage and computation speed for all sorts of data processing and made the development of new and complex software possible; invention of automatic teller machines (ATMs) made some banking services available 24 hours a day.

3. **Electronic networks**—Electronic networks, such as the Internet and World Wide Web; electronic data banks, such as statistical, economic, and demographic information provided by the Federal Government and private companies; and online information systems, such as Wikipedia, are among the most important technological developments of the recent past that made the creation and delivery of many new services possible.

Regulation/deregulation—Several important industries in the United States have been deregulated during the last three decades of the twentieth century, including airlines, trucking, telecommunications, and banking and financial services. These deregulations allowed many companies to enter into markets that had not been open to them previously and offer new services or offer consumers innovative bundling of existing services. An example is Merrill Lynch's Cash

Management Account mentioned earlier. Although some industries are being deregulated, new regulations are created such as environmental protection and consumer safety regulations. Such regulations usually create a need for improvements in consumer goods and manufacturing equipment, or new ones. They also create a need for new services such as legal, engineering, and consulting services specialized in environmental protection and safety issues.

Elimination of professional association restrictions—Paralleling deregulation of some important industries by the government, professional associations also relaxed some of their restrictions on their members' practices. For example, codes of ethics for legal, medical, accounting, and architectural professionals have been changed to allow them to advertise. Lifting of such restrictions usually leads to the development of new services and innovative delivery systems such as health maintenance organizations, franchise chains of small business accounting services, and legal clinics in shopping malls.

Growth of franchising—A franchise is a type of business in which a person (franchisee) receives a license to produce and/or sell a well-known good or service in return for an initial fee and a percentage of gross receipts to be paid to the grantor of franchise (franchisor). Some well-known franchises include McDonald's, H&R Block Tax Services, Mail Boxes, Inc., Howard Johnson hotels, and automobile dealerships. This system makes it possible for the franchisor to focus on and spend money for formal research in service innovations, product line extensions, product enhancement, and development of new delivery systems.

Balancing supply and demand—Many service organizations have limited capacities but face fluctuating demand for their services. When the demand exceeds the capacity of an organization, either customers are lost or their satisfaction level will be lower because of excessive waiting. However, when the demand falls short of supply, expensive equipment and personnel stand idle. Manufacturers can manage this problem by building inventories when the demand falls short of supply and use inventories when it exceeds supply. However, perishability of most services eliminates this practice as an alternative for service organizations. A plausible alternative is offering services that are countercyclical to the existing portfolio of services. For example, a ski resort may offer nature exploration vacations in summer months when there is no skiing. In other words, a service organization facing fluctuating demand can try developing new services that will have a high demand when the demand for the existing services is low and vice versa.

8.3 Designing Quality and Value

Humans have been designing and making tools and consumer goods for thousands of years. Technical aspects of design and manufacture of goods have been taught in engineering schools, and the process of product design and development has been studied by business scholars for many years. Service design and development, on the other hand, has never received this much scrutiny or study. Only recently, more attention is being paid to the design of services, mainly because the ever-increasing significant role of services in our economy has become obvious.

Consequently, the current level of service design and development experience and knowledge is nowhere near the level of experience and scientific knowledge accumulated for goods. This naturally leads many service researchers to the body of knowledge on goods for answers or clues for questions that concern service design and development. Hence we start from the same place and see what can be learned from manufacturing, and which tools and practices that have been successful in the design of goods can be used in designing services. First, the differences and similarities between goods and services are considered from a design perspective, and then some of the successful practices and tools employed in designing quality and value into goods that may also be used in the design and development of services are discussed.

Designing Goods and Services: Similarities and Differences

As pointed out earlier, customers don't buy goods or services; they buy solutions to their problems, satisfactions to their needs, or benefits they can enjoy. Therefore, the most important similarity between goods and services is that they are designed to provide a solution, satisfaction, or benefit. For example, George Eastman, founder of Kodak, said, "Kodak sells memories," and Charles Revson of Revlon said, "In the factory we make cosmetics; in the store we sell hope."

The second similarity is that designs of both goods and services are products of human creativity. The human mind first creates something new in concept and then figures out how this is going to be made.

The third similarity is that consumers rarely ask for the creation of a specific good or service. Consumers may express some vague needs but cannot usually articulate them in terms of goods or services; they respond only to what is offered to them. The late Steve Jobs, founder of Apple Company and one of the brilliant minds of our time, had this to say about designing new products and services:

> This is what customers pay us for—to sweat all these details so it's easy and pleasant for them to use our computers. We're supposed to be really good at this. That doesn't mean we don't listen to customers, but it's hard for them to tell you what they want when they've never seen anything remotely like it. Take desktop video editing. I never got one request from someone who wanted to edit movies on his computer. Yet now that people see it, they say, "Oh my God, that's great![3]

These unarticulated needs must be discovered and met with the benefits offered by a new product or service. We now note some of the important differences. Manufacture of goods requires many resources such as raw materials, semifinished products, labor, and energy. These resources are essential for the production of a good. The outcome of the design activity is a set of standards and specifications such as the type, grade, and quantity of materials to use, dimensions of various parts, and tolerances. Most of these specifications are expressed in a technical drawing called a **blueprint**. Conformance to standards and specifications in manufacturing is essential; deviations from them, beyond tolerances, can render the manufactured product unusable or defective and sometimes dangerous. The concept of a good can be visualized on paper, and a prototype can be made and studied, measured, tested, and finally put into actual use. After the design is finalized and manufacturing begins, all the goods will be identical with only minor variations in dimensions.

In services, raw materials are rarely used, tools and equipment are used but they are not always essential. Airplanes are essential for air transportation service, but a couch is not essential for a psychiatrist's services. The outcome of service design is a concept, or an idea, and a description of a process for performance of the concept. Service design may have standards, but usually there are few, and deviations from these standards do not necessarily make the service "defective" or create undesirable consequences. No drawing of a service is possible because a service is performance. A service can be tested in a mock trial, but each performance will be different whether in test or in actual implementation because of the involvement of different customers and service providers. After the design is finalized and the service is offered to customers, no two service performances will be the same, and each customer's experience will be unique.

Another important difference between goods and services is that changes become more and more expensive in manufacturing as the design progresses. This is usually expressed as the 85/15 percent rule, which implies that approximately 85 percent of the cost of a good is determined by decisions made during the first 15 percent of the design period. After it is finalized and frozen, the design for a good cannot be changed easily, and manufacturing will follow the same design for all units produced. Service design, on the other hand, is not a static or rigid document; modifications and adaptations on-the-fly are possible and sometimes required for meeting widely varying customer needs and requirements. Furthermore, design changes in services are not likely to be as costly as in manufacturing. On the other hand, these characteristics create a risk; instead of improving a service, accumulation of unplanned changes may cause a slow deterioration of the service in the long run.

Tools for Designing Quality and Value

The now famous adage "You cannot inspect quality into products, it must be built in" was in response to the decades of long practice in manufacturing of relying largely on inspections to make sure that poor quality goods did not leave the factory. In the early 1980s, manufacturers and quality professionals began to learn from Japanese manufacturers that many quality problems can be solved by improving the manufacturing process, but even more dramatic improvements can be obtained in the design stage.

It is clear that most services do not lend themselves to inspection. There are very few things you can inspect before or after a service performance. For example, you can inspect the appearance of service employees, measure the waiting time and time for the service, and count the number of mistakes made by service providers. These measurements, of course, do not prevent service failures or guarantee customer satisfaction. Furthermore, the service quality is not judged by quality inspectors or service employees—it is judged by customers. Consequently, inspection is not an alternative for quality assurance in services. Just like in making superior quality goods, quality must be built in to the design of a service and its delivery system.

The realization of the importance of design of goods and their manufacturing processes led many manufacturers to try new tools and practices as well as the rediscovery of old ones. In the following paragraphs, some of these concepts and tools that can be used in the design and development of services will be reviewed.

Concurrent Engineering

Design and development of goods include many steps, such as idea generation, opportunity identification, design, prototype, process design, procurement, packaging design, and the design of distribution system. The traditional approach was to conduct these activities one at a time, sequentially. One problem with the traditional approach was that it took too long. For example, American automobile manufacturers used to spend approximately 5 years to design and develop a new car, whereas Japanese manufacturers did it in 3 years. Another, equally important problem was costly design changes and quality problems. In the traditional system design engineers would "throw the design over the wall" to manufacturing engineers, who would then try to figure out how to manufacture the product. This meant designers and manufacturing engineers did not talk to each other. Usually manufacturing engineers would find many problems with the design, such as parts that cannot be produced as designers envisioned, and throw it back over the wall. It was not unusual for this to be repeated several times during the design process. After the problems between the design and manufacturing were resolved, procurement would get the design for parts to be purchased from suppliers. Inevitably, they would find problems with the design, such as parts that are too expensive or no longer made by suppliers. The design would go back to the designers.

Japanese manufacturers used a parallel approach to design, which also included cross-functional team work. American manufacturers began using this approach after seeing its benefits and called it **concurrent**, or **simultaneous engineering**. One of the major advantages of this approach is that all functions (design, manufacturing, procurement, distribution, marketing, and so on) are represented on the design team and communicate with each other. If possible, customer participation, or at least, customer input, should be solicited.

For service design and development, participation of the front-line employees is equally important for various reasons.[4] First, front-line employees are psychologically and physically close to customers and therefore can identify customer needs as the new service is developed. Second, employee involvement can increase the chances of acceptance and understanding of the new service by all front-line employees. Third, they warn designers against the possibility of organizational efficiency concerns to overwhelm the needs and interests of the customer. Finally, front-line employees are a good source of useful ideas for improvements in service quality.

Concurrent engineering also helps eliminate many quality problems. Most problems are avoided or solved early in the process before they become major headaches and lead to costly design changes. This approach avoids many design modifications by allowing product and process designs to be developed simultaneously.[5]

Concurrent engineering is a logical approach to designing goods, and there is no reason for not using it in the service design and development. For one thing, as indicated earlier, design and development of the service concept and its delivery system are inseparable, so this is a strong incentive for using concurrent engineering in services. Also, service delivery may involve interactions and hand-offs between many departments and imply potential service failures. To avoid these problems all functions or departments of an organization must participate in the design so that they understand each other and what is expected of them for seamless transitions and superior service delivery.

Quality Function Deployment

Professor Yoji Akao of Japan's Tamagawa University developed quality function deployment (QFD) as a structured approach for integrating customer requirements (that is, "customer's voice") into product design.[6] "In other words, this is a method for developing design quality aimed at satisfying the consumer and then translating the consumer's demands into design targets and major quality assurance points to be used throughout the production stage."[7] Also known as "The House of Quality,"[8] QFD involves several tables that translate customer requirements into product design characteristics, product design characteristics into part characteristics, part characteristics into process parameters, and process parameters into operating instructions for machine operators. QFD can and should be used in the design and development of services; it is actually one of the most sensible tools that can be borrowed from manufacturing. Any organization that aims at creating customer value and satisfaction has to design its services to meet customers' needs, and QFD is an effective tool for this purpose.

Exhibit 8-1 shows the structure of the House of Quality, and Exhibit 8-2 is an example of how QFD can be used to translate customer's voice into the design of a university bookstore. Customer requirements are listed on the left. The designer would like to meet all the requirements as much as possible but notices that not all requirements are equally important to customers. The most important customer requirements in this example are to find and buy textbooks easily and finish book buying as quickly as possible; both are given an importance rating of 10 out of a possible 10. The design characteristics that are needed to meet customer requirements are listed in the technical requirements section. In the middle section of the house is a matrix where the relationship between customer requirements and technical requirements is shown. For example, to meet customers' "quick in-and-out" requirement, "organization of shelves and lanes," "layout of store and signage," "number of checkout lanes," and "store hours" are essential. Also important for students to finish their book buying quickly are "informative labels on shelves," "lighting," "bags/baskets." Each cell in the roof of the house represents the relationship between two technical requirements, whether they affect each other positively or negatively. If there is no relation, it is left blank. In most applications, boxes to the right and bottom can be added for competitor evaluations. However, in this example, they are not shown because a university bookstore would not have any brick-and-mortar competitors in the immediate vicinity. As this simple example illustrates, QFD can be a powerful tool in designing a service that meets customers' needs and creates value for them.

Exhibit 8-1   The House of Quality

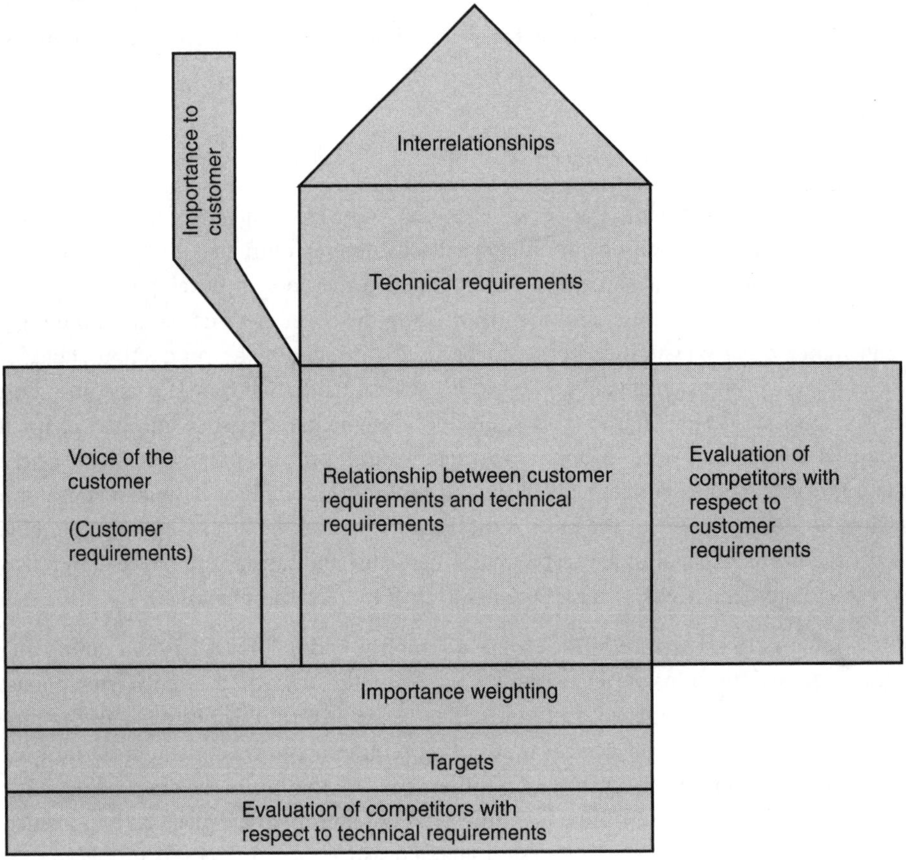

Exhibit 8-2   House of Quality for Designing a University Bookstore

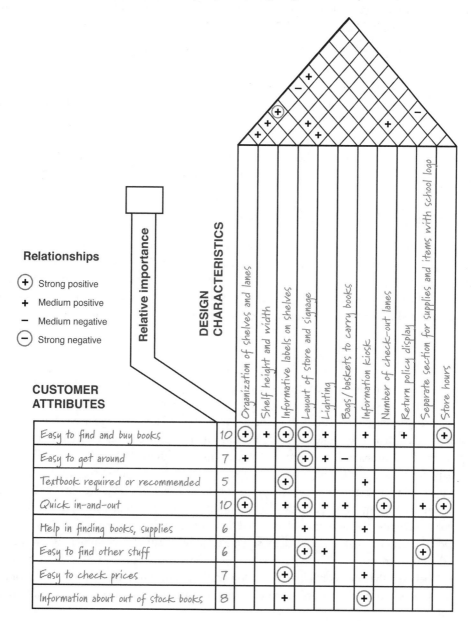

Robust Design

Robust design is a powerful idea and design practice developed for the manufacture of goods by Genichi Taguchi.[9] The basic idea behind robust design is making the product so that its performance is unaffected by adversities in the environment beyond normal operating conditions.

For example, a hand-held calculator is not supposed to be dropped, or used in a hot and steamy environment such as a steam bath. However, if the calculator endures such harsh conditions and operates as expected, it is said to be a robust product.

Service providers and customers are human. The differences in personalities and demographic characteristics they exhibit may create situations that are not normal operating conditions. Also, failures in delivery or support systems, such as a computer crash, power outage, or failure of a vendor to deliver supplies, may create these adverse conditions in which service has to be delivered. No design can make a service or a good to withstand all adverse conditions under all circumstances. However, services can be designed with possible extreme conditions in mind and measures can be taken to prevent them. Or alternative services and emergency procedures can be built into the system. The following two approaches may be helpful in making services robust.

Design Failure Mode Analysis[10]

This is a systematic procedure of examining a design to determine possible ways its parts can fail. For each potential failure, the cause, its effect on the system, and its criticality are estimated. This helps designers develop preventive measures. Failure mode analysis can be used in evaluating and improving service designs. If a blueprint of service is developed, potential failure points can be identified and measures, such as poka-yokes, can be developed and implemented.

Poka-Yoke or Fail Safe Methods[11]

This is a simple but useful concept that also came from Japan; the late Shigeo Shingo developed this approach to designing and manufacturing goods.[12] Poka-yokes are devices or procedures that signal that a mistake is about to be made. **Warning poka-yokes** signal the existence of a problem, and **control poka-yokes** stop production when a mistake is made and force the operator to correct the problem before proceeding with the operation. The concept of **fail-safing** a process is similar to a combination lock that opens only when the correct sequence of numbers are supplied. Manufacturers sometimes implement this concept by designing parts of a product so that there is only one way that they can fit, eliminating the possibility of assembly mistakes. Poka-yoke methods can and should be used in service design. However, services must be designed to prevent mistakes not only by service employees but also customers when they are involved in the process. There are many ways poka-yokes can be used in services. A bank, for example, believes that eye contact with customers is important, and to ensure eye contact, it requires tellers to mark the eye color of each customer on a checklist before they start a transaction.

Blueprints

Many years ago design specifications and standards for goods were traditionally represented in the form of technical drawings on a special blue-colored paper. The blueprint is a visualization of the designer's concept of the product together with its dimensions and tolerances. Lynn G. Shostack[13] applied this concept to the design and development of services; a service blueprint is simply a picture of a service system and its processes. Service blueprints will be discussed in more detail later in the chapter.

Value Analysis/Value Engineering

Value analysis, also known as **value engineering**, was developed by Lawrence D. Wells of General Electric in the late 1940s.[14] It is a systematic approach to identifying the function of a good or service; it establishes the value of its parts and tries to provide the function, or benefit, at the lowest possible cost without sacrificing quality or value.[15] Its basic concern is "providing good value for the customer's dollar, at a fair profit to the supplier."[16] Typical questions asked during the analysis include "Is the function necessary?", "Can the function of two or more parts, or steps of a service process, be combined into one and performed for a lower cost?", "Can the process be simplified?" These are clearly useful questions to streamline a service process for better quality and higher value for customers. Value analysis can be used effectively after a blueprint of the service has been prepared.

Benchmarking[17]

Benchmarking was developed at Xerox Corporation in the late 1970s as a result of one of various quality improvement programs. It is an approach to setting goals and standards for improvements in goods, parts, or processes. It searches for the best-in-class practice in any industry to use as a source of learning and target for the process to be improved. For example, a manufacturer may benchmark L. L. Bean for order-filling operations. Benchmarking is not simply copying ideas from other organizations. Its main objective is finding out what performance levels are possible for various processes and learning from best performers. This approach would be useful in service design and development especially reducing the learning pains of implementing a new service or process and setting standards for processes or parts of processes. Service companies already use benchmarking for their existing services. For example, Marriott benchmarked fast-food companies for its hiring, training, and pay practices, and Houston's Second Baptist Church, serving 12,000 members, benchmarked Disney World's parking and people practices in its quality improvement program.

8.4 Principles of Service Design

"Service industries" in the business literature refers to groups of organizations that offer similar services. The degree of similarity may justify the term **industry**, but even within each industry, the number and variety of services is truly staggering. For example, think about the transportation industry: It has several subindustries, such as airlines, trucking, passenger and freight rail transportation, passenger bus transportation, and marine shipping. Organizations in each of these subsectors offer hundreds or thousands of different services. The same is true for most service industries. As discussed earlier in this chapter, there are many reasons that motivate organizations to develop new services or enhance and augment existing ones. Even manufacturing firms offer many services to their internal and external customers. This immense variety raises an important question, "Are there principles that apply to designing services regardless of the industry for which they are designed, or is each service so unique that there are few principles that apply to all sectors and services?" Despite the uniqueness of each service, there are some basic principles that can and must be applied to designing services if the objective is to create customer value and satisfaction. The following are general principles for designing and developing services.

1. **Know your customers**—If the objective is creating customer value and satisfaction, the most important principle is to know your customers and their needs. A typical service organization cannot serve all potential customers; hence, it has to determine who it wants as its customers. Knowing your customer implies learning everything possible and relevant about the target market at a reasonable cost, including demographic information, such as age, sex, income, geographic distribution, and lifestyle. Information such as this can help an organization determine the needs of potential customers. When possible and economical, information about customers' needs must also be solicited from them directly. The following quote from the CEO of an excellent service company emphasizes the role "knowing your customer" plays in designing winning services:

   "One of our newest innovations—The Room That Works—grew out of a listening-to-the-customer exercise. A couple of years ago, we set out to design a better guest room for business travelers. We pulled together some focus groups and quickly discovered that high on their wish list was a change in the placement of electrical outlets in our rooms. Guests wanted them to be visible."[18]

2. **Determine which of the customers' needs will be satisfied**—It is clear that customers have many needs. It must also be clear that an organization cannot possibly meet all the needs of all its customers; therefore, it has to focus on one or a few of them it can competently meet and make a reasonable profit.

   "In response to a survey, the customers of Southwest Airlines were happy to tell the company what they wanted in airline service: low fares, on-time flights, gourmet meals with wine, large comfortable seats, in-flight movies, and so forth. The company learned that if you simply ask people what they want, they are likely to ask for everything. Southwest tried again and dug deeper into customer preferences. In these more in-depth surveys, [it] found that although customers would enjoy the extras, they really wanted the basics—low fares and on-time flights—with friendly service."[19]

   Frances X. Frei goes so far as to say "service excellence can be defined as what a business chooses not to do well."[20]

   Of course, this does not imply that service organizations should deliberately do a bad job on some aspects, but rather, to excel on the chosen, most important aspects;

excelling on less important ones may not be economical. The service that will meet the most basic and important customer need will be the core service. There are usually other services that provide additional benefits to customers. These are called **supplementary services.**

Supplementary services are designed and offered to meet needs that may not be common to all customers. They are often optional and may carry additional costs. Lovelock and Wirtz[21] identified eight clusters of supplementary services: information, consultation, order-taking, hospitality, safekeeping, exceptions, billing, and payment. Customers usually need **information** about the service especially when they use it the first time. There are a large number of items customers may need information on. Some of these include price, what is included in the service (that is, core and supplementary services), directions to the service facility, instructions about using the service, hours of operation, and payment options. **Consultation** goes beyond providing such basic facts and involves provision of information in a more customized manner. A service provider has to find out customers' needs and try to provide the best advice to meet those needs. **Order-taking** may include obtaining and recording relevant information from a customer, making reservations and providing confirmation numbers, scheduling the performance of the service, providing physical evidence (for example, a ticket) for the order. **Safekeeping** services include safekeeping of valuables in a hotel, safely transporting baggage on an airliner, safety of a customer's car in a garage or parking lot. **Exceptions** are provided when a service organization accommodates a customer with special needs, such as serving a low-salt meal on a flight to those who request it. **Hospitality** basically means "taking care of the customer"—providing a welcoming environment and treating customers with courtesy. **Billing** should provide an accurate, timely, and easy-to-understand document about the service charges. A service company should set up the payment system to make bill paying easy and convenient for customers.

Not all the supplementary services exist or are relevant for all services. Some of the supplementary services are needed for the delivery of the core service. Without them the service will be impossible. Yet others enhance the value for a customer. Relative importance of supplementary services depends on the nature of the service.

Clearly, a service organization that fails to deliver the core service often will not survive long; hence, providing the core service without failure and as expected by customers is the first and the fundamental step in creating value for customers. The core service must be the focus of the design effort. The system must be designed for flawless delivery of the core service. A failure in the core service means the failure of the service and the organization in the eyes of the customer, no matter how well supplementary services are designed and delivered. However, that is usually never enough to be competitive, because probably competitors exist that can deliver the basic service without failure. Consequently, a service organization can create more value for its customers by both increasing the variety of supplementary services that are appreciated by its customers and performing them at least as well as customers expect.

Determination of core and supplementary services leads to the service concept. In other words, a **service concept** is an expression of the outcomes or benefits to be provided, problems to be solved, or results to be achieved for a customer. An organization must also make sure that it has the basic competencies necessary to turn the service concept into reality. If these competencies do not exist in the organization, it must have a plan to acquire them before going forward with the design effort.

3. **Develop a service strategy and position the service for competitive advantage**—The basic question to be answered here is, "How do we differentiate our service from those of competitors and on what basis do we give the most value to the customer for the cost of the service?" Part of this issue relates to the "operating strategy" in the "strategic service vision" model discussed in Chapter 5, and the other part is related to "positioning." Differentiation is the major vehicle of competitiveness. An organization can differentiate its service on the basis of various benefits, including cost, reliability, uniqueness of benefits, speed, personalized service, convenience, accessibility, prestige, or long-lasting effects. **Positioning** is the act or process of creating a distinct place for the service in customers' minds. Positioning is not what marketers do to a good or service, but it is what they do to the mind of the consumer. However, positioning is not tricking customers into believing you are something that you are not. It is finding an effective way to communicate to consumers what you stand for and what they can expect from your service. It should be recalled that an organization develops a service strategy to differentiate itself and its service(s) from the competition. The service should ideally be positioned to give it a unique place in the consumers' minds relative to the competitors' services. The service strategy must support and complement the organization's overall strategy. One way this may be violated is when a new service is incompatible with the existing services. If such conflicts exist, they should be resolved to support the overall strategy.

4. **Design the service, delivery system, human resource requirements, and tangibles simultaneously**—This principle can be summarized as using a concurrent engineering approach to design. When applied to service design, concurrent engineering includes the simultaneous, or parallel, design and development of the service and its delivery system, as well as the design of physical evidence, development of personnel selection criteria, and site selection criteria if a new site is required. As discussed in the previous section, concurrent engineering requires a cross-functional approach and teamwork. In other words, the design should be a team effort by the representatives of all the parties that will be involved in the creation and delivery of the service. Input of all departments, or functional areas, is an important ingredient in the design of services that deliver superior quality and value. If possible and economical, customers should also be represented on the design team.

5. **Design service processes from the customer's/employee's perspective**—After the right service concept is developed, the most important aspect of design is the design and development of processes. Because almost all services are basically processes, process

design must receive special attention. If the customer's body (for example, a physical exam at a hospital) or mind (for example, a concert) is the recipient of the service, the process must be designed from the customer's perspective. This needs special emphasis because often the concerns of various departments, such as accounting, operations, marketing, human resources, and shipping, dictate the parameters and nature of the process, and their objectives will be optimized in the design. Often the result is extended waiting for the customer, the unnecessary tasks he has to perform, the waste of his time, and the overall frustration with the whole process.

On the other hand, if the recipient of the service is the customer's possession or information and the customer's presence is not required during the performance, processes must be designed from the service provider's perspective. The objective here is to help the service provider deliver the service with the least amount of effort possible and make the task as pleasant as possible for her so that she can deliver the highest-quality service she is capable of.

It must be emphasized that using the customer's or the employee's perspective as the guiding light for the process design does not imply a complete disregard of the other. In other words, if we take the customer's perspective in the design, this does not mean we ignore the needs of the service provider; nor does it mean that we should be unconcerned if the process is such that it would make the service employee's life miserable. Interests of both parties must be promoted and protected. The issue is finding the proper balance.

6. **Minimize hand-offs**—Many services involve processing of the customer or his possessions by more than one service employee or department. This usually increases the probability for something to go wrong. The problem is usually caused by miscommunication or lack of communication. To reduce these problems, service must be delivered by a single service provider from the beginning to the end. Recall the example of USAA discussed in Chapter 7; USAA service employees have access to all the relevant information about a customer on a computer screen, can answer any questions from a customer, and can solve practically any problem without hand-offs. If this is not possible, a team approach can be followed; a team that works together and is responsible for a particular customer from the beginning to the end.

7. **Design back room operations to support front room operations**—The front room, or office, is where most of the service encounters take place and is where the customer's opinion of the service and organization is formed. However, practically everything done in the back room has an impact on the front-room operations and hence on customer satisfaction. Consequently, it is important that this dependence is taken into consideration when the service system is designed. For most services, back-room processes are very much like manufacturing operations, and the back room can be run like a factory. The first priority, however, is that back-room operations must be designed so that the front room operates flawlessly. Once this is established, traditional operations management techniques can be used to optimize the back-room operations.

8. **Incorporate data collection in process design**—A service organization needs data for monitoring and measuring customer satisfaction, performance measurement, and for quality improvement efforts, in addition to data needed for accounting and management decision making. Data collection mechanisms installed after a service is launched may create problems and make the service provider's job harder. Data needs for various purposes must be determined during the service design and incorporated into the system to create the least amount of interference with service delivery and minimize any additional work required from the service provider or the customer.

9. **Determine the extent of customer contact and participation**—As emphasized several times throughout this book, the customer's involvement in the service process creates many challenges for management as well as opportunities for a great service experience. For most services the extent of customer contact and participation are determined by the nature of the service. However, it is usually possible to modify these parameters. For example, if an organization wants less customer involvement in the service delivery, it may automate certain aspects of the service or hire more service employees to relieve customers from some of the tasks required. On the other hand, increased involvement usually implies higher risks for mistakes and may require a higher level of customization, and therefore higher costs. The degree of customer involvement determines the type and nature of skills and information the customer must have to participate. The organization must determine these needs and provide the necessary information for effective and efficient customer participation in the service delivery.

10. **Build flexibility and robustness into the system**—There will always be customers whose needs create situations that are not anticipated by designers. Also, there may be failures caused by outside factors, such as natural disasters, power outages, and failure of vendors. Service systems must be able to respond to these unplanned situations and continue the service. A very important step in this direction is to build flexible rules and processes. Rigid rules and processes make the service employee's job harder and frustrate customers. Most important, empowered employees act quickly and decisively to respond to a situation and ensure customer satisfaction. Flexibility is important in processes in which customers are present. Back-room processes that may be characterized as "manufacturing" types can have much less flexibility for efficiency in operations and consistency in results. Marriott is one of the most successful companies in the hospitality industry and is also well known for its attention to detail and obsession with processes. Chairman and CEO J. W. "Bill" Marriott, Jr., explains this passion as follows:

"We are sometimes teased about our passion for the Marriott Way of doing things. If you happen to work in the hospitality industry, you might already be familiar with our encyclopedic procedural manuals, which include what is probably the most infamous of the bunch: a guide setting out sixty-six separate steps for cleaning a hotel room in less than half an hour. Maybe we *are* a little fanatical about the way things should be done. But for us, the idea of having systems and procedures for everything is very natural and logical: If you want to produce a consistent result, you need to figure out how to do it, write it down, practice it, and keep improving it until there's nothing left to improve. (Of course, we at Marriott believe that there's *always* something to improve.)"[22]

11. **Design employee and customer loyalty into the system**—One of the greatest assets a company may have is employee and customer loyalty. According to "The Service Profit Chain" model, "Profit and growth are linked to customer loyalty, customer loyalty is linked to customer satisfaction, customer satisfaction is linked to service value, service value is linked to employee productivity, employee productivity is linked to loyalty, employee loyalty is linked to employee satisfaction, employee satisfaction is linked to internal quality of work life."[23] Therefore, it is crucial that developing customer and employee loyalty must be one of the principles of service design. If the principles listed earlier are followed, a significant step toward customer satisfaction will be taken. Ensuring employee satisfaction would be another major step in the same direction. In addition, other mechanisms can be used to encourage customer loyalty, such as frequent flier programs airlines offer or frequent guest programs offered by hotel chains.

Fair compensation, benefits, treatment with respect, and a pleasant place to work are the main ingredients for employee satisfaction. Employee satisfaction also depends on advancement opportunities, rewards for performance beyond the standard job requirements, and empowerment. However, requirements for various tasks and the corresponding job descriptions can be developed in parallel with the service design. Another component that may play a crucial role in employee satisfaction is empowerment, which can also be designed into the delivery system and its processes during the design. Briefly, service employees must serve customers in the best way they can and solve customers' problems quickly and efficiently without waiting for authorization from management. There are many good examples of this type of empowerment. For example, the Ritz-Carlton Hotel Company, a winner of 1992 and 1999 Malcolm Baldrige National Quality Award for Service Excellence has a list of basic service standards, called Gold Standards, printed on a wallet size card carried by every employee. The following are the "Service Values" part of the Gold Standards:[24]

1. I build strong relationships and create Ritz-Carlton guests for life.

2. I am always responsive to the expressed and unexpressed wishes and needs of our guests.

3. I am empowered to create unique, memorable and personal experiences for our guests.

4. I understand my role in achieving the Key Success Factors, embracing Community Footprints and creating The Ritz-Carlton Mystique.

5. I continuously seek opportunities to innovate and improve The Ritz-Carlton experience.

6. I own and immediately resolve guest problems.

7. I create a work environment of teamwork and lateral service so that the needs of our guests and each other are met.

8. I have the opportunity to continuously learn and grow.

9. I am involved in the planning of the work that affects me.

10. I am proud of my professional appearance, language and behavior.

11. I protect the privacy and security of our guests, my fellow employees and the company's confidential information and assets.

12. I am responsible for uncompromising levels of cleanliness and creating a safe and accident-free environment.

12. **Improve continuously**—As indicated earlier, designs in manufacturing are usually difficult and costly to change. Modifications to service designs, on the other hand, are relatively easier to implement and they are generally less costly. This gives most services a significant advantage because they can be modified and improved in light of customer input and changing needs, as well as changing competitive conditions. In other words, services lend themselves to continuous improvement much more than goods. Continuous improvement[25] has become a widely accepted and well established approach to achieving superior goods and services, and it should also be a principle of service design and the process of continuous improvement must be in place for the life of the service.

8.5 Design Process

Ideas for new goods or services are products of human creativity. Although creativity cannot be programmed, or achieved as a result of a step-by-step procedure, service design and development should be a well-thought-out and organized undertaking. Research by the consulting firm Booz, Allen, & Hamilton[26] suggests that manufacturing firms that are active in designing and developing new goods follow a seven step process: 1) new product development strategy; 2) idea generation; 3) screening and evaluation; 4) business analysis; 5) development; 6) testing; and 7) commercialization. There also exist many other similar processes developed by business researchers.[27] Because service design and development does not have a long history, most models suggested for services are modifications of processes originally developed for goods. This section describes a service design and development model that goes well beyond a simple modification of a manufacturing model and takes into account the complexity of service design. The model (see Exhibit 8-3) has been suggested by Scheuing and Johnson.[28] It consists of 15 steps and can be described in four stages: direction, design, testing, and introduction. It also indicates key influences at each step both from within and outside the service organization.

Exhibit 8-3   Model of Service Design and Development

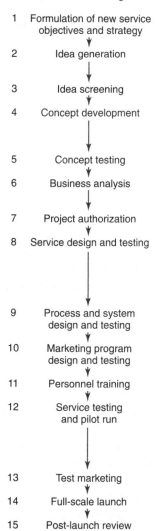

1 Formulation of new service
objectives and strategy

2 Idea generation

3 Idea screening

4 Concept development

5 Concept testing

6 Business analysis

7 Project authorization

8 Service design and testing

9 Process and system
design and testing

10 Marketing program
design and testing

11 Personnel training

12 Service testing
and pilot run

13 Test marketing

14 Full-scale launch

15 Post-launch review

Source: Adapted from Eberhard E. Scheuing and Eugene M. Johnson, "A Proposed Model for New Service Development," *The Journal of Services Marketing*, vol., 3, no. 2 (Spring 1989), pp. 25–34.

Direction

The first stage includes activities that determine the direction of the development effort.

1. **Formulation of new service objectives and strategy**—This is the first step of the whole process. As discussed in the previous section, service strategy must support the organization's overall strategy and must be directed at satisfying selected needs of customers in the target market or solving a particular problem for them. After this determination is made, strategy is the decision as to how value will be leveraged over costs, in other words what kind of service value will be created for the customer for the price he paid. (Refer to the discussion of "A Model of Service Value" in Chapter 5.)

   Customers make their purchase decisions on the basis of their perception of benefits. Consequently, positioning a new service with respect to benefits and relative to competing services is critical for its success. A useful tool for positioning is perceptual map. Perceptual maps are graphical representations of positions of products (goods or services) with respect to customer needs or wanted benefits. Perceptual maps help managers and designers discover opportunities for new products, or improvements in existing products, by providing a visual representation of how customers perceive and evaluate competing products in a category with respect to important benefits. Consider the following example of positioning of new transportation services.[29]

   Example: Suppose you are a public transit manager considering the introduction of new services to increase the utilization of public transportation. First, you need to find out what your customers' needs are. This can be done through one-on-one interviews, focus groups, or other formal and informal methods. Suppose that the following three primary needs have been discovered from customer research: 1) speed and convenience; 2) ease of travel; and 3) psychological comfort, together with how consumers rate each of the four existing modes of transportation. The results of how consumers perceive various modes of transportation are shown in Exhibit 8-4. Careful examination of this map reveals that there may be a need for a transportation service that provides ease of travel and psychological comfort. This is indicated by the fact that there is no transportation service in that sector of the perceptual map.

2. **Idea generation**—Ideas for new services may come from many different sources, including customers, customer complaints, service employees, competitors, and suppliers.

3. **Idea screening**—Naturally, not every idea for a new service is viable. There may be many ideas but only a few will be successful as new services in the market place. This step involves a crude sorting procedure separating promising ideas from others. Feasibility and potential profitability are the main concerns behind this activity. Care must be exercised not to throw out ideas just because they seem to be unusual.

Exhibit 8-4   Perceptual Map of Transportation Services

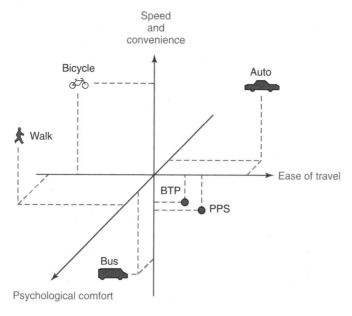

Source: Glen L. Urban and John R. Hauser, *Design and Marketing of the New Products*, 2nd ed. (Upper Saddle River, NJ, Prentice Hall, Inc., 1993), p.218.

Design

The design stage consists of steps 4 through 11 and focuses on designing a new service and its delivery system.

4. **Concept development**—Ideas that survived the screening process are developed a step further into service concepts. A service concept is a description of the bundle of benefits, solutions, and value the service is supposed to provide to a customer. The following are examples of two service concepts:

    "*A professional financial counseling service offered by your bank.* This counseling service is designed to assist you in determining and developing priorities for your financial goals (such as children's college education, retirement, purchase of a home) and to aid in the selection of a program tailored to achieve these goals. Your overall financial situation would be confidentially reviewed (including insurance policies, pension benefits, and savings) so that various investment alternatives could be explored. The service would provide for periodic review. Price for average yearly usage would be $100 for the initial year and $25 for each year thereafter.

Vision care insurance. A plan that pays $20 for each of the following annual vision care expenses: eye examination, single lens prescription, bifocal lens prescription, trifocal lens prescription, and a set of frames."[30]

5. **Concept testing**—The purpose of concept testing is to determine potential consumers' response to the service concept so that service ideas that are not attractive to consumers may be eliminated from further consideration. It also helps designers sharpen and focus the benefits of attractive concepts on what consumers really want. "A concept test of a new service is a research technique designed to evaluate whether a prospective user (1) understands the idea of the proposed service, (2) reacts favorably to it, and (3) feels it offers benefits that answer unmet needs."[31]

Example (continued): After discovering the gap in the coverage of consumers' needs, particularly, the unmet needs of ease of travel and psychological comfort, you decide to consider two new service concepts. The first concept is Budget Taxi Plan (BTP), which provides a service similar to that provided by taxi services but at a lower price. Also the driver may pick up or drop off other passengers on the way to your destination. BTP is to be provided by a private company. A second new service concept is called Personalized Premium Service (PPS). This is the same as BTP except instead of taxis minibuses are used, and it is to be publicly owned and operated. These concepts can be tested by asking potential customers to evaluate them with respect to the three dimensions: speed and convenience, ease of travel, and psychological comfort. The results of testing these two concepts are as BTP and PPS (refer to Exhibit 8-4). These two service concepts are perceived to be significantly higher than bicycle, walking, and bus on the speed and convenience, and ease of travel dimensions. On the psychological comfort dimension, however, they are perceived to be better than auto, equal to bicycle, but lower than walking and bus.

6. **Business analysis**—If a new service survives the concept testing, it is next subjected to a much closer scrutiny. The most important question designers try to answer, "Is this service concept economically sound?" In other words, is there a large enough market for it and can it be produced and sold for a reasonable profit? Consequently, this step includes market assessment, demand analysis, revenue projections, and cost analysis. If the result of this analysis is promising, the new service is recommended to top management for implementation.

7. **Project authorization**—If the results of the business analysis and profit projections meet the top management's criteria, the project will be approved and resources will be committed to the design and implementation of the new service and its delivery system.

8. **Service design and testing**—This is the stage at which a detailed service description is developed together with the specific features and characteristics of the service that differentiates it from its competitors. Although steps 8 and 9 are listed separately, they must be performed simultaneously, or in parallel, if two different teams are responsible for them. This is where the application of concurrent engineering principles must

begin, if it has not been in place already. A cross-functional team approach should be used for the entire design process, steps 1 through 15. However, if that has not been the case, this is where the team approach to design must begin, as well as parallel design efforts on other components, such as marketing program, development of employee selection criteria, site selection criteria, and the design of physical evidence.

9. **Process and system design and testing**—As emphasized earlier, most services are performances, and therefore they are the outcomes of processes. In other words, service processes create the service. This is the stage where the most detailed design work is done. This is also where quality and value can be built into the service, and hence concepts and tools for building quality and value into services can and should be used at this stage.

Before those concepts and tools are discussed, however, there are some general issues to consider. First, designers must take into consideration the influence of the following service characteristics on process design: (1) the nature of customer contact, (2) the degree of customer participation in the service production, (3) the degree of customization, (4) the role of goods and equipment in service delivery, (5) the recipient of the service (that is, customer's body, mind, or possessions), and (6) anticipated demand. Second, designers must also be conscious of the influence of these characteristics on what is above and below the line of visibility, the imaginary line that separates the front room and back room. The front room consists of what the customer would be seeing, or in contact with, during the service encounter. The back room includes all the personnel, facilities, and processes that support the front-room operations but need not be visible to the customer.

For example, if the customer's body is the recipient of the service, say a visit to the hospital for a physical exam, the customer (patient) has to be present in the facility. The front room consists of the doctors, nurses, receptionists, waiting rooms, examination rooms, nurses' station, X-ray room, and so forth. Some of the front-room processes include gathering information from the patient (for example, filling out forms), preparing the patient for doctor's exam (for example, taking blood pressure, temperature, providing an examination gown, and so on), physical exam, and drawing a blood sample for test. Back-room processes include tests performed in the lab, ordering, receiving, and stocking of medical supplies, maintenance of the facility, and billing. Most of the important services in this example are created and delivered by the processes of the front room. In this case they have to be designed for one patient at a time, and the performance is customized for each patient. The operational rule of the front room is an appointment or first-come, first-served.

Consider another service, say dry cleaning, where a customer's possession is the recipient of the service. Here the front room consists of a counter and an employee behind it to receive the items to be cleaned, give the customer a receipt, and a date when the items can be picked up. There is no need for a waiting room or elegant facilities because the customer will be in the store for only a few minutes. The back room consists of the equipment used for cleaning operations and the personnel who operate them, supplies, customers' items waiting to be cleaned, and those that have been cleaned and are waiting to be picked up. Although sometimes visible, customers are not allowed in the back room, which is organized for optimum operational efficiency. Unlike the hospital, items in a dry cleaner can be cleaned in any order, they can be processed in batches, and there is little customization.

As mentioned earlier, this is the design stage where the tools and concepts discussed in section 8.3 should be used to build quality and value into a service. Probably the most important tool for the purpose is quality function deployment, or the house of quality. This tool not only requires that designers find out customers' needs, but it also forces them to study and evaluate competitors' services. Consequently, it helps designers develop a service that meets customers' needs and determine performance levels they need to achieve to beat competitors. If the service designers also perform a benchmarking study to determine the best performances relevant to the new service, they can use those as their design targets instead of competitors' performances.

A tool that was briefly mentioned in section 8.3 is the service blueprint. A blueprint is a picture of a service system and its processes; it provides a bird's-eye view of the service system. It shows the steps of processes and interactions among processes as well as the interaction of a customer with the system. One of the most important benefits of blueprints is that they are more precise than verbal descriptions of service processes and therefore reduce ambiguity and the likelihood of misunderstandings that may originate from them. Blueprints are also educational. Preparing a service blueprint forces one to learn more about that system and probably helps him realize how little he actually knows about the functioning of the entire system.[32]

Another important advantage is that service blueprints allow the creation, study, and testing of services conceptually on paper before a costly implementation. Service blueprints are task-oriented. They display activities involved in a process. This characteristic makes them useful for training, communication, and quality improvement purposes. These last characteristics allow the application of value analysis to the evaluation of new or existing services for cost reductions and efficiency improvements. Service blueprints also allow the application of failure mode analysis (discussed in section 8.3) to determine potential areas where service failures may occur. These are called **fail points**, and they are where poka-yoke methods can be applied.

Although there are some differences, service blueprints use the flowcharting conventions. Exhibit 8-5 presents a sample blueprint of a florist service.[33]

The importance of building quality and value into the service at the design stage has been emphasized and several concepts and tools suggested. Application of these tools and concepts will also help make the new service more robust.

Exhibit 8-5   Blueprint for Florist Service

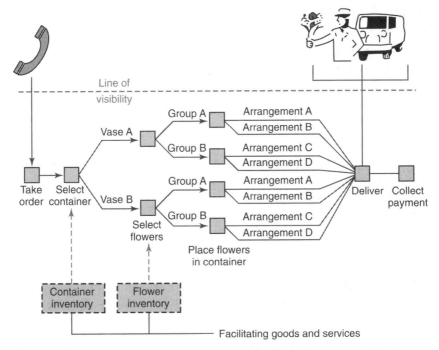

Source: Reprinted from G. Lynn Shostack, "Service Positioning through Structural Change," *Journal of Marketing*, vol. 51, no. 1, published by the American Marketing Association, January 1987.

Although the model represented in Exhibit 8-3 suggests an orderly and smooth progression of steps, the reality is never orderly or smooth; at the least it involves many iterations, revisions, redefinitions of concepts, and redesigns. Even when all these have been done several times, the process is not over; what has been designed must be tested. Tests at this stage correspond to prototype testing in manufacturing. However, they do not involve offering the service to the public—they are done internally. If possible, service and process designs must be tested under as realistic conditions as possible with real customers. When this is not possible, service may be offered to employees and their families.

10. **Market program design and testing**—A marketing program for the introduction, distribution (if relevant), and sale of the new service must be developed and tested with potential customers.

11. **Personnel training**—As previously indicated, criteria for employee selection (new hires or current employees) must be developed in parallel with the service and process design. After the selection is completed, employees must be trained not only in their specific tasks, but they also must be knowledgeable about the whole service system. They should also be given as wide authority as possible to serve customers and solve their problems.

Testing

12. **Service testing and pilot run**—This is live testing, where the service is offered on a limited basis at one or a few locations, but the service, employees, and customers are real. The purpose of this step is to determine consumer acceptance from first-hand knowledge. Another goal is to make necessary refinements and adjustments based on the information collected from customers.

13. **Test marketing**—Test marketing investigates the salability of the new service. In this case service is offered on a limited basis but at a larger scale than in step 12, (for example, at a few branches or in one region). The marketing program is also tested for its effectiveness. Information collected in this step include customers' reactions to the new service and results of different marketing mixes, such as demand corresponding to different prices charged for the service. These results are reviewed, and if necessary, modifications to the marketing plan are made.

Introduction

14. **Full-scale launch**—With all tests completed and adjustments and modifications implemented, the service is ready for a full-scale launch, the service is offered to the entire market.

15. **Post-launch review**—The purpose of this step is to determine the degree of achievement of the objectives and decide if further adjustments and modifications are needed. This step should not be the termination of the design and development process. Reviews should be conducted at regular intervals, with input from customers and frontline employees, to evaluate the success of the new service and adjust the service to changing conditions and make improvements.

8.6 Summary

This chapter focused on the design and development of services and their delivery systems. Service design is an important step in creating value and satisfaction for the customer. A service is supposed to satisfy the needs of customers, or solve their problems; the purpose of the design is to determine the best and most profitable way for doing this. Service design is also important because it influences quality, costs, customer value, and the image of the organization. Various categories of "newness," or innovation, in services were reviewed: major innovations, start-up businesses, new products for the currently served market, product line extensions, product improvements, and style changes.

In addition to meeting customers' needs, sometimes organizations are motivated by other factors to design and develop new services. Among the factors reviewed were financial goals, competitive actions, globalization, technology, changes in government regulations, elimination of professional association restrictions, growth of franchising, and balancing demand and supply.

Experience in manufacturing makes it clear that the best way to achieve quality and value in services is to build them in at the design stage. To provide an appropriate background for understanding how this can be done, the similarities and differences between goods and services were first reviewed with respect to design. Then a brief review of tools and concepts that were successfully used in designing, developing, and manufacturing goods that provide superior value and quality was provided. Included among them are concurrent engineering, quality function deployment (or the house of quality), robust design, design failure mode analysis, poka-yoke (or fail safe methods), blueprints, value analysis (or value engineering), and benchmarking. Suggestions were provided regarding how these concepts and tools may be used in designing and delivering services that provide superior value and quality.

Section 8.4 provided 12 basic principles for design and development of services that provide superior value and quality. These principles are (1) Know your customers; (2) Determine which of the customers' needs will be satisfied; (3) Develop a service strategy and position the service for competitive advantage; (4) Design the service, delivery system, human resource requirements, and tangibles simultaneously; (5) Design service processes from the customer's/employee's perspective; (6) Minimize hand-offs; (7) Design back-room operations to support front- room operations; (8) Incorporate data collection in process design; (9) Determine the extent of customer contact and participation; (10) Build flexibility and robustness into the system; (11) Design employee and customer loyalty into the system; and (12) Improve continuously.

In the last section, all these principles were put together to develop services that provide superior value and quality. Scheuing and Johnson's model for service design and development process was used. The model consists of 15 steps that can be accomplished in four stages: direction, design, testing, and introduction. Through this model, how the 12 design principles can be implemented and how concepts and tools for building value and quality can be used in the process were explained.

Endnotes

1. These categories were suggested by Donald F. Heany, "Degrees of Product Innovation," *Journal of Business Strategy* (Spring 1983), pp. 3–14, adopted to services by Christopher H. Lovelock, "Developing and Implementing New Services," in W. R. George and C. E. Marshall (Eds.), *Developing New Services* (Chicago, Illinois, American Marketing Association, 1984), pp. 44–64.

2. These factors have been adopted from the following two sources: Glen L. Urban and John R. Hauser, *Design and Marketing of New Products*, Second Edition (Upper Saddle River, NJ, Prentice-Hall, 1993), pp. 6–12, and Christopher H. Lovelock, "Developing and Implementing New Services," in W. R. George and C. E. Marshall (Eds.), *Developing New Services* (Chicago, Illinois, American Marketing Association, 1984), pp. 44–64.

3. Steve Jobs, "Apple's One-Dollar-a-Year Man," *Fortune* (January 24, 2000).

4. Benjamin Schneider and David E. Bowen, "New Services Design, Development and Implementation and the Employee," in George, W. R. and Marshall, C. E. (Eds.), *Developing New Services* (Chicago, Illinois, American Marketing Association, 1984), pp. 82–101.

5. For more information on concurrent engineering see: Alfred Rosenblatt and George F. Watson (Eds.) "Special Report: Concurrent Engineering," *IIIE Spectrum*, July 1991, pp. 22–37; Biren Prasad, *Concurrent Engineering Fundamentals*, Vols. I and II (Upper Saddle River, NJ, Prentice Hall, 1996 and 1997); J. W. Dean & G. I. Susman, "Organizing for Manufacturable Design," *Harvard Business Review* (January February 1989), pp. 28–36.

6. Yoji Akao (Ed.), *Quality Function Deployment: Integrating Customer Requirements into Product Design* (Cambridge, MA, Productivity Press, 1990).

7. Yoji Akao, "An Introduction to Quality Function Deployment," in Yoji Akao (Ed.), *Quality Function Deployment: Integrating Customer Requirements into Product Design* (Cambridge, MA, Productivity Press, 1990), pp. 3–24.

8. John R. Hauser and Don Clausing "The House of Quality," *Harvard Business Review* (May–June 1988), pp. 63–73.

9. Genichi Taguchi and Don Clausing "Robust Quality," *Harvard Business Review* (January–February 1990), pp. 65–75.

10. Joseph M. Juran and Frank M. Gryna, *Quality Planning and Analysis*, Third Edition (New York, NY, McGraw-Hill, 1993), p. 266, and Joseph M. Michalek and Richard K. Holmes, "Quality Engineering Techniques in Product Design/Process," *Quality Control in Manufacturing, Society of Automotive Engineers*, SP-483, pp. 17–22.

11. For more information on the application of poka-yoke methods in services see: Richard B. Chase and Douglas M. Stewart "Make Your Service Fail-Safe," *Sloan Management Review* (Spring 1994), pp. 35–44.

12. Shigeo Shingo, *Zero Quality Control: Source Inspection and the Poke-yoke Systems* (Cambridge, MA, Productivity Press, 1986).

13. G. Lynn Shostack, "How to Design a Service," *European Journal of Marketing*, Vol. 16, No. 1, 1982, pp. 49–63.

14. Lawrence D. Wells, *Techniques of Value Analysis and Engineering* (New York, NY, McGraw-Hill, 1961).

15. Edward D. Heller, *Value Management: Value Engineering and Cost Reduction* (Reading, MA, Addison-Wesley, 1971), pp. 13–14. Also see pp. 187–208 for some applications of value analysis/value engineering in services.

16. Carlos Fallon, "The All Important Definition," in William D. Falcon (Ed.), *Value Analysis Value Engineering: The Implications for Managers* (New York, NY, American Management Association, 1964), pp. 9–24.

17. For more information on benchmarking see Robert C. Camp, *Benchmarking: The Search for Industry Best Practices That Lead to Superior Performance* (Milwaukee, Wisconsin, ASQC Quality Press, 1989), and Robert C. Camp, *Business Process Benchmarking: Finding and Implementing Best Practices* (Milwaukee, Wisconsin, ASQC Quality Press, 1995).

18. J. W. Marriott, Jr. and Kathi Ann Brown, *The Spirit to Serve: Marriott's Way* (New York, NY, Harper Business, 1997), p. 57.

19. Robert C. Ford, Cherrill P. Heaton, and Stephen W. Brown, "Delivering Excellent Service: Lessons from the Best Firms," California Management Review, Vol. 44, No. 1 (Fall 2001), pp. 39–56.

20. Frances X. Frei, "The Four Things a Service Business Must Get Right," *Harvard Business Review* (April 2008), pp. 70–80.

21. Christopher Lovelock and Jochen Wirtz, *Services Marketing: People, Technology, Strategy*, 7th Edition (Upper Saddle River, NJ, Prentice Hall, 2011), pp. 86–93.

22. J. W. Marriott, Jr. and Kathi Ann Brown, *The Spirit to Serve: Marriott's Way* (New York, NY, Harper Business, 1997), p. 16.

23. J. L. Heskett, T. O. Jones, G. W. Loveman, W. E. Sasser, Jr., and L. A. Schlesinger, "Putting the Service-Profit Chain to Work", *Harvard Business Review* (July–August 2008), pp. 118–129; Also, see, James L. Heskett, W. Earl Sasser, Jr. and Leonard A. Schlesinger, *The Service Profit Chain* (New York, The Free Press, 1997).

24. Ritz-Carlton's Gold Standards, from http://corporate.ritzcarlton.com/en/About/GoldStandards.htm (07/15/2012).

25. Most books on quality cover continuous improvement process, however, probably the most detailed and comprehensive treatment of the subject can be found in Masaaki Imai, Kaizen: *The Key to Japan's Competitive Success* (New York, NY, McGraw-Hill, 1986).

26. Booz, Allen, and Hamilton, *New Products Management for the 1980s* (New York, NY, Booz, Allen, and Hamilton Inc., 1982).

27. Other product development processes may be found in Edgar A. Pessemier, *Product Management* (New York, NY, John Wiley, 1977); Yoram J. Wind, *Product Policy: Concepts, Methods and Strategy* (Reading, MA, Addison-Wesley, 1982); Glen L. Urban and John R. Hauser, *Design and Marketing of New Products* (Upper Saddle River, NJ, Prentice-Hall, Inc., 1993).

28. Eberhard E. Scheuing and Eugene M. Johnson, "A Proposed Model for New Service Development," *The Journal of Services Marketing*, Vol. 3, No. 2, Spring 1989, pp. 25–34.

29. This example has been adopted from Glen L. Urban and John R. Hauser, *Design and Marketing of New Products* (Upper Saddle River, NJ, Prentice-Hall, Inc., 1993), pp. 205–218.

30. Yoram J. Wind, *Product Policy: Concepts, Methods and Strategy* (Reading, MA, Addison-Wesley, 1982), pp. 281–282.

31. Scheuing and Johnson, op. cit. p. 32.

32. G. Lynn Shostack, "Understanding Services Through Blueprinting," in T. A. Swartz, D. E. Bowen, and S. W. Brown, (Eds.) *Advances in Services Marketing and Management: Research and Practice* (Greenwich, Connecticut, JAI Press Inc., 1992), Vol. 1, pp. 75–90.

33. For more information on service blueprinting, in addition to Shostack's previously cited works, see: G. Lynn Shostack, and Jane Kingman-Brundage, "How to Design a Service," in Carole A. Congram, and Margaret L. Friedman (Eds.), *Handbook of Marketing for the Service Industries* (New York, NY, American Management Association, 1991), pp. 243–261; G. Lynn Shostack, "Service Design in the Operating Environment," in W. R. George, and C. E. Marshall (Eds.), *Developing New Services* (Chicago, Illinois, American Marketing Association, 1984), pp. 27–43; Jane Kingman-Brundage, "The ABCs of Service System Blueprinting", in Mary Jo Bitner, and L. A. Crosby (Eds.), *Designing a Winning Service Strategy* (Chicago, Illinois, American Marketing Association, 1989).

9

SUPPLY CHAINS IN SERVICES AND THEIR MANAGEMENT*

9.1 Introduction

Anyone who is even remotely interested in business must be aware that there has been a lot of discussion about supply chains during the past two decades. During this period, a large number of academic and trade publications were started focusing on issues and challenges concerning supply chain management. Even newspapers and news magazines frequently carry news and articles about supply chains. It is clear that supply chain management is one of the hottest topics in the business world. Most of this attention is on supply chains for goods. However, service organizations also have supply chains, and they exhibit significantly different characteristics from supply chains for manufactured goods. This chapter introduces the basic concepts of supply chains and supply chain management and then provides a detailed look at service supply chains and their management.

To orient the reader for the following discussion, we offer the following brief definition of a supply chain for manufactured goods:

A supply chain is a system consisting of all activities, organizations, and facilities involved in the value adding transformation of raw materials, parts, and supplies into goods and delivery to final customers.

The next section reviews the developments that led to the emergence of supply chains as a focus of many business firms as well as nonprofit and public organizations. Section 9.3 summarizes some basic information about supply chains in general and traditional manufacturing supply chains in particular. The discussion of manufacturing supply chains will also include some of the most important challenges their managers face. This section is presented in case the reader is not familiar with the topic, and also to provide a background for better understanding as to the contrast between manufacturing and service supply chains. Section 9.4 presents a discussion of

---

*   We would like to thank Dr. Tan Miller of Rider University for his review of an earlier version of this chapter and his insightful comments.

service supply chains and their most basic characteristics. Section 9.5 reviews further important characteristics of supply chains of service organizations. The next section focuses on the challenges service supply chain managers face. The final section summarizes the main points of the chapter.

9.2 Developments Leading to the Emergence of Supply Chain Management

The world of business witnessed several significant developments in the last three decades. One of these was the advances in computer and telecommunications technologies, which not only increased the power and availability of computers but also made the world a more connected place through the Internet and telecommunications networks. This accelerated the globalization process; national borders are rapidly becoming less of a hindrance for people and organizations to communicate and conduct business. Also, many countries are no longer markets for domestic companies only but have become part of a global market.

One impact of these developments has been the significant increase in both the extent and severity of competition in the United States as well as in most global markets. In the 1980s and early 1990s, American companies were under tremendous pressure from Japanese competition; quality was the major competitive weapon Japanese companies wielded during this period. Loss of market share and profits forced American companies to embark upon a quality and productivity crusade, which is known as Total Quality Management (TQM). As a result, by the mid-1990s most U.S. manufacturers had achieved or sometimes surpassed Japanese quality levels in most products.

The success of TQM movement helped American manufacturers stop the loss of market share and profits, and often helped them become competitive and profitable. However, this did not change the intensity of competition in domestic or worldwide markets; to remain competitive and prosper, many U.S. companies embarked upon a massive cost cutting initiative, which often meant reducing the workforce. This was facilitated, in part, by the investment in and the use of new and enhanced technology (information systems, software, and hardware). The downsizing of corporate America did generate significant cost-savings and increases in efficiency for many companies, while at the same time some realized that they had lost valuable employees and thereby organizational competencies.

Many companies soon realized that downsizing cannot be a permanent source of efficiency gains or cost-savings, hence the fury of downsizing subsided at the end of the 1990s, but not the intensity of competition and pressure from investors for continued high levels of profits. The recession that started in 2008 has led to another massive round of layoffs in the United States and elsewhere.

Downsizing of corporations often meant hiring other firms or independent contractors to perform tasks that used to be performed by employees who were let go. This outsourcing of some functions increased the dependency of companies on suppliers and increased the size and complexity of supply chains. Improvements in computer and telecommunication technologies, and transportation, low wages in developing countries coupled with their adoption of advanced production technologies made some companies in these countries good candidates for supplying manufacturers in industrialized countries. Consequently, the supplier base of many manufacturers in the United States and industrialized countries became multinational and thereby even more complex.

As a result, American managers, as did their counterparts in other industrialized countries, had embarked upon another quest for new sources of efficiency and cost-savings. They quickly discovered that there is much to be gained from streamlining, coordinating, and integrating the flow of goods, services, and information in their supply chains. They also realized that for this to happen organizations along the supply chain must cooperate and coordinate their activities. Managers of many manufacturers discovered that, under the current competitive conditions, the success of their companies was determined by not only how they performed, but also how the entire supply chain performed.

Another development of the 1980s and 1990s was the change in consumer expectations and consumption habits. Today's consumer expects high quality, low price, variety, and when offered at a reasonable price, customization of products they plan to purchase. To a large extent these new expectations have been driven and accelerated by the advent and availability of the Internet and the vast amount of information available on World Wide Web. It has also become extremely easy to shop from your living room, and have practically anything delivered to your door. This made manufacturers become more dependent on their supply chains for providing all the things the modern consumer demanded. It is now clear to most managers that to remain competitive, it is no longer enough to make their own companies competitive, but they must also help make the members of their supply chain competitive. This means they must work with suppliers and suppliers' suppliers and with customers and customers' customers closely and coordinate their operations. Hence was born a new concept and a new area of management specialization: supply chain management.

It should also be emphasized that supply chains and their management did not materialize overnight. Of course, supply chains and their importance, especially in military operations, were known for thousands of years. However, the evolution of supply chain management can be traced back to "physical distribution" in the '60s and '70s, "integrated logistics management" in the '80s and the '90s, before it emerged as a separate branch of operations management in the later part of '90s and 2000s.

9.3 What Is a Supply Chain?

We now expand the brief definition given earlier. The starting point of a goods supply chain is the raw material extraction, such as mining, agriculture, or animal husbandry that supplies the materials to other companies for further processing and value adding. Actually, it is easy to see that even these activities have suppliers, such as mining equipment manufacturers that supply machines to mining companies; chemical manufacturers that supply fertilizers to farmers; and feed suppliers for dairy farms. Processing usually involves several operations (that is, transformations) performed by a sequence of companies in several facilities.

Activities of any organization, private or public, for profit or nonprofit, manufacturing or service, may be considered as value adding transformation of inputs into outputs. The most common inputs are land, labor, capital, raw materials, component parts (that is, outputs of other manufacturing organizations), supplies (for example, lubricants, coolants, paper, and ink for printers), energy, technology, customers, and management (Exhibit 9-1). Outputs include goods, services, and environmental impact (for example, air, water, and noise pollution). There are five main types of transformations:

Exhibit 9-1   General Model of an Organization

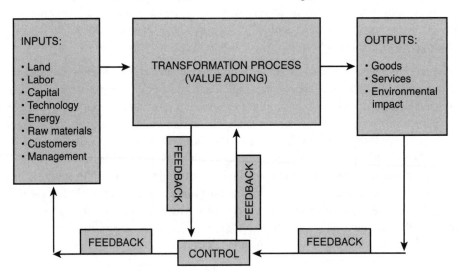

Physical transformation changes one or more physical characteristics of inputs into desirable ones. For example, steel sheets in automobile manufacturing are cut, bent, welded, and painted into a car body; tonsillectomies are performed in a hospital.

Locational transformation changes the location of humans (for example, air travel) or goods (for example, package delivery) from one location to another.

Psychological transformation changes the mood of humans (for example, a comedy movie).

Intellectual transformation changes the mind, such as developing problem-solving skills, developing new perspectives, and new knowledge (for example, higher education).

Informational transformation processes data to provide information (for example, newspapers, magazines, TV news, audit reports, consulting reports, and monthly statement of a checking account).

Manufacturing Supply Chains

Service organizations perform one or more of these transformations in their operations; however, the main function of manufacturing firms is almost exclusively physical transformations (see Exhibit 9-2). As material flows through value adding activities and various firms, information is generated in both directions. Demand information flows from downstream supply chain members (for example, ultimate customers, retailers, distributors, manufacturers) to upstream members (for example, distributors, shippers, manufacturers, suppliers, and suppliers' suppliers). Also, information from upstream supply chain members (for example, suppliers, manufacturers, distributors, retailers) flows toward downstream chain members.[1] The type of information in this case may be price, availability of products, shipping terms, date, delivery, and so on.

Exhibit 9-2   Manufacturing Supply Chains

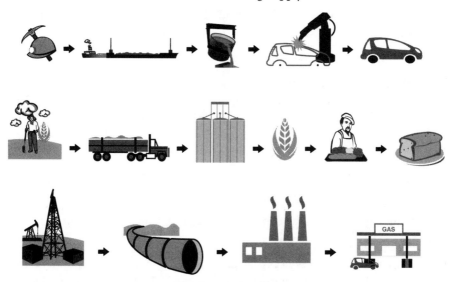

A third type of flow in a manufacturing supply chain is funds; as material moves through the supply chain (for example, raw material from suppliers to manufacturers, component parts from manufacturers to other manufacturers, finished product from retailers to final customers) recipients transfer funds for their purchases to upstream members.

Finally, a fourth type of flow is returns. Defective products or products that do not meet customers' expectations are returned to the retailer or the manufacturer for refunds. This process creates a funds flow from upstream to downstream supply chain members. Depending on the reason and the product, returned products may require repackaging, repair, or disposal.

If you think about most products, it becomes clear that the term supply chain is not an accurate description of the systems that create these products. In other words, although the image created by the term is a linear sequence of companies (that is, supplier, manufacturer, distributor, and retailer) involved in adding value to materials to create a good for the final customer, the reality is much different. Most products are created and delivered by a network of multiple suppliers, manufacturers, shippers, distributors, and retailers. Consequently, "*a multilevel web of suppliers, manufacturers, and service organizations, their facilities, and activities involved in the value adding transformation of raw materials, parts, and supplies into goods and deliver to final customers*" may be a better description of a manufacturing supply chain. However, because the term **supply chain** has been accepted and widely used by the industry and academia, we will continue to use it in the rest of this book.

Supply chain management as a field of study and practice can be considered as an outgrowth or expansion of logistics management. To a certain extent this is true; some of its tools and techniques are borrowed from logistics management, some from operations management and operations research. Logistics as a function has its origin in the military as the following definition indicates:

> The aspect of military science dealing with the procurement, maintenance, and transportation of military materiel, facilities, and personnel.[2]

In the civilian world logistics can be defined as

> The process of planning, implementing, and controlling procedures for the efficient and effective transportation and storage of goods including services, and related information from the point of origin to the point of consumption for the purpose of conforming to customer requirements. This definition includes inbound, outbound, internal, and external movements.[3]

In other words,

> The mission of logistics is to get the right goods or services to the right place, at the right time, and in the desired condition, while making the greatest contribution to the firm.[4]

Logistics management activities typically include inbound and outbound transportation management, fleet management, warehousing, materials, handling, order fulfillment, logistics network design, inventory management, supply/demand planning, and management of third-party logistics services providers.

The Council of Supply Chain Management Professionals (CSCMP) defines logistics management as one of the functions of supply chain management. It is clear that logistics plays an important role in both supply chain and in the economy of any country. Some supply chain professionals consider logistics in a much broader sense to overlap or even include many of the operations management responsibilities. (See the sidebar, "The Importance of Logistics.")

However, supply chain management is broader in scope and takes a more strategic approach to supply chain operations including the traditional logistics activities. Furthermore, supply chain management aims to optimize the flow of goods and information not only for one organization, but also for the entire chain; therefore, it takes a systems approach to the management of supply chain activities.

Supply Chain Management in Manufacturing

Supply Chain Management encompasses the planning and management of all activities involved in sourcing and procurement, conversion, and all logistics management activities. Importantly, it also includes coordination and collaboration with channel partners, which can be suppliers, intermediaries, third-party service providers, and customers. In essence, supply chain management integrates supply and demand management within and across companies. Supply Chain Management is an integrating function with primary responsibility for linking major business functions and business processes within and across companies into a cohesive and high-performing business model. It includes all of the logistics management activities noted above, as well as manufacturing operations, and it drives coordination of processes and activities with and across marketing, sales, product design, finance and information technology.[5]

Although it is not a widely embraced idea, some supply chain practitioners and academicians believe that the competition in the twenty-first century will not be company versus company, but rather supply chain versus supply chain.[6] Research has indicated that this may be true only to a very limited extent.[7] Even if it does not reflect the reality completely, the idea elevates the importance of supply chain management and the challenges it faces to a new level.

The Importance Of Logistics

Principle #1: Logistics plays a key role in supply chain management.

Supply chain management involves three major activities: sourcing, transformation, and logistics. Sourcing finds the raw materials, parts, and supplies to make goods or locates the equipment. Transformation converts materials into the correct form, and logistics moves and stores the goods from the point of origin to the point of use, sale, or service delivery.

Principle #2: Logistics benefits society.

Logistics benefits society in three major ways:

- It makes goods and services available to businesses, not-for-profit organizations, governments, and consumers.

- It influences the price of goods and services. A well designed and operated logistics system is essential for making goods available at low cost.

- It helps a society respond to the needs of its citizens, whether in daily living-by raising the standard of living, or in emergencies when the need for food, medical care, and shelter becomes acute.

Principle #3: Logistics is pervasive.

Logistics affects every aspect of business. Businesses use logistics to reach their customers and deliver goods and services. Manufacturers need parts and supplies for production and assembly; retailers need goods to sell; services need equipment and supplies. Even not-for-profit organizations must reach their clients with goods and services.

Principle #4: Logistics contributes to a company's revenues and growth.

Logistics positively affects a company's return on investment (ROI). Logistics constitutes a substantial part of costs in many industries. Using good logistics practices provides better customer service and potentially lowers costs, thereby raising profits.

Principle #5: Logistics plays a key role in marketing strategy.

Logistics can be the focal point of a marketing strategy. It can play an important role in supporting strategies based on price, product development, service or promotion. Incorporating logistics into marketing strategies can help them create a competitive advantage.

Principle #6: Logistics activities affect one another and other functions of marketing.

Logistics is not one activity but a combination of activities that affect one another and all functions of marketing. When a company promotes a product, logistics activities ensure that it is available to consumers. Decisions on production scheduling and inventory levels influence transportation.

Principle #7: Logistics fulfills the promises made by other facets of marketing.

Marketing often makes promises to customers about performance, availability, and price. Logistics plays a major role in keeping those promises and satisfying customers by placing goods where advertising and other forms of promotion say they will be, and by giving customers access to the benefits derived from the product.

Source: Adapted from Council of Supply Chain Management Professionals—CSCMP Toolbox.

Challenges for Manufacturing Supply Chain Managers

Supply chain managers face significant challenges in their jobs. Some of the most common challenges are as follows:

Uncertainty—This is probably the most serious challenge and implies risk. There are several kinds of uncertainty and associated risks. First is the uncertainty of demand; for most products demand fluctuates throughout the year. Not having enough supply of a product has the risk of losing profits and some customers forever. Probably the best way to meet this challenge is to have accurate demand information from downstream supply chain members, such as point of sale (POS) information from retailers. This requires close cooperation among the supply chain members. When actual demand information is not available, manufacturers and suppliers may base their forecasts on the magnitude of the orders from their customers. Slight fluctuations in order quantities may be misinterpreted as a surge or decline in long-term demand. Consequently, the supply chain member receiving the order from downstream places an even larger order to its supplier. This type of behavior may be repeated along the supply chain, thereby causing much larger fluctuations in the orders to upstream members, creating the **bullwhip effect**.[8]

Absence of actual demand information makes capacity and production planning difficult. Without this information supply chain managers have to rely on forecasting and inventories. It is well known that there is no perfect forecasting technique and forecasts almost always have errors. One reason inventories are held is to meet demand when demand exceeds forecasts and production capacity. The downside of this measure is that holding inventories involves significant costs; hence, there is a trade-off managers have to deal with. For manufacturing firms increasing capacity to meet demand in the short run may be possible with overtime if employees agree to work overtime. Also, manufacturing firms may use a subcontractor to produce the item to supplement the existing supply. The disadvantage of this practice is that if the item is proprietary, the manufacturer must reveal some trade secrets to the subcontractor; naturally, this is not advisable from competitiveness considerations. Another possible practice to meet demand when it exceeds supply is backordering, or backlogging; that is, meeting current demand from future production. For this to be a viable option, customers must be willing to wait.

A second type of uncertainty is supply uncertainty. Even when a company has a reliable supplier, unforeseen events, such as an earthquake, tsunami, flood, or a fire in a supplier's plant may create havoc in a supply chain. A company using a single supplier runs this type of risk. Many firms have tried to address this trade-off by using only a limited number of suppliers on a global basis for any particular item or part. Using multiple suppliers has its disadvantage that suppliers will not enjoy economies of scale; consequently, the cost will be higher than if a single supplier provided the item.

The most effective way to deal with these two uncertainties is to have a centralized information system. Other uncertainties originate from economic fluctuations, such as changes in prices of raw materials, oil, services such as transportation, and currency fluctuations.

Complexity of supply chains is caused by two factors. The first is the globalization of business; there are few major companies in developed countries that are completely domestic in terms of their suppliers and customers; basically, almost every company has some global connection. This means that companies have global as well as domestic suppliers, customers, and competitors.

Another source of complexity is the sheer number of supply chain members. For example, aircraft manufacturer Boeing has approximately 1,200 first-tier suppliers supplying parts directly to the manufacturer from 5,400 factories in 40 countries.[9] The advantages of specialization and economies of scale increased the practice of outsourcing and hence the number of suppliers a company has; this number is increased even more when a company uses multiple suppliers for the same item.

A third source is the fact that most companies have several customers with different supply chains of their own and different requirements. Finally, a company usually has several supply chains, which serves as a multiplier of the complexity originating from the first three sources. The simple reason that a company usually has several different supply chains is that different products may require different types of supply chains. For example, innovative products require responsive supply chains, whereas functional (that is, commodity type) products require efficient supply chains.[10]

Coordination/cooperation—The principle of synergy implies that a supply chain that operates as a whole will be more effective and efficient than individual members making decisions to optimize their own operations. It also means that the total profit generated will be more than the sum of the profits members make acting on their own.[11] Obviously, this requires close coordination of the activities of the entire supply chain, which requires close cooperation among them. The most important requirement is sharing of actual demand information, forecasts, and production plans, and plans for special initiatives such as promotional campaigns. If it can be established, a centralized information system as previously mentioned would be an effective way to coordination and cooperation.

Alignment of goals and incentives—The most effective way to achieve coordination and cooperation is when supply chain members focus on increasing the surplus for the entire supply chain rather than increasing their individual profits. This, of course, should be accompanied with a fair distribution of risks and profits among the members. Given the traditional focus of firms on optimizing their own operations, achieving this is a great challenge for all supply chain managers.[12] Also, supplying the right quality and quantity of material when they are needed and where they are needed is extremely important for all members of the supply chain. The smooth operation of the supply chain largely depends on this requirement, and that requires close coordination and cooperation among the members.

Other challenges include sourcing, supplier relationships, customer relationships, and setting up and operating distribution networks, all of which play important roles in determining the success of supply chain operations. A 2010 McKinsey & Company Global Survey of 639 executives on challenges for supply chains found that the top three challenges are rising pressure from global competition, consumer expectations, and increasingly complex patterns of customer demand.[13]

9.4 Supply Chains in Services and Their Characteristics

It should be remembered that service organizations exhibit great variety in terms of nature, character, size, and the services they offer. First, recall that service organizations may be private or public; they may be for profit or nonprofit (or not-for-profit). Public service organizations exist at local, state, or federal level; they are all nonprofit service organizations. On the other hand, there are many nonprofits that are not public organizations, such as hospitals owned by charities. Consequently, the following discussion about service supply chains does not necessarily apply to all service organizations; some of the organizations relevant to the discussion will be made clear with examples.

The most important characteristic of service supply chains is what flows through them: customer, customer's possession, customer's data/information, funds, and supplies. This is also the most important difference between service and manufacturing supply chains. As discussed earlier, raw materials, component parts (for example, outputs of other manufacturers), supplies (for example, lubricants, coolants, packaging material, and RFID tags), information, returns, and funds constitute main flows in a manufacturing supply chain.

Recall the general model, presented earlier, of an organization as a value adding transformation process. A manufacturing firm mainly performs physical transformations on materials; in other words, value adding transformation processes are applied to inanimate objects. A service organization may perform one or more of the five types of transformations: physical, psychological, intellectual, locational, and informational. The recipient of the service may be the customer (that is, customer's body, mind, or both), customer's possession (that is, car, house, pet, and funds), or customer's data/information. In any case it is the customer who ultimately receives the benefit of the service. Depending on the service, it may be more appropriate to use terms such as **client**, **patient**, **passenger**, **student**, **member**, **subscriber**, and so on instead of **customer**. However, the word customer will be used when distinction is not critical. It should also be emphasized that in some cases the customer is not a person but another organization; an example is an airline receiving severe weather and hurricane reports from the National Oceanic and Atmospheric Administration (NOAA).

Next, we discuss how service supply chains differ from manufacturing supply chains depending on the recipient of service.

Service Recipient: Customer

In some services the customer's body is the recipient of the service. For example, consider a patient who is scheduled to have an operation in a hospital. The patient arrives at the hospital, goes to the admissions office, fills out required forms, and in general provides all the required information such as her name, address, date of birth, Social Security number, name of the insurance carrier, medical history, medications she is using, and allergies. The patient's information becomes one of the flows in the hospital's supply chain. Then the patient will probably be seen by a nurse for other preadmission procedures (for example, checking blood pressure and taking the patient's pulse and temperature), and there may also be some tests. When these procedures are completed, she'll be admitted. If the surgery is scheduled for the same day, the patient will be prepared for the surgery, and she will be moved to the operating room. In the operating room services of a surgeon, anesthesiologist, and nurses will be needed to perform surgical processes, and surgical supplies will be the part of the supplies of the hospital's supply chain. After the surgery, the patient will be moved to a recovery room if further hospitalization is not required. When ready, the patient will be discharged with post-operation instructions. In a few days paperwork and a bill will be prepared and sent to the patient and/or to the insurance company. When the patient or the insurance company pays the bill, funds will flow upstream to the surgeon, anesthesiologist, hospital, and hospital's suppliers (see Exhibit 9-3).

Exhibit 9-3   A Surgical Patient in Hospital Supply Chain

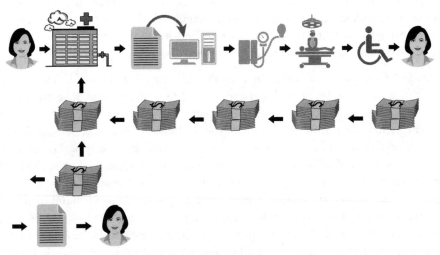

In this example physical and informational transformations were performed. Assuming that the operation was a success, it is natural to expect that a psychological transformation also took place and that the patient's mood has been transformed; she is now happier because she has regained her health.

This is an extremely simplified example of processes for surgery in a hospital. However, it demonstrates how starkly different a service supply chain may work compared to a manufacturing supply chain. In this example the patient's body, her information, hospital and surgical supplies, billing information, and funds were the main flows through the supply chain.

This example shows how customer plays a **triple** role in some services: First, the patient was the **supplier**; second, the patient's body was, to use a manufacturing term, the **material** supplied; and third, the patient was the recipient, or beneficiary, of the service, and therefore was the **customer**.

In a manufacturing supply chain, the customer is the last link. That is also true for some service supply chains. For example, someone purchasing a movie DVD, a book, or downloading software is the last link for these services. However, in most service supply chains the customer is the first and the last link. In a manufacturing supply chain, the customer demand starts the entire process from downstream; the customer buys something from a retailer, the retailer orders the good from a wholesaler to replace the sold one, the wholesaler from a distributor, the distributor from a manufacturer, and the manufacturer orders supplies from its suppliers. In a service supply chain, the customer initiates the process as a supplier of his body, possession, or information for a service from upstream and receives the service as the last member of the chain downstream.

The triple role a customer plays in some service supply chains creates significant challenges for managers. The most important challenges are related to the customer's safety and psychology. In a manufacturing supply chain, if material is damaged or incorrectly processed, it may have to be discarded or reworked, and the company incurs the cost of poor quality. Usually there will be no other consequences. If a customer is harmed physically or psychologically in a service process, there are serious consequences. First, there is an implicit contract between a customer and the service organization that the organization is to ensure the safety and well-being of its customers while in service. Violation of this contract has legal and ethical consequences. Bodily and/or psychological harm a customer suffers because of the service almost certainly trigger a lawsuit against the organization. If the incident becomes public, reputation of the organization will suffer, and the organization will most likely lose customers and profits. Hence, it is clear that physical and psychological safety and well-being of customers should be the utmost concern in service supply chains.

Of course, the seriousness of the risk of harm to customers is not the same for all services. The risk is inherent for services in which customer's body and/or mind are the recipients of service; in general healthcare providers, airlines, cruise lines, and restaurants are some examples of service organizations that should be aware of this risk. For some other services during which the customer is present but his mind is the recipient of the service, bodily harm from the service is not likely, but his psychology could be the issue. For example, an airline passenger's psychology and comfort will suffer if the airplane sits on the tarmac for hours in the heat of the summer; consequently, complaints and lawsuits about the service may ensue. Other examples of services in which psychological damage may occur include psychiatric or counseling services, movie in a theater, theatrical production, or an educational institution.

Managers of service organizations should consider all possible risks, take preventive measures, and develop plans to remedy the situation as quickly as possible, including alternatives to continue the service and compensation for customers' sufferings.[14]

Service Recipient: Customer's Possessions

Many services exist to provide services for customer's possessions, such as a car, house, pet, package, and funds. In these cases the customer is again the initiator and supplier to the service supply chain; and because she is the beneficiary of the service, she is also the **customer**. Then the customer assumes a **dual role** when her possession is serviced. In addition to supplies needed to perform the necessary service, the customer's possession and information are now the main flows in the supply chain. When payment is made funds will flow from the customer to the service organization and its suppliers.

After the customer explains the service needed, usually he leaves the service facility and entrusts his possession to the service organization. In a manufacturing supply chain, the material that flows through it is usually owned by the company that is processing it, until it is transferred to the next company in the chain. Then that company assumes possession and ownership of the material, and so on. In a service supply chain, the service organization does not assume ownership of the material (that is, the customer's possession) but only the guardianship of it while it is in the organization. Just like in the case of the customer's body, the service organization is legally and ethically responsible to make sure that the customer's possession is not harmed or damaged.

The two cases discussed separately so far, that is, the customer's body being the recipient and the customer's possession being the recipient of service, may occur together in services such as air travel, cruise vacation, hospitality services, and car rental. The issues and principles discussed for the two cases are valid when both are in service together.

One type of customer possession is funds, or money. Financial organizations, such as banks, investment banks, and mutual funds, are involved in managing customers' funds, such as 401(k), IRA, or other types of investments. Consider a mutual fund customer. After a customer fills out a form with the required information, she sends a check to a mutual funds company, or makes an electronic funds transfer, and buys shares in a mutual fund of her choice. The rest of the process is fairly straightforward; the company invests the money and sends her periodic statements about the performance of the investment and charges a service fee. There is usually no need for a face-to-face meeting between the customer and the company; interactions between them are usually through mail, e-mail, or telephone. In this case the major flows through the supply chain are funds and information; they flow both ways. The supply chain may be simple but the risks are not. As well known, there are no guarantees in investing. Investors may lose part or all of their investments due to bad decisions of financial managers, or worse, due to fraud as many scandals and ponzi schemes that rocked the financial world as recent years have shown. However, the service provider again has the responsibility to manage the customer's money with her best interests in mind.

Service Recipient: The Customer's Data/Information

Some service organizations transform the customer's data into useful information and information into reports. Some examples are public accounting firms, credit card companies, Internal Revenue Service, insurance companies, Social Security Administration, and Medicare. Even as this small set of examples may indicate, service organizations in this category exhibit great variety in their objectives and services they provide. As an example consider a public accounting firm.

Public accounting firms provide certified public accounting (CPA) services, for which they collect, maintain, and review their client's financial data and prepare financial statements. They also prepare and submit tax returns. Other services they may provide are auditing and consulting services. Their clients may be individuals or companies. The most important flow in this service supply chain is the client's data, and the client is the supplier of data. The data will be transformed into information by the public accounting firm in the form of financial statements, tax returns, or consulting reports. Again, the company has the responsibility to safeguard and protect the client's data. The client will receive this service output as the last link in the supply chain and start a fund flow to upstream for the payment of the services received. Although a public accounting firm may have many other suppliers (for example, legal counseling, office supplies, janitorial services, and security services) the most important supplier is the client, and the supply chain is simple: The client as the supplier-public accounting firm as the service provider-client as the customer; as a result the client plays a dual role.

9.5 Some Other Characteristics of Service Supply Chains

When customers are present in some service systems, they may be required to perform some tasks, such as self-checkouts in supermarkets and other stores and self-check in at a kiosk at some airports. This implies customers become suppliers of part of the labor required for the service. If tasks required of customers are complicated, or customers are not already familiar with them, customer involvement may create a risk of frustrating and alienating customers. In these systems the customer performed tasks must be kept simple, accompanied with clear, relevant information, and free of inherent dangers to customers or their possessions.

Network design and the number and location of facilities, such as plants, warehouses, and distribution centers, are important decisions in manufacturing supply chains. For example, increasing the number of warehouses and locating them closer to retail stores or population centers increases the responsiveness of the supply chain but increases inbound transportation costs. It also increases the costs of warehousing operational costs due to loss of economies of scale. Operating from a few warehouses will reduce inbound transportation costs but increase outbound transportation costs, and reduce responsiveness; hence, there is a trade-off.

In general, for some service supply chains this trade-off does not exist. Service facilities have to be easily accessible to potential customers; service organizations have no choice but to locate their facilities close to their customers. For example, service organizations such as banks, hospitals, fast food restaurants, firehouses, emergency response teams, and post offices are located where people traffic is high. Another example is The UPS Store that provides shipping services mainly for individuals and small businesses; for easy access UPS Store has more than 4,300 independently owned locations in the United States, Puerto Rico and the U.S. Virgin Islands.[15]

However, for some services locating facilities close to population centers is not an issue; these are services such as insurance companies, brokerage services, investment companies, mail order businesses (for example, Amazon.com) because they do not need to meet customers face to face to provide their services. Also, many public service organizations do not need to have facilities where customers can visit. Some examples include the National Highway Traffic Safety Administration, Federal Aviation Administration, Centers for Disease Control and Prevention, and Internal Revenue Service. Most of the services of these organizations can be obtained over the Internet, over the telephone, or by mail.

Manufacturing supply chains have many suppliers; however, the number of suppliers is finite. Actually, in recent years manufacturers have been trying to reduce the number of suppliers so that they can have long-term relationships, or partnerships, with their suppliers and thereby help them achieve economies of scale by giving them a larger share of their business. With few suppliers, they can also help suppliers improve the quality of material they supply by providing technical help. In previous sections it was emphasized that for some service organizations the major supplier is the customer. Unless the service requires a long-term and continuous relationship with customers, such as car, home, or health insurance, or telephone service, a service organization does not know who these people are until they become their customers. Consequently, a service organization has, at least theoretically, an infinite number of potential suppliers.

Unless a service organization is large and has extensive operations, it is not likely to appoint a **supply chain manager**. However, whatever their title may be, service organizations have managers in charge of supply chain-related tasks. As discussed in previous sections, the most important supplier for a service organization is the customer; hence a manager in charge of marketing the services of the organization could be considered to be in supplier relationships.

A service organization may have other suppliers. Companies that supply **material** to a service organization form the second group of suppliers, however, they are not necessarily unimportant; some supply critical material. The variety of material supplied to service organizations is almost infinite: it can range from office supplies, such as pens, pencils, paper, and ink for printers, to fuel, meals, and replacement parts for airlines, medical and surgical equipment, pharmaceuticals, chemicals, meals, and blood for hospitals.

9.6 Challenges for Service Supply Chain Managers

Challenges for manufacturing supply chain managers were discussed in section 9.3: uncertainty, complexity, coordination/cooperation, and alignment of goals and incentives. Uncertainty is the biggest challenge also for most service organizations. The last three may exist for some service supply chains but not all.

Uncertainty of demand is due to the variability of demand. There may be many factors that create variability: seasons, weather, special events, news, and state of the economy to mention a few. For example, a snowstorm is likely to keep shoppers at home and instead shop online; this will decrease demand for retailers in the area but may cause a surge of demand for some online merchants. A college football game is likely to create a huge demand for rooms at hotels in and around the town where the game is played, albeit for a day or two. Some of the events that cause a spike in demand for some services can be known and can be prepared for, such as high demand for air travel during holidays, or a big convention coming to town. Others, however, may occur suddenly and unexpectedly, and responding to them could be quite a challenge for services. For these events service organizations may develop contingency plans.

In addition to these, demand for services may also have random variation or a seasonal pattern. Using historical data and forecasting techniques (Chapter 15, "Forecasting Demand for Services") a service organization may successfully handle uncertainty due to these two factors.

In discussing the challenge of uncertainty for manufacturing supply chains, several possible remedies were mentioned: holding inventory, overtime, subcontracting, and backordering. For most services, these remedies do not exist. As discussed in Chapter 2, "The Nature of Services and Service Encounters," most services are perishable; they cannot be inventoried. Overtime cannot increase the capacity of most services; a restaurant may temporarily extend its hours to meet additional demand, but asking employees to work overtime will not increase a hotel's capacity to accept additional guests. Finally, subcontracting and backordering are just not possible for most services.

Uncertainty of supply also exists for service organizations, and some may be critical for service operations. For example, uncertainty in blood supply could create a major challenge for a hospital; uncertainty of supply of vaccine for a disease could be a major problem for healthcare organizations and may cost lives. In general, supplier uncertainty should be handled following good practices developed for manufacturing supply chains.

Complexity may be a challenge for large service organizations that have many facilities and global operations. This is because they usually have to obtain supplies from the countries in which they operate, which may be due to the host country's laws and regulations or for economic and practical reasons. For example, airlines that have international routes have to rely on local suppliers in countries they fly for fuel, ground operations, meals, cleaning services, and hospitality services for their crews. Other examples are pharmaceutical firms that have research labs, production facilities, and sales and marketing operations around the world; banks that have banking and other financial operations in other countries; and insurance companies that operate on a global scale.

There is another group of service organizations that face a different kind of complexity challenge. Public organizations at federal, state, and local level face complexity in obtaining supplies due to their nature: They are public organizations. Because they are financed by tax money, basically everything they do is subject to scrutiny by news organizations, politicians, and public in general. Almost all their activities, including choosing suppliers and purchasing supplies, are governed by laws and regulations. Consequently, public administrators in charge of purchasing supplies have to follow the laws and regulations and also deal with all the issues manufacturing supply managers deal with.

Coordination/Cooperation

Coordination and cooperation between a service organization and its suppliers, other than customers (acting as suppliers), could be critical when the availability of supplies, their quality, or timing of delivery negatively affects service efforts. For example, lack of supplies, or delay in their delivery, could cripple disaster aid and recovery efforts of service organizations[16] such as Federal

Emergency Management Agency (FEMA) as was observed in the aftermath of hurricane Katrina in 2005.

Alignment of goals and incentives—Suppliers to manufacturers have an interest and incentive in the final product's success in the market place; if the product sells well, that will most likely lead to more orders from the manufacturer, more business, and more profit to the supplier. If the product fails in the market place, the supplier is likely to lose business from the manufacturer and profits. If the failure of the product is due to poor quality of what the supplier sold to the manufacturer, it could certainly end the business relationship between them, not to mention the destruction of the reputation of the supplier. The benefits of working together toward a common goal by a supplier and its customer apply to the entire supply chain, and when their goals and incentives are aligned, they all benefit.

Interestingly, this type of synergistic relationship does not exist in most service supply chains. The simple reason is that in most cases the materials supplied by suppliers do not become part of the final product: the service, which is not a physical item. It should be clear that the quality and quantity of supplies, and when and where they are delivered, could play a significant role in the performance of a service. But as long as the service is delivered without any problems, customers would not know, or care, about supplies, the brand, or the supplier. Even if a failure occurs in the delivery of a service due to a material, customers would hold the service organization responsible.

9.7 Summary

This chapter presented a brief description of manufacturing supply chains and then focused on supply chains of service organizations. First, definitions of manufacturing supply chains from various academic and professional sources were given. Then a general model of an organization was presented as a transformation process in which inputs are transformed into goods, services, and environmental impacts. Five types of transformations were identified: physical, locational, psychological, intellectual, and informational transformation. Manufacturing performs, almost exclusively, physical transformations, whereas services perform all five.

Raw materials, component parts, supplies, information, and funds are the main flows through a manufacturing supply chain. Uncertainty, complexity, coordination/cooperation, and alignment of goals and incentives were identified as the major challenges for manufacturing supply chain managers. It has been emphasized that when supply chain members have their goals and incentives aligned, and they cooperate and coordinate their activities, the resulting profits to the supply chain will be more than the total of profits when each member optimizes its own operations.

Service supply chains and their characteristics were reviewed with respect to the recipient of service: customer (the customer's body, or mind, or both), customer's possession, customer's information. It was emphasized that in all three cases a customer is the supplier to the service supply chain. When the customer's body is in service, she plays a triple role; she is the supplier, the material, and the customer. When the customer's possession or data is the recipient, the customer plays a dual role: supplier and the customer. In addition to these discussions, some other significant characteristics of service supply chains were also reviewed.

Finally, against this background, challenges facing managers of service organizations were reviewed: uncertainty, complexity, coordination/cooperation, and alignment of goals and incentives. These are the same challenges manufacturing supply chain managers face, but in services their nature is different. Uncertainty exists for almost all service organizations and generally originates from demand variation. The other three challenges usually exist for large-scale service organizations with many facilities around the country or around the world. They may also exist when supplies play a critical role in the service.

Endnotes

1. Characterization of a supply chain member as in upstream or downstream may change depending on where the flow starts and its direction.

2. *Miriam Webster's Collegiate Dictionary*, 10th Edition, 1996.

3. *Council of Supply Chain Management Professionals, Supply Chain Management Terms and Glossary*, 2010. http://cscmp.org/digital/glossary/glossary.asp (07/27/2012).

4. Ronald H. Ballou, *Business Logistics Management*, 4th Edition (Prentice Hall, 1999), p. 6.

5. *Council of Supply Chain Management Professionals, Supply Chain Management Terms and Glossary*, 2010. http://cscmp.org/digital/glossary/glossary.asp (07/27/2012).

6. See for example Douglas M. Lambert and Martha C. Cooper, "Issues in Supply Chain Management," *Industrial Marketing Management*, 29, 65–83, 2000.

7. James B. Rice, Jr. and Richard M. Hoppe, "Supply Chain vs. Supply Chain: The Hype and the Reality," *Supply Chain Management Review*, September–October 2001, 47–54.

8. Lee, Hau L., Padmanabhan, V., and Whang, Seungjin, "The Bullwhip Effect in Supply Chains," MIT *Sloan Management Review*; Spring 1997; 38, 3; pg. 93.

9. "Faster, faster, faster," *The Economist*, January 28, 2012.

10. Fisher, Marshall L. "What is the Right Supply Chain for Your Product?" *Harvard Business Review*, March–April 1997, pp. 105–116.

11. Martin Christopher, *Logistics and Supply Chain Management*, Third Edition (Financial Times, Prentice Hall, Harlow, Great Britain, 2005), p. 5.

12. Chopra, S. and Meindl, P. *Supply Chain Management: Strategy, Planning and Operation*, 5th Edition (Prentice Hall, Upper Saddle River, NJ, 2013); Also see Narayanan, V.G and Raman, A. "Aligning Incentives in a Supply Chain," *Harvard Business Review*, November 2004, pp. 94–102.

13. (http://www.mckinseyquarterly.com/The_challenges_ahead_for_supply_chains_ McKinsey Global_Survey_results_2706 (07/26/2012); Also see "Supply Chain Challenges: Building Relationships," A Panel Discussion, *Harvard Business Review* (July 2003).

14. There is extensive literature on service failures, recovery efforts, and consequences. Some of the journals for finding relevant research are *Journal of Service Research, Journal of Services Marketing, Journal of Applied Psychology, Journal of Marketing*, and *International Journal of Service Industry Management.*

15. http://www.theupsstore.com/Pages/index.aspx (07/27/2012).

16. "The rising cost of catastrophes," *The Economist*, January 14, 2012.

10

LOCATING FACILITIES AND DESIGNING THEIR LAYOUT

10.1 Introduction

One of the most important long-term revenue decisions a service organization makes is where to locate its operation. This decision follows the design of the service and service delivery systems (the topic of Chapter 8, "Design and Development of Services and Service Delivery Systems,") and consists of two parts: finding a *location* and then finding a *site* within it for the service delivery system. After the location and site have been selected, the facility layout must be designed. The layout problem involves finding the best arrangement of the physical components of the service system possible within the time, cost, and technology constraints of the situation. Attention in this chapter first focuses on the location options available and then turns to facility layout.

Service organizations may have to make location decisions for various reasons. Offering service at new locations may be part of a growth strategy the organization is pursuing. Another reason may be increased demand; the current service facility may be unable to meet the additional demand; hence a new facility or expansion may be needed. Of course, the opposite may also be true. That is, demand at one location may fall below the level at which the service organization can survive; hence a new location with sufficient demand may be needed. When a service organization faces a location decision, there are basically three options:

1. Enlarge an existing facility at the present site.

2. Close the present facility and construct one or more new ones on new sites.

3. Open a new site or sites.

Location selection is a macrodecision involving which countries, regions within a country, and communities (within a region, county, or city) are appropriate for locating the service units. **Site selection** is a microdecision as to the specific piece of property (or properties) on which to establish the service. This chapter first examines the location selection decision by describing the effect of the following:

- The business profile

- Dominant location factors

- General selection criteria

- Common mistakes made in selection

- Multiple locations

A variety of quantitative methods for evaluating locations, ranging from simple factor weighting to complex mathematical models, are examined. Designing the layout of service facilities will be discussed in the second half of this chapter.

10.2 Location Selection

Location and site selection is a strategic decision because it is usually a decision that will have long-term effects on costs, demand, and profitability. Because location is such a significant cost driver, the consulting firm McKinsey believes "location ultimately has the power to make (or break) a company's business strategy."[1] Also, after a location is selected and a facility is built, the investment is basically a sunk cost. This is because if the chosen location turns out to be a mistake, selling the facility to another company may not be possible because it was not a good location for a business. Location and site selection is a particularly important decision for service organizations because most services are produced and consumed simultaneously. Also, most services require the customer's presence. These characteristics of services make service location an extremely important factor in consumers' buying decisions. Service organizations have no choice but to make their facilities accessible to as large a customer group as possible.

Business Profile

Before considering alternative locations (and sites), a business profile should be prepared. The profile describes the nature of the business and the needs of the business in terms of location and site. It also includes an analysis of the dominant location factors presented in the next section. A comparison is then made of the profile versus the firm's strategic plan, as shown by the model in Exhibit 10-1. The overall strategy of the organization should serve as the guiding principle and framework for locating any business.

Exhibit 10-1 Location and Site Selection Evaluation

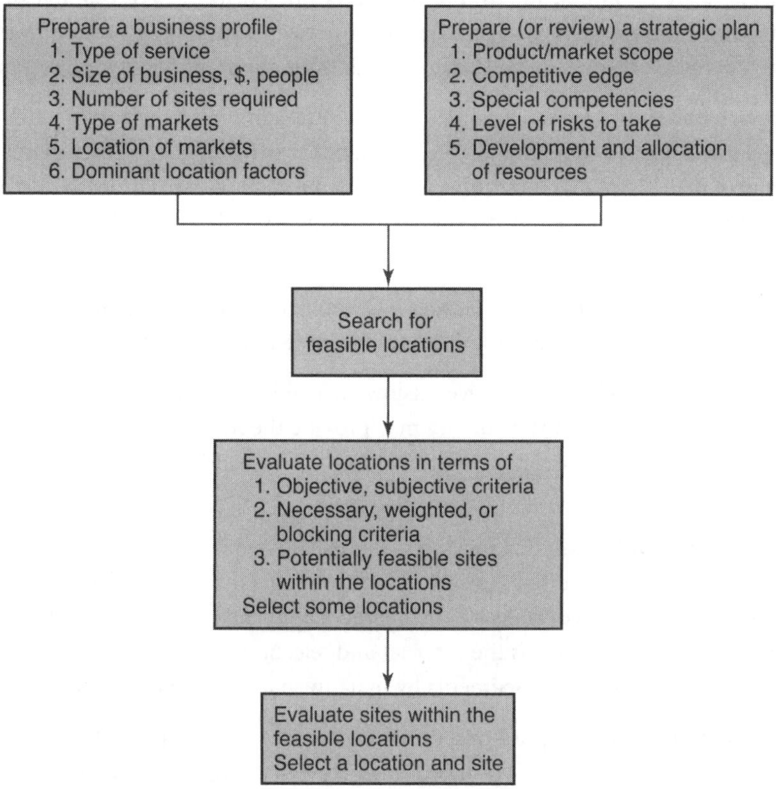

Dominant Location Factors

The selection of location and site for a service obviously depends on a number of factors and trade-offs among benefits and costs. However, there may be a particular factor that dominates the selection process and limits the number of feasible locations to be evaluated. Following are nine dominant factors relating to location and site selection.

1. **Customer-based**—If convenience of location determines where a customer shops, banks, or dines, the service is said to be customer-based. Hence, the service should be located in close proximity to its customers. Retail stores, healthcare, and other personal services, theaters, branches of banks, and restaurants are examples of organizations with customer-based locations.

2. **Cost-based**—Most specialty shops, wholesalers, and clerical services find that operating cost is their dominant location factor.

3. **Competitor-based**—Some businesses prefer to locate near their competition to observe, share resources, and draw customers from a distance. For example, in manufacturing, there are garment districts, furniture towns, and textile areas. Similarly, in services you see clusters of car dealerships, antique shops, and fast-food restaurants.

4. **Support systems**—Many companies locate in areas in which support systems are available. For example, a hotel may locate near a university medical research center. A bullion firm may locate in a city with good police protection. For Disney World, location at a site with good airline and road support systems, as well as a good electric utility service, was essential.

5. **Geographic or environmental factors**—Ocean resorts, ski resorts, and outdoor health ranches or spas illustrate geographic or environmental constraints on location.

6. **Business climate**—When a service business has only minor constraints on its location, the business climate of a state or city may provide the major factor in site location. Insurance companies, private educational institutions, and gaming resorts are likely to fall in this category.

7. **Communication-based**—Financial services usually require rapid communication with other companies and perhaps even with governments throughout the world. This is one of the reasons that large banks locate in large, highly developed cities with excellent communications. Further, as the Internet and telecommunication systems continue to replace transportation of documents by mail, this factor will become more important.

8. **Transportation-based**—Mail-order businesses and private express delivery services tend to make location decisions based on entry to a good transportation network.

9. **Personal desires of the CEO**—Despite the preceding factors, many companies have moved their headquarters based on the desire of the president or CEO.

General Criteria for Location Selection

In addition to dominant location factors, there are many other general criteria that should be considered in selecting a location, such as labor availability/cost, climate/weather, and state taxes (see Exhibit 10-2). Many of the items listed apply regardless of the type of service business. In making comparisons among locations, it is well to group the criteria according to the following:

1. Subjective Criteria
   a. Quantifiable (for example, management's estimate of risk)
   b. Nonquantifiable (for example, acceptance by the community, zoning, and legal factors)
2. Objective Criteria
   a. Quantifiable (for example, cost of construction)
   b. Nonquantifiable (for example, lower cost of living)

Common Mistakes

Oversights and common mistakes in the location decision have been identified by various writers.[2] Some of these errors are

- Failure to forecast trends—Too often, the long-range location decision is based on factors at the present time without regard to potentially adverse changes or future opportunities. The growth of the Sun Belt in the 1970s and the decay in the North Central states are examples.

- Failure to develop a company profile—In this case, the company simply looks for a place to put a building rather than a place to enhance its business.

- Paying too much attention to land costs—High land costs may accompany a highly desirable area. Also, they may indicate the possibility of large growth in value in case the company decides to move its business at some future time.

- Failure to understand the costs of moving people.

- Allowing prejudices of executives to override what should be a business decision; loss of key people who do not favor the new location.

- Failure to take into account the culture of the workers at the location.

- Paying too much attention to wage rates rather than productivity.

- Failure to coordinate construction and moving with the ongoing operations of the business.

Exhibit 10-2   General Criteria for Location Selection

1. Labor availability and costs

2. Labor history and culture

3. Educational centers

4. Recreational and cultural centers

5. Electric power

6. Transportation and road networks

7. Health and welfare system

8. Climate and weather

9. Geography and environmental protection management

10. State business climate and incentives

11. State taxes

12. Health care system

13. Suppliers and supporting service companies

14. Population and population trends

15. Communication systems

16. Preference of management

17. Cost of living

18. Community attitudes

19. Cost of land and construction

20. Potential for expansion

Multilocations

Multilocation selection decisions differ in some important aspects from single-location selection decisions. For example, a new competitor to Club Med could lay out a plan for locations all over the world taking into account many factors. But when Club Med adds a new location, consideration must be given to its present locations and the specific recreations offered at each. As another example, suppose yet another competitor to Federal Express were to start up. It may want to limit the first 50 locations of its offices to a specified region of the United States. Federal Express, on the other hand, must take into account present locations served throughout the United States to avoid overlapping and to provide synergy. Banking firms, resorts, TV networks, motel chains, franchise services, and airlines all face the multilocation as well as the single-location problem.

10.3 Quantitative Methods for Location Selection

Quantitative techniques for location selection vary from the simple to the complex. Following is an overview of a few common methods,[3] starting with factor weighting.

Factor Weighting

Factor weighting is a simple numerical method that has six steps:

1. Develop a list of relevant factors.

2. Assign a weight to each factor to reflect its relative importance in the firm's objectives.

3. Develop a scale for each factor (for example, 1 to 5, 1 to 10, or 1 to 100 points).

4. Have management score each location for each factor, using the scale in step 3.

5. Multiply the score times the weights for each factor, and total the score for each location.

6. Make a recommendation based on the maximum point score, considering the results of qualitative approaches as well.

A simplified illustration is provided in Exhibit 10-3 for location of a new ski resort. The rating sheet in that exhibit provides a list of not easily quantifiable factors that management has decided are important, their weights, and their ratings for three possible sites: California, Colorado, and New England. The factor-weighting analysis indicates that New England, with a total weight of 147, is preferable to both the California and Colorado locations. By changing the weights slightly for those factors about which there is some doubt, the sensitivity of the decision can be analyzed.

Exhibit 10-3   Factor Weighting in Selection of Ski Resort Location

Factor	Importance Weight	Location Scores			Weighted Scores		
		California	Colorado	New England	California	Colorado	New England
Average snowfall/year	8	5	4	3	(8)(5) = 40	(8)(4) = 32	(8)(3) = 24
Topography	9	4	5	4	(9)(4) = 36	(9)(5) = 45	(9)(4) = 36
Size of nearest market	7	3	2	5	(7)(3) = 21	(7)(2) = 14	(7)(5) = 35
Transportation to ski resort	5	4	4	5	(5)(4) = 20	(5)(4) = 20	(5)(5) = 25
Government incentives	3	3	4	4	(3)(3) = 9	(3)(4) = 12	(3)(4) = 12
Number and size of competitors	3	2	5	5	(3)(2) = 6	(3)(5) = 15	(3)(5) = 15
				Totals	132	138	147

Factor scoring scale: 5 = excellent, 4 = good, 3 = fair, 2 = poor, 1 = unacceptable.

Center of Gravity Method

The center of gravity method is a mathematical technique used for finding a location for a single distribution center that services a number of retail stores. The method takes into account the location of markets, the volume of goods shipped to those markets, and shipping costs in finding a best location for a distribution center.

By way of an example, consider the case of Barry's Discount Department Stores, a chain of four large Target-type outlets.[4] The firm's store locations are in Chicago, Pittsburgh, New York, and Atlanta. They are currently being supplied out of an old and inadequate warehouse in Pittsburgh, the site of the chain's first store. Data on demand rates at each outlet are shown in Exhibit 10-4.

Exhibit 10-4   Demand at Barry's Discount Stores

Store Location	Number of Containers Shipped per Month
Chicago	2,000
Pittsburgh	1,000
New York	1,000
Atlanta	2,000

The firm has decided to find some "central" location in which to build a new warehouse. Because the number of containers shipped each month affects cost, distance alone should not be the principal criterion. The center of gravity method assumes that cost is directly proportional to both distance and volume shipped. The ideal location is that which minimizes the weighted distance between the warehouse and its retail outlets, where the distance is weighted by the number of containers shipped.

The first step in the center of gravity method is to place the existing store locations on a coordinate system, as shown in Exhibit 10-5. The origin of the coordinate system and the scale used are arbitrary, just as long as the relative distances are correctly represented. This can be done easily by placing a grid over an ordinary map. The center of gravity is determined by Formulas 10.1 and 10.2. This location (66.7, 93.3) is shown by the crosshair in Exhibit 10-5. By overlaying a U.S. map on this exhibit, we find that this location is near central Ohio. The firm may want to consider Columbus, Ohio, or a nearby city as an appropriate location.

$$C_x = \frac{\sum_i d_{ix} W_i}{\sum_i W_i}$$

(10.1)

$$C_y = \frac{\sum_i d_{iy} W_i}{\sum_i W_i}$$

(10.2)

Where

$C_x =$ x-coordinate of the center of gravity

$C_y =$ y-coordinate of the center of gravity

$d_{ix} =$ x-coordinate of location i

$d_{iy} =$ y-coordinate of location i

$W_i =$ volume of goods moved to or from location i

For example, location 1 is Chicago, and from Exhibits 10-4 and 10-5, we have

$D_{1x} =$ 30

$D_{1y} =$ 120

$W_1 =$ 2,000

Exhibit 10-5   Coordinate Locations of Four Barry's Department Stores

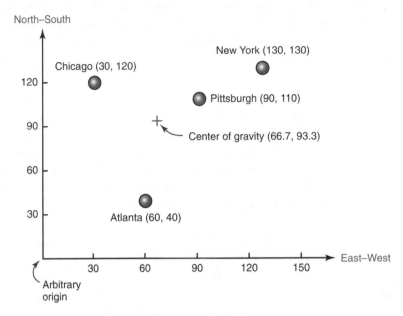

Using the data in Exhibits 10-4 and 10-5 for each of the other cities, in equations (10.1) and (10.2), we find

$$C_x = \frac{(30)(2,000) + (90)(1,000) + (130)(1,000) + (60)(2,000)}{2,000 + 1,000 + 1,000 + 2,000} = \frac{400,000}{6,000} = 66.7$$

$$C_y = \frac{(120)(2,000) + (110)(1,000) + (130)(1,000) + (40)(2,000)}{2,000 + 1,000 + 1,000 + 2,000} = \frac{560,000}{6,000} = 93.3$$

This location (66.7, 93.3) is shown by the crosshair in Exhibit 10-5. By overlaying a U.S. map on this exhibit, we find that this location is near central Ohio. The firm may well wish to consider Columbus, Ohio, or a nearby city as an appropriate location.

Warehouse Multisite Locations and Sizes

Bowman and Stewart developed a warehouse location model that can be readily adapted to a wholesaling service company that wants to set up warehouses to cover a regional area such as New England.[5] Their technique answers the question of how many square miles of area each warehouse should serve. The more warehouses in the system, the smaller is the area served by each and hence the smaller are the warehouses.

Here are the economics of the problem as analyzed by Bowman and Stewart. Warehousing costs per dollar of goods handled tend to decrease with increasing volume (because costs of supervision and other overhead are spread over more units and because labor can usually be used with a lower proportion of idle time). They further reasoned that the distance traveled would be the main factor determining costs associated with the area and that this cost would tend to vary approximately with the square root of the area. (Radius and diameter vary with the square root of the area of a circle.)

The following terms for the model are defined:

$C =$ Total cost per dollar of goods distributed in warehouse region

$K =$ Sales density, in dollar volume of goods per square mile handled by a warehouse

$A =$ Area in square miles served by warehouse

$a =$ Cost, per dollars' worth of goods, which is not affected either by warehouse volume or area served (variable cost per dollar unit)

$b =$ Fixed costs associated with warehouse operation

$c =$ Costs that vary with the distance from the warehouse

The total costs per dollar of merchandise handled are

$$C = a + \frac{b}{KA} + c\sqrt{A}$$

(10.3)

To minimize cost, take the first derivative of C with respect to A, set it equal to 0, and solve for A. The following formula results:

$$A = \left[\frac{2b}{cK} \right]^{2/3}$$

(10.4)

Also dealing with warehouse location and sizing decisions, Effroymson and Ray developed a branch-and-bound algorithm,[6] whereas Atkins and Shriver tackled the problem through linear programming.[7]

10.4 Site Selection

Site selection may sometimes be divided into two stages: community (within the location area) and specific site selection. The site chosen should be appropriate to the nature of the service operation, so clearly the factors involved will differ depending on the type of business. Exhibit 10-6 provides a sample listing of some criteria for site selection.

Exhibit 10-6   A Guide to Criteria for Site Selection

1. Area available relative to area required

2. Appropriateness of buildings, if any on site

3. Zoning

4. Traffic, access, and parking

5. City road network

6. Neighborhood character

7. Labor availability, history, and costs

8. Taxes

9. Community attitudes

10. Educational, recreational, and cultural centers

11. Air and water pollution

12. Communications network

13. Banking system

14. Fire and police protection

15. Sewage and waste removal

16. Proximity to airports

17. Local market for the company's services

Locating a Retail Store with the Gravity Model

When deciding where to locate a retail outlet such as a furniture or appliance store, a firm's objective is usually to maximize profits. The size and site of the store are two decision variables. The retailing literature is rich with variations of the so-called gravity or spatial interaction model, first proposed by Reilly in 1929, which can be used to estimate consumer demand.[8] Based on the work of Reilly and many others, a number of empirical observations have been found to affect retail trade:

1. The proportion of consumers patronizing a given shopping area varies with their distance from the shopping area.

2. The proportion of consumers patronizing various shopping areas varies with the breadth and depth of merchandise offered by each shopping area.

3. The distances that consumers travel to various shopping areas vary for different types of product purchases.

4. The "pull" of any given shopping area is influenced by the proximity of competing shopping areas.

The probability that a consumer at a given place of origin i will shop at a particular shopping center j is expressed by David L. Huff[9] in the following model:

$$P_{ij} = \frac{S_j / T_{ij}^{\lambda}}{\sum_{j=1}^{n} (S_j / T_{ij}^{\lambda})}$$

(10.5)

where

P_{ij} = Probability of a consumer at a given point of origin i traveling to a particular shopping center j

S_j = Size of a shopping center j (measured in terms of square footage of selling area devoted to sale of a particular class of goods)

T_{ij} = Travel time involved in getting from a consumer's travel base i to a given shopping center j

λ = A parameter that is to be estimated empirically to reflect the effect of travel time on various kinds of shopping trips

In Huff's initial pilot study, λ was found to be 2.7 for furniture shopping trips and 3.2 for trips involving clothes purchases. The greater the value of λ, the less time expenditure for a given trip purpose.

The expected number of consumers at a given place of origin i that shop at a particular shopping center j is equal to the number of consumers at i multiplied by the probability that a consumer at i will select j for shopping. That is

$$E_{ij} = P_{ij}C_i$$

(10.6)

where

E_{ij} = Expected number of consumers at i likely to travel to shopping center j

C_i = Number of consumers at i

The Gravity Model in Nonretail Services

Variations of Huff's and Reilly's gravity models also have been applied to the services supplied by hospitals, recreational facilities, and colleges. For example, the model was used to determine the service areas of existing hospitals in St. Louis by Ault, Bass, and Johnson.[10] Attractiveness of each hospital complex was estimated to be proportional to the total number of services offered there, and cost was measured in minutes to reach the hospital from each sector of the city. Morrill and Kelley[11] used a similar gravity model to study flows of patients to hospitals. Cesario[12] developed a model to measure competition among northeastern Pennsylvania state park facilities in drawing vacationing residents of that state. As a measure of trip cost, he employed road mileages from each county to each park. Finally, Render and Shawhan's model examined the competition among 70 public colleges in Ohio in attracting students from each county to attend their school.[13] All these applications indicate the potential for the use of gravity models in locating a wide variety of service-sector facilities and determining their success in drawing clients away from existing competition.

Factor-Weighting Method

Just as cities and communities can be compared for location selection by the factor-weighting model, as we saw earlier in this chapter, so can actual site decisions be helped. Exhibit 10-7 illustrates four factors of importance to Washington, DC health officials charged with opening that city's first public AIDS clinic. Of primary concern (and given a weight of 5) was location of the clinic so it would be as accessible as possible to the largest number of patients. The annual lease cost also was of some concern due to a tight budget. A suite in the new City Hall, at 14th and U Streets, was highly rated because its rent would be free. An old office building near the downtown bus station received a much lower rating because of its cost. Equally important as lease cost was the need for confidentiality of patients and, therefore, for a relatively inconspicuous clinic. Finally, because so many of the staff at the AIDS clinic would be donating their time, the safety, parking, and accessibility of each site were of concern as well.

Exhibit 10-7 Potential AIDS Clinic Sites in Washington, DC

| Factor | Importance Weight | Potential Locations* | | | Weighted Scores | | |
		Homeless Shelter (2nd and D, SE)	City Hall (14th and U, NW)	Bus Terminal Area (7th and H, NW)	Homeless Shelter	City Hall	Bus Terminal Area
Accessibility for patients	5	9	7	7	45	35	35
Annual lease cost	3	6	10	3	18	30	9
Inconspicuous	3	5	2	7	15	6	21
Accessibility for health staff	2	3	6	2	6	12	4
				Total scores	84	83	69

* All sites are rated on a 1 to 10 basis, with 10 as the highest score and 1 as the lowest.

From the three rightmost columns in Exhibit 10-7, the weighted scores are summed. It appears that the bus terminal area can be excluded from further consideration, but that the other two sites are virtually identical in total score. The city may now consider other factors, including political ones, in selecting between the two remaining sites.

Multisites

Within a city or metropolitan area, various services require multiple sites for offices, warehouses, outlets, branches, or service areas for vehicles. Examples range from fire stations to branch banks to auto quick-lube shops. The measures of benefits that arise from an arrangement of sites within a metropolitan area are (1) distance, (2) time, and (3) cost. These three criteria are not necessarily related. For example, a customer may travel a longer distance by bus to reach the service site than traveling by cab. Again, a longer route over an expressway may be much quicker than driving through crowded inner-city streets.

The preceding criteria of distance, time, and cost may apply to a service business (1) that delivers goods or services where time is not a factor, (2) that must service people quickly (as in the case of a private ambulance business), or (3) when transportation costs are high and visits to clients frequent. On the other side of the coin, the sites selected may depend on the distance, time, and cost criteria taken from the point of view of the customer who must travel to the service site.

A trade-off occurs when a service business adds more sites at a greater total cost to the firm. This may reduce the value of one or more of the preceding criteria. Also, the greater the proximity of sites, the more likely it is that some will draw trade from others.

Quantitative methods for finding the minimum number of sites to cover a specified market area are rough in terms of meeting multiple realistic criteria. For example, the geometric distance on a grid is sometimes used as a substitute for the actual distance or time of travel. In one method, a table is set up in which markets served and potential sites are matched. When we want to find the minimum number and location of facilities to serve all customers within a specified service time or distance, we face the **location set-covering problem**.

To illustrate, Arlington County, Virginia, which currently has five fire stations, wants to place highly sophisticated emergency medical vehicles in one or more of those stations. The county's objective is to find a site or sites that will minimize response times to medical emergencies. Although regular firefighters and firetrucks are equipped to deal with minor medical problems, the county now wants to provide its residents with a higher level and quality of care for severe cases. Exhibit 10-8 identifies the location of each of the current fire stations, its zone of the county, and the distance in time along major roads between zones. The question faced is where the medical vehicle or vehicles should be located. If the objective is to select a site so that the maximum response time to any other zone is as small as possible, the analysis in Exhibit 10-9 provides several insights.

Exhibit 10-8   Zone Connections for Arlington County

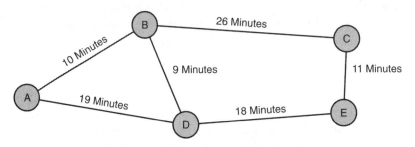

For example, if the county is satisfied responding to all medical calls within 30 minutes, then one station located in either zone B or zone D will suffice. If a 15-minute response time is the county's objective, then locating medical units in zones B and C or B and E will suffice. Finally, if a 10-minute response time is desired, the county must place units at three stations, with one each in zones B, C, and E.

Exhibit 10-9   Possible Site for Arlington County Emergency Medical Units
with Differing Response Rates

Set of Zones Served from Stations in This Zone

Zone in County	Within 10 Minutes	Within 15 Minutes	Within 30 Minutes
A	A, B	A, B	A, B, D
B	A, B, D	A, B, D	A, B, C, D, E
C	C	C, E	B, C, D, E
D	B, D	B, D	A, B, C, D, E
E	E	C, E	B, C, D, E
Possible locations to meet time constraints	B, C, E	B, C or B, E	B or D

Another version of the location set-covering problem is called **maximal covering.** The goal of maximal covering is to maximize the population covered within a desired service distance. First described by Church and Revelle,[14] the approach begins by mapping the population density for a metropolitan area. The first site selected is the one that maximizes the population served within a specified travel distance. Then a second site is selected that serves the maximum of the remaining population. This process is continued until the population served by the last site meets the criterion for the level of population to be served.

10.5 Objectives of Facility Layout[15]

After the location and site have been selected, the facility layout must be designed. The layout problem involves finding the best arrangement of the physical components of the service system possible within the time, cost, and technology constraints of the situation. The objectives of designing a good layout are

1. **Movement of people, materials, and paperwork must be over the minimum distance possible**—One of the largest components of cost in many wholesalers' warehouses is the handling and movement of materials.

2. **High utilization of space, balanced with means for expansion**—There should be some space available for growth that will have low utilization, or else the building should be constructed so that a wing or floor may be easily added on.

3. **Flexibility for rearrangement, services, and growth**—Changes in product or service, changes in output required, and improvements in layout make modification of the layout desirable from time to time.

4. **Satisfactory physical environment for workers**—This includes good lighting, temperature control, low noise, cafeterias, rest rooms, and exits. Fixed equipment, such as boilers, should be external to the work area.

5. **Convenience for customers during the service.**

6. **Attractive appearance of room office arrangements for management and customers**—An example is the use of planter boxes and foliage to separate areas in banks and offices.

A variety of layout strategies are available to management depending on whether the firm is dealing with arranging processes, stores, warehouses, assembly lines, or offices. Exhibit 10-10 provides examples of five types of service layouts.

Exhibit 10-10   Some Types of Layout Strategies in the Service Sector

	Product	Process	Office	Retail	Warehouse
Example	Cafeteria serving line	Insurance company	Hospital	Retail store	Distributor
Problem	Balance work from one serving station to the next	Locate workers requiring frequent contact close to one another	Flow to various services differs with each patient	Expose customer to high margin items and impulse items at exit	Lower cost of storage and material handling

10.6 Inputs to the Layout Problem

This section presents a brief discussion of six issues that need to be addressed before tackling service layout problems. Richard Muther developed a five-item key to unlocking *factory* layout problems.[16] Exhibit 10-11 shows a six-item service variation called the **OPQRST key.** The inputs are as follows:

O. **Objectives of the company**—Those objectives related to layout are diversification plans, cost objectives, expansion plans, and so on.

P. **People/services**—Nature and number. Whether the company is providing a single service or a mix of heterogeneous services, the degree of customer contact and personalization will have an impact on the layout.

Q. **Quantity demanded**—Layout will be affected by whether high volume or low volume throughput is required.

R. **Routing**—Processes, equipment, materials, information, and customer participation in the process.

S. **Space and services**—The square feet, the cubic feet, and the shape (rectangular, square, and L-shaped) of the space available or desired are important to layout decisions. The type and location of services are also inputs.

T. **Timing**—Flexibility for change over time and timing for additional space needed.

Exhibit 10-11   The Key—OPQRST—for Unlocking Layout Problems

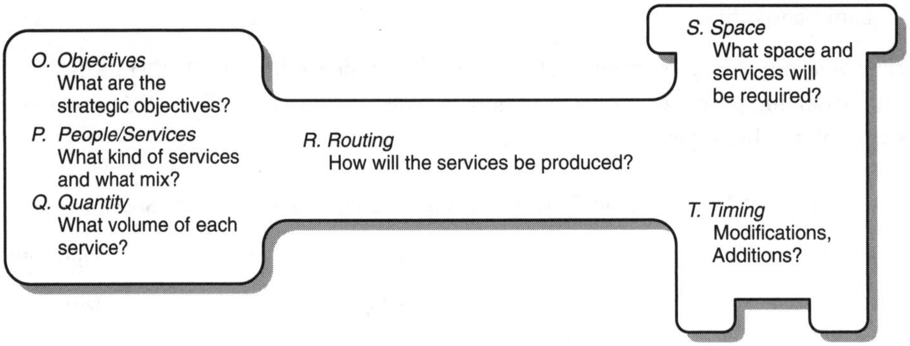

O. Objectives
What are the strategic objectives?

P. People/Services
What kind of services and what mix?

Q. Quantity
What volume of each service?

R. Routing
How will the services be produced?

S. Space
What space and services will be required?

T. Timing
Modifications, Additions?

10.7 Layout Strategies

Now that these six inputs to the layout decision have been addressed, each of the strategies available to managers will be introduced.

Product Layout

A **product layout** is one in which a limited number of services is provided, one after the other, to a large number of customers. These services, such as food stations in a student cafeteria, are arranged in the sequence in which they are to be performed. The idea is to maintain a smooth flow of customers through the stations so that bottlenecks can be avoided and the time needed by each individual server or station is equalized. This is the familiar assembly-line layout problem found in the manufacture of cars, toasters, and even jet fighter airplanes.

Assembly lines can be "balanced" by moving tasks from one individual to another. The central problem in product layout planning is to find the ideal balance, so a continuous flow of customers is maintained along the service line with a minimum of idle time at each workstation.

To illustrate, assume that you enter your cafeteria, pushing your tray ahead of you, and request various items for your meal. The line is inflexible and some servers may even have specializations that cannot be assigned to others (such as being trained to act as cashier). The ideal (that is, balanced) line is one where each server is assigned tasks that take an equal amount of time. Exhibit 10-12 indicates that there are six service stations in the cafeteria.

Exhibit 10-12   Cafeteria Service Times

Sequence	Service Station	Average Service Time
1	Serve vegetables	20 seconds
2	Serve entree	30 seconds
3	Serve soup	20 seconds
4	Serve dessert	15 seconds
5	Serve drink	10 seconds
6	Collect money	60 seconds

Exhibit 10-13(a) illustrates how five workers have currently been assigned to staff the service stations. Workstation (WS) 4 consists of one employee who serves both desserts (15 seconds) and drinks (10 seconds). The problem, however, is that this line is poorly balanced. Workstation 5, the cashier, requires 60 seconds per customer on average, meaning that only 60 customers per hour can be served. The other workers are idle anywhere from 30 to 40 seconds of every minute or customer "cycle."

Exhibit 10-13   Cafeteria Line-Balancing Layouts

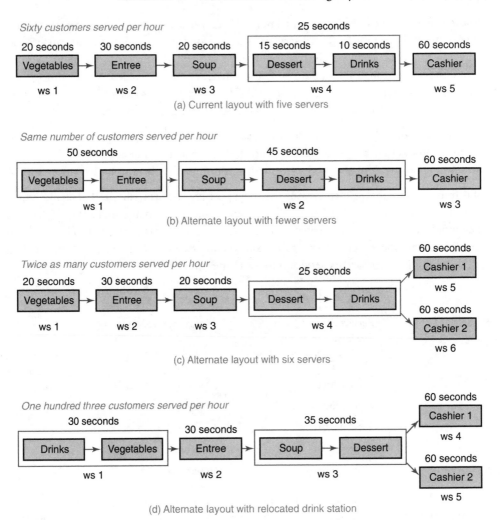

Sixty customers served per hour

25 seconds

20 seconds	30 seconds	20 seconds	15 seconds	10 seconds	60 seconds
Vegetables	Entree	Soup	Dessert	Drinks	Cashier
ws 1	ws 2	ws 3	ws 4		ws 5

(a) Current layout with five servers

Same number of customers served per hour

50 seconds		45 seconds			60 seconds
Vegetables	Entree	Soup	Dessert	Drinks	Cashier
ws 1		ws 2			ws 3

(b) Alternate layout with fewer servers

Twice as many customers served per hour

60 seconds — Cashier 1 — ws 5

20 seconds	30 seconds	20 seconds	25 seconds	
Vegetables	Entree	Soup	Dessert	Drinks
ws 1	ws 2	ws 3	ws 4	

60 seconds — Cashier 2 — ws 6

(c) Alternate layout with six servers

One hundred three customers served per hour

60 seconds — Cashier 1 — ws 4

30 seconds		30 seconds	35 seconds	
Drinks	Vegetables	Entree	Soup	Dessert
ws 1		ws 2	ws 3	

60 seconds — Cashier 2 — ws 5

(d) Alternate layout with relocated drink station

In Exhibit 10-13(b), management has reduced costs by eliminating two workstations (and hence two workers) by merging vegetables and entrees into one station (50 seconds) and soup, dessert, and drinks into a second station (45 seconds) and placing a cashier at the third (still 60 seconds). Although this first alternative lowers costs, service is still slowed to a pace of 60 customers per hour, or one per minute, on average.

If the real problem is the need for increased throughput, alternatives 2 and 3 may be explored, as shown in Exhibit 10-13(c) and (d). In Exhibit 10-13(c), the current layout is retained but for the opening of a second cashier station. With the reduction of that bottleneck, 120 customers may now be served, albeit at a higher labor cost because there are now six workers.

The final alternative shown is one in which the drink equipment is relocated to the beginning of the cafeteria line and assigned to the worker currently serving vegetables. The soup and dessert tasks are assigned to workstation 3, and the freed worker is trained to work as a second cashier. There will be some costs of reconfiguring the service line, but labor costs will not increase. Now 103 customers can be handled per hour. The new bottleneck is workstation 3, which requires 35 seconds per customer.

Many services can be viewed in the context of product layout, even though they are not as rigid as this assembly-line example. Oil change/lube shops, for example, provide well-defined services, require special equipment for different tasks, and work well with a division of labor. Again, the service output is limited to the slowest activity.

Process-Oriented Layout

Whereas product layouts are arranged to deliver a specific product, **process-oriented layouts** are arranged by similar process function. Most service organizations use this approach because it can simultaneously handle a wide variety of services. It is efficient when dealing with customers of law offices, insurance companies, or travel agencies, typical situations in which each customer has a different need. Another good example of the process-oriented layout is a hospital or clinic. A continuous inflow of patients, each with his or her request, requires routing through records areas, admissions, laboratories, operating rooms, intensive care areas, pharmacies, nursing stations, and so on.

A big advantage of the process layout is its flexibility in equipment use and in employee assignments. In the hospital example, there may be several obstetricians on duty available to deliver an unexpected baby in a number of similar delivery rooms. However, if a specialist is unavailable, there are other doctors with broad enough skills to step in during an emergency. The service provided is enhanced by the personalization found in the process approach. The downside of this approach is that while operational efficiency is being optimized, customers' convenience, time, and travel distances are probably sacrificed. In Chapter 8 the principles of service and delivery system design were discussed. One of those principles is "Design service processes from the customer's/employee's perspective." Process layout will probably violate this principle. However, if the cost-savings from increased operational efficiency are reflected in the prices charged, customers may prefer such a compromise.

In process layout planning, the most common tactic is to arrange departments or service centers in the most convenient locations. This often entails placing departments with large interdepartmental flows of people or paperwork next to one another. Costs in this approach depend on (1) the number of people or documents moving during some period of time between two departments and (2) the distances between departments. The best way to understand the steps of process layout is to look at an example.

Example: North Slope Hospital

The North Slope Hospital is a small emergency-oriented facility located in a popular ski resort area. Its new administrator decides to reorganize the hospital using the process layout method she studied in business school. The current layout of North Slope's eight rooms is shown in Exhibit 10-14. The only physical restriction perceived by the administrator is the need to keep the entrance and initial processing room in its current location. All other departments or rooms (each 10 ft ×15 ft) can be moved if the layout analysis indicates it would be beneficial.

Exhibit 10-14   North Slope Hospital Layout

Entrance/ Initial processing	Exam room 1	Exam room 2	X-ray	15'
Laboratory tests/EKG	Operating room	Recovery room	Cast-setting room	15'

|←———————— 40' ————————→|

The first step is to analyze records to determine the number of trips made by patients between departments in an average month. The data are shown in Exhibit 10-15. The objective is to lay out the rooms to minimize the total distance walked by patients who enter for treatment. The administrator writes her objective as

$$\text{Minimize patient movement} = \sum_{i=1}^{8} \sum_{j=1}^{8} N_{ij} D_{ij}$$

where

N_{ij} = Number of patients (or trips) per month moving from department i to department j and from department j to department i

D_{ij} = Distance in feet between departments i and j (which, in this case, is the equivalent of cost per load to move between departments)

i, j = Individual departments

Exhibit 10-15   Number of Patients Moving Between Departments in 1 Month

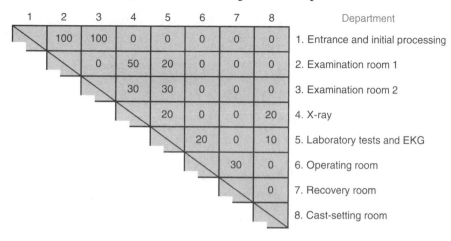

	1	2	3	4	5	6	7	8	Department
1		100	100	0	0	0	0	0	1. Entrance and initial processing
2			0	50	20	0	0	0	2. Examination room 1
3				30	30	0	0	0	3. Examination room 2
4					20	0	0	20	4. X-ray
5						20	0	10	5. Laboratory tests and EKG
6							30	0	6. Operating room
7								0	7. Recovery room
8									8. Cast-setting room

Departments next to one another, such as the entrance and examination room 1, are assumed to carry a walking distance of 10 feet. Diagonal departments are also considered adjacent and assigned a distance of 10 feet. Nonadjacent departments such as the entrance and examination room 2 or the entrance and recovery room are 20 feet apart, while nonadjacent rooms such as the entrance and X-ray are 30 feet apart. (Hence 10 feet is considered 10 units of cost, 20 feet is 20 units of cost, and 30 feet is 30 units of cost.)

Given this information, we can redo the layout of North Slope Hospital and improve its efficiency in terms of patient flow. Using North Slope's current layout flow, as shown in Exhibit 10-16, the patient movement may be computed.

Exhibit 10-16   Current North Slope Patient Flow

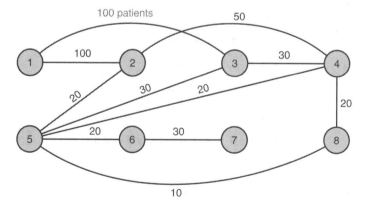

$$\text{Total movement} = (100 \times 10 \text{ ft}) + (100 \times 20 \text{ ft}) + (50 \times 20 \text{ ft})$$

$$\qquad\quad \text{1 to 2} \qquad\qquad \text{1 to 3} \qquad\qquad \text{2 to 4}$$

$$+ (20 + 10 \text{ ft}) + (30 \times 10 \text{ ft}) + (30 \times 20 \text{ ft})$$

$$\quad \text{2 to 5} \qquad\qquad \text{3 to 4} \qquad\qquad \text{3 to 5}$$

$$+ (20 \times 30 \text{ ft}) + (20 \times 10 \text{ ft}) + (20 \times 10 \text{ ft})$$

$$\quad \text{4 to 5} \qquad\qquad \text{4 to 8} \qquad\qquad \text{5 to 6}$$

$$+ (10 \times 30 \text{ ft}) + (30 \times 10 \text{ ft})$$

$$\quad \text{5 to 8} \qquad\qquad \text{6 to 7}$$

$$= 1{,}000 + 2{,}000 + 1{,}000 + 200 + 300 + 600 + 600$$

$$+\ 200 + 200 + 300 + 300$$

$$= 6{,}700 \text{ feet}$$

It is not generally feasible to arrive at an "optimal" solution, but we should be able to propose a new layout that will reduce the current figure of 6,700 feet. Two useful changes, for example, are to switch rooms 3 and 5 (reducing patient movement by 1,000 feet) and to interchange rooms 4 and 6 (reducing patient movement by an additional 900 feet). The revised layout is shown in Exhibit 10-17.

The revised patient movement is calculated as

$$\text{Total movement} = (100 \times 10 \text{ ft}) + (100 \times 10 \text{ ft}) + (50 \times 10 \text{ ft})$$

$$\qquad\quad \text{1 to 2} \qquad\qquad \text{1 to 3} \qquad\qquad \text{2 to 4}$$

$$+ (20 \times 10 \text{ ft}) + (30 \times 10 \text{ ft}) + (30 \times 20 \text{ ft})$$

$$\quad \text{2 to 5} \qquad\qquad \text{3 to 4} \qquad\qquad \text{3 to 5}$$

$$+ (20 \times 10 \text{ ft}) + (20 \times 20 \text{ ft}) + (20 \times 10 \text{ ft})$$

$$\quad \text{4 to 5} \qquad\qquad \text{4 to 8} \qquad\qquad \text{5 to 6}$$

$$+ (10 \times 10 \text{ ft}) + (30 \times 10 \text{ ft})$$

$$\quad \text{5 to 8} \qquad\qquad \text{6 to 7}$$

$$= 1{,}000 + 1{,}000 + 500 + 200 + 300 + 600 + 200$$

$$+\ 400 + 200 + 100 + 300$$

$$= 4{,}800 \text{ ft}$$

Further improvement may be possible. Do you see where it could take place?

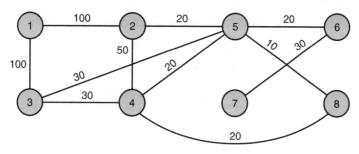

Exhibit 10-17   Improved Layout

Computerized Layout

The graphic approach we have been discussing is adequate for finding a reasonable layout for small service centers.[17] When 20 departments are involved in a layout problem, more than 2.43 quintillion (or 20!) different department configurations are possible. Fortunately, computer programs have been written to handle layouts of up to 40 departments. The best-known of these is CRAFT (Computerized Relative Allocation of Facilities Technique),[18] a program that produces "good," but not always "optimal" solutions. CRAFT is a search technique that systematically examines alternative departmental rearrangements to reduce the total movement cost. CRAFT has the added advantage of not only allowing the number of people and distance to be examined, but also introducing a third factor, a difficulty rating. Two other software packages are Automated Layout Design Program (ALDEP), and Computerized Relationship Layout Planning (CORELAP).

Computerized techniques have been developed for both two-dimensional and three-dimensional cases. The two-dimensional case is a one-story facility successfully addressed by CRAFT; the three-dimensional case is a multistory facility addressed by SPACECRAFT.[19] And, as we have discussed, manual as well as computer techniques exist.

Another computerized approach to facility layout design is simulation. (The supplement to Chapter 11, "Managing Demand and Supply in Services" discusses simulation.) Various simulation packages exist to help decision makers review alternative layouts. ServiceModel and MedModel are two of these packages that have been developed by ProModel Corporation. ServiceModel is a full-scale simulation program for service system modeling. In addition to simulating various operations of service organizations, one of its capabilities is to assist decision makers in facility layout and design. With this software a decision maker can create an office layout, locate service employees and machines in the layout, observe the operation of the system, such as movement of customers and bottlenecks in various processes, and collect data on important performance measures for intelligent decision making. ServiceModel has been used in designing the layout of service facilities such as banks and airport terminals. MedModel has been developed for similar purposes of healthcare organizations.

10.8 Office Layout

Office workers are concerned with the movement of information. Movement of information is carried out by

- Individuals in face-to-face conversations
- Individuals conversing by phone and computers simultaneously
- Mail, hard copy documents
- Electronic mail
- Group discussions or meetings
- Intercom speakers

A Checklist for Office Layout Design

If all work were carried out by phone and telecommunications, the layout problem would be greatly simplified. It is the movement of people and hard documents that largely dictates the nature of office facility layouts. A design checklist to consider in laying out office facilities is as follows:

1. Workers within groups usually have frequent contacts with each other.

2. Some groups interact frequently with certain other groups.

3. Some firms require conference rooms, especially those who supply professional services to clients.

4. Some service work is best done in private offices, whereas other work, such as high-volume routine processing of paper forms, is best suited to large open areas (frequently called "bullpens").

5. Areas visited by customers should be more aesthetic than standard work areas.

6. Aisles should be designed so that all offices may be quickly reached, and yet high traffic past private offices should be avoided to the extent possible.

7. Individual offices usually reflect the status of the workers by size, location, and window space.

8. Shared facilities such as printers, copy machines, and file cabinets should be convenient for users.

9. Reception areas may be required, and they should be attractive and convenient for customers.

10. Rooms for storage of supplies may be needed.

11. Generally, rest rooms, and coat rooms for employees are required. If the service is in a suite of an office building, rest rooms may be provided already.

12. A central computer room or an information center may be required.

Workstations

The office layout depends on the total office area, its shape, the process to be performed, and the relationships among the employees. Each employee has a workstation designed for (hopefully) optimal efficiency in terms of the work system as a whole and the tasks of the worker at the station. Different types of jobs require different kinds of working surfaces, equipment, space, and privacy.

Workstation variations are

- Desks packed together in rows in an open area

- Desks or work areas separated by bookcases, foliage, or file cabinets

- Partitions about the work area-metal and glass varying in height from approximately 4 to 8 feet, which can be installed in about one day

- Floor-to-ceiling partitions around a group of workstations

- Offices that are built as part of the building construction

By making effective use of the vertical dimension in a workstation, some office designers expand upward instead of outward. This keeps each workstation unit (what designers call the "footprint") as small as possible.

10.9 Retail Store Layout

In retail organizations, the objective is to maximize the net profit per square foot of display space. Because the retail grocery store is pervasive and widely studied, it will be used as an example in this section. Most grocery stores target a wide range of customer groups, and this discussion of retail store layout is based on that assumption. However, this is not the only possible strategy; the retail store layout may be tailored for a particular segment of consumers.

A hypothesis that has been widely accepted for the retail case is that sales vary directly with customer exposure to products. Consequently, a requirement for good profitability is to expose customers to as many products as possible. Studies do show that the greater the rate of exposure, the greater the sales, hence the higher return on investment. The service manager has two distinct variables to manipulate: the overall arrangement or flow pattern for the store and the allocation of space within that arrangement to various products.

Although some authors suggest that there is no longer any set pattern for store layouts, we can still note six ideas that are helpful for determining the overall arrangement of many stores.

1. Locate the high-draw items around the periphery of the store. Thus, we tend to find dairy products in one corner of a supermarket and bread and bakery products in another.

2. Use prominent locations such as the first or last aisle for high-impulse and high-margin items such as housewares, beauty aids, and shampoos.

3. Remove the crossover aisles that allow customers the opportunity to move between aisles. Place continuous shelves the length or width of the store. In the extreme case, customers are allowed only one path through the store.

4. Distribute what are known in the trade as "power items"—items that may dominate a purchasing trip—to both sides of an aisle, and disperse them to increase the viewing of other items. This results in a "bounce" pattern of shopping that increases exposure and hence sales of those items located adjacent to the power items.

5. Use end-aisle locations because they have a high exposure rate.

6. Convey the image of the store by careful selection in the positioning of the lead-off department. Produce remains a popular choice in stores, but managers who want to convey a low-price message may want to start off with a wall of values. Others will position the bakery and deli up front to appeal to convenience-oriented customers who want prepared foods.

With these six ideas in mind, we move to the second phase of retail store layout, which is to allocate space to various products.[20]

The objective is to maximize profitability per product per square foot of shelf space. The criteria may be modified to the needs of the product line by using linear foot of shelf space in lieu of square foot of shelf space. "Big-ticket," or expensive, items may yield greater dollar sales, but the profit per square foot may be lower. In addition, determining the actual cost per item means determining spoilage, pilferage, breakage, and returns, as well as the necessary labor to stock and sell. There are, of course, other issues, such as having a full line of merchandise regardless of margin. A drug store selling only high-margin shampoo would have met the criteria, but it would have a different set of problems.

Rapid manipulation of data by means of computers, accurate reports, and the capture of sales data through point-of-sale terminals allow retail store managers an opportunity to find optimal allocation of space. A number of computer programs exist that can assist managers in maximizing sales.

Two such programs are SAS Retail Space Management and AVT/Oracle Retail Focus Merchandizer. Another group of shelf space management software is Planograms. These are software packages that provide visual representation of a store's products or services and are considered a tool for visual merchandising. Planograms help organizations to plan how their stores are going to look. Some of the available software in this category include SmartDraw, ezPOG, PlanoGraphics, and Shelf Logic.[21]

10.10 Warehousing and Storage Layouts

The objective of warehouse layout is to find the optimal trade-off between handling cost and warehouse space (Exhibit 10-18). Consequently, management is to maximize the utilization of the total "cube" of the warehouse, that is, utilize its full volume while maintaining low materials handling costs. **Materials handling costs** are all the costs related to the incoming, storage, and outgoing transport of the materials.

Exhibit 10-18   Minimizing Storage and Materials Handling Costs (Note That Both Lines Shift Up or Down Depending on Investments and Variable Costs)

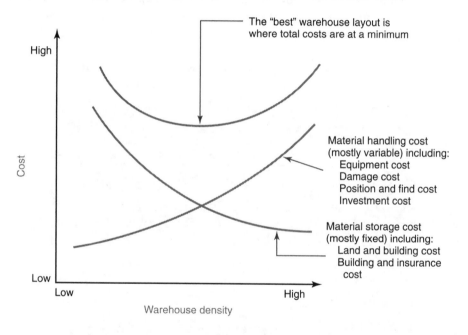

These costs are related to equipment, people, type of materials, supervision, insurance, obsolescence, shrinkage, spoilage, and depreciation. Management minimizes the sum of the resources spent on finding and moving materials plus the deterioration and damage to the materials themselves. The variety of items stored and the number of items "picked" have direct bearing on the optimal layout. A warehouse storing a few items lends itself to higher density more than a warehouse storing a variety of items. Modern warehouse management is, in many instances, an automated procedure utilizing automatic stacking and picking cranes, conveyors, and sophisticated controls that manage the flow of materials, for example, Amazon.com, which recently acquired robot maker Kiva Systems, Inc. and uses its robots in its fulfillment centers. These robots bring the product shelves to a warehouse worker, rather than a worker walking to the shelves. The robots locate the items in a customer's order, move the products around warehouses, and help get packed boxes to a final loading dock.[22] Of course, with the recently demonstrated success of Just-in-Time concepts in cutting inventory costs, the whole issue of warehousing costs needs to be reexamined. We suspect, however, that there will always be some situations in which inventory storage is unavoidable.

Using POM for Windows to Solve Location Decision Problems

The Location module in POM for Windows includes two different models. The first, the qualitative weighting model (also known as the factor weighting method), is used to solve the Ski Resort Location Selection example shown in Exhibit 10-19. The second is the center of gravity method applied to the Barry's Discount Department Store example, as shown in Exhibit 10-20.

Exhibit 10-19   POM for Windows Factor Weighting Model
Applied to Ski Resort Location Selection Example

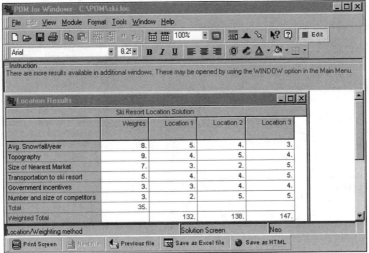

Exhibit 10-20   POM for Windows Center of Gravity Method Applied to
Barry's Discount Department Store Example

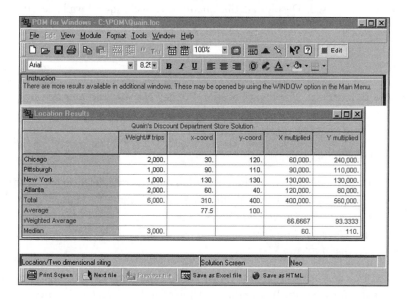

10.11 Summary

Part of the design of the service conversion or delivery process consists of location and site selection. Location selection is the macrodecision about the general regions or metropolitan areas in which the business is to be established. Site selection is the microdecision for the specific pieces of property for the business location.

Several methods for evaluating locations, including factor weighting, center of gravity, Bowman and Stewart's warehouse model, and optimization criteria were discussed. For the site-selection problem, a variety of gravity or spatial interaction models, along with another factor-weighting example, and the location set covering approach were presented.

Service location analysis differs in many ways from industrial location analysis. The focus in the industrial sector is usually on minimizing cost, whereas revenue maximization is the focus of most private-sector service firms. This is because manufacturing costs tend to vary substantially between locations, but in service firms, costs vary little within a region. The location decision focus for service firms should thus be on determining the volume of business and revenue.

The layout problem is the determination of the most nearly optimal arrangement of the physical components of the service system within time, cost, and technology constraints. A six-point list of inputs to the layout problem (called OPQRST) was given in this chapter, and a number of layout strategies were described. Different approaches to designing layout in service facilities have been discussed including product layout, process layout, and computerized layout. In addition approaches to designing layouts for efficient operations in offices, retail establishments, and warehouses were discussed. Despite all the quantitative techniques available and substantial research effort, layout decisions remain something of an art.

Endnotes

1. Andrew D. Bartness, "The Plant Location Puzzle," *Harvard Business Review* (March–April 1994).

2. See, for example, Richard Muther, *Systematic Layout Planning*, Second Edition (Boston, MA: Cahners Books, 1973).

3. For more information on quantitative models and their applications to facility location decisions, see Reza Zanjirani Farahani and Masoud Hekmatfar (Eds.), *Facility Location: Concepts, Models, Algorithms and Case Studies* (Physica Verlag Heidelberg, 2009); and Zvi Drezner (Ed.), *Facility Location: A Survey of Applications and Methods* (New York, Springer-Verlag, 1995).

4. This example has been adopted from Jay Heizer and Barry Render, *Production and Operations Management*, Tenth Edition (Upper Saddle River, NJ: Prentice Hall, 2011), pp. 322–323.

5. E. H. Bowman & J. B. Stewart, "A Model for Scale of Operations," *Journal of Marketing* (January 1956), pp.242–247.

6. M. A. Effroymson and T. L. Ray, "A Branch and Bound Algorithm for Plant Location," *Operations Research* (May–June 1966).

7. Robert J. Atkins and Richard H. Shriver, "A New Approach to Facilities Location," *Harvard Business Review*, Vol. 46, No. 3 (May–June 1968).

8. W. J. Reilly, *The Law of Retail Gravitation* (New York: Putnam and Son, 1931).

9. David L. Huff, "Defining and Estimating a Trading Area," *Journal of Marketing*, Vol. 28 (1964), pp. 34–38.

10. David Ault, Stephen Bass, and Thomas Johnson, "The Impact of New Hospital Construction on the Service Areas of Existing Hospital Complexes," *Proceedings of the American Institute for Decision Sciences* (St. Louis, 1971).

11. R. L. Morrill and M. B. Kelley, "The Simulation of Hospital Use and the Estimation of Location Efficiency," *Geographical Analysis*, Vol. 2 (1970), pp. 283–300.

12. Frank J. Cesario, "A Generalized Trip Distribution Model," *Journal of Regional Science*, Vol. 13 (1973), pp. 233–248.

13. Barry Render and Gerald Shawhan, "A Spatial Interaction Model for the Allocation of Higher Education Enrollments," *Socio-Economic Planning Sciences*, Vol. 11 (1977), pp. 43–48.

14. Richard Church and Charles Revelle, "The Maximal Covering Location Problem," *Papers of the Regional Science Association* (Fall 1974), pp. 101–118.

15. Portions of the rest of this chapter were adapted from Jay Heizer and Barry Render, *Production and Operations Management*. Copyright © 1988 by Allyn and Bacon.

16. Richard Muther, *Systematic Layout Planning*, Second Edition (Boston, MA: Cahners Books, 1976).

17. Also see Richard Muther, *Systematic Layout Planning*, for a similar approach to what the author calls simplified layout planning.

18. E. S. Buffa, G. S. Armor, and T. E. Vollman, "Allocating Facilities with CRAFT," *Harvard Business Review*, Vol. 42, No. 2 (March–April 1964), pp. 136–159.

19. R. V. Johnson, "SPACECRAFT for Multi-Floor Layout Planning," *Management Science*, Vol. 28, No. 4 (1982), pp. 407–417. A discussion of CRAFT, COFAD, PLANET, CORE-LAP, and ALDEP is available in James A. Tompkins and James M. Moore, *Computer Aided Layout: A User's Guide*, Publication Number I in the Monograph Series (Norcross, Ga.: American Institute of Industrial Engineers, 1977), p. 77–1.

20. "Computers Revolutionize Shelf Allocation," *Chain Store Age/Supermarkets* (November 1980), p. 66.

21. For more information on a state-of-the-art overview and research framework for integrated assortment and shelf space planning, and software applications see, Alexander H. Hübner and Heinrich Kuhn, "Retail category management: State-of-the-art review of quantitative research and software applications in assortment and shelf space management," *Omega*, 40. 2 (Apr 2012).

22. John Letzing, "Amazon Adds That Robotic Touch," *The Wall Street Journal*, March 20, 2012.

11

MANAGING DEMAND AND SUPPLY IN SERVICES

11.1 Introduction

One of the biggest challenges service operations managers face is matching demand for service and the capacity (or supply) of the service. This is also a challenge for manufacturing managers, but they have a few more tools and strategies—such as inventories, overtime work, adding another shift, or back ordering—available to them to help meet the challenge. When the demand and supply are matched for a period of 1 to 3 years, the activity is known as **aggregate planning**. Aggregate planning involves determining the resource capacity that a firm needs to meet its demand. The role of aggregate planning is to convert the strategic types of marketing plans or demand forecasts associated with long-range planning into overall capacity requirements. These aggregate capacity requirements will subsequently serve as a framework for the short-range allocation (that is, disaggregation) of overall capacity to individual services.

Exhibit 11-1 indicates the general characteristics of aggregate planning, planning disaggregated by resources and outputs, and the short-term scheduling of resources. The distinction between manufacturing-like and service-like firms refers to the tangibility of the output. Manufacturing-like firms are those that have tangible outputs or have distinct front-office/back-office operations.

This chapter focuses on strategies and tools available to service organizations to meet the demand for service. Some of these strategies can be implemented over a span of 1 to 3 years and therefore are aggregate planning strategies. Others, however, can be implemented within much shorter periods, such as months, weeks, or days. The discussion of matching demand and supply has been organized in two parts. First, strategies for managing demand are discussed, and then strategies for supply, or capacity, management.

Exhibit 11-1   Levels of Planning Disaggregation

Level of Planning	Manufacturing-Like Firms	Service-Like Firms
Level 1 Aggregate planning	Translation of strategic decisions into productive capacity over 1 to 3 years	Translation of strategic decisions into technology and resource planning over 1 to 3 years
Level 2 Disaggregate planning	Decisions on the individual product lines with regard to capacity and timing for each Decisions on capacity disaggregated into facilities, equipment, and human resources with timing for 1 year ahead Make or buy decisions	Decisions on basic service designs and markets to be matched Decisions on how capacity will be expanded or limited and demand will be managed for 1 year ahead
Level 3 Scheduling of resources	Weekly, monthly, and quarterly (or rolling 3-month) plans for production to match capacity to short-term fluctuations in demand Raw materials and finished goods inventory decisions Decisions on priorities for products, filling of orders, and assignment of work to individual operations	Weekly, monthly, and quarterly (or rolling 3-month) plans for production to match capacity with managed demand Decisions on raw materials inventory Decisions on assignment of work to individuals

Forecast of demand is, of course, very important for effective demand management. Forecasting is a broad subject that includes a variety of approaches and techniques that can appropriately be covered in an independent chapter; forecasting issues and techniques are presented in Chapter 15, "Forecasting Demand for Services." Before the important issue of matching demand and supply is discussed, however, the reasons that make this such a challenge for service operations managers should be reviewed.

11.2 Why Matching Demand and Supply Is Such a Challenge in Services

It was mentioned earlier that some of the strategies and tools operations managers use in manufacturing to match demand and supply are not available in services. In this section, the reason is explained, and some other reasons that make this a difficult task are discussed.

1. **Most services are perishable**—They are consumed as they are produced. Thus, it is impossible to produce the service early in anticipation of higher demand at a later time. This eliminates inventory as a tool in managing demand fluctuations or uncertainties for most services. An exception is when a service is embedded in a physical item, such as books, music CDs, and movie DVDs. Backordering of goods is possible when customers are willing to wait. For example, a car buyer is likely to wait a few weeks if his preferred model with all the options he wants is not available on the dealer's lot. A patient with a toothache, however, will probably not wait if her dentist is on vacation. Of course, there are exceptions to these generalizations; for example, a reservation system that services use may be seen as a form of backordering.

2. **Maximum capacity of some service systems has no flexibility**—Capacity of manufacturing systems can be increased in the short term through such practices as overtime work or additional shifts. Some services can similarly increase their maximum capacity by extending their hours of operation, like amusement parks do in summer months, but not all services can do that. For example, if you are making TV sets, working overtime or adding another shift will increase the number of sets produced, but a hotel manager cannot increase the number of rooms by overtime, or second shift, when all the rooms are booked for the night.

3. **Demand for many services is more difficult to predict**—Compared to predicting demand for most goods, predicting demand for many services is much more difficult, and demand variations are typically more severe and frequent—that is, they occur over shorter time periods. One reason for this is that consumption decisions for some services, such as eating out, going to a movie, having a haircut, are usually spur of the moment decisions, induced by the circumstances of the day or week. In other words, people normally don't make long-range plans for some services. Also, demand for some services, such as a visit to a pediatrician for a child's ear infection, is never planned. This makes prediction of demand difficult. Another reason is that the demand for some services occurs in peaks and valleys; in some services, such as fast food, public transportation, and electric power, these peaks and valleys are known and predictable, but in others they are not.

4. **Variability in service time**—Because of (1) the variety of services offered, (2) the individualized nature of services, and (3) the variability of each customer's needs and requirements, the time needed to serve an expected number of customers is difficult to

predict. For example, the time required to serve a customer at a bank can vary considerably depending on the number and type of transactions requested by the customer. This may lead to underestimation or overestimation in determining the required capacity. *Units* of capacity also may be hard to define. For instance, should a hospital define capacity in terms of number of beds, number of patients, size of nursing or medical staff, or number of patient hours at each level of care?

5. **Most services are location bound**—Because most services cannot be transported, service capacity must be available at the appropriate *place* as well as at the appropriate time. For a multisite service organization, this may mean while one unit is overwhelmed with customers, another unit at a different location may be underutilized. When such an imbalance occurs for goods, they can be transported from one location to another with relative ease; however, service customers cannot be easily transported or may not be willing to go to another service unit.

11.3 Managing Demand

Demand management is usually within the realm of marketing management. However, as pointed out earlier in this book, in service organizations many operations and marketing management tasks overlap, and frequently operations managers have to perform those tasks. Hence, they must be knowledgeable about options available to their colleagues in marketing. Furthermore, even when operations and marketing duties are clearly separated, managers on both sides must coordinate their activities and cooperate for superior service and a profitable organization. Therefore, they must be well versed in the tools of each other's field.

Understanding Customers and Their Needs

The simplest and probably the most important requirement for managing demand effectively is knowing who the customers are and understanding their needs. This may be a simple requirement, but it is an often overlooked ingredient of demand management. A service organization must collect data on its customers' demographic characteristics, such as age, sex, income, occupation, as well as lifestyle characteristics, and their needs and requirements, or any other relevant data that can be found. It must also know what motivates them to buy the service. Collecting data on these dimensions is neither easy nor inexpensive; therefore, it is not always economically feasible to build a complete data set. However, whatever information can be economically gathered about the customers is better than no information.

Understanding customers and their needs can help a service organization decide which of the strategies and tools discussed in this section can be most effective in managing demand for its services. For example, lower prices may be used to shift service demand from peak to off-peak periods. However, if the customers are affluent people insensitive to small price changes, this strategy may be ineffective and, worse yet, may lead to a perception of lower quality by those customers.

Understanding customers and their needs will also help identify and separate, if they exist, different components of demand. For example, hospital or health clinic managers discovered long ago that demand for their services can be grouped as emergency and regular care. To meet these two types of demand more effectively they allocate part of their facilities and some of their doctors and nurses to emergency cases while the rest attend to regular visits. Clearly, each component has a different demand pattern. For example, most people do not schedule a hospital visit for a check-up on weekends, but emergency room visits may actually increase on weekends.

Studying the Nature and Pattern of Demand

Knowing the customers and understanding their needs is necessary but not sufficient for effective demand management. Service managers must also study the nature and pattern of the demand because many factors, such as weather, social, political, or sporting events in the community or in the country, influence the demand for services. Some of these influences may be regular, some may not be. Discovering patterns and understanding the behavior of demand requires data. Again, data may not always be easy or inexpensive to collect, but without an understanding of the nature and patterns of demand, effective management is not possible. Clearly, knowing the demand pattern not only helps the operations manager determine which strategies to use to influence demand, it also helps her manage service supply effectively.

Strategies for Influencing Demand

Demand for services is not under the direct control of the service organization; it is influenced and shaped by many factors such as price, competitors' offerings and prices; income level of potential customers; accessibility; and so forth. A service organization, however, may exert some influence on demand by using one or more of the strategies discussed in this section. We must point out, however, that not all these strategies are appropriate or feasible for every service organization.

Pricing—This is probably the most obvious of strategies; for most services reducing the price will increase demand, and increasing it will create the opposite effect. Another common use of pricing is in short-term price changes. Some service organizations offer their services at lower than normal prices to shift peak period demand to off-peak periods. Price incentive may be strong enough for some customers to use the service during periods of low demand, thereby reducing the severity of fluctuations in demand. Examples of this practice include reduced-rate long distance or cellular telephone service at night and on weekends, movies before 6 P.M., and red-eye specials on airlines. Shifting peak period demand, of course, is important for efficient use of resources, such as workforce and facilities. If demand cannot be smoothed by shifting, the service organization either has to build enough capacity to meet the maximum demand, or lose customers who demand service during the peak period. The result of the first alternative will be inefficient use of resources; facilities and employees will be underutilized during the off-peak period. And the consequence of the second may be a significant reduction in profits or even failure of the company.

Reservations/appointments—Another common strategy in demand management used by many service organizations is to offer their services through reservations or appointments. This can be seen as "inventorying" or "backlogging" demand for service. This practice is viable for services that are not widely available but highly valuable to customers. Airlines, hotels, healthcare providers, legal services, and elegant restaurants offer their services through reservations or appointments; service is not guaranteed to walk-in customers. Reservations/appointments usually provide a steady level of demand, and they guarantee that the demand will not exceed a previously set limit. However, there is no guarantee that customers who cannot get an appointment soon enough will come back. This practice also has benefits for the customers. The most important benefit is probably the guarantee of service at the scheduled time. Also it helps customers save time; they don't have to wait in line. Another benefit a reservation system provides is that it eliminates customer anxiety about if and when the service will be available, or how long they will have to wait for the service.

A disadvantage of a reservations system is no-shows, that is, customers who make a reservation or appointment but fail to show up. This, of course, means loss of revenue for the service organization if it cannot immediately replace the no-show by another customer. This is a problem frequently faced by airlines and hotels. Because finding a new customer on short notice is usually not possible, these service organizations use a practice called **overbooking**. They accept more reservations than they have room for. This reduces the chances of having many empty seats on airplanes or empty hotel rooms but may also lead to a difficult situation when the number of people who show up exceeds the number of available seats or rooms. The general practice in these cases is to offer some compensation to the passenger whose reservation has not been honored, such as free plane tickets to anywhere in the United States and put him on the next flight, or in the case of a hotel guest, to find her a room at a comparable hotel nearby at no charge.

Communication efforts—Sometimes a simple message to customers may help reduce the peaks in the demand. Signs, advertising, and sales messages may convince customers that using various services, such as public transportation, national parks, museums, and the post office at off-peak periods has many benefits, including lower prices, smaller crowds, and a more comfortable ride or visit. We are all accustomed to seeing TV commercials of the U.S. Postal Service reminding us to "Mail early for Christmas."

Offering services that have countercyclical demand patterns—Some services present extreme challenges in demand management. Demand for these services has a definite and inflexible seasonal pattern and price incentives. Reservations or communications will not usually be effective in changing the pattern or smoothing the peaks of demand. Demand for these services is either extremely low or nonexistent during the "off" season. One possible remedy is to offer additional services that use the same facilities and possibly the same personnel but have countercyclical seasonal pattern. For example, many landscaping services offer snow removal services during the winter months when there is not much landscaping to be done. Another example is a ski resort offering a dry ski run or an alpine slide, offering the ski slopes for mountain biking enthusiasts, or nature discovery tours.

Offering complementary services—Loss of patrons because of long waiting lines may be reduced by diverting them to complementary services. During periods of peak demand, complementary services may make the wait for service more bearable for customers and increase the likelihood for their staying in the system or returning at a later date. Thus a bar or lounge may hold a surge of patrons for a restaurant. A putting green or driving range may keep golfers occupied when starting times are delayed. In essence, a complementary service represents one stage of a two-stage queue.[1] The service time for the first stage may stretch out for a considerable time before a client leaves the service stage to exit from the system.

Advertising and sales promotion—Promotional offers and advertising are two additional tools to stimulate demand when the demand is below what is desired. Promotions may offer additional benefits or a reduced price for a limited period of time. Holiday tours with extended features and the promotion of late-night movie theater showings with prizes are examples.

Yield Management

Yield management may be considered as a specialized area of revenue management. While yield management focuses on generating the maximum yield, or revenue, from a perishable inventory, such as seats on a flight, revenue management considers a wide range of strategies and practices to optimize revenue.[2]

Yield management is an approach that originated in the airline industry but is used in hotel and car rental businesses as well. The objective of yield management is to maximize the revenue, or yield, from revenue-generating units that are limited in number for a given time period, such as seats on a flight or rooms in a hotel on a particular day. The principle of yield management can be summarized as *to sell perishable inventory, such as airline seats or hotel rooms, to the right customer at the right time for the right price.*

Yield management is an appropriate approach when (1) the firm is operating with a relatively fixed capacity, (2) demand can be segmented into clearly identified partitions, (3) inventory is perishable, (4) the product is sold well in advance, (5) demand fluctuates substantially, and (6) marginal sales costs and production costs are low, but capacity change costs are high.[3]

The basic idea behind the yield management is to partition the inventory of revenue generating units and sell them to different customer segments. For example, airlines have identified different customer segments such as affluent travelers for whom the cost is not the primary concern, business travelers who have to go somewhere on short notice and be back on a certain date, vacationers for whom cost is an important issue, and people who would visit family and friends or travel for pleasure if the price is right. Airlines offer different levels of service for these groups such as first class, business class, economy, and super-savers, respectively.

All these different levels of service are offered on the same plane; therefore, the problem is how to allocate the available seats on a particular flight to each one of these groups. Obviously, an airline would like to fill all seats with first-class passengers or full-fare paying business travelers, but because this is not likely to occur, many seats will be empty on most flights. Consequently, they offer the remaining seats to economy and super-saver passengers at reduced prices. This is justified because the marginal cost of flying another passenger when there is an available seat on a flight is almost negligible. Because seats are sold long before the departure date, the issue is how many discount tickets to sell and make sure that there are enough seats left for late-booking travelers who will be willing to pay the full fare.

A yield management system has to address four basic issues to optimize revenues: demand patterns for various rates/fares, overbooking policy, demand elasticities, and information system.[4] Yield management has been successfully used by many companies such as Holiday Inn, Ryder truck rental company, Amtrak, and American Airlines. For example, it is estimated that yield management at American Airlines provided more than $1.4 billion quantifiable benefits for a 3-year period in the early 1990s.[5] More recently, InterContinental Hotels Group, the world's largest hotel group by the number of rooms, has generated $145 million additional revenue by implementing an advanced version of revenue management in more than 2,000 of its hotels.[6]

The use of yield management is not limited to airlines and hotels. A company called Uber and several other competitors have recently started a phone app-based service to summon a private car for a taxi service; a service which may be especially useful during rush hour in large cities when finding a taxicab seems impossible. "It does this by engaging yield-management principles that tie together smartphones, GPS locations, existing licensed drivers, user ratings, all-in-one billing, and back-office organization. Uber maintains an inventory in the form of potential rides and uses demand-based pricing to increase supply during peak periods."[7] Not surprisingly, yield management applications are spreading to many other areas, such as renting unused meeting rooms, private offices, or executive suits in companies, as well as restaurant reservations: "Like airline seats or co-working desks, a restaurant forgoes profits each time a table is empty."[8]

Management Science Techniques

Management science provides powerful techniques to help service operations managers manage both demand and supply. Two of these, queuing theory and simulation, are especially useful in making decisions in managing both demand and supply. Queuing models help determine some important performance characteristics of a service system related to waiting lines that form at peak periods of demand or when demand exceeds service capacity for a limited period of time. Queuing models provide performance measures such as the average time each customer spends in the waiting line and in the system, average number of customers in the system, average queue length. Knowledge of such important performance measures can help operations managers make intelligent decisions concerning capacity and demand. Simulation is also a powerful and popular tool often used with queuing models. Simulation helps managers collect important information about system performance and provide answers to "what if" questions concerning capacity expansion or reduction. These techniques are discussed in the supplement to this chapter.

Management of Demand in Waiting

Lines that form at cash registers, box offices, toll booths, bank tellers, and post offices are resented by many people, but seen by most as part of daily life. Strategies for managing demand are effective for some service organizations but they don't completely eliminate waiting. In other words, waiting lines, or queues, form even at well-managed service facilities.

Among the many disadvantages of waiting is balking; that is, some customers may give up and leave the system. This may mean loss of some customers in the short term; that is, they may come back at another time, but some may leave the system forever and go to a competitor. Whatever the case might be, it means loss of revenue for the service organization.

Reducing waiting time may be an important component of both demand and supply management. It was mentioned that management science techniques are available to help operations managers make system-related decisions to reduce waiting and its negative impact on customers and service organization. Now let's look at other, nontechnical approaches to managing demand when waiting lines are formed. The main focus of these approaches is to make waiting a less painful experience for customers as well as service providers. To accomplish this we must understand the psychology of people in waiting lines. David Maister[9] formulated eight propositions about the perceptions and psychology of people in waiting. In the following paragraphs, these propositions are summarized, and suggestions are offered as to what management can do to alleviate the problem.

1. **Unoccupied time feels longer than occupied time**—Many service organizations have discovered this perception and provide distractions to keep customers occupied. Some restaurants have a bar where patrons can have a drink and socialize while waiting for their table. Newspapers and magazines found in doctors' and dentists' offices, or TV sets in waiting rooms of auto repair shops all serve the same purpose: take customer's mind off waiting. A recent innovation for doctors' waiting rooms is health information provided by a Tampa, Florida company: "…in many doctor's offices these days, the standard television offerings like daytime talk shows are giving way to a more focused kind of programming: health content. A company called AccentHealth has been providing programming to 12,300 doctor's offices in the United States on subjects like mental health, allergies and diabetes."[10]

2. **Preprocess waits feel longer than in-process waits**—Waiting seems to be shorter once the service has begun. Anxiety may be higher when waiting to be served. There is the fear of being forgotten by the servers, but once you are in the system and the process is underway, these feelings can easily go away. Some restaurants give menus to patrons waiting for a table, which gives them the impression that service has begun and keeps them occupied. Sometimes a simple acknowledgment is enough to give the same impression; a letter from the admissions office of a college you have applied may make waiting feel shorter especially if an approximate date for decision is also provided.

3. **Anxiety makes waits seem longer**—As mentioned in the previous paragraph "being forgotten" may be one source of anxiety; not knowing how long the wait is going to be, what the service will be like, if you are in the right line, or if you'll be able to get in before all tickets are sold out at a sporting event are some other sources. Anything management can do to reduce the customer's anxiety will make the wait feel shorter and less painful.

4. **Uncertain waits are longer than known, finite waits**—Waiting feels longer when you don't know when the service will begin, and as just mentioned, this increases anxiety. Providing an estimate for the wait usually helps customers calm down and accept the situation. Estimates, however, must be carefully made and close to actual and overestimating usually pleasantly surprises the customer. Disney World and Disneyland, for example, post estimates for each attraction and they generously overestimate them.

5. **Unexplained waits are longer than explained waits**—When people are told of the reasons for the wait, they can feel more comfortable and be more understanding, but when they are kept in the dark as to the reason for delay, they may get upset. For example, if a nurse explains to patients in the waiting room that the doctor is going to be late because he is attending an emergency case, most people will understand and judge the delay as justifiable. Consequently, service organizations must be honest and forthcoming with customers and explain the reason(s) when there is a delay in the service.

6. **Unfair waits are longer than equitable waits**—Most people would be upset if they see someone cutting in the line, or any other practice that violates the common concept of fairness. Unfortunately, these practices are common at some service organizations. For example, an employee who opens up a new cashier line at a supermarket may take customers from the end of another check-out line rather than the next person in line, or an employee at the service counter who interrupts your service to answer a phone and serves the customer on the line violates people's expectations of fairness. These practices not only anger customers, but they also make the wait feel longer than it actually is.

7. **The more valuable the service, the longer the customer will wait**—In Chapter 5, "Service Strategy and Competitiveness," a model of value was presented, which defined nonmonetary price as any sacrifice a customer has to make to receive a service. We also included waiting time as part of this price. Consequently, time spent in waiting is part of the sacrifice consumers are willing to make for the service, and just like monetary price paid for services, the higher the value of the service, the higher the nonmonetary price customers will be willing to pay. Service managers must have a good idea how valuable the service is to customers to make sure that waiting does not exact too high a price from customers.

8. **Solo waits feel longer than group waits**—Waiting for most services is in the company of other customers; hence customers are not alone in the line in a strict sense. However, because customers normally don't know each other, they may feel like waiting in

isolation, especially if there is no conversation among customers or no distractions. Service operations managers should create opportunities, when possible, for customers to socialize and converse among themselves. This will create a sense of community and provide a distraction and make the wait feel shorter.

Research on customer perceptions of waiting conducted at a bank branch in Boston confirmed that as perceptions of waiting time increase, customer satisfaction tends to decrease. Researchers also found that the most important issues for customers include the following:

- "**Fairness**—Can newcomers cut in front of customers who arrived before them, or is the line first come, first served?

- **Interest level**—Are interesting things happening that the customer can watch?

- **Customer attitudes**—What time pressures do customers face?

- **Environment**—Is waiting comfortable? Does the customer have to freeze in the cold or bake in the sun?

- **Value of service**—How important is the result of the transaction to the customer? Could it easily be obtained elsewhere? Can the customer come back another time, or is the transaction urgent?"[11]

11.4 Managing Supply

Capacity is the extent of the ability of a system to deliver the service it was designed to deliver. Hence, managing supply means managing the capacity. Before strategies for managing supply are discussed, capacity must first be defined and difficulties surrounding the measure of capacity understood. Then, the components that make up or influence capacity will be examined. When there is a solid understanding of capacity and its components, the various strategies for managing demand and the process of aggregate planning may be discussed.

Capacity

Capacity is usually defined as the maximum rate of output. This simple definition, however, hides an inherent difficulty with the concept, and that is the measure of output in services. As discussed in Chapter 2, "The Nature of Services and Service Encounters," two of the characteristics of services are that they produce an intangible output, and the output is not standard and may exhibit considerable variability. A third reason for the difficulty is that service organizations rarely offer a single, uniform service. For example, how is the output of a hospital measured? Should the number of beds occupied, number of patients treated, number of physician hours, or number of nurse hours be used? None of these measures provides a satisfactory measure to truly reflect the service provided at a hospital. For example, if the number of beds occupied is used, this measure does not tell anything about the difference in resources needed to treat a patient with cancer and a patient who is in the hospital with a broken leg. Even if two cancer patients are compared, the severity of their cases, required treatments, and the resources needed for their treatment and their costs can be very different.

Another interesting fact, and a challenge for service operations managers, is that even with the same number of employees and same facilities, capacity of a service organization may not be the same from day to day. This is so because of the variability customers exhibit in terms of their needs and requirements as well as variability due to service employees. For example, two customers who arrive at a bank teller may require considerably different amounts of service from the teller; one may be just depositing his paycheck and take 30 seconds of the teller's time. The second customer, on the other hand, may be depositing 15 checks for a small business and transferring money between accounts of the company and may take several minutes. When the bank has too many of the second type of customers on a particular day, say Friday, the capacity of the bank will be reduced. Thus, it is clear that a service organization must choose its output measure carefully, if possible, to avoid all these problems.

Components of Capacity

The seven basic components of capacity are human resources, facilities, equipment, tools, time, customer participation, and alternative sources of capacity.

Human resources—Human resources are directly related to aggregate output. The number of people, the level of skills, and the mix of skills are major factors. Highly skilled people organized into motivated groups and supplied with the best equipment can have an enormous impact on productivity. Further, if the leadership is excellent and the environment is rewarding, the twin factors of leadership and motivation may increase capacity. Human resources are also a highly flexible capacity component. Workers can be hired and fired easier than equipment can be bought and sold. Labor can work full-time, part-time or overtime. Workers can be cross-trained to perform a variety of jobs.

Facilities—Facilities are needed to house employees and equipment. Some services are provided over the phone, through computer networks, through mail, or through air such as TV broadcasts; hence they do not need to consider customers in facility design. However, many other organizations receive customers in their facilities to deliver a service.

Equipment and tools—Although much of equipment planning has already been determined in the design of the service delivery system and capital budgeting stage of the strategic plan, sometimes simple, inexpensive equipment substitutions or modifications may yield increases in productivity and thereby expand capacity. Advances in technology, especially new gadgets that take advantage of the Internet and high-speed telecommunication networks, may increase service productivity and capacity. For example, some restaurants in the United States, Europe, and Japan are using "technology that allows diners to order food directly off screens at their tables, instead of depending on fellow human beings to note their choices, sometimes grumpily or erroneously."[12]

Time—Time is a component in two ways. First, capacity may be altered by changing the mix between two time periods or shifting output to another time period. This is especially appropriate for services subject to peak demand periods. Second, in a larger sense, extending the hours of operation increases the total capacity relative to demand for a specified time period.

Customer participation—Another important component of capacity in some services is customer participation. Many services rely on customers' labor for service delivery. For example, a customer does all the work at an automated teller machine to withdraw money from his account. In other services the customer may supply only part of the required labor.

Alternative sources—Alternative sources of capacity may be internal or external. Internal sources may consist of mothballed machines or facilities, extended work hours, or multiple shifts. External sources may consist of subcontracting, acquiring another company, or increasing automation. The leasing of resources also allows for a wide range of capacity expansion alternatives.

Strategies for Management of Supply

Service operations managers have a much greater control of and influence on the supply of services than they have on the demand. However, even a higher degree of control of the supply of services does not guarantee a perfect match between the demand and supply. Following are some strategies operations managers can use to increase or decrease the supply of services. These strategies inevitably rely on skillful use of one or more capacity components in changing the service capacity and hence the supply. As with demand management strategies, it must be pointed out that not all these strategies are appropriate or feasible for all service organizations.

Changing the level of workforce—This is a strategy that can be used effectively only in the medium-term, that is, over a planning period of 3 to 12 months. Anticipating an increasing or decreasing trend in demand, managers can gradually increase or decrease the number of employees. Also, anticipating seasonal peaks and valleys in demand, a service organization may hire workers for the length of the season. The major disadvantage of this strategy is the high cost of hiring, training, and termination of employees, and the difficulty of developing loyalty among employees.

Cross-training employees—Most services involve several tasks. The level of demand for each task may not be equal at all times. Training employees in tasks other than their regular assignments and empowering them to serve can help increase service capacity during peak demand periods. This has an additional advantage; it helps employees develop themselves by gaining additional skills and reduces boredom that results from doing the same job day-in and day-out.

Part-time workers—Many service organizations today rely on part-time employees for a significant portion of their labor needs. It is estimated that in 2011 approximately 19.5 percent of the workforce in the U.S. is employed on a temporary, part-time basis.[13] Part-time employees may be most appropriate when the daily labor needs of the service exhibit a clear and pronounced pattern, as is the case in fast food restaurants and package delivery services. When feasible, the use of part-time workers adds significant flexibility to service capacity and gives operations managers better control of service supply.

Increasing customer participation—As mentioned earlier, customers may be a valuable source of labor in the delivery of some services, and some service organizations make clever use of this source. For example, in some restaurants patrons prepare their own salad at the salad bar, but a waiter brings their food to the table. At Shouldice Hospital, patients are encouraged to walk out of the operating room to a rest area after a hernia operation, rather than hospital personnel transporting the patient in a wheelchair as done in most hospitals after a surgery. Increasing customer participation, in general, reduces the labor input from the service organization and increases the service speed, thereby increasing the capacity. However, there is also a risk in increasing customer participation; if customers are not skillful in performing their tasks, they may slow things down and cause a reduction in the capacity.

Renting equipment—Equipment is an important component of service capacity in many services. Hence, just increasing the number of employees may not be enough to increase the capacity. An increase in the equipment availability must usually accompany the increase in employment. When the increase in employment is only temporary, purchase of equipment may not be economically justified. When this is the case, the service organization may rent or lease the necessary equipment. This is a common practice in the airline industry; airlines that face increased demand during summer rent or lease airplanes from other airlines or freight carriers.

Expanding/renovating facilities—Often output may be increased by moving to a new building with a better space pattern or by developing a better layout of equipment in the old building. Better lighting, air-conditioning, and heating improvements also may contribute to productivity and thereby expand capacity.

Automation—Automation of tasks performed by humans has been used in manufacturing for many years. Major advantages of automation are lower cost, higher output, consistency of output, and hence higher quality. Automation has not always been seen as desirable in services because it usually implies impersonal service. However, speed and lower cost, in addition to other benefits it provides, are making automation an attractive alternative to human delivery of some services. For example, many hotel chains have installed kiosks for quick check-ins and check-outs. Also, customers of auto rental company Hertz rent cars at automated kiosks, just as airlines have for some time allowed passengers to check in without talking to anyone.[14]

Extending service hours—Some service organizations may increase their capacity by extending their hours of operation under special circumstances or during periods of increased demand. For example, some retailers stay open all night during Christmas shopping; some post offices receive mail until midnight on April 15 to help taxpayers make the deadline; and amusement parks have extended hours in summer months and on weekends.

Better scheduling tools and practices—Significant increases in capacity may be obtained from better scheduling of service personnel and their activities. Many management science techniques are available to optimize scheduling of service employees, such as nurses at a hospital, airline flight crews, and locating and scheduling emergency medical services. Also, performing nonurgent tasks, such as cleaning and maintenance, during periods of low demand are simple but effective ways to increase service capacity.

11.5 Summary

The development of a service system proceeds from the design of the service, to aggregate planning of resources, to building of the system. The basic objective of aggregate planning is to plan a firm's resources so that the firm's capacity and demand for outputs are matched. Thus aggregate planning may alternatively emphasize adjusting the demand side or the supply side to achieve a desired balance. In this chapter, strategies and tools that operations managers can use in accomplishing the challenging task of balancing demand and supply in services were discussed.

The major reasons that make this a particularly difficult task in services were first reviewed. For effective performance of this task, an operations manager must be equipped with a sound knowledge of her customers and an understanding of their needs. Then, she must study the nature and pattern of demand to select and implement the appropriate strategies for managing demand. Strategies and tools that help a service organization influence demand include price, advertising and promotions, offering services that have countercyclical demand patterns, using reservations or appointments, communication efforts, and offering complementary services. Yield management as a special form of demand management used by airlines, car rental companies, and hotel chains was also briefly discussed. The discussion of demand management concluded by focusing on the psychological aspects of waiting and what operations managers can do to make waiting less painful, or maybe even an enjoyable experience for customers.

Capacity is the extent of the capability of a system to deliver the service it was designed to deliver and is usually defined as the maximum rate of output. Hence managing supply means managing the capacity. After pointing out the difficulties surrounding the capacity measurement in services, the major components of capacity for a service organization were discussed. Strategies for managing supply rely on the management of these components of capacity and include changing the level of workforce, cross-training employees, hiring part-time workers, increasing customer participation, renting equipment, expanding/renovating facilities, automation, extending service hours, and using management science techniques for better scheduling and implementing good scheduling practices.

Endnotes

1. Queuing theory is discussed in the supplement to this chapter.

2. For more information on Revenue Management see, Robert G. Cross, *Revenue Management: Hard-core Tactics for Market Domination* (Broadway Books, New York, 1997); for a comprehensive treatment of revenue management topics, see Robert L. Phillips, *Pricing and Revenue Optimization*, Stanford Business Books (Stanford, California, 2005).

3. Sheryl E. Kimes, "Yield Management: A Tool for Capacity-Constrained Service Firms," *Journal of Operations Management*, Vol. 8, No. 4 (October 1989), pp. 348–363.

4. Kimes, "Yield Management: A Tool for Capacity-Constrained Service Firms," *Journal of Operations Management*, Vol. 8, No. 4 (October 1989), pp. 348–363.

5. Barry C. Smith, John F. Leimkuhler, and Ross M. Darrow, "Yield Management at American Airlines," *Interfaces*, Vol. 22, No. 1 (January–February, 1992), pp. 8–31.

6. Dev Koushik, Jon A. Higbie, and Craig Eister, "Retail Price Optimization at InterContinental Hotels Group," *Interfaces*, Vol. 42, No. 1 (January–February 2012), pp. 45–57.

7. G.F., "A digital fare tale," *The Economist* (June 14, 2012).

8. G.F., "Lofty goals," *The Economist* (February 28, 2012).

9. David H. Maister, "The Psychology of Waiting Lines," in Czepiel, J. A., Solomon, M. R., and Surprenant, C. F., (Eds.), *The Service Encounter: Managing Employee/Customer Interaction in Service Businesses* (Lexington, MA: Lexington Books, 1985), pp. 113–123.

10. Tanzina Vega, "AccentHealth Puts Medical Content on Waiting Room TVs," *The New York Times* (April 8, 2012).

11. Karen L. Katz, Blaire M. Larson, and Richard C. Larson, "Prescription for the Waiting-in-Line Blues: Entertain, Enlighten, and Engage," *Sloan Management Review* (Winter 1991), pp. 44–53.

12. Rebecca Harrison, "E-waiter, Where's My Food?" *The New York Times* (Monday, February 25, 2008.)

13. Bureau of Labor Statistics, Current Population Survey, Employed Persons by Sex, Occupation, Class of Worker, Full- or Part-Time Status, and Race, http://www.bls.gov/cps/cpsaat12.pdf (08/05/2012).

14. "Hard Times, Lean Firms: How Much Longer Can America Keep Increasing Productivity?" *The Economist* (December 31, 2011).

11 Supplement
QUEUING AND SIMULATION

S11.1 Introduction

The body of knowledge about waiting lines, often called **queuing theory**, is a valuable tool for the service operations manager. Waiting lines are a common situation—they may, for example, take the form of cars waiting for repair at an auto service center, printing jobs waiting to be completed at a print shop, or students waiting for a consultation with their professor. Exhibit S11-1 lists just a few uses of waiting-line models. Analysis of waiting-line length, average waiting time, and other factors helps to understand service system capacity.

Service operations managers recognize the trade-off that must take place between the cost of providing good service and the cost of customer waiting time. Managers want queues that are short enough so that customers do not become unhappy and either leave without buying or buy but never return. However, managers are willing to allow some waiting if the waiting is balanced by a significant savings in capacity costs.

Exhibit S11-1   Common Queuing Situations

Situation	Arrivals in Queue	Service Process
Supermarket	Grocery shoppers	Checkout clerks at cash register
Highway toll booth	Automobiles	Collection of toll at booth
Doctor's office	Patients	Treatment by doctors and nurses
Computer system	Programs to be run	Computer processes jobs
Telephone company	Callers	Switching equipment to forward calls
Bank	Customers	Transactions handled by teller
Machine maintenance	Broken machines	Repair people fix machines
Harbor	Ships and barges	Dockworkers load and unload

One means of evaluating a service facility is to look at total expected cost, a concept illustrated in Exhibit S11-2. Total cost is the sum of capacity costs plus expected waiting costs.

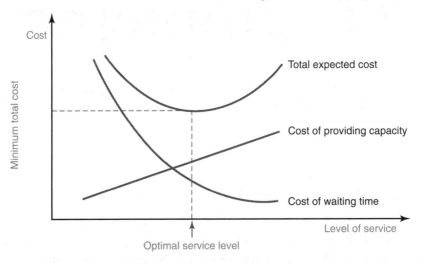

Capacity costs increase as a firm attempts to raise its level of service. Managers in some service centers can vary their capacity by having standby personnel and machines that can be assigned to specific service stations to prevent or shorten excessively long lines. In grocery stores, managers and stock clerks can operate extra checkout counters when needed. In banks and airport check-in points, part-time workers may be called in to help. As service improves (that is, speeds up), however, the cost of time spent waiting in lines decreases. Waiting cost may reflect lost productivity of workers while their tools or machines are awaiting repairs or may simply be an estimate of the cost of customers lost because of poor service and long queues. In some service systems (for example, emergency ambulance service), the cost of long waiting lines may be intolerably high.

S11.2 Basic Queuing System Configurations

Service systems are usually classified in terms of their number of channels (for example, number of servers) and number of phases (for example, number of service stops that must be made). A single-channel queuing system with one server is typified by the drive-in bank that has only one open teller or by a drive-through fast-food restaurant. If, on the other hand, the bank had several tellers on duty and each customer waited in one common line for the first available teller, then we would have a multichannel queuing system at work. Most banks today are multichannel service systems, as are most large barber shops, airline ticket counters, and post offices.

A single-phase system is one in which the customer receives service from only one station and then exits the system. A fast-food restaurant in which the person who takes your order also brings you the food and takes your money is a single-phase system. So is a driver's license agency in which the person taking your application also grades your test and collects the license fee. However, if the restaurant requires you to place your order at one station, pay at a second, and pick up the food at a third service stop, it becomes a multiphase system. Likewise, if the driver's license agency is large or busy, you will probably have to wait in a line to complete the application (the first service stop), then queue again to have the test graded (the second service stop), and finally go to a third service counter to pay the fee. To help you relate the concepts of channels and phases, Exhibit S11-3 presents four possible configurations.

Exhibit S11-3   Basic Queuing System Configurations

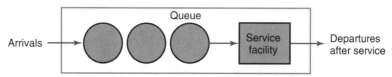

Single-channel, single-phase system

Single-channel, multiphase system

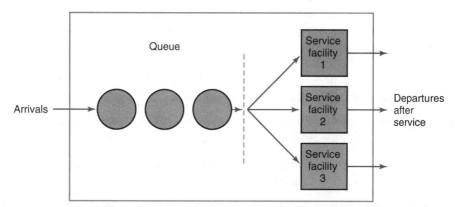

Multichannel, single-phase system

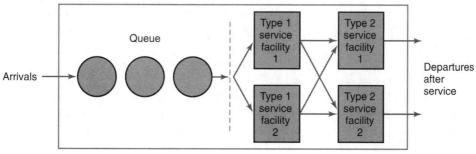

Multichannel, multiphase system

S11.3 Measuring the Queue's Performance

Queuing models help managers make decisions that balance desirable capacity costs with waiting-line costs. Some of the many measures of a waiting-line system's performance that are commonly obtained in a queuing analysis are the following:

- The average time each customer or object spends in the queue

- The average queue length

- The average time each customer spends in the system (waiting time plus service time)

- The average number of customers in the system

- The probability that the service facility will be idle

- The utilization factor for the system

- The probability of a specific number of customers in the system

S11.4 A Single-Channel Queuing Model

The most common case of queuing problems involves the single-channel, or single-server, waiting line. In this situation, arrivals form a single line to be serviced by a single station (refer to Exhibit S11-3). It is often possible to assume that the following conditions exist in this type of system:

1. Arrivals are served on a first-come, first-served basis, and every arrival waits to be served, regardless of the length of the line or queue.

2. Arrivals are independent of preceding arrivals, but the average number of arrivals (arrival rate) does not change over time.

3. Arrivals are described by a Poisson probability distribution and come from an infinite (or very, very large) population.[1]

4. Service times vary from one customer to the next and are independent of one another, but their average rate is known.

5. Service times occur according to the negative exponential probability distribution.[2]

6. The average service rate is faster than the average arrival rate.

When these conditions are met, the equations shown in Exhibit S11-4 can be developed. These equations enable you to calculate the seven measures of a waiting line system's performance mentioned earlier. Note that all the calculations are based in some way on the average number of arrivals per time period (λ) and the average number of customers served per time period (μ). The following example illustrates how this single-channel model may be used.

λ = Mean number of arrivals per time period

μ = Mean number of people or items served per time period

L_s = Average number of units (customers) in the system (waiting line + service)

$$= \frac{\lambda}{\mu - \lambda}$$

W_S = Average time a unit spends in the system (waiting time + service time)

$$= \frac{1}{\mu - \lambda}$$

L_q = Average number of units in the queue

$$= \frac{\lambda^2}{\mu(\mu - \lambda)}$$

W_q = Average time a unit spends waiting in the queue

$$= \frac{\lambda}{\mu(\mu - \lambda)}$$

ρ = Utilization factor for the system

$$= \frac{\lambda}{\mu}$$

P_0 = Probability of 0 units in the system (that is, the service unit is idle)

$$= 1 - \frac{\lambda}{\mu}$$

$P_{n>k}$ = Probability of more than k units in the system, where n is the number of units in the system

$$= \left(\frac{\lambda}{\mu}\right)^{k+1}$$

Golden Muffler Shop—Jones, the mechanic at the Golden Muffler Shop, can install new mufflers at an average rate of three per hour (or approximately one every 20 minutes), according to a negative exponential distribution. Customers seeking this service arrive at the shop on the average of two per hour, following a Poisson distribution. The customers are served on a first-in, first-out basis and come from a large population of possible buyers.

From this description, we can obtain the operating characteristics of Golden Muffler's queuing system:

$$\lambda = 2 \text{ cars arriving per hour}$$

$$\mu = 3 \text{ cars served per hour}$$

$$L_s = \frac{\lambda}{\mu - \lambda} = \frac{2}{3-2} = \frac{2}{1}$$

$$= 2 \text{ cars in the system, on average}$$

$$W_s = \frac{1}{\mu - \lambda} = \frac{1}{3-2} = 1 \text{ hour}$$

$$= 1\text{-hour average waiting time in the system}$$

$$L_q = \frac{\lambda^2}{\mu(\mu - \lambda)} = \frac{2^2}{3(3-2)} = \frac{4}{3(1)} = \frac{4}{3}$$

$$= 1.33 \text{ cars waiting in line, on average}$$

$$W_q = \frac{\lambda}{\mu(\mu - \lambda)} = \frac{2}{3(3-2)} = \frac{2}{3} \text{ hour}$$

$$= 40\text{-minute average waiting time in the queue per car}$$

$$\rho = \frac{\lambda}{\mu} = \frac{2}{3}$$

$$= 66.6 \text{ percent of time mechanic is busy}$$

$$P_0 = 1 - \frac{\lambda}{\mu} = 1 - \frac{2}{3}$$

$$= 0.33 \text{ probability there are 0 cars in the system}$$

$$P_{n>3} = \left(\frac{\lambda}{\mu}\right)^{k+1} = \left(\frac{2}{3}\right)^{3+1}$$

$$= .198 \text{ or a } 19.8 \text{ percent chance that more than 3 cars are in the system}$$

After we have computed the operating characteristics of a queuing system, it is often important to do an economic analysis of their impact. The waiting-line model previously described is valuable in predicting potential waiting times, queue lengths, idle times, and so on, but it does not identify optimal decisions or consider cost factors. As stated earlier, the solution to a queuing problem may require management to make a trade-off between the increased cost of providing better service and the decreased waiting costs derived from providing that service.

S11.5 A Multichannel Queuing Model

The next logical step is to look at a multichannel queuing system, in which two or more servers or channels are available to handle arriving customers. Assume that customers awaiting service form one single line and then proceed to the first available server. An example of such a multichannel, single-phase waiting line is found in many banks today. A common line is formed, and the customer at the head of the line proceeds to the first free teller. (Refer to Exhibit S11-3 for a typical multichannel configuration.)

The multichannel system presented here again assumes that arrivals follow a Poisson probability distribution and that service times follow a negative exponential distribution. Service is first-come, first-served, and all servers are assumed to perform at the same rate. Other assumptions listed earlier for the single-channel model apply as well.

The queuing equations for this model are shown in Exhibit S11-5. These equations are obviously more complex than the ones used in the single-channel model, yet they are used in exactly the same fashion and provide the same type of information as the simpler model.[3]

Golden Muffler Revisited—The Golden Muffler Shop has decided to open a second garage bay and hire a second mechanic to handle muffler installations. Customers, who arrive at the rate of about $\lambda = 2$ per hour, will wait in a single line until one of the two mechanics is free. Each mechanic installs mufflers at the rate of approximately $\mu = 3$ per hour.

Exhibit S11-5   Equations for the Multichannel Queuing Model

M = Number of channels open

λ = Average arrival rate

μ = Average service rate at each channel

P_0 = Probability that there are 0 people or units in the system

$$= \cfrac{1}{\left[\sum_{n=0}^{M-1}\dfrac{1}{n!}\left(\dfrac{\lambda}{\mu}\right)^n\right] + \dfrac{1}{M!}\left(\dfrac{\lambda}{\mu}\right)^M \dfrac{M\mu}{M\mu-\lambda}} \quad \text{for } M\mu > \lambda$$

L_s = Average number of people or units in the system

$$= \frac{\lambda\mu(\lambda/\mu)^M}{(M-1)!(M\mu-\lambda)^2}P_0 + \frac{\lambda}{\mu}$$

W_s = Average time a unit spends in the waiting line
or being service (namely, in the system)

$$= \frac{\mu(\lambda/\mu)^M}{(M-1)!(M\mu-\lambda)^2}P_0 + \frac{1}{\mu} = \frac{L_s}{\lambda}$$

L_q = Average number of people or units in line
waiting for service

$$= L_s - \frac{\lambda}{\mu}$$

W_q = Average time a person or unit spends in the
queue waiting for service

$$= W_s - \frac{1}{\mu} = \frac{L_q}{\lambda}$$

To find out how this system compares to the old single-channel waiting-line system, compute several operating characteristics for the M = 2 channel system and compare the results with those found in the first example.

$$P_0 = \cfrac{1}{\left[\displaystyle\sum_{n=0}^{1}\frac{1}{n!}\left(\frac{2}{3}\right)^n\right] + \frac{1}{2!}\left(\frac{2}{3}\right)^2 \frac{2(3)}{2(3)-2}}$$

$$= \cfrac{1}{1 + \cfrac{2}{3} + \cfrac{1}{2}\left(\cfrac{4}{9}\right)\left(\cfrac{6}{6-2}\right)} = \cfrac{1}{1 + \cfrac{2}{3} + \cfrac{1}{3}} = \frac{1}{2}$$

$= 0.50$ probability of 0 cars in the system

Then

$$L_s = \frac{(2)(3)(2/3)^2}{1![2(3)-2]^2}\left(\frac{1}{2}\right) + \frac{2}{3} = \frac{8/3}{16}\left(\frac{1}{2}\right) + \frac{2}{3} = \frac{3}{4}$$

$= 0.75$ average number of cars in the system

$$W_s = \frac{L_s}{\lambda} = \frac{3/4}{2} = \frac{3}{8}\text{ hour}$$

$= 22.5$-minute average time a car spends in the system

$$L_q = L_s - \frac{\lambda}{\mu} = \frac{3}{4} - \frac{2}{3} = \frac{1}{12}$$

$= 0.083$ average number of cars in the queue

$$W_q = \frac{L_q}{\lambda} = \frac{0.083}{2} = 0.0415\text{ hour}$$

$= 2.5$-minute average time a car spends in the queue

We can summarize these characteristics and compare them to those of the single-channel model as follows:

	Single Channel	Two Channels
P_0	0.33	0.5
L_s	2 cars	0.75 car
W_s	60 minutes	22.5 minutes
L_q	1.33 cars	0.083 car
W_q	40 minutes	2.5 minutes

The increased service has a dramatic effect on almost all characteristics. In particular, time spent waiting in line drops from 40 minutes to only 2.5 minutes. This is consistent with the trade-off curve illustrated earlier in Exhibit S11-2.

S11.6 More Complex Queuing Models and the Use of Simulation

Many practical waiting-line problems that occur in service systems have characteristics like the models just described. Often, however, variations of this specific case are present in an analysis. Service times in an automobile repair shop, for example, tend to follow the normal probability distribution instead of the exponential distribution. A college registration system in which seniors have first choice of courses and hours over all other students is an example of a first-come, first-served model with a preemptive priority queue discipline. A physical examination for military recruits is an example of a multiphase system, one that differs from the single-phase models discussed earlier. A recruit first lines up to have blood drawn at one station, then waits to take an eye examination at the next station, talks to a psychiatrist at the third, and is examined by a doctor for medical problems at the fourth. At each phase, the recruit must enter another queue and wait his turn.

Models to handle these cases have been developed by operations researchers. The computations for the resulting mathematical formulations are more complex than the earlier ones, though. And many real-world queuing applications are too complex to be modeled analytically. When this happens, analysts usually turn to computer simulation.

Simulation, the next topic, is a technique in which random numbers are used to draw inferences about probability distributions (such as arrivals and services). Using this approach, many hours, days, or months of data can be developed by a computer in a few seconds. This allows analysis of controllable factors, such as adding another service channel, without actually doing so physically. Basically, whenever a standard analytical queuing model provides only a poor approximation of the actual service system, it is wise to develop a simulation model instead.

S11.7 Simulation as a Scheduling Tool

When a system contains elements that exhibit chance in their behavior, the **Monte Carlo** method of simulation may be applied. The basis of Monte Carlo simulation is experimentation on the chance (or **probabilistic**) variables through random sampling.

The simulation technique breaks down into five simple steps:

1. Set up a probability distribution for important variables.

2. Build a cumulative probability distribution for each variable.

3. Establish an interval of random numbers for each variable.

4. Generate random numbers.

5. Actually simulate a series of trials using the random numbers to obtain values for the variables.

We demonstrate a Monte Carlo simulation with the aid of Exhibits S11-6 through S11-8. Assume that a single-channel, single-phase queuing system, such as that at a postal substation, is being analyzed. The analyst makes a number of observations of the number of arrivals per 5-minute period and the number of services per 5-minute period. The data are classified into frequency distributions and then represented as probability distributions, as shown in Exhibit S11-6(a) and (c). Next, the cumulative probability distributions for Exhibit S11-6(a) and (c) are computed, as shown in Exhibit S11-6(b) and (d). We now proceed as follows.

Exhibit S11-6 Probabilities for a System Simulation

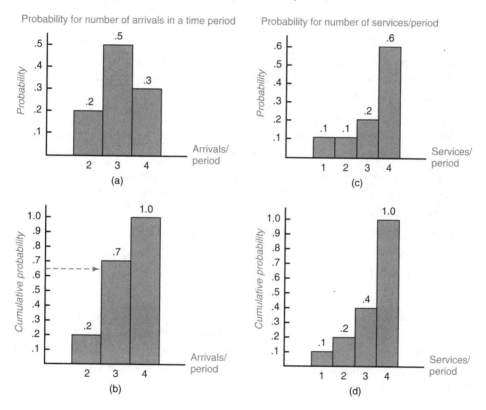

Exhibit S11-7   Simulation of a Postal Substation for Three Time Periods

Period	Random Number	Units Arriving During the Period	Random Number	Units Serviced During the Period*	Units in Line Waiting to Be Serviced at End of Period
1	—	0	—	0	0
2	0.63	3	0.17	2	1
3	0.87	4	0.03	1	4
4	0.11	2	0.42	3	3

* These would proceed to the next station.

1. Set up headings for the time and status of each item in the system, as in Exhibit S11-7. (Items in this case are the number of people arriving or being served.)

2. Obtain a table of random numbers found in management science texts. A portion of such unrelated numbers is shown in Exhibit S11-8.

3. Select a row and column, and then proceed to the random number table. We selected the second column to start and decided to read down. Enter the number 0.63 for the second column and 0.17 for the fourth column in Exhibit S11-7.

4. Go to the first cumulative probability chart (Exhibit S11-6(b)), and find 0.63 on the vertical scale. Draw a horizontal line to the bar it first meets. This is the three-arrivals-per-period bar. Enter 3 in the table in Exhibit S11-7 in the appropriate column.

5. Go to the second cumulative probability chart (Exhibit S11-6(d)) and find 0.17 on the vertical scale. Draw a horizontal line to the bar it first meets. This is the two-units-serviced-per-period bar. Enter 2 in the appropriate column in Exhibit S11-7.

6. Units arriving minus units serviced in the period gives a surplus of one waiting to be served in the next period.

7. Repeat steps 3 through 5, keeping track of units left to be serviced in each following period, if any.

Note that no matter how complex the system may be, simulation consists of examining the inputs, waiting lines, services, and output at one particular time period. Then the "clock" is moved up one time period and the system is examined again. After hundreds (or thousands) of simulations, average waiting periods or average total service times through many different transactions may be found.

S11.8 The Role of Computers in Simulation

Computers are critical in simulating complex tasks. They can generate random numbers, simulate thousands of time periods in a matter of seconds or minutes, and provide management with reports that make decision making easier. A computer approach is almost a necessity to draw valid conclusions from a simulation.

5497	6317	5736	9468	5707	8576	2614
0234	8703	2454	6094	1760	3195	0985
9821	1142	6650	2749	3677	4451	4959
9681	5613	9971	0081	7249	3016	1385

Computer programming languages can help the simulation process. General-purpose languages such as FORTRAN, BASIC, COBOL, C++, or PASCAL are one approach.

Special-purpose simulation languages, such as GPSS, and SIMSCRIPT, have a few advantages: (1) they require less programming time for large scale simulations, (2) they are usually more efficient and easier to check for errors, and (3) they have random-number generators already built in as subroutines.

Commercial, easy-to-use prewritten simulation programs are also available. Some are generalized to handle a wide variety of situations ranging from queuing to inventory.

The names of a few such programs are Extend, Modsim, Witness, MAP/I, Enterprise Dynamics, Simfactory, ProModel, Micro Saint, and ARENA. There are also packages specifically designed for simulating various aspects of service systems. Two such programs are ServiceModel and MedModel developed by ProModel Corporation. ServiceModel can be used to simulate facility layout and design, capacity planning, staff and service scheduling, complex paperwork and customer flow, and distribution and logistics of service organizations. MedModel has been developed for the healthcare industry to evaluate, plan, and design/redesign the processes, procedures and policies of hospitals, clinics and labs. Spreadsheet software can also be used to develop simulations quickly and easily. Such packages have built-in random-number generators (through the @ RAND command) and develop outputs through "data-fill" table commands.

Using POM for Windows for Queuing Problems

POM for Windows Waiting Lines (queuing) module can be used to solve problems that fit any one of the models discussed in this chapter. Exhibit S11-9 illustrates the solution of the single channel waiting line model of Golden Muffler Shop example (select model M/M/1 from the menu) and a graph of probabilities for the number of customers in the system. In addition, the Waiting Lines module provides a table of probabilities for $P (n = k)$. Exhibit S11-10 has the output of the Golden Muffler Shop problem with two servers (multichannel model, M/M/s).

Exhibit S11-9 POM for Windows Solution of the Single-Channel Golden Muffler Shop Example

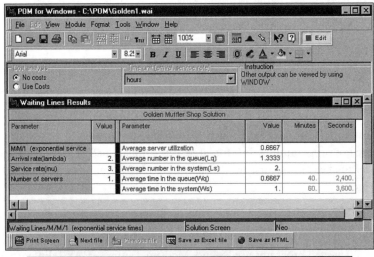

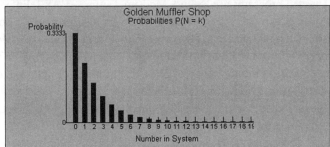

Exhibit S11-10 POM for Windows Solution of the Two-Channel Golden Muffler Shop Example

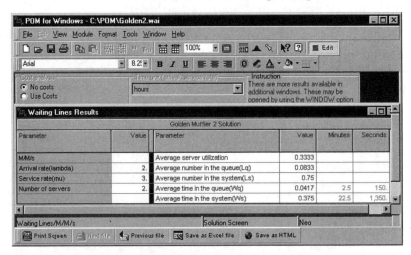

S11.9 Summary

Two management science tools were examined, queuing theory and simulation, which are often useful in scheduling capacity. They can both provide information about the capacity needed so that customers are not forced to wait an unreasonable length of time. When certain mathematical conditions can be met, a series of queuing formulas may describe the parameters of the wait. When the situation at hand does not fit the assumptions of queuing theory, Monte Carlo simulation can be employed as a scheduling tool.

Endnotes

1. The Poisson distribution is established by the formula

    $$P(x) = \frac{e^{-\lambda}\lambda^x}{x!} \quad \text{for } x = 0,1,2,...$$

    Where $P(x)$ = probability of x arrivals per unit of time

    x = number of arrivals per unit of time

    λ = average arrival rate

    e = 2.7183 (which is the base of natural logs)

2. This distribution takes the form

    Probability (service takes longer than x minutes) = $e^{-\mu x}$ for $x \geq 0$

    μ = average number served per minute

3. See either Barry Render and R. M. Stair, *Quantitative Analysis for Management*, 11th ed. (Upper Saddle River, NJ, Prentice Hall, 2012); or Jay Heizer and Barry Render, *Production and Operations Management*, 11th ed. (Upper Saddle River, NJ, Prentice Hall, 2014), for details.

12

SERVICE QUALITY AND CONTINUOUS IMPROVEMENT

12.1 Introduction

Quality has been one of the most talked about topics in the business world during the 1980s and 1990s. There is, of course, good reason for this. During the late 1970s and 1980s many large U.S. corporations were affected; some were virtually devastated by competition from foreign companies. Japanese firms, for example, increased their U.S. market share in practically every industry they entered, while consumer confidence in goods produced by American companies diminished. Loss of customers led to loss of profits for many American companies and loss of jobs for many of their employees, and hardship for their families. Japanese companies achieved this success in the United States, as well as in many other countries, largely due to the superior quality of their goods and efficient production methods.

The shock caused by this situation initiated a quality revolution in the U.S. industry. As a result today most American manufacturers have significantly improved the quality of their goods. The quality revolution that started in the early 1980s was not limited to manufacturing industries. Practically all service organizations, including government organizations at all levels, were also impacted by the movement as consumers demanded quality in everything they purchased; both goods and services.

This chapter discusses basic issues that determine quality and continuous improvement in services. The supplement to the chapter focuses on the tools and techniques of service quality and continuous improvement.

12.2 Why Quality Is So Important

Quality is no longer a strong competitive advantage possessed by only a relatively few firms in any manufacturing industry. Today it is simply a prerequisite for being in business. Manufacturers who do not produce quality products will not survive in the years to come. Is this also true for the field of services? We believe the answer is "yes." Although service companies do not have as much foreign competition as manufacturers do, domestic competition is fierce enough to make quality a prerequisite for survival in many services. Thus, the answer to the question as to why service quality is so important is simply, "survival," and "competitiveness." Now take a look at some of the reasons that make quality so essential for survival and competitiveness.

Higher customer loyalty—Quality is a vital ingredient of customer satisfaction. Superior quality leads to higher satisfaction, and higher satisfaction in turn leads to loyal customers. As emphasized earlier, customer loyalty leads to higher profits and growth.

Higher market share—Loyal customers provide a solid customer base for the organization. Their word-of-mouth advertising brings new customers leading to a larger market share for the organization.

Higher returns to investors—Research indicates that companies known for their high-quality goods and/or services are profitable companies, and therefore their stocks are good investments. A recent study by the National Institute of Standards and Technology (NIST) involving the applicants of Baldrige Performance Excellence Program (formerly Malcolm Baldrige National Quality Award Program) found a benefit-to-cost ratio of 820-to-1 to the U.S. economy using only the benefits for the surveyed group of applicants for the National Quality Award since 2006 but using *all* the social costs of the award program.[1]

Loyal employees—When an organization produces superior quality goods and/or services, its employees take pride in their work and gain high levels of satisfaction from their jobs. Satisfied employees tend to be loyal and productive. In addition, the organization enjoys low employee turnover.

Lower costs—Superior quality means doing things right the first time, which means the organization will spend relatively little money to correct mistakes or give refunds to dissatisfied customers. Preventing mistakes increases productivity and lowers cost.

Lesser vulnerability to price competition—Companies like Ritz-Carlton Hotels, known for their superior quality, can usually charge premium prices because they offer something their competitors don't. Consequently, they usually don't have to compete primarily on the basis of price, and when they do have to compete on the basis of price, they are usually in good condition to do so because of their high productivity and low costs.

No organization will enjoy these competitive advantages if its goods and/or services do not have the quality customers want. Another consequence of poor quality is liability for damages or injuries caused by poorly designed or produced goods and/or services. Medical malpractice suits and their financial impact on physicians and healthcare providers are well known.

12.3 Quality Defined

Quality is often talked about, and much desired but somewhat difficult to define. The problem lies not in finding definitions as many definitions exist, but in making sure that in any particular situation, customers, service providers, and suppliers understand each other's definitions. Most definitions of quality fall short of reflecting all the relevant perspectives. However, this is not necessarily bad; multiple definitions of quality make us aware of the multiple perspectives that should be considered and multiple requirements that must be met to achieve superior quality.

David Garvin identified five categories of quality definitions that reflect five different perspectives:[2]

1. **Transcendent**—According to the transcendent view, quality is innate excellence and can be recognized only through experience. In other words, it can be summarized as "You cannot define quality but you know it when you see it." This, however, provides little practical guidance to managers in the quest for quality.

2. **Product-based**—Product-based definitions rely on measurable quantities to define quality. For goods, the measures may include length of useful life, amount of a desirable ingredient (e.g., "100% cotton") or amount of a desirable output (e.g., "it gets 45 miles per gallon"). Examples for services include number of entries in an encyclopedia, number of days within which your order will be shipped, or number of rings before your call will be answered. Since it is based on measurable quantities, this definition allows an objective assessment of quality. The disadvantage of a product-based definition is that it assumes that all customers desire the same attributes and hence fails to account for differences in tastes and preferences of individual consumers.

3. **User-based**—This approach to defining quality begins where the product-based definition ends; it defines quality from an individual consumer's perspective. The "fitness for use" definition of quality is consistent with this approach. In other words, it is based on the premise that "quality is in the eyes of the beholder." For example, a tastefully prepared and presented meal that takes half an hour to deliver to a customer's table may be seen as a sign of poor quality if the meal is for lunch and the customer is in a hurry. The subjectivity of this approach leads to two problems: (1) how to decide which attributes should be included in a good or service to appeal to the largest number of customers; (2) how to differentiate between attributes that provide satisfaction and those that imply quality.

4. **Manufacturing-based**—Manufacturing-based definitions view quality as an outcome of engineering and production processes. According to this approach quality is "conformance to requirements." In other words, how well does the output match the design specifications. For example, if an airline service specifies arrival within fifteen minutes of the schedule, the level of quality in terms of this specification can easily be determined by comparing actual flight arrivals with schedule. The disadvantage of this approach is that, unless specifications are based on customers' needs and preferences, quality becomes an internal issue that helps simplify production control but fails to deliver what customers want.

5. **Value-based**—This approach incorporates value and price into the definition of quality. Quality is defined as a balance between conformance or performance and an acceptable price to the customer.

These different quality definitions represent differences in perspectives of business functions such as marketing, manufacturing, and design. For example, user-based definitions are closest to the marketing viewpoint. Designers, on the other hand, prefer a product-based approach, but manufacturing-based definitions reflect the manufacturing manager's primary concerns.

Finally, here's the formal definition developed jointly by the American National Standards Institute (ANSI) and the American Society for Quality (ASQ): Quality is "*the totality of features and characteristics of a product or service that bears on its ability to satisfy given needs.*"

12.4 Dimensions of Service Quality

Despite the value of the different definitions of quality discussed, managers of service organizations still have a difficult time understanding the exact meaning of service quality. Garvin[3] identified eight dimensions of quality that help develop a more precise understanding of the concept.

1. **Performance**—The basic operating characteristics of a product that can be measured constitute the performance dimension. For example, the number of seconds it takes a car to reach 60 miles per hour can be considered a performance measure for an automobile.

2. **Features**—These are extras or "bells and whistles" that come with the product but normally not part of the standard package in similar products, such as a Global Positioning System (GPS) navigation device and antilock-braking system in a car.

3. **Reliability**—The probability that a product will perform its intended function for a specified period of time under specified environmental conditions, such as the probability that the transmission system will not require a repair for 6 years when maintained according to the manufacturer's guidelines.

4. **Conformance**—The degree to which a product meets design specifications, such as actual number of miles per gallon (mpg) as compared to the mpg design specifications.

5. **Durability**—Durability is the amount of use a consumer gets from the product before it physically deteriorates or continued use becomes uneconomical.

6. **Serviceability**—The ease and speed of repairs and the courtesy of repair personnel.

7. **Aesthetics**—This dimension includes subjective traits such as how a product looks, feels, sounds, and for food items, tastes, or smells.

8. **Perceived quality**—Perceptions that have been formed in the consumer's mind as a result of advertising, brand promotion, word-of-mouth, or personal experience in use.

Although the meaning of the word "product" includes both goods and services, these dimensions seem more easily interpreted or understood for goods. Zeithaml, Parasuraman and Berry[4] identified five dimensions with which consumers judge services:

1. **Reliability**—Reliability in services is defined as the ability to perform the promised service dependably and accurately. It means that the service organization performs the service right the first time and also means that the organization honors all its promises. Some examples include accuracy in billing, keeping records correctly, and completing the service at the promised time.

2. **Responsiveness**—This concerns the willingness or readiness of employees to provide service. It includes timeliness of service such as giving prompt service, mailing a transaction slip immediately, and returning customer calls quickly.

3. **Assurance**—This dimension relates to the knowledge, competence, and courtesy of service employees and their ability to convey trust and confidence. Competence means possession of the required skills and knowledge to perform the service. Courtesy involves politeness, respect, consideration, and friendliness of contact personnel. This dimension also includes trustworthiness, believability, and honesty of service employees.

4. **Empathy**—Empathy is defined as the caring and individualized attention provided to customers. It includes the approachability and ease of contact with the service providers and making the effort to understand the customers and their needs.

5. **Tangibles**—Tangibles include the physical evidence of the service such as physical facilities, appearance of service providers, tools or equipment used to provide the service, physical presentation of the service, and other customers in the service facility.

When Zeithaml, Parasuraman, and Berry asked more than 1,900 customers of five nationally known companies to allocate 100 points across the five service quality dimensions, they averaged as follows: reliability 32 percent, responsiveness 22 percent, assurance 19 percent, empathy 16 percent, and tangibles 11 percent. Then the researchers asked these customers to evaluate the company they had a service experience with. Customers indicated that their service company's most serious shortcoming was lack of reliability. These results seem to indicate that the most important service quality dimension for customers is reliability. This also seems to be where many service companies fail.

It should be noted that some researchers believe these dimensions do not necessarily apply to all services, whereas others conclude that only two of the dimensions are significant.[5] These should be seen as dimensions for services in general. An in-depth understanding of quality in any particular service requires a closer study of its characteristics and what customers expect from the service. However, one should not be surprised to find commonalties among the different sets of quality dimensions for different services. For example, a National Consumer Study on Service Quality in Banking identified the following eight dimensions of quality in bank services:

accessibility, appearance, clarity, competence, courtesy, features, reliability, and responsiveness.[6] When AT&T designed the Military Card, a special calling card service for military personnel (many of whom do not have local service), it identified the following eight dimensions based on customers' needs: reliability, responsiveness, competence, access, courtesy, communications, credibility, and tangibles.

12.5 The Gaps Model of Service Quality

The research project that helped Zeithaml, Parasuraman, and Berry to identify the five service quality dimensions also led them to develop a model of service quality, which is commonly known as the "gaps" model. This model conceptualizes service quality on the basis of the differences between customers' expectations with respect to the five dimensions and their perceptions of what was actually delivered. If a difference exists it is characterized as a "gap." To measure these gaps they developed a 22 item questionnaire called SERVQUAL.

The gaps model and its SERVQUAL instrument is probably the most frequently used approach to discuss and measure service quality. However, this approach also has some risks. One problem is it does not allow the possibility that customers can have low quality expectations.[7] For example, if a customer expected poor quality and got slightly better service from a service organization, we cannot logically characterize the service as quality service. Also, the satisfaction approach to measuring quality runs into difficulty when services high in credence characteristics are evaluated. For example, complex legal or medical services present particular challenges because customers usually don't know what to expect, and even after the service is delivered, they may never know with certainty how good the service was.[8] Another limitation of the gaps model is that it is appropriate for large service organizations. It may not be an accurate representation of service quality in small firms.[9]

Despite these limitations, the gaps model provides valuable insight into understanding challenges of delivering quality service. There have been numerous applications of SERVQUAL as well as criticisms.[10] A graphical representation of the gaps model is given in Exhibit 12-1.[11]

Exhibit 12-1　Service Quality Model

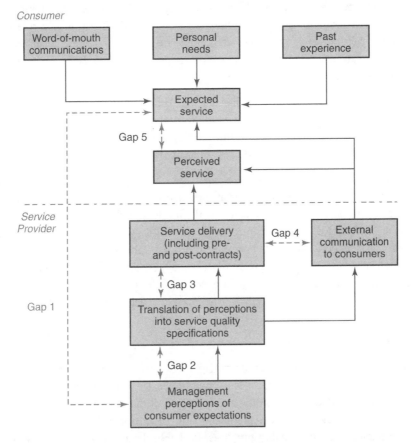

Source: A. Parasuraman, Valarie A. Zeithaml, and Leonard L. Berry, "A Conceptual Model of Service Quality and Its Implications for Future Research," *Journal of Marketing* (Fall 1985), p. 44. Reprinted from *Journal of Marketing*, published by the American Marketing Association.

Gap 1: Not knowing what customers expect—According to the model, the first gap occurs because of the difference between what customers expect and what managers perceive they expect. Major reasons for this gap are a lack of marketing research orientation, evidenced by insufficient marketing research; inadequate use of research findings; and lack of interaction between management and customers. Inadequate upward communication from contact personnel to management and too many levels of management separating contact personnel from top managers are the other two reasons for this gap.

Gap 2: The wrong service quality standards—The difference between what managers think customers expect and the actual specifications they establish for service delivery leads to the second gap. Reasons for the emergence of this gap are inadequate commitment to service quality, lack of perception of feasibility, inadequate task standardization, and absence of goal setting.

Gap 3: The service performance gap—The discrepancy between service specifications and the actual service delivered creates this gap. In general, this gap is created when employees are unable and/or unwilling to perform the service at the desired level. Various reasons are role ambiguity; role conflict, poor employee-job fit, poor technology-job fit, inappropriate supervisory control systems leading to an inappropriate evaluation/compensation system, lack of perceived control on the part of employees, and lack of teamwork.

Gap 4: When promises do not match delivery—The difference between what an organization promises about a service and what it actually delivers is described as Gap 4. Two factors contribute to this gap: (1) inadequate communication among operations, marketing, and human resources, as well as across branches, and (2) propensity to overpromise in communications.

Gap 5: Expected service—perceived service gap. Gaps 1 through 4 contribute to the emergence of Gap 5, which is the difference between what the customer expected to receive from the service and what she believes she actually did receive. As the model in Exhibit 12-1 indicates, customers' perceptions are influenced by many sources, which include word-of-mouth communications, personal needs, past experiences, and communications from the service organization. This is the most important gap because if the perceived service falls short of the customer's expectations, she will be disappointed and dissatisfied. Conversely, if the perceived service exceeds the customer's expectations, she will be not only satisfied, but also delighted.

12.6 Achieving Quality

The American quality revolution that started in the 1980s was to a large extent sparked by Japanese competition. Japanese companies learned the basics of quality from American experience. Quality experts W. Edwards Deming and Joseph M. Juran taught quality to many Japanese managers after World War II. In turn, American quality practitioners learned several things from Japanese companies and their quality practices. Probably the most important lesson was that quality cannot be achieved simply by the mechanical application of a few quality techniques in our factories or service establishments. Creating quality goods and services requires a fundamental change in management philosophy. A second important lesson was that this change cannot be accomplished quickly or easily. It is an endless journey. The third lesson was that we must produce goods and services that are desired by customers, rather than try to sell them what we produce. In other words, we should be customer-focused. This also required a fundamental change in how we design and produce goods and services. We must listen to customers and find out what they need and require.

These observations, combined with the accumulated theoretical and practical knowledge of quality of American industry, led to the development of a new philosophy of management initially known as Total Quality Management (TQM). Although most elements of TQM are not new, the way they are put together and practiced today is considered by many as revolutionary because of the fundamental changes it requires in management philosophy. TQM has evolved from the ideas of many quality experts and practices of highly successful companies in the

United States and Japan, and it will probably continue to evolve in the future as the needs of customers and the realities of the market place change. In this section we briefly review the basic principles of this philosophy.

Focus on Customer Satisfaction

The first and foremost principle of TQM is customer focus, which means meeting and exceeding customer requirements and expectations the first time and every time. This principle must be embraced by all employees and must become part of an organization's culture. It requires systematic and continual inquiry into customer wants and desires, for their requirements and expectations are ever-changing. It must be emphasized that this is quite different from the practice of the past, which pretended to acknowledge the significance of customers with slogans like, "The Customer Is King," but in actuality focused on what managers thought customers needed.

Leadership

Strong and dedicated leadership is one of the prerequisites for successful TQM implementation. Leadership must come from the highest levels of the organization. The leadership needed goes far beyond writing a memo emphasizing the organization's need for quality or hiring a manager to be "in charge" of quality. These approaches don't work. The type of leadership needed is the kind that starts a revolution in the corporate culture; such a leader is actively and personally involved in the implementation of all the TQM principles and provides examples of the desired behavior.

Senior leadership must create clear quality values, policies, strategies, and high expectations. Among these are innovation, risk-taking in trying new ideas, and methods to improve product quality and customer satisfaction, pride in work, employee involvement, and continuous improvement of products, processes, and individuals. Finally, there is a need for change in the way managers do their jobs; managers must shift their focus from directing and controlling to identifying and removing barriers that prevent employees from meeting customer requirements and expectations the first time and every time. Managers must become facilitators.

Commitment to Training and Education: Creating a Learning Organization

A major reason for many quality problems is a lack of proper employee training. In some industries service employees are paid the minimum wage because of the minimum skills required. However, some employees do not have even the basic reading and math skills that are needed for any job. Furthermore, employees also need to be trained in the technical requirements of the job they are performing. Of course, these basics are not enough to guarantee quality service delivery.

Employees also need to be given training in problem solving and the use of continuous improvement tools. The amount and the type of training should be determined according to the nature of the work.

Participation, Empowerment, Teamwork, and Recognition

Top management involvement and leadership are essential for success, however, they alone are not sufficient. TQM succeeds only when it is embraced by the whole organization. Therefore, employee involvement at every level is another vital principle.

Empowerment is giving employees the authority to make and implement decisions and change the environment in which they work. Teamwork is another way employee involvement can be achieved. Teams may be formed to address operational and quality problems. The advantage of this approach is that people who perform the task usually have the best ideas for solving task-related problems. When their suggestions are implemented and problems are eliminated, team members experience the satisfaction of making a contribution to the success of the firm and are motivated to seek continuing improvements.

Whether they are the result of an individual effort or teamwork, achievements in improving quality and customer satisfaction must be recognized and rewarded. Recognition is probably the best way for management to reinforce the new values and practices TQM requires. Rewards do not have to be monetary, but they must be meaningful and timely.

Benchmarking

As discussed in Chapter 8, "Design and Development of Services and Service Delivery Systems," benchmarking is one of the essential methods of determining what to aim for in quality improvements. It helps a service organization determine what is possible in terms of customer satisfaction and quality. Benchmarking does not have to be in one's own industry, it must be global in its scope. The purpose of benchmarking is to determine who is doing the best job in a particular area of interest and learn from the best performer.

Long-Term View and Strategic Approach

It must be clear from the discussion of the TQM principles so far that TQM requires significant changes in an organization's culture. However, the experiences of many large firms indicate that positive results will not be apparent immediately. Hence, an organization on the quality journey needs to take a long-term perspective. This requires strategic thinking and planning on the part of the top management. A strategic plan will identify major tasks to achieve the necessary changes in the organizational culture and the way of doing business. The plan should establish goals and methods for the implementation of TQM. The plan should be updated as the conditions within and outside the organization change.

Management by Fact: Measurement and Analysis

Intuition and experience are two of the most valuable assets of managers. However, intuition and experience alone are not always sufficient for achieving customer satisfaction. To be effective, decisions must be based on facts and results must be measured. Facts can be obtained from data gathered from customers, service delivery processes, and competitors. In other words, a service organization must have a system of collecting and processing relevant data to determine what the customers' requirements are, how well the service design and delivery system conform to these requirements, and the degree with which the services satisfy customers' needs.

Fast Response

The nature of competition, especially in consumer services, has changed in recent decades. It now includes a faster introduction of new services, greater variety, and higher quality and value. Consequently, a service organization must be flexible and agile to respond to changing customer needs and requirements as well as competitive threats.

Continuous Improvement

A fundamental view in TQM is that whatever success a company may have achieved in its quality efforts and competitiveness, it has not reached its destination, for there is no destination to reach. TQM is best understood as a journey with no particular end. However, there is a direction to this journey; it is toward customer satisfaction. The reason why there is no end to the journey is that the needs and expectations of customers are constantly changing, and competition is pushing standards to higher levels; hence, customer satisfaction is a moving target. Another reason is that new services are being introduced at a faster pace in recent years. New products tend to use more advanced technology, offer higher quality and value than existing products, and sometimes make some services obsolete. As an organization gains experience with its existing services and improves their quality, it may also introduce technologically advanced new services, which bring new challenges in quality and customer satisfaction. Consequently, continuous improvement is a natural requirement for superior quality and sustained customer satisfaction.

A few points must be emphasized with regard to TQM. The items previously listed do not constitute a recipe. They are the principles of quality and continuous improvement as expressed as a management philosophy. Implementing them is a strategic issue, but they *all* should be implemented. There is no one right way to implement TQM; each organization must tailor its quality program to its needs according to these principles. Implementation should not be rushed, but it should proceed with determination.

Another strategic issue is the design and development of service and its delivery system. The principles and tools discussed in Chapter 8 must be used for this purpose under the guidance of TQM principles.

12.7 Other Approaches to Achieving Service Quality

This section reviews two other approaches to achieving service quality: ISO standards and the Baldrige Performance Excellence Program.

ISO 9000 Standards

ISO is the acronym for the International Organization for Standardization of Geneva, Switzerland. Founded in 1947, this organization has members from 161 countries. Each country is represented by its national organization. The United States is represented by the American National Standards Institute (ANSI).

ISO International Standards have been developed to ensure that products and services are safe, reliable, and of good quality. Its standards aim to be strategic tools for business to reduce costs by minimizing waste and errors and increase productivity. They help companies to access new markets, level the playing field for developing countries, and facilitate free and fair global trade.[12]

ISO 9000 standards are designed to define and implement management systems by which organizations design, produce, deliver, and support their products. In other words, they are standards for building a management system that ultimately produces quality goods and/or services, but they are not related to any product or technical specifications.

There are many standards in the ISO 9000 family, including

- **ISO 9001:2008**—Sets out the criteria for a quality management system and is the only standard in the family that can be certified to (although this is not a requirement). It can be used by any organization, large or small, regardless of its field of activity.

- **ISO 9000:2005**—Covers the basic concepts and language.

- **ISO 9004:2009**—Focuses on how to make a quality management system more efficient and effective.

- **ISO 19011**—Sets out guidance on internal and external audits of quality management systems.

The standards known as ISO 9000 series have been developed by ISO to achieve uniformity among standards of member countries. The impetus was provided by the globalization of business. The economic unification of Europe under the banner of European Union helped the rapid acceptance of common standards throughout the world. When implemented, these standards serve to eliminate nontariff barriers to international trade that arise from differences among national or company standards. Consequently, ISO 9000 standards tend to facilitate international trade.[13]

ISO quality management standards are based on eight quality principles:[14]

Principle 1: Customer focus—Organizations depend on their customers and therefore should understand current and future customer needs, should meet customer requirements, and should strive to exceed customer expectations.

Principle 2: Leadership—Leaders establish unity of purpose and direction of the organization. They should create and maintain the internal environment in which people can become fully involved in achieving the organization's objectives.

Principle 3: Involvement of people—People at all levels are the essence of an organization and their full involvement enables their abilities to be used for the organization's benefit.

Principle 4: Process approach—A desired result is achieved more efficiently when activities and related resources are managed as a process.

Principle 5: System approach to management—Identifying, understanding, and managing interrelated processes as a system contributes to the organization's effectiveness and efficiency in achieving its objectives.

Principle 6: Continual improvement—Continual improvement of the organization's overall performance should be a permanent objective of the organization.

Principle 7: Factual approach to decision making—Effective decisions are based on the analysis of data and information.

Principle 8: Mutually beneficial supplier relationships—An organization and its suppliers are interdependent, and a mutually beneficial relationship enhances the ability of both to create value.

An organization that adopts one of the ISO standards (ISO 9001 or ISO 14009) may want to be certified by an independent agency as evidence of its compliance with the standards. ISO defines certification as: "the provision by an independent body of written assurance (a certificate) that the product, service or system in question meets specific requirements." Registration is the term used in North America for certification.

Essentially, the ISO standards require that an organization document what it does, do what it documents, review the process, and change it when necessary.

Originally, service organizations did not show much interest in ISO 9000 standards because they were known as standards for manufactured goods. However, competitive pressures led more service organizations to adopt these standards and seek certification. Despite the fact that ISO 9000 standards have a manufacturing flavor, and some aspects of them may not be applicable to services, they can be adopted by service organizations.

The Baldrige Performance Excellence Program

The Malcolm Baldrige National Quality Award was created by Public Law 100-107, signed into law on August 20, 1987. In 2010, the program was renamed the Baldrige Performance Excellence Program to reflect the evolution of the field of quality from a focus on product, service, and customer quality to a broader, strategic focus on overall organizational quality.[15] The Award Program led to the creation of a new public-private partnership. Principal support for the program comes from the Foundation for the Malcolm Baldrige National Quality Award, established in 1988. National Institute of Standards and Technology (NIST) of the Department of Commerce manages the award program with the assistance of the American Society for Quality (ASQ).

The Baldrige Program

- Raises awareness about the importance of performance excellence in driving the U.S. and global economy
- Provides organizational assessment tools and criteria
- Educates leaders in businesses, schools, health care organizations, and government and nonprofit agencies about the practices of best-in-class organizations
- Recognizes national role models and honors them with the only Presidential Award for performance excellence

Mission

To improve the competitiveness and performance of U.S. organizations for the benefit of all U.S. residents, the Baldrige Performance Excellence Program is a customer-focused federal change agent that

- Develops and disseminates evaluation criteria
- Manages the Malcolm Baldrige National Quality Award
- Promotes performance excellence
- Provides global leadership in the learning and sharing of successful strategies and performance practices, principles, and methodologies

Vision

To be the partner of choice for excellence in every sector of the economy.

Core Values

- Deliver a consistently positive customer experience
- Value and empower our workforce
- Think and act ethically
- Think and act strategically[16]

Originally the Malcolm Baldrige National Quality Award (MBNQA) was given to for-profit businesses in three categories: manufacturing, services, and small business; a maximum of two awards were given in each category. However, the award program has been expanded and awards are given in healthcare and education organizations (in 1999) and to nonprofit/government organizations (in 2005) in addition to the original categories.

The maximum number of awards in each category is currently three.

The Baldrige Award has had a positive effect on many American companies as well as government and private nonprofit organizations. Participants have shown significant improvements in productivity, employee relationships, market share, and profitability. The sound principles and criteria of the program help organizations develop systems, processes, and a management philosophy for producing superior quality goods and services. Many states have established their own quality award programs based on Baldrige criteria. In addition to the general service category, the expansion of eligibility to nonprofit and for-profit educational organizations and healthcare providers creates a greater opportunity for service organizations to improve their services and create more value for their customers by adopting the Baldrige criteria and competing for the award.

12.8 Reinforcing Quality Service

On several occasions throughout this book, the importance of keeping customers has been emphasized; that is the question of customer loyalty. This section discusses two measures a service organization should take to achieve customer loyalty and reinforce its overall quality efforts.

Service Recovery

Even the best service organizations experience service failures once in a while. Inexperienced or rude service employees, equipment breakdowns, power system failures, flight cancellations, and late delivery by a vendor are just some examples of how a service organization may experience failures. Whether the organization is responsible for the failure, it is crucial that it take the necessary steps to solve the problem and restore the service. If that is not possible, it should at least make it less inconvenient for the customers.

Some service failures may occur during the delivery and are obvious to managers and service providers, but some failures may go unnoticed. Some customers may later complain and bring the service failure to the attention of management. Whenever such failure may be discovered, the service organization must act quickly and decisively and resolve the problem as soon as possible to the customer's satisfaction. Failing to do so means a second failure in the service delivery and will probably lead to the loss of that customer. Resolving the problem quickly and to the customer's satisfaction usually means winning that customer's business for the long term.

Customer complaints must be considered as "opportunities" for winning customer loyalty because there is evidence that a well-handled service failure may ensure the loyalty of many customers. Kent C. Nelson, former chairman and chief operating officer of United Parcel Service (UPS), reaches the same conclusion as a result of a service recovery effort undertaken by his organization:

> One of our customers is the chairman of several Midwestern banks...an avid map collector. He owns many rare and valuable maps, and collects maps that will increase in value over time. Some time ago, he got the idea of sending a die-cut map of the lunar surface to each of the nine astronauts who had walked on the moon, asking them to sign at the spot where they had walked. Over the course of many months, he gathered all of their signatures, ending with Neil Armstrong, who signed it in Las Vegas. It was now one of a kind, and very valuable.
>
> The finished map was shipped from Las Vegas to the bank chairman. It was shipped via UPS. The map never arrived. The banker was devastated. We were embarrassed.
>
> It was one of our customer service managers who decided that the only way to satisfy their customer would be to duplicate the map. He bought a die-cut map of the lunar surface and sent it around to the business development managers in each UPS district where one of the nine astronauts lived. Over the course of several weeks, we obtained each of their signatures and delivered the finished map to the customer. He was delighted. And impressed. And completely satisfied. In fact, I think he was more satisfied by what we did to make up for our mistake than he would have been if the original map had been routinely delivered.[17]

Recovering from service failures does not happen automatically; an organization must carefully prepare for it. Hart, Heskett, and Sasser recommend the following approach:[18]

1. **Measure the costs**—The old adage "What gets measured gets managed" is the principle here. Service failures have costs both to the customer and the service organization. Some of the costs customers incur include time and money they spend in writing letters or calls to the organization, and the anguish they feel. The organization may have to give a refund or repeat the service and in extreme cases may have to face a lawsuit and punitive damages that may result from it. Probably the most important cost is the permanent loss of the customer. Most managers underestimate the costs of service failures. When they understand the magnitude of their losses, they are more likely to focus on prevention measures.

2. **Break the silence and listen closely for complaints**—It is well known that many customers do not complain if they are not happy with a good or service. Among the most frequently given reasons researchers found are

- It's not worth the time or effort.

- No one would be concerned with my problem or interested in acting on it.

- Don't know where to go or what to do.

Clearly, if a service organization does not know about service failures, it will not do anything about them. Hence, it is important that customers are encouraged to complain when they are not satisfied with the service. There are many ways to hear the customer's voice. Some organizations have 800 numbers for complaints and questions, whereas others offer rewards for suggestions. Regular surveys, focus groups, and interviews of lost customers are additional ways of uncovering service problems. Another way organizations can find out about customer complaints as well as praise is the Internet. Many companies selling on the Internet post comments from their customers on products they sell or services they provide.

3. **Anticipate needs for recovery**—Managers who understand the service and its delivery system can anticipate where failures may occur and can make plans for recovery. In Chapter 8 it was recommended that service process and the delivery system be represented by a blueprint on which the failure points are indicated. A plan and a procedure for each potential failure must be developed and employees must be trained in these procedures.

4. **Act fast**—A service organization that acts quickly to correct the situation will probably impress the customer and make him forget the incident. Long, drawn-out processes and weeks of waiting are not going to make the customer forget the failure easily even if it is eventually resolved satisfactorily.

5. **Train employees**—Effective service recovery is not possible if the employees who handle complaints are not prepared for occasional service failures. Preparation involves training and empowerment. Employees who know what to do in response to various types of service failures and who are authorized to take corrective measures quickly are indispensable for effective recovery. Training should include developing good communication skills, creative thinking, quick decision making, and developing an awareness of customers' concerns. One of the most effective training methods is simulated situations and role playing.

6. **Empower the front-line**—Quick and decisive action to remedy a service failure is not possible without empowered employees. If employees have to check the rule book and seek authorization from a supervisor every time they have to handle a complaint, recovery will neither be quick nor satisfactory in customers' eyes. In addition, employee enthusiasm in solving customers' problems will quickly diminish. Many rules and limits on authority are established because of a fear that employees will "give away the store." However, this will not happen with a well-trained and motivated employee, but losing a customer is more likely to happen when her problem is not solved.

7. **Close the loop**—Recovery and complaint handling must be brought to a closure. If the condition that led to the problem cannot be remedied, the customer must be given an explanation. If the complaint leads to a change in the service and/or the delivery system, the customer should be told so. Other ways of effectively closing the loop include asking the customer for suggestions and letting him know what is being done with his suggestions.

Service Guarantees

An effective way to improve the quality image of a service organization in the eyes of its customers and improve service quality is to offer service guarantees, especially unconditional ones. Most service guarantees have financial consequences for the organization. If the organization cannot deliver what it promised, there will be an immediate financial loss, such as refunding customers' money. This makes the cost of poor quality unbearable.[19] Consequently, when they are done right, service guarantees will help an organization focus on delivering superior quality service. Only a few service companies offer unconditional service guarantees, but their number will be increasing in the future because of competition and because there are good reasons for offering them. Christopher Hart[20] identifies five reasons for service guarantees:

1. **A guarantee forces you to focus on customers**—Guaranteeing something customers don't want or value is not meaningful, and worse it may just backfire. Therefore, a service organization has to find out first what its customers want in a service.

2. **A guarantee sets clear standards**—A meaningful service guarantee must be unambiguous and clear, such as FedEx's delivery promise "absolutely, positively by 10:30." Such clear promises also force the organization to clearly identify the service expectations for its employees, and they in turn, know what to shoot for.

3. **A guarantee generates feedback**—When an organization fails to satisfy a customer, it does not necessarily hear from her as indicated in the previous section. In addition to the reasons given earlier, because services are intangible, customers lack evidence for their complaints and many may not know what the standards are. (Is 45 minutes too long for pizza delivery?) When customers don't complain the service organization gets no feedback. A service guarantee significantly increases the chances of hearing from its customers when something goes wrong. The feedback as well as payouts to customers provide invaluable data for quality improvement efforts.

4. **A guarantee forces you to understand why you fail**—Data about failures and their costs forces management to look for causes in the way the service and its delivery system is designed and/or employees are selected and trained. Finding the causes of poor quality and eliminating them is the best way to improve quality.

5. **A guarantee builds marketing muscle**—When they are done right, an organization will attract new customers and keep existing ones by offering service guarantees. Especially

in services about which customers do not have much knowledge, such as auto repair, existence of a guarantee gives most customers peace of mind and provides a good reason for selecting that organization for the service.

Another benefit is that service guarantees level the field for customers in their relationship with a service provider. Services are intangible and many are hard to evaluate before the actual experience, and some even after they have been delivered. Because of this, customers of some services feel they are at a disadvantage in their relationship with the service organization. Service guarantees play the role of an equalizer and help the organization demonstrate its fairness.[21]

For these benefits to accrue to the service organization, a service guarantee must meet five criteria:[22]

1. **Unconditional**—A guarantee with conditions loses its power and attractiveness to customers. The best service guarantee is without any conditions, such as the one by L. L. Bean, which guarantees 100 percent satisfaction, no strings attached. L. L. Bean, the Freeport, Maine retailer, probably has the ultimate in guarantees. Its customers can return any merchandise any time and get a refund, credit or replacement (Exhibit 12-2).

Exhibit 12-2   L. L. Bean's Guarantee Statement[23]

Guaranteed to Last

Our products are guaranteed to give 100% satisfaction in every way. Return anything purchased from us at any time if it proves otherwise. We do not want you to have anything from L. L. Bean that is not completely satisfactory.

---

2. **Easy to understand and communicate**—A guarantee should not look like a legal document. It should be simply worded and easy to understand by any customer. "Delivery by 10:30, or your money back" rather than "Prompt delivery" leaves no doubt as to what is guaranteed.

3. **Meaningful**—A guarantee must promise what is important to the customer. A promise of error free bank statement is probably more meaningful than a promise to deliver them before the end of each month. A guarantee must also be meaningful financially. If it promises a payout when the customer is not satisfied, the payout must be in proportion with the cost of the service and the inconvenience to the customer.

4. **Easy to invoke**—If a service guarantee requires the customer to jump through many hoops to invoke it, it loses all its advantages and probably makes an already unhappy customer even more unhappy, or angry.

5. **Easy to collect**—A customer invoking a guarantee should not have to wait too long or go to different units of the organization to collect a payout. The best way for a payout is on the spot, if possible, or automatic credit.

12.9 Summary

Service quality and customer satisfaction are closely related. Satisfaction is a likely outcome when customers perceive they have received superior quality service. Superior quality also leads to higher customer and employee loyalty, higher market share, higher returns to investors, lower costs, and lower sensitivity to price competition. Even a single one of these reasons is sufficient motivation for a service organization to seek quality and continuous improvement.

In this chapter various definitions of quality were reviewed. We pointed out that each one of these definitions, in addition to representing the viewpoint of different organizational areas, makes a valuable contribution to our understanding of the meaning of quality and related issues.

A definition of quality, however useful it might be, is never sufficient to guide managerial action for customer satisfaction. Managers need to understand what quality means to customers and what characteristics are perceived to contribute to the quality of a service. In other words, managers need to understand the dimensions of quality. We reviewed various approaches to defining the dimensions of service quality. One set of dimensions (reliability, responsiveness, assurance, empathy, and tangibles) may serve well for most services as a generic set, but articulation of additional dimensions for a proper understanding of quality may be needed when closer attention is paid to a particular service. The gaps model is another device to guide managers in delivering high-quality service. This model conceptualizes service quality on the basis of the differences between customers' expectations with respect to the five dimensions and their perceptions of what was actually delivered.

Achieving quality is not a matter of using a particular method or technique; it requires a change in the philosophy of management and organizational culture. Total Quality Management has been developed through the 1980s and 1990s to meet that need of American manufacturing and service organizations. Its principles form a whole new approach to managing and require a long-term commitment from both management and employees.

Even the best service organizations occasionally experience failures in their service delivery. Most customers will forgive these mishaps if the organization manages to solve the problem quickly. Actually, some service organizations manage to win lifelong customers when they masterfully recover from failures. Every service organization must have a recovery system and must train its employees for such emergencies.

An increasing number of service organizations offer unconditional service guarantees to their customers. The last section of this chapter reviewed the reasons why service guarantees make sense for many service organizations. The characteristics of effective service guarantees were also discussed.

Endnotes

1. Albert N. Link and John T. Scott, "Planning Report 11-2, Economic Evaluation of the Baldrige Performance Excellence Program," National Institute of Standards, U.S. Department of Commerce (December 16, 2011).

2. The discussion of the five perspectives has been adapted from David A. Garvin, *Managing Quality* (New York, NY: The Free Press, 1988), pp. 40–46.

3. David A. Garvin, "Competing on the Eight Dimensions of Quality," *Harvard Business Review* (November–December 1987), pp. 101–109.

4. The discussion of the five dimensions has been adapted from Valarie A. Zeithaml, A. Parasuraman, and Leonard L. Berry, *Delivering Quality Service: Balancing Customer Perceptions and Expectations* (New York, NY: The Free Press, 1990), pp. 15–33.

5. See, for example, Emin Babakus and Gregory W. Boller, "An Empirical Assessment of the SERVQUAL Scale," *Journal of Business Research*, Vol. 24 (May 1992), pp. 253–268; James M. Carman, "Consumer Perceptions of Service Quality: An Assessment of the SERVQUAL Dimensions," *Journal of Retailing*, Vol. 66 (Spring 1990), pp. 33–35; and Gerhard Mels, Christo Boshoff, and Deon Nel, "The Dimensions of Service Quality: The Original European Perspective Revisited," *The Service Industries Journal*, Vol. 17, No. 1 (January 1997), pp. 173–189.

6. Penny Lunt, "Just What, Exactly, Is Quality Service?" *ABA Banking Journal* (June 1992), pp. 78–81.

7. Richard L. Oliver, "A Conceptual Model of Service Quality and Service Satisfaction: Compatible Goals, Different Concepts," in T. A. Swartz, D. E. Bowen, and S. W. Brown, (Eds.) *Advances in Services Marketing and Management: Research and Practice* (Greenwich, Connecticut: JAI Press Inc.), Vol. 2, 1993, pp. 65–-85.

8. Christopher H. Lovelock, *Services Marketing*, Fourth Edition (Upper Saddle River, NJ: Prentice-Hall, 2001), p. 364. Also see Christopher H. Lovelock and Jochen Wirtz, *Services Marketing*, Seventh Edition (Upper Saddle River, NJ: Prentice-Hall, 2011), p. 408.

9. See, for example, Cengiz Haksever, Ronald G. Cook, and Radha Chaganti, "Applicability of the Gaps Model to Service Quality in Small Firms," *Journal of Small Business Strategy*, Vol. 8, No. 1 (Spring 1997), pp. 49–66.

10. For a review of applications and criticisms of SERVQUAL see, Riadh Ladhari, "A Review of Twenty Years of SERVQUAL Research," *International Journal of Quality and Service Sciences*, Vol. 1 No. 2 (2009), pp. 172–198.

11. The discussion of the gaps model is adapted from Valarie A. Zeithaml, A. Parasuraman, and Leonard L. Berry, *Delivering Quality Service: Balancing Customer Perceptions and Expectations* (New York, NY: The Free Press, 1990), pp. 51–133.

12. About ISO: http://www.iso.org/iso/iso_9000/ (08/09/2012).

13. Donald W. Marquardt, "Background and Development of ISO 9000 Standards," in Robert W. Peach (Ed.), *The ISO 9000 Handbook*, Third Edition (Chicago, Irwin, 1997), pp. 9–30.

14. This section consists of excerpts from ISO's Quality Management Principles, http://www.iso.org/iso/qmp_2012.pdf (08/09/2012).

15. Wikipedia, "Malcolm Baldrige National Quality Award," http://en.wikipedia.org/wiki/Malcolm_Baldrige_National_Quality_Award (08/10/2012).

16. http://www.nist.gov/baldrige/about/index.cfm (08/09/2012).

17. Kent C. Nelson, "Quality in a Service Organization: Beyond Grand Gestures," Executive Speeches (August–September 1995), pp. 11–14.

18. Christopher W. L. Hart, James L. Heskett, and W. Earl Sasser, "The Profitable Art of Service Recovery," *Harvard Business Review* (July–August 1990), pp. 148–156.

19. Christopher W. L. Hart, *Extraordinary Guarantees* (New York, NY: American Management Association, 1993), p. 17.

20. Christopher W. L. Hart, "The Power of Unconditional Service Guarantees," *Harvard Business Review* (July–August 1988), pp. 54–62.

21. Leonard L. Berry, A. Parasuraman and Valarie A. Zeithaml, "Improving Service Quality in America: Lessons Learned," *Academy of Management Executive*, Vol. 8, No. 2 (1994), pp. 32–52.

22. These criteria are adapted from C. W. L. Hart, "The Power of Unconditional Service Guarantees."

23. From L. L. Bean company website: http://www.llbean.com/customerService/aboutLLBean/company_values.html?nav=s1-ln (08/10/2012).

12 Supplement
TOOLS AND TECHNIQUES OF TOTAL QUALITY MANAGEMENT

S12.1 Introduction

Implementing Total Quality Management (TQM) requires a long-term commitment by the management and hard work. As indicated in Chapter 12, "Service Quality and Continuous Improvement," there is no recipe, or one "right way" to implement TQM. Each organization must develop its own model that responds to its needs and supports its strategy. However, there exist a variety of effective tools and techniques we can rely on for successful implementation of TQM. In this supplement some of the most widely used tools and techniques are reviewed.

S12.2 Plan-Do-Study-Act Cycle

The conceptual basis for most TQM processes is what is known as **Shewhart**, or the **plan-do-study-act (PDSA) cycle** (Exhibit S12-1).

Exhibit S12-1   The Shewhart (PDSA) Cycle

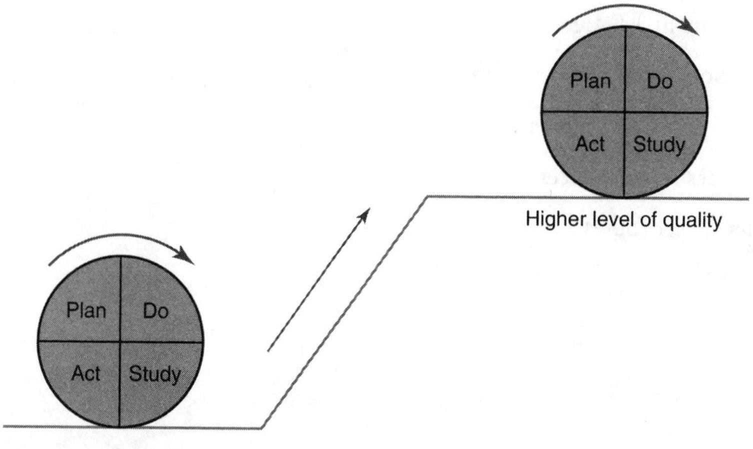

Higher level of quality

Plan—The first step of the process is to collect data and study the problem to be solved or process to be improved. This is needed to develop an in-depth understanding of the problem. Next, develop a plan for the solution of the problem or for improvement in the current situation. Then set goals and develop criteria to measure success.

Do—Implement the plan in a laboratory setting or on a small scale (for example, in a branch, or small unit of the organization). Collect data on the results of the implementation.

Study—Evaluate the data and study the results in light of criteria to determine if the objectives have been achieved.

Act—If the small scale implementation created the desired results, standardize the solution and implement it in the whole system. If the results do not meet the success criteria, revise the plan and repeat the process. If the plan is successful, the new improvement cycle starts at the new level, which has become the standard. The cycle is continuous.

S12.3 Tools of TQM

A number of simple but effective graphical tools have been developed through the years for improvement of quality in manufacturing. Most of them are simple and straightforward, so practically anyone can learn and use them. They are equally effective for quality improvement efforts in services. Their simplicity and flexibility give them their worldwide appeal. This section reviews seven of these tools, which are sometimes called the "magnificent seven."

Histograms—Histograms are graphical tools to represent data summaries. Large data sets can be summarized into frequency distributions for detecting patterns, central tendencies, and variability, as well as for further processing. Histograms for variables can be constructed from frequency distributions, or for attribute data, such as complaint categories, from check sheets. Exhibit S12-2 shows two histograms of the time required by different airlines to clean a particular aircraft and prepare it for the next flight. From the histograms we can tell that the variation of Company A's service is smaller than Company B's. Possible reasons are

- A's equipment is better
- A's employees have had more thorough training
- A's procedures are more effective
- A provides fewer services
- A offers fewer routes

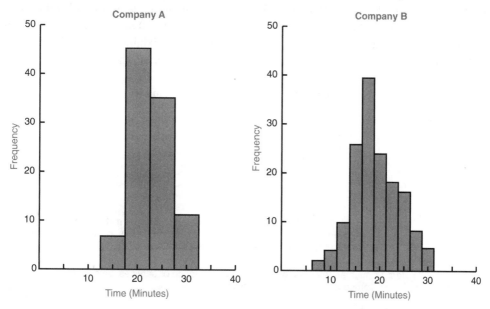

Now that we have identified that Company B has a problem with service variability, we can investigate the possible causes with a cause-and-effect diagram or collect more data using check sheets.

Flowcharts—Flowcharts are diagrams consisting of pictorial symbols connected by directed line segments. Their purpose is to show the sequencing of activities, operations, tasks, materials flow, data/information flow, people movement, logic flow, or authority flow in organizations. They are useful in designing and describing services and processes. The service blueprint, discussed in Chapter 8, "Design and Development of Services and Service Delivery Systems," is just one example of flowcharts. Various types of flowcharts exist. One of the most frequently used flowcharts is the process flowchart. These charts are useful in quality improvement efforts because they help us develop a better understanding of the process we are trying to improve.

The flow process chart is the primary tool for developing and describing a system that converts inputs into goods and services. It provides two essential types of information about the conversion process: (1) the actions performed on materials, information, or people in providing the service and (2) the relationships among processes. Relationships refer to the order in which actions are performed, what processes have to be performed first, which can be performed in parallel, and what has to be completed before the next step can begin.

For flow process charts, five standardized pictorial symbols are used to describe the processes. These are operations, transportation, inspection, storage, and delay, as shown in Exhibit S12-3. The chart can track the flow of products, customers, or information. An example of a flow process chart for mortgage application and approval is given in Exhibit S12-4. In this example, the flows of information and paperwork for a particular customer are charted.

Exhibit S12-3   Flow Process Chart Symbols

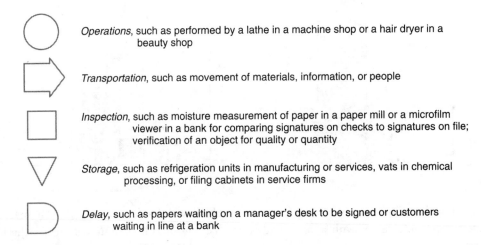

Operations, such as performed by a lathe in a machine shop or a hair dryer in a beauty shop

Transportation, such as movement of materials, information, or people

Inspection, such as moisture measurement of paper in a paper mill or a microfilm viewer in a bank for comparing signatures on checks to signatures on file; verification of an object for quality or quantity

Storage, such as refrigeration units in manufacturing or services, vats in chemical processing, or filing cabinets in service firms

Delay, such as papers waiting on a manager's desk to be signed or customers waiting in line at a bank

Flow process charts often include data on the distance a customer or item is moved, the time required to process a customer or item, and the time a customer or item spends waiting. This additional information helps managers to analyze the efficiency of a specified order of operations. Hopefully, tasks can be identified that should be eliminated, combined, resequenced, or simplified. Often the flow process chart is also superimposed on a floor plan of a facility as an aid to improving facility layout and eliminating bottlenecks.

Exhibit S12-4 Flow Process Chart for Mortgage Application and Approval

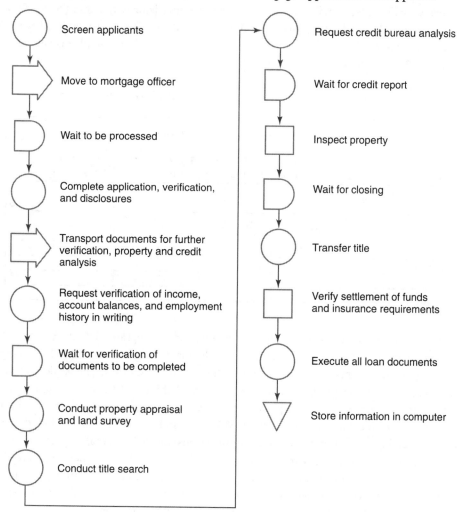

Screen applicants

Move to mortgage officer

Wait to be processed

Complete application, verification, and disclosures

Transport documents for further verification, property and credit analysis

Request verification of income, account balances, and employment history in writing

Wait for verification of documents to be completed

Conduct property appraisal and land survey

Conduct title search

Request credit bureau analysis

Wait for credit report

Inspect property

Wait for closing

Transfer title

Verify settlement of funds and insurance requirements

Execute all loan documents

Store information in computer

Check sheets—A check sheet is a simple tool for collecting data about problems or complaints. Check sheets are designed to make data collection and summarizing easy. Exhibit S12-5 shows a check sheet designed for collecting data on complaints about a pizza delivery service. The exhibit also contains hypothetical data for one day. A logical next step in this example may be the construction of a Pareto diagram as discussed next.

Exhibit S12-5   Check Sheet for Complaints About a Pizza Delivery Service

				TYPE OF COMPLAINT				
		Delivery Took Too Long	Cold Pizza	Wrong Topping	Wrong Size	Underbaked Pizza	Overbaked Pizza	TOTAL
DAY	TIME							
M	4–5 P.M.			///	/	卌		9
	5–6	/	//	/			/	5
	6–7	卌	/	///		///		12
	7–8	//		/		//		5
	8–9			//				2
	9–10							0
	10–11 P.M.	///		//	/	卌		11
	TOTAL	11	3	12	2	15	1	44

Pareto diagrams—A Pareto diagram is an ordered form of a histogram that attempts to isolate the few dominant factors affecting a situation from the many insignificant ones. The rectangles of the histogram are arranged from the tallest on the left to the shortest. The vertical axis may represent frequencies or relative frequencies (percentages). Exhibit S12-6 shows a Pareto diagram that continues the pizza delivery example and indicates the number of complaints in each category as obtained from column totals in Exhibit S12-5. As can be seen from the exhibit, the most frequently occurring complaint, therefore the most serious one, is "underbaked pizza." The next most frequent two categories are "wrong topping" and "delivery time." The other three categories of complaints seem less serious compared to these three. This fact has been emphasized by the ordering of the rectangles representing the frequency of complaints. A quality improvement team would normally first focus and try to solve the most serious problem.

Scatter diagrams—Scatter diagrams are used to provide a quick check if a relationship exists between two variables. For example, a quality improvement team may want to know if the number of underbaked pizza complaints is related to the number of orders per day. In this case, number of orders per day may be represented on the horizontal axis and the number of complaints on the vertical axis. If a scatter diagram indicates a relationship, a formal model may be developed using regression techniques (see Exhibit S12-7).

Exhibit S12-6 Pareto Chart for Complaints About a Pizza Delivery Service

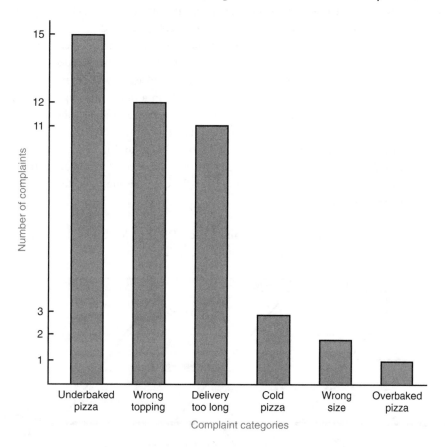

Exhibit S12-7 Scatter Diagram for the Complaints About Pizza Delivery Service

Cause-and-effect diagrams—Developed by the Japanese quality expert Kaoru Ishikawa, these diagrams are also called **fishbone diagrams**. They are effective tools that help quality improvement efforts to focus on finding the causes of a selected problem. The diagram has a center line, or the "spine," which leads to the "effect" or the problem, and a few major categories of possible causes connected to the spine. Causes for most quality problems can be grouped in general categories such as personnel, equipment, methods, materials, processes, and environment, or categories specific to the problem may be used. Then, usually in a brainstorming session, possible subcauses and their subcauses, and so on in each category are identified. At the end of the session, each item in the diagram is examined and eliminated if it is not a factor that contributes to the problem. The remaining causes are examined more closely, and if a link is found between them and the "effect," the quality improvement effort is directed at eliminating them. As an example refer to Exhibit S12-8, which was developed for determining the causes of passengers' dissatisfaction with air travel.

Exhibit S12-8 Ishikawa (Cause-and-Effect) Diagram for Understanding
Airline Passenger Complaints

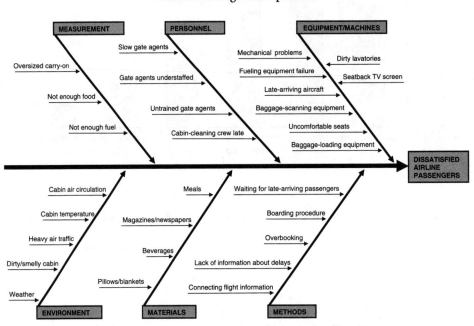

Control charts—Control charts are statistical graphical devices that are used to monitor the performance of a manufacturing or service process over time. Because of this process focus, they are also called **process control charts**. A control chart has a center line, and an upper and a lower limit. The center line represents the long term process average. Control limits are determined so that any sample data point that is above the upper limit or below the lower limit is a possible indication of the process being out of control, or not performing satisfactorily. If the data point falls between the two limits, it is concluded that the process in is statistical control, or performing satisfactorily. The control chart is one of the most important tools for quality and continuous improvement efforts. For this reason we present a more detailed discussion of this tool in the next section.

S12.4 Process Control Charts

In many cases, production and consumption of a service occur simultaneously. This leaves little opportunity for the service provider to test or inspect the quality of the service before it is delivered to the customer. That is why the importance of service design and its delivery system was emphasized in many places in this book, especially in Chapter 8. Also in the same chapter, and in many other occasions, the crucial role service employees play in achieving service quality and customer satisfaction was emphasized. Achieving quality and customer satisfaction in services is different; it has to start with the design of the service and its delivery system with selecting and hiring the right people. Hiring the right people is just one step; you have to give them all the necessary training and preparation and then empower them to do their best for customers.

All these advance a service organization a considerable distance on the road to quality and customer satisfaction. However, there is still much more to be done on the technical side to complement these efforts. Many services involve manufacturing-like activities and processes, such as check clearing operations in a bank, preparation and mailing of bank statements, cooking and assembling meals in a fast food restaurant, performing tests on blood samples in a medical lab, processing insurance claims, and enplaning and deplaning passengers of an airline. Many of these processes, but not all, take place in the back room and out of sight. Regardless of where they are performed, they are an essential part of the delivery system and without them quality service is not possible.

Because of their manufacturing-like nature, outputs of these activities and processes can be measured, standardized, and controlled. Process control charts are effective in such settings for monitoring conformance to standards. Output data in services may be in one of three types:

- **Measurable data**, such as time spent in a service or time spent waiting for service

- **Percentages**, such as the percent of goods damaged or the percent of customers complaining

- **Counting data**, such as the number of typos in a report or the number of mistakes in an insurance claim

The first type is used when the output is a variable (a measurable characteristic of a service process), and the other two are used when the output is an attribute (a characteristic a service performance may or may not possess). In this section, control charts for each one of these data types are presented and discussed.

Normally, there is some degree of variation in all processes. A control chart that appears to be in control implies that variations in samples of the outcome of a service process taken over time are, for the most part, random, due to common causes. In building control charts, averages of small service samples (often of five accounts or customers or daily averages) are used, as opposed to data on individual service encounters. Individual measurements tend to be too erratic to make trends quickly visible. The purpose of control charts is to help distinguish between natural (random) variations and variations due to assignable causes. **Random variations** affect almost every service process to some degree and are to be expected. As long as output precision remains within specified limits, this fact of life can be tolerated.

Assignable variation in a service process can usually be traced to a specific reason. Factors such as misadjusted equipment, fatigued or untrained employees, or new procedures, are all typical sources of assignable variations. Control charts identify when a problem is occurring and help the employee pinpoint where a problem may lie.

Control Charts for Variables

Two types of control charts, one for the sample mean ($\bar{X}$) and another for the range (R), are used to monitor processes that are measured in continuous units. For example, these control charts may monitor the time that it takes to serve a customer or the length of time that a customer waits before being served. The $\bar{X}$ (X-bar) chart would tell us whether significant changes have occurred in the average service time or waiting time. The R-chart values would indicate the amount of variability in service time or waiting time customers experience. The two charts go hand in hand when monitoring variables.

$\bar{X}$ Charts

The theoretical foundation for $\bar{X}$ charts is the **central limit theorem.** In general terms, this theorem states that regardless of the distribution of the population of all parts or services, the distribution of $\bar{X}$s (each of which is a mean of a sample drawn from the population) will tend to follow a normal curve as the sample size grows large. And fortunately, even if n is fairly small (say 4 or 5), the distributions of the averages will still roughly follow a normal curve. It is also known that (1) the mean of the distribution of the $\bar{X}$s (called $\bar{\bar{X}}$) will equal the mean of the overall population (which is called μ), and (2) the standard deviation of the sampling distribution $\sigma_{\bar{x}}$ will be the population standard deviation σ_x divided by the square root of the sample size n, when all possible samples of size n is taken, or when sampling is repeated for a very large number of times. In other words,

$$\bar{\bar{X}} = \mu \text{ and } \sigma_{\bar{x}} = \frac{\sigma_x}{\sqrt{n}}$$

(S12.1)

Exhibit S12-9 shows three possible population distributions, each with its own mean μ and standard deviation σ_x. If a series of random samples ($\bar{X}_1, \bar{X}_2, \bar{X}_3, \bar{X}_4$, and so on) each of size n is drawn from any of these populations, the resulting distribution of $\bar{X}_i$ will appear as in the bottom graph of the exhibit. Because this is a normal distribution, we can state that if the process has only random variations

1. 99.7 percent of the time the sample averages will fall within $\pm 3\,\sigma_{\bar{x}}$.

2. 95.5 percent of the time the sample averages will fall within $\pm 2\,\sigma_{\bar{x}}$.

In other words, if a point on the control chart falls outside of the $\pm 3\,\sigma_{\bar{x}}$ control limits, then we are 99.7 percent confident that the process has changed. Similarly, if a point on the control charts falls outside of the $\pm 2\,\sigma_{\bar{x}}$ control limits, we are 95.5 percent sure that the process has changed. This is the theory behind control charts.

Exhibit S12-9   Population and Sampling Distributions

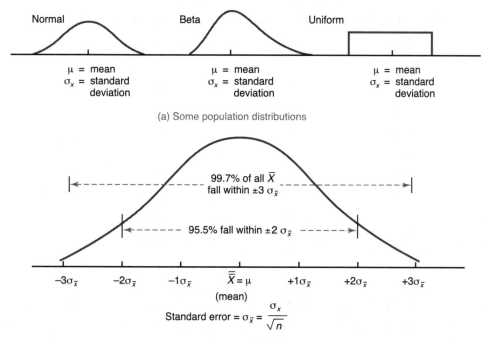

(a) Some population distributions

(b) Sampling distribution of sample means (approaches normal as sample size increases)

In practice, the standard deviation of the service process may be difficult to determine, but it can be estimated by the **range** of the service process. The range is the difference between the highest and lowest measurement in a sample.

An $\bar{X}$ *chart* is simply a plot of the means of the samples taken of a process. $\bar{\bar{X}}$ is the average of about 25–50 sample means. To set upper and lower control limits for the $\bar{X}$ chart, use the following formulas:

$$\text{UCL}_{\bar{x}} = \bar{\bar{X}} + A_2\bar{R} \quad \text{and} \quad \text{LCL}_{\bar{x}} = \bar{\bar{X}} - A_2\bar{R}$$

where

$\bar{\bar{X}}$ = the average of the sample means.

$\bar{R}$ = the average range of samples.

A_2 = a constant factor that depends on the sample size (see Exhibit S12-10).

$UCL_{\bar{x}}$ = upper control limit for the mean.

$LCL_{\bar{x}}$ = lower control limit for the mean.

$A_2\bar{R}$ = provides an estimate of $3\,\sigma_{\bar{x}}$.

Exhibit S12-10   Control Limit Factors

Sample Size n	A_2 (Mean Factor)	D_3 (Upper-Range Factor)	D_4 (Lower-Range Factor)
2	1.880	3.267	0
3	1.023	2.574	0
4	0.729	2.282	0
5	0.577	2.114	0
6	0.483	2.004	0
7	0.419	1.924	0.076
8	0.373	1.864	0.136
9	0.337	1.816	0.184
10	0.308	1.777	0.223
11	0.285	1.744	0.256
12	0.266	1.717	0.283
13	0.249	1.693	0.307
14	0.235	1.672	0.328
15	0.223	1.653	0.347
20	0.180	1.585	0.415
25	0.153	1.541	0.459

$\bar{R}$ Charts

In addition to being concerned with the process average, managers are interested in the process variability. Even though the process average is under control, the variability of the process may not be. The theory behind control charts for ranges is the same as for the process average. Limits are established that contain ± 3 standard deviations of the distribution for the average range $\bar{R}$. With a few simplifying assumptions, you can set the upper and lower control limits for ranges as follows:

$$UCL_R = D_4\bar{R} \quad \text{and} \quad LCL_R = D_3\bar{R}$$

where

UCL_R = upper control limit for the range.

LCL_R = lower control limit for the range.

D_3 and D_4 = values from Exhibit S12-10.

Mail-order business example: A mail-ordering business wants to measure the response time of their operators in taking customer orders over the phone. Listed next is the time recorded in minutes from five different samples of the ordering process with four customer orders per sample. We will construct three standard deviation $\bar{X}$ and R control charts for this process and determine if any points are out of control.

Sample	Observations	Sample Average $\bar{X}$	Sample Range R
1	5 3 6 10	24/4 = 6	10 – 3 = 7
2	7 5 3 5	20/4 = 5	7 – 3 = 4
3	1 8 3 12	24/4 = 6	12 – 1 = 11
4	7 6 2 1	16/4 = 4	7 – 1 = 6
5	3 15 6 12	36/4 = 9	15 – 3 = 12
		$\Sigma\ \bar{X} = \overline{30}$	$\Sigma R = \overline{40}$

$$\bar{\bar{X}} = 30/5 = 6$$

$$\bar{R} = 40/5 = 8$$

$$UCL_{\bar{x}} = 6 = 0.729(8) = 11.832$$

$$LCL_{\bar{x}} = 6 - 0.729(8) = 0.168$$

The $\bar{X}$ chart is shown in Exhibit S12-11.

$$UCL_R = 2.282(8) = 18.256$$

$$LCL_R = 0(8) = 0$$

The R chart is shown in Exhibit S12-12.

Examining Exhibits S12-11 and S12-12, we can see that no $\bar{X}$ or R points are out of control. The operators are performing their work within reasonable time limits.

What other measures of service quality would you recommend for this process?

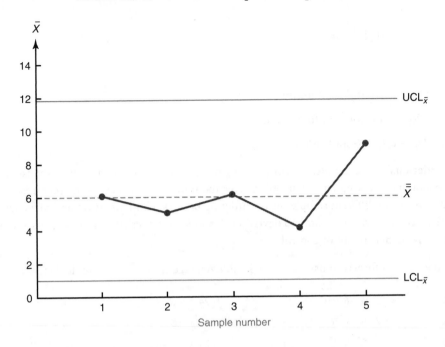

Exhibit S12-11 $\bar{X}$ Chart for Operator Response Time

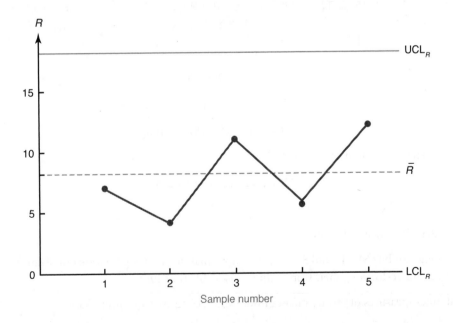

Exhibit S12-12   R Chart for Operator Response Time

Control Charts for Attributes

Control charts for variables, $\bar{X}$ and R, do not apply when we sample attributes, in which items are typically classified as defective or nondefective. Measuring defectives involves counting them (for example, the number of bad light bulbs in a given lot or the number of data entry records typed with errors), whereas variables are usually measured for length, volume, weight, or time. There are two kinds of attribute control charts: those that measure the percent **defective** in a sample—called **p charts,** and those that count the number of **defects**—called **c charts.**

p Charts

The principal means of controlling attributes are p charts. Although attributes that are either good or bad follow the **binomial distribution,** the normal distribution can be used to calculate p chart limits when sample sizes are large. The procedure resembles the $\bar{X}$ chart approach, which also was based on the central limit theorem. The formulas for p chart upper and lower control limits are

$$UCL_{\hat{p}} = \bar{p} + Z\sigma_{\hat{p}} \tag{S12.2}$$

$$LCL_{\hat{p}} = \bar{p} + Z\sigma_{\hat{p}} \tag{S12.3}$$

where

$\bar{p}$ = mean percent defective in the samples

Z = number of standard deviates (Z=2 for 95.5 percent control limits,

   Z=3 for 99.7 percent control limits)

$\sigma_{\hat{p}}$ = standard deviation of the distribution of sample percent defectives ($\hat{p}$)

$\sigma_{\hat{p}}$ is estimated by the formula

$$\sigma_{\hat{p}} = \sqrt{\frac{\bar{p}(1-\bar{p})}{n}} \tag{S12.4}$$

$$\hat{p}_i = \frac{number\ of\ defectives\ in\ sample\ i}{number\ of\ observations\ in\ sample\ i}$$

$$\bar{p} = \frac{sum\ of\ \hat{p}_i's}{number\ of\ samples} = \frac{\sum_{i=1}^{m}\hat{p}_i}{m}$$

or

$$\bar{p} = \frac{total\ number\ of\ defectives}{total\ number\ of\ observations}$$

where

n = number of observations in a sample (sample size

m = number of samples

---

p chart example: Using a popular database software package, 20 data entry clerks at ARCO key in thousands of insurance records each day. A sample of 100 records entered by each clerk was carefully examined to make sure they contained no errors. The percent defective in each sample was then computed as shown in Exhibit S12-13. We will develop a *p* chart that plots the percent defective and sets control limits to include 99.7 percent of the random variation in the entry process when it is in control.

$$\bar{p} = \frac{total\ number\ of\ errors}{total\ number\ of\ records\ examined} = \frac{80}{(100)(20)} = 0.04$$

$n =$ sample size $= 100;$ $m =$ number of samples $= 20$

$$\sigma_{\hat{p}} = \sqrt{\frac{\bar{p}(1-\bar{p})}{n}} = \sqrt{\frac{(0.04)(1-0.04)}{100}} \cong 0.02$$

$UCL_{\hat{p}} = \bar{p} + Z\sigma_{\hat{p}} = 0.04 + 3(0.02) \cong 0.10$

$LCL_{\hat{p}} = \bar{p} - Z\sigma_{\hat{p}} = 0.04 - 3(0.02) \cong -0.02$ or 0

(because we cannot have a negative percent)   (S12.5)

Exhibit S12-13   Data Entry Errors

Sample Number	Records with Errors	Percent Defective	Sample Number	Records with Errors	Percent Defective
1	6	0.06	11	6	0.06
2	5	0.05	12	1	0.01
3	0	0.00	13	8	0.08
4	1	0.01	14	7	0.07
5	4	0.04	15	5	0.05
6	2	0.02	16	4	0.04
7	5	0.05	17	11	0.11
8	3	0.03	18	3	0.03
9	3	0.03	19	0	0.00
10	2	0.02	20	4	0.04
			Total	80	

The control limits and percent defective are plotted in Exhibit S12-14. Notice that only one data entry clerk (number 17) is out of control. The firm may want to examine that individual's work a bit more closely to see if a serious problem exists. In addition, it might be interesting to investigate the working habits of clerks 3 and 19. Do they make no errors because they work too slowly or have they developed a superior procedure?

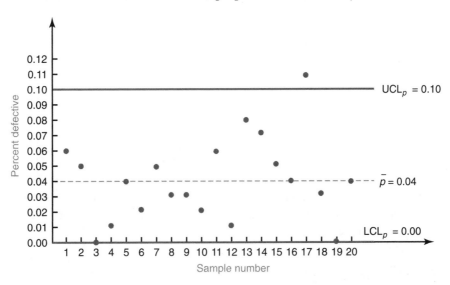

Exhibit S12-14   Example p Chart for Data Entry

c Charts

In the preceding example, we counted the number of defective database records entered. A defective record was one that was not exactly correct (that is, with one or more errors, or defects). A bad record may contain more than one defect, however. We use c charts to control the number of defects per unit of output (or per insurance record in the preceding case).

Control charts for defects are helpful for monitoring processes in which a large number of potential errors can occur, but the actual number that does occur is relatively small. Defects may be typographical errors in newspapers, imperfections or blemishes on a table, or missing pickles on a fast-food hamburger. Hence, we focus on defects on an observation unit (or unit of measure), such as typographical errors on a page, blemishes on a dining table, and dents or scratches on a car body. A few defects normally do not necessarily make a product defective; a few dents or scratches on a new car do not make it a defective car, they can easily be repaired.

The **Poisson probability distribution,** which has a variance equal to its mean, is the basis for c charts. Because $\bar{c}$ is the mean number of defects per unit, the standard deviation is equal to $\sqrt{\bar{c}}$. The limits of a c chart can be computed using the following formulas:

$$UCL_c = \bar{c} + Z\sqrt{\bar{c}} \qquad LCL_c = \bar{c} - Z\sqrt{\bar{c}}$$

(S12.6)

To compute 99.7 percent control limits, use these formulas with Z=3:

$$UCL_c = \bar{c} + 3\sqrt{\bar{c}} \quad LCL_c = \bar{c} - 3\sqrt{\bar{c}} \text{ lim}$$

c chart example: Red Top Cab Company receives several complaints per day about the behavior of its drivers. Over a 9-day period (where days are the units of measure), the owner received this number of calls from irate passengers: 3, 0, 8, 9, 6, 7, 4, 9, and 8, for a total of 54 complaints.

To compute 99.7 percent control limits, find the average number of complaints:

$$\bar{c} = \frac{54}{9} = 6 \text{ complaints per day}$$

Thus

$$UCL_c = \bar{c} + 3\sqrt{\bar{c}} = 6 + 3\sqrt{6} = 6 + 3(2.45) = 6 + 7.35 = 13.35$$
$$LCL_c = \bar{c} - 3\sqrt{\bar{c}} = 6 - 3\sqrt{6} = 6 - 3(2.45) = 6 - 7.35 = -1.35 \text{ or } 0.$$

After plotting a control chart summarizing this data and posting it prominently in the drivers' locker room, the number of calls received dropped to an average of three per day. Can you explain why this may have occurred?

Interpretation of Control Charts

We indicated earlier that when sample data points, such as sample averages, fall within the control limits, the process is considered to be in statistical control, which means variations from the process average are due to common, or natural, causes. When they fall outside the limits, it is concluded that the process might be out of control, which requires an investigation as to the cause of the out of control sign. However, this is not the only case that an investigation is warranted. Data points may fall within the limits, but if they exhibit an unusual, nonrandom pattern, this may be a sign of a process out of control or about to go out of control. Consequently, process control charts must be examined not only for points that fall outside the limits, but also for unusual patterns. Exhibit S12-15 provides some examples of possible patterns in control charts.

Exhibit S12-15   Patterns to Look for on Control Charts

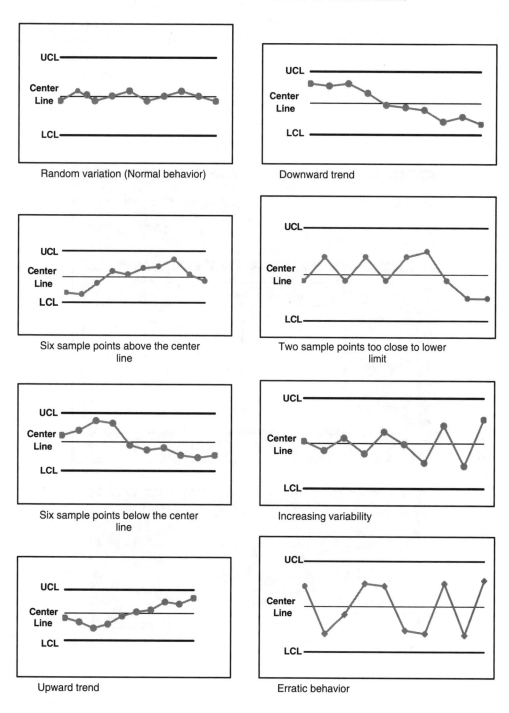

Random variation (Normal behavior)

Downward trend

Six sample points above the center line

Two sample points too close to lower limit

Six sample points below the center line

Increasing variability

Upward trend

Erratic behavior

Using POM for Windows for SPC

POM for the Windows' Quality Control module has the capability to compute and plot all the SPC control charts introduced in this supplement. Exhibit S12-16 illustrates POM for Windows output for the ARCO Data Entry Errors example. In addition to the relevant computational output for a p-chart, POM for Windows can plot the sample points in a separate control chart, as shown in the second half of Exhibit S12-16. As another example, Exhibit S12-17 contains the limits of the c-chart and other sample information for the Red Top Cab Company problem.

Exhibit S12-16   POM for Windows Output of ARCO's Data Entry Errors Example

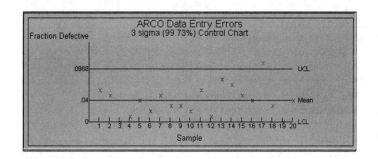

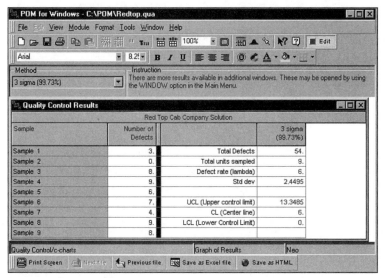

S12.5 Summary

This supplement presented some of the most widely used tools and techniques of quality and continuous improvement. Most quality improvement projects can be based on the plan-do-study-act cycle. In solving quality problems and improving existing systems, one or more of the tools, known as the "magnificent seven," can be used. These are simple and straightforward graphical tools that are easy to learn and use; they are also effective in uncovering quality problems. We discussed one of these tools, the process control chart, in more detail because of its applicability in many services.

The process control chart is a quality control technique constructed to detect unacceptable levels of output variability in a process. $\bar{X}$ and R charts are used together to measure changes in the central tendency and variability of a process. The percent defective in a sample taken from a process is measured by p charts, and c charts help monitor the number of defects.

Service employees can monitor the quality of the service they are providing by sampling their work and recording such data as the time it takes to process a customer, the number of errors made, or the percentage of customers who are satisfied. If the data point recorded falls outside prespecified control limits, or an unusual pattern is observed, an investigation of the causes needs to be undertaken.

13

SERVICE PRODUCTIVITY AND MEASUREMENT OF PERFORMANCE

13.1 Introduction

> The single greatest challenge facing managers in the developed countries of the world is to raise the productivity of knowledge and service workers. This challenge, which will dominate the management agenda for the next several decades, will ultimately determine the competitive performance of companies. Even more important, it will determine the very fabric of society and the quality of life in every industrialized nation.[1]

These were the words that began a *Harvard Business Review* article by the management philosopher the late Peter F. Drucker. Some researchers and management practitioners may not agree with Professor Drucker on the extent of the impact of service productivity on society. However, most, if not all, would agree that raising productivity in general, and service productivity in particular, is indeed one of the most important issues public policy makers and managers face.

This chapter focuses on the important topic of productivity, especially service productivity, and efficiency as a measure of performance in service organizations. A brief background on productivity is presented; then this chapter discusses why raising productivity is so crucial for the well-being of a country as well as individual public and private organizations. Also discussed is how service productivity can be raised. Finally, a brief discussion of data envelopment analysis as a powerful tool in measuring efficiency of service organizations is presented.

13.2 A Brief Background on Productivity

Productivity represents the relationship between outputs (goods, services, or outcomes) and inputs used to produce the outputs. It is an indicator of how well an organization converts its inputs (for example, resources) into outputs. The organization may be producing goods or services, or it may be the whole economy of a country producing all kinds of goods and services. Hence the concept of productivity can be applied to an economy, to an industry (for example, airline industry) to a particular organization, or to any operation in any of these economic units.

Productivity

Productivity is defined as a ratio of output to input:

$$\text{Productivity} = \text{Output/Input}$$

The components in this ratio may be in their natural physical units, such as number of 60-inch TV sets produced and number of labor hours used to produce those sets. Whether it is goods or services that are represented in the numerator, output must include only those of good quality. In other words, goods that are later found out to be defective, or services that had to be repeated because they were not satisfactory the first time, should not be included in the output.

Productivity may be computed for a single output and a single input or multiple outputs and multiple inputs. Most organizations produce more than one kind of output and use several kinds of inputs. Outputs are usually measured in different units; therefore they must be converted to a common unit. Similarly, when there is more than one type, inputs must also be converted to a common unit, usually to dollars. In practice, both the output and input are calculated as weighted index numbers.[2]

A productivity ratio with a single input is called **partial productivity**, such as total output divided by number of labor hours, or capital, or the number of kilowatt hours of energy, or any relevant quantity of input used. A labor productivity ratio, for example, represents units of output produced per unit of labor hour. Care should be exercised not to attribute the result entirely to labor in such ratios because other inputs are also needed to produce a unit of a good or deliver a service.

Multifactor, or total productivity, measures are useful when it is important to assess the outcome from the use of all the relevant inputs. Total productivity is the ratio of total output to total inputs. Clearly, a total productivity index provides more information. It makes available information on trade-offs among various inputs and allows senior managers to make more informed decisions.[3] An increase in the total productivity ratio represents savings achieved in one or more of the inputs. Changes in labor productivity ratio reflect not only the changes in the efficiency of labor, but also the substitution effect of other inputs, such as capital, for labor. In other words, improvements in labor productivity may be due to the use of more efficient or labor-saving machines, which is substitution of capital for labor. Because total factor productivity measure includes all the inputs, all changes in inputs are represented.

Efficiency

A related concept is efficiency. Although sometimes used interchangeably, productivity and efficiency are different concepts. As mentioned earlier, productivity of an economic unit is the ratio of its output to its input used to produce that output. Efficiency, on the other hand, indicates the degree of attainment of an optimum outcome, a preselected goal, or the best practice.

Efficiency can be measured as the ratio of output obtained from a process to the maximum output that is possible for the amount of input used. Alternatively, efficiency can be measured as the ratio of the minimum input needed to produce the observed output to the actual amount of input used. It is also possible to set performance targets, such as output volume, cost, revenue, or profits, and measure the performance of an economic unit against these goals.[4] Although the productivity measure can theoretically be any nonnegative number, efficiency is expressed as a percentage and cannot be greater than one. Also, productivity of economic units can be compared even if they use different technologies. Efficiency comparisons, however, are meaningful only among economic units using similar technologies and inputs to produce similar outputs.

13.3 Why Productivity Is Important

Productivity ratio, as a number, is not very meaningful unless it is considered over time. In other words, productivity ratio is only meaningful when its change through regular intervals of time is considered. Clearly, the desired change is an increase in productivity. Also, it is meaningful and useful when two similar organizations are compared. In this section we review the relationship between productivity and several economic and business indicators.[5]

- **Standard of living**—At the national level, labor productivity is the most frequently used productivity measure. Output in this ratio represents all goods and services produced by the private sector of the economy. Input represents the number of hours worked in the private sector. Labor productivity is used as an index of standard of living in a country. The change in productivity through time shows if the standard of living in a country is improving.

  Probably, there is nothing more important for the welfare of the citizens of a country than a steady increase in productivity in the long run. An increase in productivity means there will be more goods and services to consume for the citizens of a country. It also means that, everything else being equal, the prices of these goods and services will be decreasing; hence the society will be better off in general. Although there may be a lag, an increase in productivity usually leads to a rise in wages. On the other hand, if the productivity growth falls consistently below that of other countries, it will experience a relatively (although not absolutely) lower standard of living.

  The real impact of productivity increases is observed in the long run. Annual productivity increases are usually limited to a few percentage points. However, their impact becomes immense in the long run because of the effect of compounding. Examples of this effect can be seen in Exhibit 13-1, which presents estimates of productivity growth for 16 industrialized countries between 1870 and 1979.

- **Costs and competitiveness**—Productivity growth contributes to a country's competitiveness in international trade due to its cost lowering effect. It has the same effect on a company's costs.

An increase in productivity helps reduce the rise in the level of prices; that is, inflation.

Exhibit 13-1   Growth in Productivity of Industrialized Countries 1870–1979:
Top Ten Performers (GDP per Person-Hour)

Country	Growth in Real GDP per Capita (%)	Growth in Real GDP per Person-Hour (%)
Japan	1,653.0	2,480.0
Sweden	1,084.0	2,060.0
Finland	1,016.0	1,710.0
France	694.0	1,590.0
Norway	872.0	1,560.0
Germany	1,396.0	1,510.0
Austria	642.0	1,260.0
Italy	493.0	1,220.0
Denmark	650.0	1,090.0
United States	691.0	1,080.0

Source: Adapted from William J. Baumol, Sue Anne Batey Blackman, and Edward N. Wolf, *Productivity and American Leadership: The Long View* (Cambridge, MA, MIT Press, 1989), p. 13.

- **Unemployment**—Productivity growth is sometimes blamed for an increase in unemployment. It is true that as productivity increases, some employees will be displaced from their regular line of employment in the short run. However, there is no evidence to indicate that productivity growth causes unemployment in the long run.

- **Social programs**—Productivity growth also makes it possible for governments to allocate resources to combating poverty and provide for elderly, education, arts, environmental protection, or programs that in general benefit many of its citizens and contribute to a nation's well-being.

- **Resource conservation**—As an economy grows it produces more goods and services. This may mean an increase in the use of natural resources and an increase in adverse impact on the environment. However, if the growth in output is achieved through productivity increases, fewer resources will be used and environmental impact will be reduced.

13.4 Review of the Slowdown of U.S. Productivity Growth in the Recent Past

Between 1966 and 1980, the United States experienced a slowdown in the growth of its productivity. The slowdown got even worse after 1973. For example, while the average annual productivity increase between 1950 and 1973 was 2.8 percent, the rate of growth was only 0.9 percent between 1973 and 1979. Another closely related development of the period was that the rate of growth of the U.S. productivity not only slowed down, but also fell behind the rates of some other industrialized countries such as Japan, Germany, Sweden, France, and Italy. If it is persistent, such a shortfall may mean loss of competitiveness in the long-run and deterioration in the standard of living. Naturally, these developments caused concern among business leaders and public policy makers. However, it was later realized that the slowdown in the productivity growth was a temporary, short-run phenomenon.[6] In other words, the long-run U.S. productivity growth rate has not fallen below its historical level. On the other hand, we must emphasize that the consequences of these developments, pain and suffering they caused among the population, were real and there is no guarantee that the United States will always maintain its historical level of productivity or its growth rate.

Major reasons for the slowdown have been identified as follows:[7]

- **A slowdown in the rate of capital formation**—The rate of capital formation in the form of plant and equipment began to decline in 1966, and, more important, the growth of capital per worker slowed down after 1973. American workers had less equipment to work with on the average.

- **Composition of the labor force**—Women joined the labor force in increasing numbers and the relative share of young workers increased. These new additions were less experienced than the existing workforce. However, overall educational level of the new entrants into the labor force was higher; hence it made a positive contribution.

- **Decline in research and development investments**—It is estimated that approximately 10 percent of the slowdown in productivity growth was due to a slowdown in the rate of investment in research and development (R&D) that create cost-saving technological innovations.

- **Composition of output**—The composition of output shifted from manufacturing, whose productivity grows relatively rapidly, to services, whose productivity typically grows relatively slowly.

- **The availability and cost of energy**—Many researchers believe that the significant increase in energy prices, especially oil, which started in the early 1970s had a negative impact on the productivity growth.

- **Government regulations**—Government regulations, in general, have a negative impact on productivity because they require more paperwork, distract managers from their normal duties, extend the fruition period of new investment projects, and increase uncertainty about the future.

- **Cyclical factors**—Some economists believe that the slowdown in productivity growth during the period of 1966 to 1980 was due to the business cycle. They argue that productivity growth tends to decline at the tail end of an economic expansion and during recessions but increases rapidly in the early stages of an economic expansion.

These possible causes have been supported in varying degrees by statistical evidence found by various researchers. There are, however, other causes, mostly based on general observation and judgment, that have been suggested to explain the phenomenon in question: excessive preoccupation of top business executives with the short-term results; a management reward system that encourages avoidance of risk rather than innovation and causes a decline in the spirit of entrepreneurship; inflation, which created uncertainty, absorbing the time and effort of management, and increasing the cost of investments; growth of parochialism and protectionism in the form of rescue plans for domestic firms that were in financial trouble, both of which reduce the pressures on management to be more productive and to innovate; financing difficulties of small firms; and the role of unions, including resistance to change.[8]

13.5 Raising Productivity

Productivity is influenced by many factors. First among the factors that improve productivity in the long run are technological developments that reduce labor requirement in the production of goods and services, or increase output without increasing labor input. Another factor that has both long- and short-term implications for increasing productivity is the organization and management of productive activities. However, behind these are the basic values and institutions of society that are relevant to "attitudes toward work, propensities to save and invest, willingness to innovate, take risks, and adapt to changes wrought by scientific and technological progress.... The important point is that the values of a people and its leaders condition the rate of technological progress and other forces directly affecting productivity."[9] For example, in a competitive private-enterprise environment, firms have strong incentives to improve productivity for survival. In such an environment, firms undertake R&D projects, innovate, and take risks in trying out new ideas and technologies, all of which may lead to improvements in productivity and profitability. Actions of central and local governments also have a significant effect on the productivity of organizations. Incentives by government for investment into R&D and new technologies usually end up increasing the productivity of private enterprises.

Naturally, productivity improvements at the firm level determine what happens at the national level. Organizations can increase productivity in the long run by introducing new technologies and innovations in existing technology. They can also achieve productivity improvements from economies of scale. As organizations grow, their productive resources, such as machines, equipment, and workforce, also grow in scale and tend to specialize. Growth in capacity does not necessarily require a growth of all inputs in the same proportions. For example, when an organization increases its capacity by 25 percent, it does not necessarily need an equal expansion in the number of employees in its accounting department. Specialization of equipment and employees also lead to an increase in productivity because of the increased output volume specialization generates.

Short-run conditions also influence productivity. Cyclical, seasonal, or erratic fluctuations in demand can influence productivity of an industry or an organization. However, organizations can achieve significant increases in efficiency in the short term by implementing better work methods and better management practices. Overall, good relationships between management and labor, common objectives adopted by both, can create the right environment for productivity increases in the work place. In general investments into developing human resources contribute to productivity growth. Recruiting workers with the right skills and attitude, paying them competitive wages and providing attractive benefits, giving them the appropriate training and education to help them achieve their maximum potential, and motivating them to be their best are some of the most effective human resource practices that can improve productivity. Teamwork and empowerment encourage participation of employees in problem solving and making suggestions for improvements in production methods. Employees are usually the best source of ideas for improvement in production processes and methods, and eliminating waste and defects.

Another factor that contributes to productivity growth in manufacturing is the development and introduction of new products. Productivity increases faster in the early stages of production of new products than in later stages due to the learning curve effect.[10]

In summary, improving productivity largely depends on good management practices. All the factors listed, other than cultural and environmental factors and activities of government, depend on management action. Without the right managerial approach and decisions, productivity increases will be difficult to achieve.

13.6 Service Productivity

It is clear that raising productivity is one of the biggest challenges for public policy makers whose decisions influence the productivity performance of the economy, as well as for managers, whose decisions influence the productivity performance of their organization. Services, on the other hand, present a special challenge. It is not only difficult to increase service productivity, but it is also difficult to measure it and measure it accurately. First, this section briefly reviews some of the reasons for the measurement problem. Then it discusses why service productivity growth is slower than manufacturing productivity. Finally, some suggestions for raising productivity of services are presented.

Measurement of Service Productivity

Recall that productivity is defined as the ratio of output to input. The most common way to measure service productivity is to divide output by aggregate labor hours. Labor input is the sum of hours worked by all persons involved in producing the given output. Although by no means an easy task, measuring labor input in services is relatively straightforward. However, measurement of output presents certain challenges in some services. Difficulties emerge when we try to define the output of a service. Major problems are (1) identifying the elements of a complex bundle of services; (2) choosing among alternative representations of an industry's output; (3) accounting for the consumer's role in the production of a service; and (4) quality differences.[11]

1. **Identifying the elements of a service**—Many services consist of a set of services that are jointly produced. It is usually difficult, if not impossible, to separate the bundle into individual services. For example, banks provide several different services when a customer opens a checking account. Safekeeping of money, record keeping, and making payments, such as bill payments, are some of the services jointly produced and difficult to separate.

2. **Alternative representations of service output**—The second problem arises from the nature of services. Services are performances and usually there is no physical evidence or output when a service is performed. Consequently, what to measure and how to measure it becomes a thorny issue. For example, in healthcare a logical output measure for a hospital would be the number of patients cured, but that is not an easy output to measure and usually no such data exist. Furthermore, not everything a hospital does is directed at curing, some hospital activities are aimed at keeping patients healthy. Some hospital activities may be aimed at diagnosing problems, such as X-rays, lab tests, and CAT scans. After the problem is diagnosed, the treatment may be performed by another healthcare provider. There are still other activities hospitals perform, such as training of interns and nurses. Because of this difficulty, output in some services may be measured indirectly by measuring relevant activities. For example, output of hospitals may be represented by the number of patient-days. In banking, demand deposits are sometimes considered as part of a bank's output (safekeeping, accounting, and payment services provided to customers) and sometimes its input. (They are a source of funds for the bank.)

3. **Accounting for consumer's role**—Customers are involved in the creation and delivery of many services. Customer involvement creates at least three challenges in the measurement of service productivity. First, in some services, the customer supplies the labor for the delivery of service. It may be difficult to separate the contribution of the customer to the service output from that of the service organization. Normally, the labor provided by the customer is not included in the labor input, thereby causing an underestimation of labor input and overestimation of productivity. It can be argued that because the customer provides part of the labor, price of the service will be lower thereby alleviating the estimation problem. On the other hand, inexperienced customers may adversely affect the efficiency of service delivery.[12]

   Second, service output may depend on the number of customers served. For example, the output of an airline may be measured by the number of passenger-miles. The number of passenger-miles on a particular flight, however, depends on the number of passengers on board. Similarly, if an orchestra plays to an empty concert hall, no output is produced because there are no consumers to hear it.

Finally, demand in many services is not uniform and is difficult to predict, but the service organization must maintain its facilities and personnel must be available. For example, retail stores must remain open even if the demand is low during certain hours of the day and tolerate its salespeople to be idle during those hours. Thus, the availability of the facility and personnel during those nonproductive periods must somehow be included in the store's output because they exist for the customers' convenience. Ignoring the necessity of the idle time or excess capacity may lead to wrong conclusions or decisions. Can you imagine what would happen to a fire department's budget and personnel if its productivity is measured by the number of fires extinguished per firefighter?

4. **Quality differences**—Intangibility and nonstandard nature of service output makes the measurement of quality difficult. For example, legal services provided by lawyers are usually measured in number of hours a lawyer spends on a particular case. However, the outcome of this service, winning the case, depends largely on the knowledge and skills of the lawyer rather than the number of hours spent on the case. Also, the quality of some services is difficult to judge by consumers because they do not have the specialized knowledge, as is usually the case in healthcare and legal services. This, together with the fact that many services require payment before delivery, may lead to an overestimation of service productivity because poor-quality service becomes part of total output. Finally, quality of the output in some services may depend on the customer and her behavior. For example, a student who is not well prepared and not motivated to do the necessary work will learn little in a course even if the teacher is competent.

Slow Rate of Service Productivity Growth

Services are known for their resistance to productivity improvement efforts. As discussed earlier in this chapter, increased share of services in gross national product (GNP) has been identified as one of the reasons for the slowdown in productivity growth. However, this generalization can be misleading; not all services are stagnant in productivity growth. Professor William J. Baumol points out that services are too heterogeneous to lend themselves to such generalizations and suggests three categories of services with respect to their amenability to productivity growth: (1) the stagnant personal services, (2) the progressive impersonal services, and (3) asymptotically stagnant impersonal services.[13]

The stagnant personal services—In this category are the services that are by their nature most resistant to productivity improvement efforts. An extreme example would be the performance of a Mozart quartet that today requires the same number of musicians and time as it did approximately 200 years ago. No productivity improvement effort can change those input requirements without a significant decrease in quality. Other, less extreme examples also exist. Some of the stagnant services are nonstandard and cannot be provided in mass quantities; for example, services provided by a lawyer or a physician fall in this category. Each case handled by a lawyer is different, as is each patient seen by a doctor. Usually an increase in output, or reduction in input, cannot be obtained unless quality is sacrificed. The quality of most services in this category is often judged by how much time the service provider spends with the client or patient.

The progressive impersonal services—These are the services at the other extreme of the spectrum. They do not necessarily require the customer's involvement. It may be possible to substitute capital for labor in these services and hence some of them can be automated. Telecommunications is an example for this category of services. Until approximately 50 years ago, most telephone connections were made with the aid of switchboard operators. Today, telephone calls are connected by automatic switchboards. Unless a customer requires an operator's assistance, no contact with the personnel of the telephone company is needed in making the call. The productivity increase in this service sector is phenomenal. Although the technology started with open wire transmission of calls, it moved to microwave, coaxial cable, and satellite transmission, while the costs declined steadily over the years.

Asymptotically stagnant impersonal services—This category includes services whose characteristic is a mixture of the first two categories. The most important aspect of a service in this category is that it exhibits an extraordinary growth in productivity and decrease in cost during the early stages of its lifecycle. The productivity growth of such a service is self-extinguishing; the greater its initial productivity growth, the more quickly it can be expected to come to an end. Computational and data processing services constitute a good example for this category. These services require two major inputs: computer hardware and software. The first component is a product of a progressive sector of the economy. As is well-known, cost of computer hardware has been declining continuously for decades mainly due to technological development and productivity growth in this industry. The other component, computer software, is a product of a stagnant sector, where costs have been steadily increasing.

Another example is the production of television programs, such as sitcoms and soap operas. The production of these programs consists of two main components: First is the creation of the program, which involves writing, casting, rehearsals, actual performance, and taping. The second is the broadcasting of the program. The first component is the stagnant component; productivity improvements are hard to achieve in making these programs. The second component is technology-driven, and significant productivity and quality improvements have been achieved over many years through research and development in broadcasting technology.

Probably the most interesting aspect of these services is what happens to the costs of the two components through time. Usually the progressive part is the expensive component at the outset. While it becomes less and less expensive because of fast productivity growth, the stagnant component experiences very little or no improvement in productivity but becomes more and more expensive. There are two reasons for this. One is inflation, which affects most goods and services. The second reason is that while the input quantities of progressive component decrease due to productivity growth, the input quantities of the stagnant part do not change or decrease less; hence, the stagnant part becomes relatively more expensive. Because of this, stagnant services will become relatively more expensive even if there is no inflation.

Another interesting fact is that the productivity improvements in the progressive component may quickly become less significant in the overall cost picture. This is because of the shrinking share of the progressive component in the total cost. Eventually, the stagnant component becomes dominant and the service takes on the characteristics of that category.

Raising Productivity in Services

It is clear that not all services are resistant to efforts for improving productivity; only stagnant personal services and asymptotically stagnant services that later become stagnant provide the greatest challenges to managers. However, even those services may benefit from the outcomes of technological progress, such as computers and advanced telecommunications systems. In this section, general approaches to raising the productivity of services are discussed.

As discussed earlier in this chapter, increasing productivity depends to a large extent on managerial decisions and actions. Better organization of work, efficient work methods, better relationships between the management and employees, training, teamwork, and empowerment are only a few steps management can take to raise productivity in manufacturing as well as service organizations. A *Harvard Business Review* article emphasized this point by placing the blame for slow growth of the service sector productivity on the ineffectiveness of many American managers and the inherent complexity of the service sector. Van Biema and Greenwald, the authors of the article, indicate that the first compelling piece of evidence for this assertion is that external competitive pressures on manufacturing managers led to significant improvements in productivity and quality.[14] The second major piece of evidence is the existence of wide and persistence differences in performance between the successful service companies and their competitors. Third, the authors of the article observe that productivity growth at many companies fluctuates widely in both duration and magnitude. This much fluctuation in the short run, they argue, cannot be explained by the usually cited factors of capital, labor, and technology but must be due to management's attention and inattention to productivity at various times. Finally, "the success of most leveraged buyout firms...stems from their ability to concentrate management's attention on the efficiency of basic business operations."

Then what should managers do to raise the productivity of service work? Drucker takes a macro approach to raising productivity and offers some suggestions that would help managers improve productivity in most services.[15] He observes that an important difference between services and manufacturing is that capital and labor-saving technology can be substituted for labor in manufacturing because capital and labor are "factors of production," and they can be substitutes for each other. However, in service and knowledge work, they are "tools" of production and may or may not be substituted for labor. How skillfully the tools are used determines if they help increase productivity in services. Therefore, we cannot depend on capital and technology investments alone to raise the productivity of service work. Instead we must learn to "work smarter," which means working more productively without working harder or longer. Drucker recommends the following for working smarter: (1) define the task; (2) concentrate work on the task; (3) define performance; (4) form a partnership with employees; and (5) make continuous learning part of the organization's culture.

1. **Define the task**—The first thing we must do is to question why we do what we do. In other words, ask "What is the task? What are we trying to accomplish? Why do it at all?" Frequently, we may find that the task in question can be simplified, or combined with other tasks or completely eliminated with no negative impact on the outcome, which is customer satisfaction. Investigating these questions, we may find that the task was established for a reason in the past, but the reason had disappeared or conditions had changed long ago, but managers forgot to eliminate the task.

2. **Concentrate work on the task**—Employees in many services are usually required to perform many different tasks, some of which are not essential to their main function. A common complaint heard from nurses provides a good example. Many hospitals require nurses to perform clerical duties such as completing paperwork for Medicare, Medicaid, insurers, the billing office, and for the prevention of malpractice suits. These duties are unproductive work for nurses and take considerable time and keep them from doing what they are supposed to be doing, which is patient care. A clerk can be hired for completing paperwork, and the nurses can concentrate on patient care. Such a simple step should improve nurses' productivity. This is a common problem for many service providers. To avoid this problem we must ask, "What do we pay for? What value is this job supposed to add?"

3. **Define performance**—Sometimes services are treated as if they are a homogeneous group. Services range from R&D, creating new knowledge and inventing new products, to flipping burgers at a fast food restaurant. Clearly, they include a huge variety of tasks and require skills, knowledge, and training that vary widely from one job to another. Performance criteria are different in each service, and we cannot expect all services to respond positively to the same productivity improvement effort. In some services, such as R&D, performance depends on the quality of the output rather than the quantity. For example, a research lab that produces a breakthrough product in a year is more valuable for an organization than a lab that produced several "me too" products. In other words, this category includes "stagnant" services. It is not clear if there is a common process that consistently creates quality results in the services of this category. Therefore, we must look into each specific area to determine "what works?"

   Quantity may be the desired output in some other services. For example, the number of offices cleaned per hour may be the appropriate measure for a team of custodial service employees. These services closely resemble manufacturing tasks and therefore may benefit most from methods used for improving manufacturing productivity. Most of the services in this group can be characterized as "progressive," and capital investments may lead to significant productivity increases in these services.

A third category consists of services for which both the quality and the quantity define performance. Most service work falls into this category and most can be characterized as "asymptotically stagnant." A bank teller's performance may be measured by the number of transactions he completes during his shift as well as the quality of his work as measured by a customer satisfaction survey. The number of transactions can be increased by investing into computers and automated systems. Customer satisfaction, on the other hand, may depend entirely on the attitude of the teller and how much time he spends with a customer.

In these services we must try to determine "what works" as well as apply traditional operations management and industrial engineering methods to aspects that resemble manufacturing tasks to boost productivity.

4. **Form a partnership with employees**—The days when managers did the thinking and workers implemented their commands are long gone. Before Frederick Taylor developed his scientific management, and even long after, the average worker had little education or training; hence managers told them what to do and closely controlled them. Today's employees, especially in industrialized countries, are much better educated and well informed through mass media and the Internet. Many organizations and managers are discovering that they can be an invaluable source of good suggestions for improving quality and increasing productivity. Teamwork, employee participation, and empowerment discussed earlier in this book are all aimed at making good use of this valuable source as well as making employees happy and satisfied. The goal must be to make quality, customer satisfaction, and productivity both employees' and management's responsibility. The experience of most of the successful American manufacturers in the 1980s and 1990s indicates that employee-management partnership is the *best* way to achieve these goals. Drucker emphasizes that for knowledge and service work it is the *only* way.

5. **Make continuous learning part of organization's culture**—Rapid pace of technological development, fast new product introductions, shortening of product lifecycles, and increasing sophistication of new goods and services make continuous learning a necessity for survival for both managers and employees. Learning should include education and training; both are necessary for breakthrough as well as small continuous improvements in productivity. By their nature some service jobs are knowledge jobs, hence a culture of continuous learning may come naturally to those organizations, but for others it must be developed strategically.

13.7 Data Envelopment Analysis for Measurement of Service Efficiency

A service organization that achieves high levels of customer satisfaction is an effective organization. An efficient organization is the one that produces its output with minimum expenditure of resources. Effectiveness and efficiency must go hand-in-hand together. Effectiveness without efficiency in a profit-seeking organization would eventually lead to bankruptcy, or to lower than normal profits, if the organization cannot charge enough for its services to cover its costs. Conversely, efficiency without effectiveness will lead to loss of customers, and eventually the organization will go out of business. Naturally, public service organizations and some not-for-profit services are subject to different rules. Nevertheless, we can assume that efficiency and effectiveness of operations are dual goals shared by management of all service organizations.

A Brief Background on Data Envelopment Analysis

Measuring efficiency and productivity, or any aspect of performance, is an indispensable part of any productivity improvement effort because, as the well-known adage goes, "what gets measured gets managed." As mentioned earlier, productivity and efficiency are related but different concepts. Productivity can be measured as a ratio of output to input, and a typical service organization may construct a large variety of partial and total productivity ratios. Tracking these ratios through time can help an organization determine its productivity improvements. However, when the purpose is to compare similar units of a service organization, such as branches of a large bank, ratios may not provide the needed information.

Sometimes executives would like to know not only how units within their organization are performing in an absolute sense, but also relative to each other. Also, some managers would like to compare their organizations to others in the same service industry. In such cases the use of productivity ratios may not be possible because not all organizations compute the same ratios or may be willing to share the data with others. Comparison of similar units within the same organization or comparison of similar service organizations can be accomplished through the measurement of their relative efficiencies. Data envelopment analysis (DEA) is a linear programming based management science technique that has been developed for such purposes. This section presents a brief background on DEA as a powerful technique for measuring the relative technical efficiency of service organizations as well as a technique that may help managers identify the sources and amounts of inefficiencies in their organizations and orient them toward improvements in performance.

DEA was developed by Charnes, Cooper, and Rhodes as a response to a need to evaluate the efficiency of not-for-profit organizations where some inputs and outputs cannot be measured in monetary units, and therefore usually no "bottom line" is available for performance measurement.[16] The first application of DEA was in education[17] but others quickly followed in both the public and private sectors.

Various efficiency concepts exist in economics such as technical efficiency, scale efficiency, and allocative efficiency. **Technical inefficiency** exists for an organization if any of its inputs or any of its outputs can be improved without worsening any other input or output. **Scale efficiency** is related to the scale of productive facilities. If the average output (that is, output per unit input) increases as a firm increases its input quantity, the firm enjoys increasing returns to scale; however, if the average output decreases, the firm exhibits decreasing returns to scale. If the average output per unit input remains the same with increasing input, constant returns to scale exist. **Allocative efficiency** is concerned with the right mix of inputs for producing the outputs of an economic entity at a minimum cost and therefore requires price data.

These entities, such as bank branches, hospitals, and school districts, responsible for converting inputs into outputs, are referred to as decision-making units (DMUs) in the DEA literature. The management of a DMU has inputs at its disposal and is responsible for deciding how to use them for producing the desired outputs. Various DEA models exist to measure each type of efficiency as well as the overall efficiency. Efficient DMUs define an empirical efficiency frontier. In some DEA models this frontier is piecewise linear, and the segments between points representing the efficient DMUs indicate alternative input-output combinations for efficient operations. Each DEA model determines a different efficiency frontier from the data of DMUs included in the analysis. Decision-making units that are not on the frontier are inefficient, and those that are on the frontier may be efficient under certain conditions.

DEA is an empirical method. It uses actual data from the performance of DMUs; there is no need to convert data to a common unit (for example, dollars) as is commonly done in productivity ratios. All inputs and outputs can be expressed in their natural units. For example, a study concerning the efficiency of MBA programs included Graduate Management Admission Test (GMAT) scores, tuition in dollars, percentage of students with work experience, and the number of faculty publications as input measures, and starting salaries of graduates, percentage of students who had a job by graduation, and an index of program quality as output measures.[18]

We consider a simple one-output and one-input example to introduce some of the basic ideas relevant to DEA. In this example we have five DMUs that use different quantities of the same input to produce different quantities of the same output (refer to Exhibit 13-2). The solid line in the exhibit is the efficient frontier, which is defined by DMUs 1, 2, 4, and 5. DMUs in the exhibit are represented as points D1-D5.

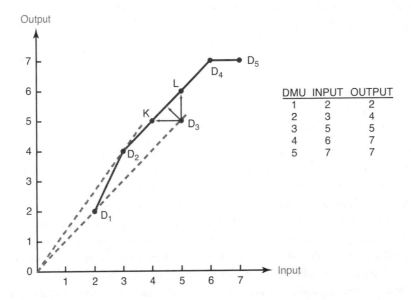

All DMUs in the data set are efficient except DMUs 3 and 5. As shown in the graph, DMU5 produces the same quantity of output as DMU4 but uses a larger quantity of input; therefore it is not fully efficient. Hence, it is clear that being on the efficient frontier is necessary but not sufficient for being efficient. When an appropriate DEA model is solved for DMU5, it will have a nonzero input "slack." Also, it can be seen from the graph that DMU3 is not efficient because it is not on the efficiency frontier.

In a simple example like this, a productivity ratio may be computed by dividing output by the input quantity. However, as noted earlier, a simple ratio may be misleading. Notice that DMUs 1, 3, and 5 all have the same output to input ratio (that is, productivity), but only DMU1 is efficient. Inefficiency exhibited by DMU3 can be eliminated if it can reduce its usage of input from 5 to 4 units without decreasing its output, and hence move to point K on the efficiency frontier, or increase its output from 5 to 6 units without increasing its input, and hence move to point L. Alternatively, DMU3 can become efficient if it can move to any point on the frontier between K and L. Any of these moves would make DMU3 technically efficient.

Scale efficiency can also be observed from the graph. Consider the slope of the dashed line from the origin to D1. Movement from D1 to D2 increases the slope and indicates a faster growth in average output for each additional unit of input, hence implies increasing returns to scale. Maximum returns to scale is reached at point D2 (that is, by DMU2). From D2 to D4 the slope of the ray decreases indicating a slower growth in average output for each additional unit of input, or decreasing returns to scale. It must be noted that returns-to-scale characterizations refer only to movement on the efficient frontier. The concept of returns-to-scale is ambiguous when applied to DMU3, which also exhibits technical inefficiencies.[19] If DMU3 can improve its efficiency and move to point K or point L on the efficiency frontier, or any point in between, it can become technically efficient; however, it will not be scale-efficient as DMU2.

The CCR Ratio Model of DEA

DEA is an extension and generalization of M. J. Farrell's work on measuring the efficiency of economic entities, or decision making units.[20] Farrell's work was focused on developing a summary efficiency measure from empirical data but was limited to a single-output case. Charnes, Cooper, and Rhodes made the extension to multiple inputs and multiple outputs and developed the mathematical programming method to determine efficiency. The original DEA model, named the CCR ratio model after its originators, in its revised form is given here.[21] The purpose of the model is to determine weights u_r and v_i so that the DMU that is being evaluated is given the maximum possible efficiency rating, on the condition that the same weights apply to all DMUs and no DMU can have an efficiency rating greater than one.[22]

$$\underset{u,v}{\text{Max}} \quad h_0 = \frac{\sum_{r=1}^{s} u_r y_{r0}}{\sum_{i=1}^{m} v_i x_{i0}}$$

(13.1)

Subject to:

$$\frac{\sum_{r=1}^{s} u_r y_{rj}}{\sum_{i=1}^{m} v_i x_{ij}} \leq 1 \qquad j = 1,...,n$$

$$\frac{u_r}{\sum_{i=1}^{m} v_i x_{i0}} \geq \varepsilon \qquad r = 1,...,s$$

$$\frac{v_i}{\sum_{i=1}^{m} v_i x_{i0}} \geq \varepsilon \qquad i = 1,...,m$$

where we assume that there are n DMUs in the data set, and each DMU uses various quantities of m different inputs to produce various quantities of s different outputs; y_{rj} is the rth observed output of the jth DMU, and x_{ij} is the ith observed input of the jth DMU; u_r and v_i are the weights associated with the rth output and ith input, respectively, and they are to be determined as the solution to the mathematical model. In other words, u_r and v_i are the variables in this model. The constant ε in the last two sets of constraints is an extremely small number, which assures that all observed inputs and outputs will have positive weights assigned to them. The subscript 0 refers to the DMU whose efficiency is being measured. The objective function represents the efficiency of DMU$_0$ and is also a part of the constraint set.

The CCR ratio model extends the engineering, or scientific, concept of efficiency to economics. This is done by generating a single "virtual" output in the numerator and a single "virtual" input in the denominator of the objective function. Also, the constraint set of the model ensures that the selection of weights does not violate the engineering principle of efficiency and that no unit can have an efficiency of more than 1.0. Because the model aims at finding u_r and v_is so that the maximum efficiency rating is assigned to DMU$_0$, DMU$_0$ is portrayed in the best possible light. The process can be repeated for any DMU in the data set. For actual computations the following transformed linear programming (LP) version may be used:[23]

$$\text{Min} \quad b_0 = \theta_0 - \mathcal{E} \left(\sum_{i=1}^{m} s_i^- + \sum_{r=1}^{s} s_r^+ \right) \tag{13.2.1}$$

Subject to:

$$\theta_0 x_{i0} - \sum_{j=1}^{n} x_{ij} \lambda_j - s_i^- = 0 \qquad i=1, 2, \ldots, m \tag{13.2.2}$$

$$\sum_{j=1}^{n} y_{rj} \lambda_j - s_r^+ = y_{r0} \qquad r=1, 2, \ldots, s \tag{13.2.3}$$

$$\lambda_j, s_i^-, s_i^+ \geq 0 \qquad j=1, 2, \ldots, n \tag{13.2.4}$$

where λ_js represent transformed variables u_r and v_is for each DMU j; s_i^-s are the slack variables for input constraints, and s_r^+s are the slack variables for output constraints.

DMU$_0$ is efficient if both of the following conditions are satisfied:

1. $\theta_0^* = 1.0$

2. All slacks (that is, s_i^- and s_r^+) are zero

where $*$ indicates an optimal value and θ_0^* represents the relative technical efficiency of DMU$_0$ $(0 \leq \theta_0 \leq 1.0)$. However, note that $\theta_0^* = 1.0$ does not necessarily mean full efficiency. For a DMU to be fully efficient, both of the above conditions must be satisfied. If $\theta_0^* < 1.0$, DMU$_0$ is inefficient, and $\theta_0^* x_{i0} \leq \sigma x_{ij} \lambda_j$ indicates that it is possible to form a combination of other DMUs, which uses less input than DMU$_0$ (that is $\theta_0^* x_{i0} < x_{i0}$) to produce the same output; this implies excess in one or more inputs used by DMU$_0$. If any input slack s_i^{-*} is not zero, it implies that input i can be further reduced by an amount equal to s_i^{-*} without changing the amount of any other input or output. To determine the quantities of inputs and outputs that would make DMU$_0$ efficient, the following CCR projection formulas can be used: $x_{i0}^* = \theta_0^* x_{i0} - s_i^{-*}$; $i=1,\ldots,m$, and $y_{r0}^* = y_{r0} + s_r^{+*}$;

$r=1,\dots,s$, where x^*_{i0} and y^*_{r0} are the projected inputs (x_{i0}) and outputs (y_{r0}), respectively. Such projection places DMU_0 on the efficient frontier.

Example: First Bank of Gotham City has six branches around the city. Executives of the bank would like to evaluate the efficiency of these branches.[24] The purpose of the evaluation is to reward the managers and employees of the efficient branches and guide inefficient branches to efficiency. Branch managers have agreed that the number of transactions performed per month, such as checks cashed or deposited, cash withdrawals and deposits, accounts opened, accounts closed, and so on constitutes a reasonable representation of the output of a branch. They also agreed that the rent paid by each branch and the number of teller hours are two of the most important inputs. The rent has been selected as an input measure because it is proportional to the area of office space occupied and accurately represents the branch size and the magnitude of all resources used. Because tellers perform most of the work related to transactions, it was felt that it represented the labor input into the operations of a branch.

Data from the operations of the last year have been collected, as shown in Exhibit 13-3(a). Output represents the number of transactions, in thousands, performed at each branch last year. Annual rent is in thousands of dollars and the number of teller hours is the sum of full-time and part-time teller hours, also in the thousands. To help represent the efficiency frontier graphically, we next divide the rent and the number of teller hours for each branch by the number of transactions performed.[25] This enables us to express quantities of each input per unit output (transaction) and make a two-dimensional graph possible for representing the efficiencies of bank branches. The results are shown in Exhibit 13-3(b).

Exhibit 13-3   Annual Output and Input Quantities of the Six Branches of the First Bank of Gotham City

a.　　Original data:

	OUTPUT	INPUTS	
Branch (DMU)	**Number of Transactions (Thousands)**	**Rent ($1,000)**	**Number of Teller Hours (Thousands)**
1	30	6	1.5
2	40	8	1.6
3	70	28	2.1
4	50	20	1.0
5	60	36	1.2
6	40	24	0.4

b.   Transformed data:

Branch (DMU)	y Transactions	x_1 Rent (per Unit Output)	x_2 Teller Hours (per Unit Output)
1	1	0.2	0.05
2	1	0.2	0.04
3	1	0.4	0.03
4	1	0.4	0.02
5	1	0.6	0.02
6	1	0.6	0.01

We need to set up and solve a linear programming (LP) model for each branch to determine its efficiency. However, only a few coefficients will be different in each LP problem. Now set up the model for DMU3 for illustration:

$$\text{Min } h_0 = \theta_0 - \varepsilon s_1^- - \varepsilon s_2^- - \varepsilon s_3^+$$

Subject to:

$$0.4\theta_0 - 0.2\lambda_1 - 0.2\lambda_2 - 0.4\lambda_3 - 0.4\lambda_4 - 0.6\lambda_5 - 0.6\lambda_6 - s_1^- = 0$$

$$0.03\theta_0 - 0.05\lambda_1 - 0.04\lambda_2 - 0.03\lambda_3 - 0.02\lambda_4 - 0.02\lambda_5 - 0.01\lambda_6 - s_2^- = 0$$

$$\lambda_1 + \lambda_2 + \lambda_3 + \lambda_4 + \lambda_5 + \lambda_6 - s_3^+ = 1$$

$$s_1^-, s_2^-, s_3^+, \lambda_j \geq 0 \; j = 1, 2, \ldots, 6$$

Exhibit 13-4 shows all six branches and the efficiency frontier. Note that each point in the graph represents a DMU using different combinations of transformed rent dollars and teller hours to produce one transaction. Branches 1, 2, 4, and 6 are on the efficiency frontier; however, only 2, 4, and 6 are efficient. Branches 1, 3, and 5 are inefficient.

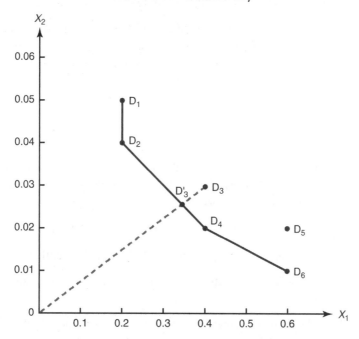

The first two constraints of the above problem correspond to the constraint set (13.2.2) of the LP model. The coefficients of these constraints are x_{ij}s that are given in Exhibit 13.3b, and the coefficients of θ_0 are the x_{ij}s of DMU3. The third constraint corresponds to the constraint set (13.2.3) of the LP model; because DMUs generate a single output (transactions) there is only one constraint of this type. The coefficients of the third constraint (y_{rj}) are all ones, as shown in Exhibit 13.3b. The right-hand side value of the constraint is the output quantity of DMU3. This problem can be solved on any commercially available LP software to obtain the following optimal solution:[26]

$\theta_0{}^* = 0.857143 \cong 0.86$, $\lambda^*_2 = 0.2857$, $\lambda^*_4 = 0.7143$, and all other variables equal to zero. As expected, Branch 3 is not fully efficient, but only 86 percent efficient. The optimal solution also indicates that Branches 2 and 4 form a peer group for Branch 3 because its mix of two inputs is closest to these two branches. In other words, input quantities used and the output quantities produced by Branches 2 and 4 serve as benchmarks for Branch 3 for its style of production. Consequently, Branch 3 can emulate them to become fully efficient. One way Branch 3 can become efficient is indicated by the projection formulas given earlier. Specifically, Branch 3 can become efficient if it reduces its inputs (per unit output) to the following quantities, without reducing its output:

$$x^*_1 = \theta_0{}^* x_1 - s_1{}^{-*} = 0.857143 \, (0.4) - 0 = 0.3428572 \cong \$0.34 \text{ per transaction;}$$

or $70,000(0.3428572) = \$24,000$ annual rent.

$$x^*_2 = \theta_0{}^*x_2 - s_2{}^{-*} = 0.857143(0.03) - 0 = 0.02571429 \cong 0.026 \text{ hr per transaction;}$$

or $70,000(0.02571429) = 1800$ hours per year.

Note that (0.34 and 0.026) are the coordinates of D'$_3$ in Exhibit 13-4. In other words, D'$_3$ represents the projection of the inefficient Branch 3 to the efficiency frontier. Because the output slack is zero the projection formula for output $y^*_{r0} = y_{r0} + s_r{}^{+*}$ would give us $y^*_{r0} = y_{r0}$, the same output value for DMU3 to become efficient. Also note that the efficiency of Branch 3 can be calculated as the ratio of the distance between the origin and D'$_3$ on the frontier, to the distance between the origin and D$_3$.

$$\theta_0{}^* = OD'_3 / OD_3$$

The same results can be obtained if a linear combination of inputs of the branches in the peer group is formed. Specifically, if Branch 3 combines 0.2857 of the input quantities of Branch 2 and 0.7143 of the input quantities of Branch 4 as its new input quantities:

$$x^*_{13} = x_{12}\,\lambda^*_2 + x_{14}\,\lambda^*_4 = 0.2(0.2857) + 0.4(0.7143) = 0.05714 + 0.28572 = 0.34286;$$

$$x^*_{23} = x_{22}\,\lambda^*_2 + x_{24}\,\lambda^*_4 = 0.04(0.2857) + 0.02(0.7143) = 0.011428 + 0.014246 = 0.025714.$$

In other words, D'$_3$ is a convex combination of points D$_2$ and D$_4$, which represent Branches 2 and 4.

Similar LP models can be set up and solved to determine the efficiencies of other branches. The results are given in Exhibit 13-5. As can be seen from the exhibit, Branch 1 is not efficient. Although it has an efficiency rating of 1.0, not all slacks are zero; hence Branch 1 does not meet all the conditions for efficiency. The slack value of 1.0 indicates that Branch 1 should reduce its usage of Input 2 (rent) by one unit to become efficient.

Exhibit 13-5 Efficiencies of the Branches of the First Bank of Gotham City

Branch (DMU)	Variables in the Optimal Solution	θ^*	Efficient?	Peer Group if Not Fully Efficient
1	$\lambda^*_2 = 1.00$ $s_2{}^{-*} = 0.01$	1.00	No	Branch 2
2	$\lambda^*_2 = 1.00$	1.00	Yes	
3	$\lambda^*_2 = 0.2857$ $\lambda^*_4 = 0.7143$	0.86	No	Branch 2 Branch 4
4	$\lambda^*_4 = 1.00$	1.00	Yes	
5	$\lambda^*_4 = 0.60$ $\lambda^*_6 = 0.40$	0.80	No	Branch 4 Branch 6
6	$\lambda^*_6 = 1.00$	1.00	Yes	

Lambdas with positive values in the optimal solution indicate the DMUs that comprise the peer group for each inefficient DMU. If a DMU is efficient, it serves as its own peer. Identification of a peer group is very useful in providing guidance to inefficient DMUs, because DMUs in the peer group are most like the branch being evaluated and can serve as role models for that branch.

A Review of DEA and Alternative Methods for the Measurement of Service Efficiency

DEA is not the only technique for measuring the efficiency of economic entities. As mentioned earlier, many organizations use ratios for productivity and efficiency measurement. Ratio analysis may be useful for determining if a DMU's performance deviates too much from a standard, such as an industry norm. However, when multiple outputs and multiple inputs are involved, a simple ratio of one output to one input would not be very helpful for comparative purposes. A common problem arises when a decision making unit may score high on some ratios and low on others. Unless some a priori weights are assigned to various ratios, comparison would not be possible. Selection of weights, on the other hand, is usually a troublesome task because there is usually no objective way for assignment of the weights. In other words, experts or managers may disagree on relative weights. Another possible approach to handle multiple outputs and inputs is to aggregate various ratios into a single ratio. This approach also requires weights to reflect the relative importance of different ratios and hence runs into the same problem.

Another common method is the regression analysis. The regression analysis can accommodate multiple outputs and inputs. However, it also has some drawbacks. First, the least squares method used in regression finds the average relationship between an output and inputs based on data that come from both efficient and inefficient DMUs. For example, the straight line found in a simple linear regression passes through the point X-bar and Y-bar, average values for the independent variable (for example, input) and dependent variable (for example, output), respectively. The average relationship is not likely to be an efficient relationship. Another shortcoming of regression is that it does not reveal much about the scale efficiency.[27]

Data envelopment analysis is an attractive alternative to ratio and regression analyses; it not only does not have the shortcomings of those two techniques, but it also has additional advantages. We can summarize the advantages of DEA as follows:[28]

1. DEA accommodates multiple outputs and multiple inputs; each input or output quantity can be expressed in its natural units.

2. DEA provides a single comprehensive, defensible measure of performance.

3. If a DMU is less than fully efficient, DEA provides valuable information on how it can become efficient. It indicates which outputs must be increased and/or which inputs must be decreased, and by how much, for an inefficient DMU to become efficient.

4. DEA determines efficiency in a fair and equitable way. The weights in the ratio model (13.1) are determined by maximizing the objective function, which is the efficiency of the DMU being evaluated. In other words, each DMU is given the highest efficiency rating possible.

5. For each inefficient DMU, DEA also provides a peer group (or best-practice group) consisting of efficient DMUs for reference purposes. In other words, DEA performs a benchmarking study at the same time as it measures efficiency. A decision maker, then, would refer only to this relatively small group of fully efficient DMUs to determine important characteristics of efficient units.

6. DEA does not assume any specific functional form of production relationship such as Cobb-Douglas production function.

7. DEA assumes all outputs and inputs have "some" value but does not require a priori selection of weights or prices for inputs or value for outputs.

8. DEA can include external factors, such as weather or demographic factors, in the measurement of efficiency.

9. DEA can accommodate judgment and expert opinion when needed.

10. Unlike regression analysis, it focuses on individual DMUs, and it does not assume that there is only one best way for productive efficiency. It allows the possibility of being efficient with different mixes of inputs and outputs.

Like any other quantitative tool, DEA has its limitations. An important issue is the selection of output and input measures to be used in the analysis. The decision as to which input and output measures should be included in a DEA model is an important decision for at least two reasons.[29] First, efficiency ratings will not decrease when a new input or output measure is added to a DEA model; efficiency of some DMUs will remain the same, while others' ratings may increase. Therefore, too many measures may diminish the discriminatory power of a model. A rule of thumb to avoid this problem is to make sure that the number of DMUs is equal to or greater than three times the sum of inputs and outputs. The second reason the selection of input and output measures is important is that it is not possible to judge from results if a measure is a theoretically correct measure to use. In other words, as in regression analysis, spurious relationships may be obtained.

As one of the advantages, we mentioned that DEA allows DMUs to be efficient with different mixes of inputs and outputs. This may become a disadvantage when an unimportant input or output is included among the measures. A DMU may excel in minimizing the use of such an input or succeed in producing large quantities of that type of output and be declared as efficient. This may not agree with the objectives of the organization and may lead to behavior that takes the organization farther away from its targets.

Another potential problem is related to the same characteristic. As indicated earlier, the DEA model selects the weights for outputs and inputs so that the efficiency rating for each DMU is maximized. This may result in weights that are not congruent with the value system of the organization. However, this problem can be solved with proper limits on the weights.[30]

The DEA measure of efficiency is not robust with respect to errors in data. In other words, the accuracy of data in DEA is critical; errors in data may lead to identification of inefficient DMUs as efficient and efficient ones as inefficient, which may compromise the perceived fairness of the measure.[31]

Other DEA Models

Various DEA models have been developed since the inception of the CCR model. All DEA models aim to construct an empirical efficiency frontier that represents best practices among DMUs included in the data set. Each model tries to identify the DMUs that define this frontier. An efficiency frontier envelops all DMUs in the set, and the efficiency of all units is determined relative to this frontier. The efficiency frontier may be different for different DEA models; some may be piecewise linear, piecewise loglinear, or piecewise Cobb-Douglas. Models also differ with respect to whether they assume constant or variable returns to scale. CCR model presented in this chapter assumes constant returns to scale. Another way DEA models may differ is whether they are units invariant or not. Finally, some models may have two versions: an input-oriented version and an output-oriented version. For example, the model (13.2) used in our example is the input-oriented version of the CCR model. An input-oriented version focuses on reducing inputs as a way to efficient operations. Conversely, an output-oriented model focuses on output augmentation to lead inefficient DMUs to efficiency. An efficiency frontier constructed through a specific DEA model will be the same for both the input and the output-oriented versions. The difference would be the point to which an inefficient DMU will be projected on the frontier. The output-oriented version of the CCR model is as follows.[32]

$$\text{Max } h_O = \phi_o + \varepsilon \left(\sum_{i=1}^{m} s_i^- + \sum_{r=1}^{s} s_r^+ \right) \tag{13.3}$$

Subject to:

$$\phi_o\, y_{ro} - \sum_{j=1}^{n} y_{rj}\lambda_j + s_r^+ = 0$$

$$\sum_{j=1}^{n} x_{ij}\lambda_j + s_i^- = x_{io}$$

$$\lambda_j, s_i^-, s_r^+ \geq 0 \qquad\qquad i=1, 2, \ldots, m;\ r=1, 2, \ldots, s;\ j=1, 2, \ldots, n$$

and the projection formulas are given as: $y^*_{ro} = \phi_o y_{ro} + s_r^{+*}$ and $x^*_{io} = x_{io} - s_i^{-*}$.

13.8 Summary

This chapter focused on productivity and efficiency of service operations. First, we discussed the basic concepts relevant to productivity and defined productivity as the ratio of output to input. Productivity may be computed for a single output and a single input or multiple outputs and inputs. Most organizations produce more than one kind of output and use several kinds of inputs. At the national level, labor productivity is the most frequently used productivity measure. Growth in labor productivity is used as an indicator of improvement in the standard of living of a country. In addition to being an indicator of standard of living, productivity growth influences other important economic variables, such as competitiveness, unemployment, inflation, social programs, and resource conservation.

Raising productivity is an important goal at both the national and organizational level. First among the factors that improve productivity in the long run is technological developments that reduce labor requirement in the production of goods and services. Another factor that has both long-term and short-term implications for increasing productivity is the organization and management of productive activities. Naturally, productivity improvements at the firm level determine what happens at the national level. Organizations can increase productivity in the long run by introducing new technologies and innovations in existing technology. They can also achieve significant increases in productivity in the short term by implementing better work methods and better management practices.

Services present special challenges with respect to productivity. It is not only difficult to increase service productivity, but it is also difficult to measure it and measure it accurately. We reviewed some of the reasons for the measurement problem and discussed why service productivity growth is slower in some services than manufacturing productivity. Some services, called progressive, are responsive to productivity improvement efforts, however, some services are not. The main reason is that the labor requirement in the latter group usually cannot be changed without a significant deterioration in quality. These are called stagnant services. We then presented some suggestions for raising productivity of services. Raising productivity is the responsibility of management; improvements in productivity are, to a large extent, the results of management actions. Drucker proposes "working smarter" as the way to raise productivity in services. Specifically he recommends (1) defining the task; (2) concentrating work on the task; (3) defining performance; (4) forming a partnership with employees; and (5) making continuous learning part of organization's culture.

The last section of this chapter presented data envelopment analysis (DEA) as a powerful management science technique for measuring the efficiency of economic units, which produce the same types of outputs by using the same types of inputs. One of the most frequently used models, the ratio model, was presented as a medium for the discussion of issues relevant to the application of DEA. Examples were provided for insight into the concepts and advantages of DEA.

Endnotes

1. P. F. Drucker, "The New Productivity Challenge," *Harvard Business Review*, (November–December 1991), pp. 69–79.

2. Bureau of Labor Statistics of the U.S. Department of Labor computes and publishes measures of productivity and studies on productivity change in the United States. More information on the compilation of data and computation of various productivity measures can be found in their publications; for example, see "Technical Information About the BLS Major Sector Productivity and Costs Measures," March 11, 2008, http://www.bls.gov/lpc/lpcmethods.pdf; "New Service Industry Productivity Measures," February 2006, Report 993, http://www.bls.gov/lpc/iprsr06.pdf, "Chapter 11. Industry Productivity Measures," http://www.bls.gov/opub/hom/pdf/homch11.pdf (accessed on 9/12/2012).or their periodical, Monthly Labor Review.

3. J. Jurison, "Reevaluating Productivity Measures," *Information Systems Management* (Winter 1997), pp. 30–34.

4. C. A. Knox Lovell, "Production Frontiers and Productive Efficiency," in Harold O. Fried, C. A. Knox Lovell, and Shelton S. Schmidt (Eds.), *The Measurement of Productive Efficiency: Techniques and Applications* (New York, NY, Oxford University Press, 1993), p. 4.

5. This section has been adopted from the following two sources: Committee for Economic Development, "Productivity Policy: Key to the Nation's Economic Future," (New York, NY, Committee for Economic Development, 1983), pp. 23–29; and W. J. Baumol, S. A. B. Blackman, and E. N. Wolff, *Productivity and American Leadership: The Long View* (Cambridge, MA, The MIT Press, 1989), pp. 9–27.

6. For example, see the discussion in Baumol, Blackman and Wolff, *Productivity and American Leadership: The Long View*, especially Chapters 1 and 4.

7. E. N. Wolff, "The Magnitude and Causes of the Recent Productivity Slowdown in the United States: A Survey of Recent Studies," in W. J. Baumol and K. McLennan (Eds.), *Productivity Growth and U.S. Competitiveness* (New York, Oxford University Press, 1985), pp. 29–57.

8. Committee for Economic Development, *Productivity Policy: Key to the Nation's Economic Future* (New York, NY, Committee for Economic Development, 1983), p. 31.

9. J. W. Kendrick, *Improving Company Productivity* (Baltimore, The Johns Hopkins University Press, 1984), p. 13.

10. Kendrick, *Improving Company Productivity*, p. 15.

11. M. K. Sherwood, "Difficulties in the Measurement of Service Outputs," *Monthly Labor Review* (March 1994), pp. 11–19.

12. D. I. Riddle, *Service-Led Growth: The Role of the Service Sector in World Development* (New York, NY, Praeger Publishers, 1986), p. 81.

13. The discussion in this section has been adopted from William J. Baumol "Productivity Policy and the Service Sector," in Inman, R. P. (Ed.), *Managing the Service Economy: Prospect and Problems* (New York, Cambridge University Press, 1985), pp. 301–317.

14. M. van Biema and B. Greenwald, "Managing Our Way to Higher Service-Sector Productivity," *Harvard Business Review* (July–August 1997), pp. 87–95.

15. Drucker, "The New Productivity Challenge."

16. A. Charnes, W. W. Cooper, and E. Rhodes, "Measuring the Efficiency of Decision Making Units," *European Journal of Operational Research*, Vol. 2, No. 6 (1978), pp. 429–444.

17. A. Charnes, W. W. Cooper, and E. Rhodes, "Evaluating Program and Managerial Efficiency: An Application of Data Envelopment Analysis to Program Follow Through," *Management Science*, Vol. 27 (1981), pp. 668–697.

18. C. Haksever and Y. Muragishi, "Measuring Value in MBA Programmes," *Education Economics*, Vol. 6, No. 1 (1998), pp. 11–25.

19. R. Banker, A. Charnes, W. W. Cooper, J. Swarts, and D. A. Thomas, "An Introduction to Data Envelopment Analysis With Some of its Models and Their Uses," *Research in Governmental and Nonprofit Accounting*, Vol. 5 (1989), pp. 125–163.

20. M. J. Farrell, "The Measurement of Productive Efficiency," *Journal of the Royal Statistical Society*, Series A, Part III, Vol. 120, No. 3 (1957), pp. 253–290.

21. Charnes, Cooper, and Rhodes, "Measuring the Efficiency of Decision Making Units," and A. Charnes, Z. M. Huang, J. Semple, T. Song, and D. Thomas "Origins and Research in Data Envelopment Analysis," *The Arabian Journal for Science and Engineering*, Vol. 19 (1990), pp. 617–625.

22. It must be noted that optimization as used in DEA is not for planning purposes (for example, production planning for optimizing profit). Optimization in DEA models is employed to assess the past performance of DMUs based on their observed inputs and outputs.

23. Charnes, Cooper, and Rhodes, "Measuring the Efficiency of Decision Making Units" for the details of the transformation.

24. For large scale applications of DEA in banking see the following two sources: C. Parkan, "Measuring the Efficiency of Service Operations: An Application to Bank Branches," *Engineering Costs and Production Economics*, Vol. 12 (1984), pp. 237–242, and M. Oral and R. Yolalan, "An Empirical Study on Measuring Operating Efficiency and Profitability of Bank Branches," *European Journal of Operational Research*, Vol. 46 (1990), pp. 282–294.

25. The DEA model we use in this example is units invariant. That is, if we divide, or multiply, data by a positive constant, efficiency evaluations are not affected as long as the same is done to all data of the same kind.

26. An explicit value of 10–6 has been used for epsilon (ε) in solving this model. This constant must be "small enough" for accurate results. However, what is "small enough" depends on the problem data. In general, the use of any explicit value in large problems carries the risk of giving inaccurate results and is not recommended. For a discussion of alternative approaches, see I. A. Ali, "Data Envelopment Analysis: Computational Issues," *Computers, Environment, and Urban Systems*, Vol. 14 (1990), pp. 157–165, and I. A. Ali and L. M. Seiford, "Computational Accuracy and Infinitesimals in Data Envelopment Analysis," *INFOR*, Vol. 31, No. 4 (1993), pp. 290–297.

27. See H. D. Sherman "Hospital Efficiency Measurement and Evaluation: Empirical Test of a New Technique," *Medical Care*, Vol. 22, No. 10 (October 1984), pp. 922–938, for a discussion of the use of ratio and regression techniques in measuring the efficiency of hospitals.

28. A. Charnes, W. W. Cooper, A. Y. Lewin, and L. M. Seiford,(Eds.), *Data Envelopment Analysis: Theory, Methodology, and Applications* (Boston, MA, Kluwer Academic Publishers, 1994), pp. 7–10, and M. K. Epstein and J. C. Henderson "Data Envelopment Analysis for Managerial Control and Diagnosis," *Decision Sciences*, Vol. 20 (1989), pp. 90–119.

29. See B. Golany and Y. Roll "An Application Procedure for DEA," *Omega*, Vol. 17 (1989), pp. 237–250, for a formal process for DEA applications.

30. See for example R. G. Dyson, and E. Thanassoulis "Reducing Weight Flexibility in Data Envelopment Analysis," *Journal of the Operational Research Society*, Vol. 39, No. 6 (1988), pp. 563–576.

31. See A. Charnes, W. W. Cooper, A. Y. Lewin, and L. M. Seiford,(Eds.), *Data Envelopment Analysis: Theory, Methodology, and Applications*, Chapter 21, pp. 425–435, for a discussion of important issues involved in DEA studies, including model selection, implementation, and interpretation of results.

32. See A. Charnes, W. W. Cooper, A. Y. Lewin, and L. M. Seiford (Eds.), *Data Envelopment Analysis: Theory, Methodology, and Applications*, Chapter 2, pp. 23–47, for a discussion of basic DEA models. Discussion of different DEA models from a "returns to scale" perspective is presented in A. I. Ali and L. M. Seiford, "The Mathematical Programming Approach to Efficiency Analysis," in Harold O. Fried, C. A. Knox Lovell, and Shelton S. Schmidt (Eds.), *The Measurement of Productive Efficiency: Techniques and Applications*, pp. 120–159.

14

MANAGEMENT OF PUBLIC AND PRIVATE NONPROFIT SERVICE ORGANIZATIONS

14.1 Introduction

> Americans of all ages, all stations in life, and all types of disposition are forever forming associations. There are not only commercial and industrial associations in which all take part, but others of a thousand different types—religious, moral, serious, futile, very general and very limited, immensely large and very minute. Americans combine to give fetes, found seminaries, build churches, distribute books...if they want to proclaim a truth or propagate some feeling by the encouragement of a great example, they form an association. In every case, at the head of any new undertaking, where in France you would find the government or in England some territorial magnate, in the United States you are sure to find an association.[1]

Alexis de Tocqueville, French social philosopher, visited the United States for nine months in 1831. The preceding quote is from his famous book *Democracy in America*, which resulted from observations he made during the visit. What de Tocqueville observed more than a century and a half ago is still true today; Americans are still forming and managing associations for a wide variety of purposes, but more often than not for public service.

These organizations form the **nonprofit** sector. The variety of nonprofits is truly amazing. They range from the neighborhood church and local parent-teacher association to the National Rifle Association, Sierra Club, and American Bar Association. Nonprofit organizations play such an important role in the economic and social life of the United States that it is also referred to as the **third sector**, private and public sectors being the other two.

The **public** sector consists of organizations that are formed and managed by the federal, state, or local governments. In the strict sense of the term, they are also nonprofit service organizations.

For this reason, sometimes they are called **public nonprofits**, and others are called **private non-profits** (see Exhibit 14-1). In this book, the term "public" will be used for nonprofit organizations that are formed and managed by government at any level, and private nonprofits simply as "nonprofit." The tax exempt status of private nonprofits leads some scholars to claim that these are actually public organizations. They argue that the tax exemption for nonprofits represents a flow of public money to nonprofits; tax revenue that the state could rightfully collect from them.[2]

Exhibit 14-1   Categories of Nonprofit Organizations

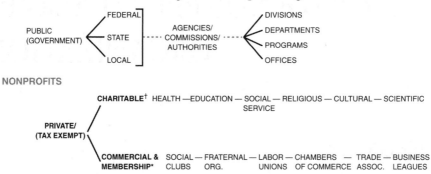

† Donor contributions are tax deductible.
* Donor contributions are not tax deductible.
Source: Adapted from Robert N. Anthony and David W. Young, *Management Control in Nonprofit Organizations*, 4th ed. (McGraw-Hill, 1988).

This chapter focuses on both types of these service organizations. The purpose is to present a synopsis of both public and nonprofit sectors and challenges their managers face. As you will discover, tasks and challenges of management in these two sectors are similar and yet they exhibit some important differences from the private sector. Organizations in both the public and nonprofit sectors need managers and managerial skills just like private firms. Although most managers in public and nonprofit organizations have their education in fields other than business, some business graduates will be working for some of these service organizations. Therefore, it is essential for service managers to understand these two important sectors of the U.S. economy.

14.2 Public and Private Nonprofit Organizations Defined

As indicated earlier, the public sector consists of agencies and organizations of the federal, state, and local governments. They are formed as a result of legislation at the appropriate level and are almost always financed by tax revenues and sometimes supplemented by fees. Most public organizations have a monopoly status. In other words, they usually have no competitors offering the same services. It is clear that they are not "profit-making" entities; actually no such concept exists for public organizations.[3] They may have a "surplus," but the surplus is not profit and is usually returned to the appropriate treasury at the end of a fiscal year.

The most important characteristic of nonprofits is that they are established for purposes other than making a profit. That is why sometimes they are called "not-for-profit."[4] It may be an over-simplification, but we assume that the major objective of private sector organizations is to make a profit. Naturally, some may have additional objectives, but without profits a private company cannot survive too long. Nonprofits, on the other hand, are distinguished by the absence of the profit objective. This does not mean that they do not make a profit from their operations. They do make profits and they are allowed to keep them. Actually, some (for example, nonprofit hospitals) at least partially depend on profits from their operations for their survival.

Perhaps the second important characteristic that defines nonprofits is the nondistribution constraint. **Nondistribution** means that no part of a nonprofit's income, profits, or assets can be distributed to its members, directors, or officers.

The third important characteristic is that nonprofits produce public goods—goods and services that provide benefits to the general public. Fourth, many nonprofits are exempt from federal corporate income tax and some are exempt from other federal, state, and local taxes, such as property tax, because they serve public purposes. There are more than 30 categories of tax exempt organizations under the U.S. tax law (see Exhibit 14-2). Only one group of nonprofits, 501(c) (3) charitable institutions, receive extra privileges that contributions to them are tax deductible for individuals and corporations. Public charities constitute the largest group among nonprofits; more than 1 million charities exist in the United States.[5] In addition to the public service aim, they are specifically designated as nonprofit when they are organized and are not allowed to distribute profits or assets to their members, officers, or directors. Nonprofits can engage in profit-making activities and keep their tax exempt status if the activity is *related* to the tax exempt purpose or unrelated but *insubstantial*.[6]

Yet another important characteristic of nonprofits is its reliance on volunteers. Some nonprofits rely only on volunteers.[7] Many individuals contribute their time and labor to nonprofits, especially charitable organizations. It is estimated that in 2010, 26.8 million individuals, approximately 26 percent of U.S. adults, volunteered 15 billion hours of their time for a nonprofit organization. Assuming a full-time employee works 1,700 hours per year, the hours they contributed was an equivalent of 8.8 million full-time employees, which is estimated to be worth $283.85 billion.[8]

Exhibit 14-2   Tax Exempt Organizations

Section of 1986 IRS Code	Description of Organization	Entities Registered with the IRS
501(c)(1)	Corporations organized under an act of Congress	100
501(c)(2)	Title-holding companies for exempt organizations	5,850
501(c)(3)	Religious, charitable, and similar organizations	984,386
501(c)(4)	Civic leagues and social welfare organizations	116,890
501(c)(5)	Labor, agricultural, and horticultural organizations	56,819
501(c)(6)	Business leagues, chambers of commerce, real estate boards, and trade boards	71,878
501(c)(7)	Social and recreational clubs	56,369
501(c)(8)	Fraternal beneficiary societies and associations	63,318
501(c)(9)	Voluntary employee-beneficiary associations	10,088
501(c)(10)	Domestic fraternal societies and associations	20,944
501(c)(11)	Teachers' retirement fund associations	14
501(c)(12)	Benevolent life insurance associations, mutual ditch or irrigation companies, mutual or cooperative telephone companies, and so on	5,901
501(c)(13)	Cemetery companies	9,808
501(c)(14)	State-chartered credit unions and mutual reserve funds	3,565
501(c)(15)	Mutual insurance companies or associations	1,646
501(c)(16)	Cooperative organizations to finance crop operations	16
501(c)(17)	Supplemental unemployment benefit trusts	300
501(c)(18)	Employee-funded pension trusts created before June 25, 1959	1
501(c)(19)	War veterans' organizations	35,113
501(c)(20)	Legal service organizations	9
501(c)(21)	Black lung benefits trusts	28
501(c)(22)	Withdrawal liability payment funds	0
501(c)(23)	Veterans associations founded prior to 1880	2
501(c)(24)	Trusts described in Section 4049 of the Employment Retirement Security Act of 1974	1
501(c)(25)	Title-holding corporations or trusts with multiple parents	1,133

501(c)(26)	State-sponsored organizations providing health coverage for high-risk individuals	10
501(c)(27)	State-sponsored workers' compensation reinsurance organizations	12
501(d)	Religious and apostolic organizations	160
501(e)	Cooperative hospital service organizations	18
501(f)	Cooperative service organizations of operating educational organizations	1
Other	Organizations not classified previously, including charitable risk pools	4,105
	Total	1,448,485

Sources: Urban Institute, National Center for Charitable Statistics, Core Files (2005) and IRS Business Master Files (2006). *Notes:* Not all Internal Revenue Code Section 501 (c) (3) organizations are included because certain organizations, such as churches (and their integrated auxiliaries or subordinate units) and conventions or associations of churches, need not apply for recognition of tax exemption unless they specifically request a ruling. Private foundations are included among 501 (c) (3) organizations. Adapted from Kennard T. Wing, Thomas H. Pollak, & Amy Blackwood, *The Nonprofit Almanac*, The Urban Institute Press, Washington, DC, (2008), pp. 2–3.

14.3 Significance of Public and Private Nonprofit Organizations

Whether they are private or public, the essence of nonprofit organizations is service; service to the public in general, but in most cases, to a subgroup of public. There is little, if any, manufacturing done by public sector organizations or nonprofits. Think about some of the well-known agencies of the federal government, for example, the U.S. Coast Guard, U.S. Secret Service, Centers for Disease Control and Prevention, National Weather Service, Federal Aviation Administration, Forest Service, Federal Highway Administration, National Park Service, Social Security Administration. These organizations constitute only a small sample of the agencies of the U.S. government, but they are all service organizations like thousands of other organizations of federal, state, and local governments.

Now consider a few examples from the nonprofit sector, such as the U. S. Tennis Association, Red Cross, Salvation Army, Girl Scouts, Boy Scouts, private colleges and universities, fraternities and sororities on college campuses, professional associations, religious organizations (churches, synagogues, mosques, and so on), United Way, American Heart Association, American Cancer Society, museums, and symphony orchestras. It is clear that these private nonprofits, just like public organizations, exist to provide a variety of services. Consequently, there is no question that public and nonprofit sectors are **service** sectors.

It must be obvious that government organizations at all three levels perform vital services such as national defense, maintaining law and order, education, healthcare, banking (for example,

Federal Reserve, Federal Deposit Insurance Corporation), safety of air, rail, highway, and maritime transportation. Hence, no matter how much we complain about the size of government, or the quality of its services, without public organizations, social and economic life as we know it would not be possible. There are more than 87,000 public organizations in the United States. Their activities create a lot of business for private sector and create many jobs for the population. The private sector is where most people work; as of 2012, 111.4 million people (approximately 84 percent of the nonfarm workforce) are employed by the private sector. The public sector is second in terms of the number of employees. The federal government is the single biggest employer; in addition to military personnel, the federal government employs approximately 3 million (2.58 million full-time) civilians, which is approximately 1.9 percent of the nonfarm workforce. State governments employ approximately 7.5 million people and local governments employ 12 million (10.78 million full time). Hence, overall the public sector provides jobs to more than 22 million people, almost 17 percent of the workforce.[9]

The nonprofit sector is also a major source of employment in the United States. More than 1.44 million nonprofit organizations exist, and more than 10 million people work for these organizations, which is approximately 9 percent of the workforce. Volunteers provide about 37 percent of the labor input to the operations of nonprofits. The amount of volunteer and paid labor together indicate that a total of about 16 million people work for nonprofits.

14.4 The Nature of Public Sector Organizations

As indicated earlier, the U.S. economy consists of three sectors: private, public, and nonprofit. Most of the economic activity takes place in the private sector. However, as the data of the previous section demonstrated, the other two sectors are also important to Americans, not only in an economic sense, but also from a political, sociological, and cultural perspectives. These two sectors also differ from the private sector in some important respects. This section discusses some of the reasons that necessitate the existence of public organizations and their characteristics that make them so different from the private firms.

Why Public Organizations Exist

Four major reasons for the existence of public organizations can be identified:[10]

Providing public goods—Public goods are those goods and services that possess two important characteristics: (1) Their consumption by an individual does not prevent others from consuming them or diminish the benefits others receive from them; and (2) exclusion of any potential consumer from the benefits of these goods is usually not possible. Some examples include national defense, clean air, a lighthouse, parks, paved roads and highways, and radio and television broadcasts on the air. Although economists coined the term **public goods**, it is clear that most public goods are services.

Private goods are those goods that you have to pay for before you can consume them. For example, if you want to listen to a music broadcast, you have to buy a radio, which is a private good. Your purchase and use of it prevents somebody else from the benefits of a radio, at least in the short term, because resources are limited. However, the radio broadcast is a public good; your enjoyment of it does not reduce its availability for others. Also, when the broadcast is on the air, those who want to listen to it cannot be prevented from listening.

But who is going to pay for the broadcast? If it is a commercial radio station, most likely advertisers will, but not the listeners. Listeners cannot be made to pay for the broadcast because it is available to anyone with a radio after it is produced. Hence, someone pays for it and most listeners enjoy it free. In other words, there are many "free riders" in the consumption of public goods; of course, there are some radio and TV stations that receive voluntary financial support from their listeners or viewers (for example, the Public Broadcasting System and National Public Radio). However, this example illustrates the basic problem with public goods; those who do not want to pay for the service can neither be made to pay nor can they be prevented from their use. On the other hand, there is no incentive for private companies to produce public goods if they are not getting paid for it. Most people need those goods, but without someone paying for them, they will not be provided by the private sector. Hence, government steps in to provide most of the public goods such as national defense, police protection, and paved streets. Governments provide these services and finance them through taxation. The fact that private companies would not produce most public goods is sometimes called **market failure** because the market mechanism that makes the production, distribution, and sale of private goods and services possible fails to provide most public goods.

Controlling externalities—Side effects of economic activities are called externalities. Externalities are the outcomes that impact third parties. They may be negative or positive. A negative externality is called a **social cost**, and a positive one is called a **social benefit**. Pollution is a well-understood negative externality. When a manufacturing process creates air pollution, for example, people who have nothing to do with this economic activity (that is, those other than the owners of the firm or its employees or customers) suffer the consequences. A well-kept house on a block may be an example of a positive externality because people who live around that house will get something positive from it even though they did not pay for the upkeep of the house. A well-kept house will provide a pleasant view, and increase the value, and hence prices, of other houses around it. Externalities are also considered a form of market failure because the market mechanism does not necessarily extract all the costs of negative externalities from those who benefit from the activity that created it. Similarly, the mechanism cannot collect payments from those who benefit from a positive externality. An effective way to solve this problem is usually government's imposition of taxes on those who create negative externalities and subsidies to those who create positive externalities. Public organizations such as the Environmental Protection Agency and Nuclear Regulatory Commission are set up to deal with negative externalities.

Equity—Another reason for the existence of government, and therefore public organizations, is the desire for equality, which is predicated on the belief that human beings must have equal rights. Various forms of inequality may result from an unlimited and uncontrolled operation of the market mechanism. For example, a private company may ignore the safety and health of its employees because taking safety precautions reduces profits. Or a company may prefer to hire only white males as employees. When there are no laws against them, some private companies may follow such practices because of their superior economic position in the transaction. This type of practice will outrage many Americans today, and they will demand government action to stop them. Clearly, this function of government originates from the value system of its citizens. Equal Employment Opportunity Commission, for example, was established in 1964 to achieve equity in employment. Specifically, it promotes equal employment opportunities and prevents discrimination in hiring based on race, color, religion, sex, national origin, age, disability, or genetic information.

Providing a framework for law and order and economic stability—An obvious function of the government is to maintain law and order and ensure the safety of its citizens. Equally important is the creation and maintenance of a stable economic environment, which is essential for the operation of the free market mechanism. The Constitution of the United States gives the federal government the right to print money and regulate commerce. Public organizations such as the Federal Reserve Board, Federal Trade Commission (FTC), and Securities and Exchange Commission (SEC) are some of the public organizations that contribute to the achievement of this objective. The FTC, for example, is charged with keeping business competition free and fair and preventing the dissemination of false and deceptive advertising, regulating the labeling and packaging of commodities, and enforcing antitrust laws. SEC, on the other hand, oversees the public issuance and sale of corporate securities and regulates the U.S. stock exchanges (New York, American, and 12 regional exchanges).

Characteristics of Public Organizations and Challenges for Their Managers

Individuals who supervise the activities of public employees and public organizations are called public managers. Some of these people are elected and some are appointed. In the federal government, the president of the United States is the highest elected official; in a state government, it is the governor, and in a city government, it is the mayor. Elected officials usually appoint people they know and trust to high administrative positions. They are political appointees, and some of these appointments need legislative approval. Political appointees may not be reappointed if the elected official loses his position. These managers may come from the inside or outside of a public organization. Levels below them are executive managers, middle managers, and supervisors who are usually appointed from among the career employees of the organization. This chapter focuses on managers, including political appointees, but not elected officials.

Public managers face tremendous challenges because most of them have to perform duties in addition to duties private sector managers in similar positions undertake. They have to face additional challenges created by the nature and environment of public organizations that are usually not related to management. To understand these challenges, the nature of public organizations and the environment they operate in are reviewed next. The challenges public managers face are compared to those faced by managers in the private sector. Characteristics of public organizations can be understood along the following dimensions.

Reason for existence—A private service company is created to make money for its owners. A public organization, on the other hand, is created by law passed by the appropriate legislative body. In general, a public organization tries to fulfill one or more of the four purposes of government discussed in the previous section by providing one or more services to the public. In other words, its mission is determined by the legislative body and is ultimately accountable to the public, or to the legislative body that created it.

Source of funds—A private company is established with capital provided by its owners. Additional funds for investments or operating expenses may be obtained through loans from financial institutions. Also, revenues from the sale of goods and/or services constitute an important source of funds for a private company. For a public company the capital (for example, buildings, furniture, and equipment) and operating funds and salaries paid to employees are provided by the government from tax revenues. Most public organizations have no revenue to speak of. Some may collect fees, but fees usually do not constitute a major source of income for public organizations. Remaining funds at the end of a fiscal year cannot be kept for the following year; they must be returned to the appropriate treasury.

Environment—A private company pursues its profit goal, and other goals, in a market environment and must follow the rules of the market. The market mechanism determines the answers to three basic economic questions: what combination of goods and services to produce, how to produce them, and for whom to produce them. Market mechanism works when buyers and sellers of a good or service interact to determine its price and quantity. Public organizations are not part of this environment; they do not seek profit and therefore they are not subject to most of the rules and forces of the market. They do not need prices to determine what services to produce and for whom. All these decisions are made by legislators. In short, public organizations are part of the government and the political system, but not the market system. They have to follow the rules of the political system, not the market system. The political system includes the laws and regulations, as well as the wishes of elected officials and legislators.

Goals[11]—The profit goal of a private organization is clear and easily understandable. Because of this clear goal, it is also relatively easy to measure efficiency in the private sector. Efficiency of operations is a significant contributor to the achievement of profitability. Consequently, efficiency, in addition to effectiveness, is an important goal for private organizations. Efficiency and effectiveness are also important for public organizations, but they have other important goals, such as responsiveness to the general public, responsiveness to the affected clientele, and political rewards for the legislature and executive. Often there is conflict among these goals. It is easy to imagine the difficult time a public manager has trying to balance these conflicting goals and satisfy demands from various stakeholders.

Public pressure—Public organizations often operate under intense public pressure due to controversial issues they sometimes have to deal with. Private companies may also come under pressure from the public, politicians, and the news media. However, what public organizations face is usually much more complicated and intense. Some public managers feel like they live in a "fish bowl." They are under constant public scrutiny because these organizations belong to the public, and they are supposed to serve the public interest.

Internal organization—Public organizations have formal hierarchical structures. However, their managers operate under a fragmented authority structure. This is mainly because there is a division of authority in federal and state governments among executive, legislative, and judicial branches. In the private sector a manager usually has only one boss. In the public sector, managers have many bosses: their direct supervisor, their supporting interest groups, and the members of the legislative overseeing committee.

Background of public managers—Public managers usually are not professional managers. In other words, their education is usually in a field other than business administration. Hence, it is not surprising to see lawyers running legal agencies, doctors running health-related agencies, and professional politicians heading a variety of other organizations. The lack of professional management training puts public managers at a disadvantage in dealing with some of the routine managerial tasks their counterparts face in the private sector.

Legal restrictions—Public organizations are bound by many legal restrictions in their external actions. They can do only what the laws and regulations allow them to do; going outside these boundaries for higher efficiency or effectiveness is usually not permitted. Internal operations of a public organization are also bound by extensive procedures and formal specifications and controls designed to ensure accountability to the taxpayer and conformance to laws and regulations. Consequently, public managers also have far more restrictions on their internal operations than managers in the private sector. Private sector managers hire, fire, promote, and demote employees with relative ease. They can add another shift to increase output or eliminate a shift to reduce output. Normally, these options are not available to public managers. They are generally bound by "merit" systems that put severe restrictions on how they manage employees. Some actions may require approval from the top authority of the administration or even from the legislative body. In short, public managers have much less flexibility and authority in decision making.

14.5 The Nature of Private Nonprofit Organizations

In this section, the nature of the third sector of the U.S. economy is reviewed: private nonprofits. First, the question of how to classify nonprofits is considered. Then, the economic reasons for the emergence of this sector are discussed. Finally, some important characteristics of nonprofits that separate them from private companies and public organizations are summarized. As these characteristics are discussed, the challenges they create for managers in this sector are also pointed out.

Types of Nonprofit Organizations

Nonprofits exhibit great variety in terms of their purposes, causes they serve, sources of funding, services they provide, use of volunteers, size, and nature of their customers. Understanding why these organizations have so much diversity may be aided if they can be categorized into meaningful groups. However, this is not an easy task, simply because on every dimension of categorization these organizations form a continuum, rather than clearly separated groups. The U.S. government classifies nonprofits for tax purposes (refer to Exhibit 14-2). Another attempt for classification is along two dimensions: (1) source of income and (2) the way in which they are controlled.[12] Two groups of nonprofits can be identified with respect to source of income: donative and commercial (Exhibit 14-3).

Exhibit 14-3   A Four-Way Classification of Nonprofit Organizations

	Mutual	Entrepreneurial
Donative	Common cause	CARE
	National Audubon Society	March of Dimes
	Political clubs	Art museums
Commercial	American Automobile Association	National Geographic Society[b]
	Consumers Union[a]	Educational Testing Service, Hospitals
	Country clubs	Nursing homes

a   Publisher of Consumer Reports.
b   Publisher of National Geographic.
Source: Henry Hansmann, "The Role of Nonprofit Enterprise," Yale Law Journal, vol. 89 (1980), pp. 835–901.

"Donative" nonprofits receive a substantial portion of their income in the form of donations, and "commercial" nonprofits receive their income primarily or exclusively from sales of goods and services. With respect to the control dimension, two groups exist: mutual and entrepreneurial. If the ultimate control of the organization is in the hands of its patrons (that is, donors, members, or customers) they fall into the first group. Nonprofits whose boards are self-perpetuating are in the second group. Of course, the four groups are not clearly separated from each other; organizations exist between the two groups along each dimension. For example, many private universities depend heavily on both donations and tuition, and some university boards of trustees include members elected by the alumni and members who are self-perpetuating.

Another useful way to categorize nonprofits is along the following four dimensions: nature of the product, nature of the market, mission focus on clients, and use of volunteers.[13]

Why Nonprofits Exist

The four major reasons discussed in the previous section are generally accepted as an explanation for the existence of public organizations. When the same question is asked for private nonprofits, however, the answer is not unique. Economists have been debating the issue for some time and have advanced various theories which can be grouped under four titles.[14]

The public goods theory—The first of these theories attributes the existence of nonprofits to the failure of both the market and government in providing public goods.[15] As discussed earlier, the private sector would not produce public goods when it does not get paid for its efforts; hence, the government steps in to provide some of those services and taxes people for the cost of provision. However, the government faces some limitations as the provider of these services; the most important one is a limited budget. Consequently, it has to choose carefully the kinds and quantities of public services to provide. In a democratic country a government normally chooses those services that would command majority support. This implies that there are services some segment of the public demands but cannot garner majority support for their provision. According to the theory, private nonprofit organizations are formed to meet the demand for such services.

The contract failure theory—Consumers have difficulty in evaluating the quality of some services, especially those that require technical knowledge and special skills and services provided by professionals. These services are said to be high in **credence qualities**.[16] The quality and the quantity of some services are even harder to evaluate when the recipient of the service is different from the purchaser. Some examples include healthcare, care for the aged, and daycare services. Economists describe the situation as a case of **asymmetric information** between the service provider and the consumer. In other words, the service provider has more information about the quality and the quantity of the service than a consumer. Consequently, when these services are provided by a profit-seeking private firm, there is an incentive to cheat. The theory predicts that the nondistribution characteristic of the nonprofit organizations, together with the fact that they are not primarily seeking a profit, makes these organizations more trustworthy in the eyes of consumers. For similar reasons, donors give money and/or their time to nonprofits because these organizations are more likely to use donations for the intended purposes.

The consumer control theory—Some nonprofits, such as mutual benefit organizations that provide services exclusively to their members or supporters, such as a country club, do not seem to result from the contract failure.[17] These organizations are formed, according to the theory, to provide more control to their members over the quality and cost of the services provided. Such control helps avoid monopolistic exploitation of members by the owners of a private company. The major reason for joining exclusive clubs is the opportunity to meet and associate with people who have qualities and connections that make them attractive companions. Consequently, a private owner of such an exclusive club would charge membership fees that cover not only the operating costs, but also the value to each member of associating with other members.[18] The theory also explains why a nonprofit form is preferred when quality rather than cost is the dominant concern in some social services or when donors are also consumers. For example, most people who serve on the boards of directors of opera companies, symphonies, and museums are also consumers of the services, and they serve to monitor the quality of the output.[19]

The subsidy theory—Governments at three levels contribute approximately 31 percent of the income of nonprofits. Contributions may be in the form of grants or contracts for the provision of services for which government has accepted some responsibility. Other forms of government contribution are loans and loan guarantees. In addition to these, tax exemption status of most nonprofits is an implicit government subsidy. Hence, subsidies constitute a major source of funding for nonprofits. It has been suggested[20] that these subsidies encourage the establishment of nonprofits especially in those industries in which nonprofits compete with private profit seeking companies. An important question is why doesn't the government provide these services but delegate the production task to nonprofits? According to one view, the major reason is that nonprofits can charge fees for these services so that the government's share of total cost is reduced. A second important reason is that nonprofits may have lower costs than public organizations, especially for labor. Another relevant question is, "Why are nonprofits preferred for the provision of the needed services, whereas many equally capable private companies exist?" Of course, sometimes the government uses the private sector for some services. For example, large defense contracts are given to private firms, and some private companies now provide prison services. In other cases nonprofits may be the only alternative, or the government may prefer to use nonprofits if costs can be lowered. For example, a nonprofit organization may come up with matching donations for the desired service.[21]

These theories present an economic perspective of nonprofits.[22] There is, however, another important noneconomic reason for the existence of nonprofits. As the quote from de Tocqueville hinted, in addition to economic reasons, Americans form nonprofit organizations to express their religious, political, social, or artistic views or promote a cause that may or may not be popular. In other words, through nonprofit organizations Americans can exercise their First Amendment freedoms. Nonprofits also limit the political impact of America's remarkable religious, ethnic, and ideological diversity and help reduce tensions that may originate from this diversity.[23]

Characteristics of Nonprofits and Challenges for Their Managers

Private nonprofit organizations not only constitute the third sector of the U.S. economy, but they also assume a role and a set of characteristics that fall somewhere between the private and public sectors. In some respects they have characteristics similar to the private sector because they are established and run by private citizens and are subject to most of the rules and forces of the market. In other respects, they are similar to the public sector because their mission is public service. This section reviews some of these characteristics and the challenges they create for their managers.

Purpose/mission—Two of the most important characteristics of nonprofit organizations are that profit is not the main purpose, and there is a nondistribution constraint on their assets; they cannot distribute any part of their income, profits, or assets to their members, directors, or officers. These organizations must be specifically designated as nonprofit in their charters when they are established.[24] Nonprofits may provide a wide variety of services, which can be grouped in six major categories: healthcare, education and research, social services, arts and culture, community development, and religion. A nonprofit organization tends to accumulate multiple purposes or missions for various reasons. Additional purposes may be added to increase the utilization of the existing fundraising and service delivery systems; with a few modifications to the existing systems additional needs may be met.[25] Multiplicity of purposes may make management's task harder, especially if the purposes are incongruent.

Ideology—Ideology may be a major reason for the establishment of many nonprofits. Many organizations have been founded by people who have a set of strongly held beliefs. These people are motivated by their ideals and spend their time and money to promote their ideals. Ideology may stem from religious faiths or from secular thoughts, political beliefs, different artistic approaches, or subscription to a particular theory in any field, such as education, science, or child development.[26]

Ownership—Nonprofits do not have owners. Private companies belong to their shareholders, public organizations belong to the government, or the public at large, but nonprofits do not have owners. This is because ownership implies a claim on assets that clearly contradicts the nondistribution constraint. If a nonprofit organization is dissolved, its assets are transferred to another nonprofit organization or to the state or municipality in which it operates, but never to private individuals.[27]

Source of funds/capital—Owners, or shareholders, provide the capital and operating funds for a private company, and for this reason they have claims on the company's assets and profits. Because nonprofits cannot have owners, the capital, and possibly some portion of operating funds, must be donated. Fundraising is a vital function for many nonprofits. However, donors are not the only source of funds for nonprofits; they may charge a fee for some of their services. Even if they are not sufficient to cover all the costs, fees may be a significant source of revenue for a nonprofit organization. For example, a nonprofit hospital may rely on revenues from its patients as well as donations. Similarly, a private university may mainly depend on tuition it receives from students for survival. Government grants and service contracts constitute the third important source of funds for nonprofits. As mentioned earlier, tax exempt status of most nonprofits can be considered as an implicit government subsidy to these organizations.

Management structure—A private corporation is governed by its board of directors, which represents the interests of its shareholders. A nonprofit organization is governed by a board of trustees, but because there are no owners, the board's main responsibility is to see that the mission of the organization is accomplished. Other responsibilities of the board include determining the mission and purpose, setting policies, making long-range plans, designing fiscal policy and plans, appointing a chief executive officer, and developing the bylaws of the organization.[28] Most trustees of a nonprofit don't receive any compensation for their services; in addition, many are also donors. They may be chosen for political or financial reasons rather than for their managerial talent or knowledge of the organization.

Volunteers—Volunteers provide approximately 37 percent of the labor input of nonprofits, and therefore constitute a significant resource. Because of this, they also create a challenge for managers. Because volunteers do not receive any compensation, they are not financially dependent on the organization. Some may even be major donors, and hence they may be difficult to manage and control. A nonprofit organization may also have paid employees. The existence of two types of employees multiplies the complexity of the tasks of management.

Internal organization—Formal hierarchical structure of public organizations or clear lines of authority in private companies may not be found in nonprofits. Especially large nonprofit organizations have a more complex and less rigid internal structure. Large nonprofits such as universities, hospitals, opera companies, and social welfare agencies lack clear lines of hierarchy.[29] For example, a university may have a hierarchical structure such as a board of trustees, president, provost, deans, and department chairs; but individual faculty members, especially tenured faculty, have considerable freedom of action and cannot be managed or controlled like employees in a private company. Another unique feature of most nonprofit organizations is that they consist of two distinct systems. One system is for the development of resources, and the other is for the provision of services (Exhibit 14-4). In a private company there is only one system for both.[30] For example, consider a nonprofit organization that runs a needle exchange program for the prevention of the spread of AIDS. Although the funds for this mission may be raised by one branch of the organization, another branch may be in charge of the distribution of clean needles to drug addicts. The main reason for this dual system is increased efficiency from specialization. It is clear that a nonprofit with such a structure has two categories of external customers: one, those who provide the funds, such as individuals, private companies, or government, and two, those who receive the services. This feature of some nonprofits also increases organizational complexity and makes the job of managers harder.

Exhibit 14-4   Internal Systems of Private and Nonprofit Enterprises

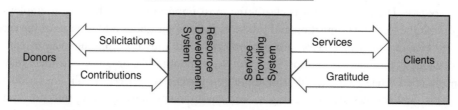

Source: Adapted from David E. Mason, *Voluntary Nonprofit Enterprise Management* (New York, Plenum Press, 1984), p.65.

Goals—Organizational goals in nonprofits are usually numerous, vague, and sometimes contradictory. One reason for this is that some nonprofits pursue multiple purposes as discussed earlier. Multiple purposes lead to multiple, and possibly, contradictory goals. For example, a nonprofit whose mission is to help victims of an incurable disease may face conflicting goals of allocating resources to the care of victims of the disease and contributing funds to ongoing research to find a cure. The existence of multiple goals may lead to a diffusion of management attention and energy, and less than ideal outcomes. Vagueness of goals, on the other hand, contributes to measurement problems as discussed in the next paragraph.

Measurement problems—Performance of a private company or its management can be assessed relatively easily by looking at the bottom line. In other words, profit is a reliable overall indicator of both effectiveness and efficiency in the private sector. Profit as a measure serves several purposes in private companies. For example, it can be used for evaluating proposed courses of action in a quantitative analysis of alternatives; as a measure of managerial performance; and as a common measure for comparing the performance of dissimilar units.[31] Such a reliable measure does not usually exist for nonprofit organizations; therefore, it is difficult to develop an effective measurement and control system in these organizations. Because goals are not usually expressed in monetary terms, assessment of organizational or managerial performance is difficult. These difficulties are in addition to measurement difficulties inherent in the provision of services because nonprofits are almost never manufacturing organizations.

Complexity—Complexity is the main source of challenges for the management of a nonprofit and therefore deserves special emphasis. We have mentioned that many nonprofits may consist of dual internal systems and may have two groups of employees and two groups of customers. In addition, nonprofits typically have multiple purposes; their goals are abstract and sometimes contradictory. Each of these multiply the complexity of internal and external relationships of a nonprofit organization and implies a variable to control or manage. Add to these the difficulties of measuring outcomes or performance, and the constant struggle to generate enough funds to survive, it becomes clear that managers of nonprofits face tremendous challenges.

14.6 Summary

The economy of the United States consists of three sectors: private, public, and nonprofit. This chapter reviewed the nature of public and private nonprofit organizations and challenges their managers face. The private sector is clearly the most important sector because it employs the majority of the working population and produces most of the goods and services of the economy. However, the other two sectors are also important, not only for economic reasons, but also for sociological and political reasons. For example, without public organizations there may not be any national defense, safe neighborhoods, safe air travel, paved streets, public education, state universities and colleges, national parks, a clean environment, warning and protection systems against natural disasters (such as hurricanes and flood), protection against epidemics and other health hazards, and many other services we take for granted. Also, without private nonprofits many museums, symphony orchestras or other classical music groups, private universities and colleges, research organizations, religious organizations, charities, fraternal organizations, professional societies, and organizations that fight incurable diseases may not exist. In short, without public and private nonprofits, the society we live in would be very different and probably not as convenient or pleasant.

Organizations in public and nonprofit sectors have some characteristics in common: They have purposes other than profit making; they serve the public in general or a subgroup of it; and they are all service organizations. Public organizations are created by law and may be federal, state, or local government organizations. Their main purposes are to provide public goods, control externalities, ensure equality and equal treatment of their citizens, and provide a framework for law and order and economic stability. Public organizations are funded by tax revenues collected by the appropriate level of government. They operate in a political environment, they are subject to many internal and external restrictions brought upon by laws and regulations, and they are under public scrutiny most of the time. These characteristics create unique challenges for the managers of public organizations. Top-level public managers are usually elected; others who serve under them are usually appointed from within the organization. Most managers in public organizations have their training in fields other than business, which complicates the already difficult task they face.

The nonprofit sector is placed somewhere between the public and private sectors. Nonprofits are not created by the government; therefore, they are not public organizations. However, their purpose, in general, is to serve the public. They not only provide a wide variety of services, but they also form an outlet for the expression of a variety of beliefs and ideologies. Nonprofits are established by private citizens, but they have no owners. They can and do make a profit from their operations but cannot distribute their profits or assets to their officers, members, or directors. Main sources of funds for nonprofits are donations, fees they collect for their services, and government grants and contracts for services. Many nonprofits have dual internal systems: one for the acquisition of resources and the other for producing service. They also have two groups of external customers: donors and those who are the consumers of the nonprofit's service. Furthermore, many nonprofits have two types of employees: volunteers and paid employees. These characteristics multiply the complexity of internal and external relationships of a nonprofit organization. Nonprofits usually pursue multiple goals that are abstract and sometimes contradictory. These characteristics make measurement of individual or organizational performance difficult. Finally, most nonprofits constantly struggle to generate funds for survival. It is clear that managers of nonprofits face tremendous challenges.

Endnotes

1. Alexis de Tocqueville, *Democracy in America*, edited by J. P. Mayer and Max Lerner, translated by George Lawrence, Harper & Row, New York, 1966, p. 485.

2. There are quite a few arguments for and against the assertion that the tax exempt status of private nonprofits makes them "public" organizations. For a detailed discussion of these views, see Andrew Stark, "The Distinction between Public, Nonprofit, and For-Profit: Revisiting the 'Core Legal' Approach," *Journal of Public Administration Research and Theory*, Vol. 21:1 (2011), pp. 3–36.

3. A few exceptions exist. For example, the U.S. Postal Service and Amtrak are quasigovernmental agencies that appear to be neither profit-making nor nonprofit.

4. Some people may see a subtle difference between the terms "nonprofit" and "not-for-profit." Actually, the latter may describe these organizations more accurately because they are established for purposes other than making profit. The term "nonprofit" may imply an organization that is incapable of making profit. However, there seems to be no real difference between these terms as they are used in the literature.

5. Katie L. Roeger, Amy Blackwood, and Sarah L. Pettijohn, *The Nonprofit Sector in Brief: Public Charities, Giving, and Volunteering* (The Urban Institute, 2011), http://www.urban.org/publications/412434.html.

6. Robert N. Anthony and David W. Young, "Characteristics of Nonprofit Organizations." in David L. Gies, J. Steven Ott and Jay M. Shafritz (Eds.), *The Nonprofit Organization: Essential Readings* (Pacific Grove, California, Brooks/Cole Publishing Company, 1990), pp. 216–235.

7. Lester M. Salamon, "Putting the Civil Society Sector on the Economic Map of the World," *Annals of Public and Cooperative Economics*, Vol. 81:2 (2010), pp. 167–210.

8. Katie L. Roeger, Amy Blackwood, and Sarah L. Pettijohn, *The Nonprofit Sector in Brief: Public Charities, Giving, and Volunteering*.

9. Unless otherwise mentioned, statistical data given in this chapter are from U.S. Department of Labor, Bureau of Labor Statistics website, http://www.bls.gov/ (accessed 09/19/2012).

10. Michael L. Vasu, Debra W. Stewart, and G. David Garson, *Organizational Behavior and Public Management*, Second Edition (New York, Marcel Dekker, 1990), pp. 8–11; W. Glen Rowe and Mary Conway Dato-On, *Introduction to Nonprofit Management* (Los Angeles, Sage Publications, Inc., 2013), p.8.

11. This and the next four dimensions have been adapted from James E. Swiss, *Public Management Systems: Monitoring and Managing Government Performance* (Englewood Cliffs, NJ, Prentice Hall, 1991), pp. 6–8.

12. Henry Hansmann, "Economic Theories of Nonprofit Organization," in Walter W. Powell, (Ed.), *The Nonprofit Sector: A Research Handbook* (New Haven, CT, Yale University Press, 1987), pp. 27–42.

13. Robert D. Hay, *Strategic Management in Nonprofit Organizations* (New York, Quorum Books, 1990).

14. See the following sources for a detailed discussion of these theories: Henry Hansmann, "Economic Theories of Nonprofit Organization"; Estelle James and Susan Rose-Ackerman, The Nonprofit Enterprise in Market Economics, (London, Harwood Academic Publishers, 1986); Lester M. Salamon, *Partners in Public Service: Government-Nonprofit Relations in the Modern Welfare State* (Baltimore, The Johns Hopkins University Press, 1995).

15. Burton Weisbrod, "Toward a Theory of the Voluntary Nonprofit Sector in a Three-Sector Economy," in Burton Weisbrod (Ed.), *The Voluntary Nonprofit Sector* (Lexington, MA, D.C. Heath, 1977), pp. 51–76.

16. See Chapter 3, "Customers: The Focus of Service Management," for a discussion of credence qualities as well as search and experience qualities.

17. Henry Hansmann, "The Role of Nonprofit Enterprise," *Yale Law Journal*, Vol. 89 (1980), pp. 835–901.

18. Hansmann, "Economic Theories of Nonprofit Organization."

19. James and Rose-Ackerman, *The Nonprofit Enterprise in Market Economics*, p. 23.

20. See, for example, Eugene Fama and Michael Jensen "Agency Problems and Residual Claims," *Journal of Law and Economics*, Vol. 26 (June 1983), pp. 327–350.

21. James and Rose-Ackerman, *The Nonprofit Enterprise in Market Economics*, p. 30.

22. There are still other theories to explain the existence of nonprofits. For a discussion of some of these see Vladislav Valentinov, "The Economics of Nonprofit Organization: In Search of an Integrative Theory," *Journal of Economic Issues*, Vol. XLII No. 3 (September 2008), pp. 745–761.

23. David C. Hammack and Dennis R. Young "Perspectives on Nonprofits in the Marketplace," in David C. Hammack and Dennis R. Young, (Eds.), *Nonprofit Organizations in a Market Economy* (San Francisco, Jossey-Bass Publishers, 1993), 1–19.

24. L. Howard Oleck, *Nonprofit Corporations, Organizations, and Associations*, Fifth Edition (Englewood Cliffs, NJ, Prentice Hall, 1988), p. 5.

25. David E. Mason, *Voluntary Nonprofit Enterprise Management* (New York, Plenum Press, 1984), p. 128.

26. James and Rose-Ackerman, *The Nonprofit Enterprise in Market Economics*, p. 51.

27. Anthony and Young, "Characteristics of Nonprofit Organizations."

28. Thomas Wolf, *Managing a Nonprofit Organization* (New York, Fireside, Simon and Schuster, 1990), p. 29.

29. James and Rose-Ackerman, *The Nonprofit Enterprise in Market Economics*, p. 75.

30. Mason, *Voluntary Nonprofit Enterprise Management*, p. 63.

31. Anthony and Young, "Characteristics of Nonprofit Organizations."

15

FORECASTING DEMAND FOR SERVICES

15.1 Introduction

Every day, managers make decisions without knowing what will happen in the future.

Making good estimates is the main purpose of forecasting. This chapter explains why forecasting is so important to service operations, what types of service outputs are forecast, and the factors that affect the choice of forecasting methods. A variety of forecasting models are also presented, such as exponential smoothing, moving averages, time series extrapolation, and linear regression.

Good forecasts are an essential input to all types of productive systems because they form the basis for planning. There are many types of services, however, that would be chaotic without careful forecasting of demand. A few situations that differ widely from manufacturing companies are described briefly.

Fixed Capacity with Widely Fluctuating Demand

If a service organization has a relatively limited range of capacity and widely fluctuating demand for its services, it must establish policies to prevent idle facilities when demand is normally low. It also must seek a means for treating customers when demand exceeds capacities. For example, tennis clubs in South Florida usually have little activity during the summer, so courts may be used only 25 percent of the time. Policies may establish lower-priced summer memberships, tennis "camps," party-tournaments, corporate tournaments, and short clinics to keep the courts in use. On the other hand, in the winter, when demand usually exceeds court time, policies may include higher prices to reduce demand. In addition, activities such as parties, tours, and matches with clubs that have available court capacity may be arranged to shift the demand to other facilities and avoid losing members.

Service Systems That Cannot Carry Inventories

One of the features of manufacturing that enables adjustments for fluctuations to be made more easily is the capability to carry inventory for extended periods of time. Although many "embedded" service outputs such as videotapes, books, maps, and blood for transfusions can be carried in inventory, most services are intangible and are consumed during production. For intangible outputs of services, capacity must be closely matched to demand. Delays in supplying the service may lead to lost sales or ill will.

15.2 The Demand Forecast as the Basis for Operations Planning

The demand forecast is the starting point for all planning. If the good or service is new for the organization, it must estimate whether it should produce such a product. It is not necessary to design the product for the preliminary demand forecast. The organization needs to determine initially if there is a latent demand for a new product or what share of an established market it can reasonably obtain. Therefore, only the product concept is needed for this forecast. After the good or service has been designed in detail, the demand forecast may be revised based on design superiorities or differences from competitors' offerings.

The demand forecast provides estimates of the number of units of services that could be sold by the organization, as bounded by the demand for the services and the potential capacity of the organization. The number of units forecasted to be sold must be based on an approximate price. Therefore, the **total annual revenue** results from the demand forecast. The forecast of revenue is important for making the decision as to whether the service should be marketed. It permits an annual budget and a breakdown analysis.

The preliminary annual budget is primarily based on the volume of production and marketing plans. Exhibit 15-1 shows income and expense items as components of profit plans for a manufacturing company and a service firm—an airline.

Exhibit 15-1　The Sales Forecast as the Basis for Operations Planning

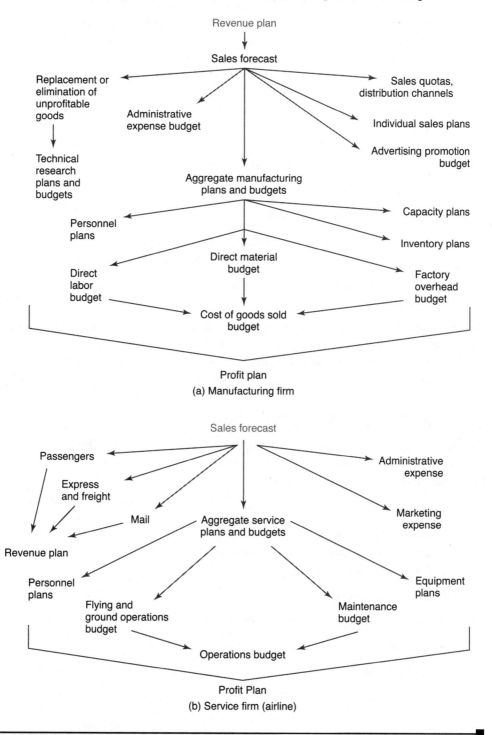

(a) Manufacturing firm

(b) Service firm (airline)

15.3 What Types of Service Outputs Are Forecast?

In manufactured products, the forecast is clearly in terms of units of product. In the manufacture of intermediate goods, the demand forecast may be in tons (steel), pounds (chemicals), square feet (textiles, wallboard), or other similar physical units, as well as product units (motors, gears, and so on). All these goods are clearly defined "countables." But what about services? The hospital may count emergency operations of accident victims, but these may vary considerably in nature and length of time. The consulting firm may want to forecast demand for services, but projects may vary in time and complexity. Although the service manager may forecast the number of customers fairly accurately, the mix of services and the nature of services may vary tremendously. The units of services forecasted therefore are

- Number of customers

- Number of hours of service supplied

- Variety of services supplied and number of each (meals, surgical operations, tailoring, real estate transactions, bank services, financial projects, repair jobs, and so on)

- Units of product supplied (gallons of gasoline, number of dial-a-song calls, number of newspapers sold)

One interesting difference between manufacturing and services forecasting is that net demand in manufacturing involves sales minus returns of goods. In most services (except retail and wholesale sales), the service has disappeared or been used up so that the only "two-way" transaction is when a customer refuses to pay for unsatisfactory services.

15.4 Factors That Affect the Choice of Forecasting Method

The choice of forecasting method, like most operating decisions, is an economic one. Therefore, each method should be reviewed from a cost-benefit perspective. The factors that should be taken into consideration in forecasting are

1. Time
   a. Span of the forecast
   b. Urgency with which the forecast is needed
   c. Frequency that updates must be made

2. Resource requirements
   a. Mathematical sophistication available to the company
   b. Computer resources
   c. Financial resources

3. Input characteristics

   a. Antecedent data availability

   b. Variability or fluctuation range and frequency

   c. External stability

4. Output characteristics required

   a. Detail or degree of disaggregation

   b. Accuracy

Choosing a Forecasting Method

The output of many services fluctuates widely according to hour of the day, day of the week, week of the month, and month of the year. Other random factors peculiar to demand for services are the weather, special news, items on sale, the economy, some famous personality, the results of a medical study, or changes in interpretations of the law, such as tax accounting services. Holidays and days before and after holidays also produce surprises many times.

Service forecasting requires, in many cases, forecasts of hour-by-hour and day-to-day activities as well as aggregate forecasts, whereas in manufacturing, weekly, monthly, and aggregate forecasts are more common. This means that in services, short-range forecasts must be made frequently. Basically, all forecasting techniques can be classified under these four groups:

- Judgment

- Counting

- Time series

- Associative or causal

Forecasting with **judgment methods**, the manager uses experience, mental estimates of the market, intuition, personal value systems, guesses, and an expert opinion to arrive at a forecast.

Counting means just that—counting the number of people who will buy or who *say* they will buy. A count may be obtained through a random sample of the target population (that is, potential customers). With such surveys, forecasts may be in error because people change their minds after the survey or did not or could not answer the survey truthfully.

Time series—A time series is a set of numerical observations on a variable of interest (for example, demand for a service and price of crude oil) obtained at regular intervals of time (for example, daily, weekly, and monthly). Techniques based on time series are quantitative models that predict future values based on the assumption that the future values of the variable of interest is a function of the past. In other words, these models look at what has happened over a period of time and use past data to make a forecast. One weakness of this method is that new factors in the future can throw off the results.

Associative or causal methods—These methods try to find a relationship between a variable of interest (that is, a dependent variable) and another variable (that is, an independent or explanatory variable), or set of variables, which may influence or cause the variable of interest to change. Linear regression methods, simple and multiple regressions, are the most commonly used techniques. A causal model for lawn mower sales might include factors such as new housing starts, advertising budget, and competitors' prices.

Although many quantitative or mathematical forecasts include some subjectivity, some researchers believe that forecasters should rely more heavily on the output of a quantitative forecast than on their own judgment. Ashton and Ashton have concluded that even simple quantitative techniques outperform the unstructured intuitive assessments of experts in many cases. In addition, using judgment to adjust the values of a quantitatively derived forecast can reduce its accuracy.[1] This is so because judgment methods are susceptible to bias, and managers are limited in their ability to process information and also to maintain consistent relationships among variables.[2]

Although each forecasting technique has strengths and weaknesses, every forecasting situation is limited by such constraints as time, funds, competencies, or data. Balancing the advantages and disadvantages of techniques for a situation's limitations and requirements is an important, but tough, managerial task. The task is to find the technique that works best for the particular situation.

15.5 Time Series Forecasting Models

A time series is a sequence of evenly spaced (hourly, daily, weekly, monthly, and so on) data points. Examples include weekly sales of laptops, quarterly revenue passenger miles on an airline, monthly admissions to a hospital, and daily ridership on a metropolitan area subway. Forecasting with time series data implies that future values are predicted *only* from past values and that other variables are incorporated into the past behavior of the time series.

Decomposition of a Time Series

Analyzing time series means breaking down past data into components and then projecting them forward. A time series typically has four components: trend, seasonality, cycles, and random variation.

1. **Trend** is the gradual upward or downward movement of the data over time. (See Exhibit 15-2.)

2. **Seasonality** is a pattern of fluctuation above or below the trend line that occurs regularly within a year or less. Seasonal variation may or may not be due to seasons. For example, toy sales are highest during November and December due to holiday season gift buying. However, the number of customers in a fast food restaurant peaks around

certain times of the day (that is, breakfast, lunch, and dinner) but this pattern can be observed any day of the year.

3. **Cycles** are patterns in the data that occur over several years; they are usually tied into business cycles.

4. **Random variations** are "blips" in the data caused by chance and unusual situations; they follow no discernible pattern. In *most* models, forecasters assume that the random variations are averaged out over time. They then concentrate on only the seasonal component and a component that is a combination of trend and cyclical factors.

Exhibit 15-2   Demand Charted over 4 Years with Trend and Seasonality Indicated

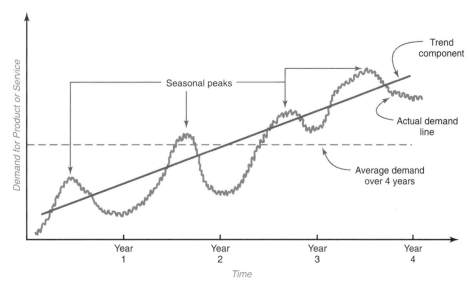

Source: Jay Heizer and Barry Render, *Operations Management,* 10th Edition (Upper Saddle River. NJ, Prentice Hall, 2011), p. 109.

Moving Averages

Moving averages are useful if we can assume that demand for services will stay fairly steady over time. We can find a 4-month moving average by simply summing the demand during the past 4 months and dividing by 4. With each passing month, the most recent month's data is added to the sum of the previous 3 months' data, and the earliest month is dropped. This tends to smooth out short-term irregularities in the data series.

Mathematically, the simple moving average (which serves as an estimate of the next period's demand) is expressed as

$$\text{Moving average} = \frac{\sum \text{demand in previous } n \text{ periods}}{n} \qquad (15.1)$$

where n is the number of periods in the moving average—for example, 4, 5, or 6 months, respectively, for a 4-, 5-, or 6-month moving average.

For example, customer demand at Donna's Garden Supply is shown in the following table. A three-month moving average forecast appears on the right.

Month	Actual Shed Sales	3-Month Moving Average
January	10	
February	12	
March	13	
April	16	$(10 + 12 + 13)/3 = 11\frac{2}{3}$
May	19	$(12 + 13 + 16)/3 = 13\frac{2}{3}$
June	23	$(13 + 16 + 19)/3 = 16$
July	26	$(16 + 19 + 23)/3 = 19\frac{1}{3}$
August	30	$(19 + 23 + 26)/3 = 22\frac{2}{3}$
September	28	$(23 + 26 + 30)/3 = 26\frac{1}{3}$
October	18	$(26 + 30 + 28)/3 = 28$
November	16	$(30 + 28 + 18)/3 = 25\frac{1}{3}$
December	14	$(28 + 18 + 16)/3 = 20\frac{2}{3}$

Weighted Moving Averages

When there is a trend or pattern, weights can be used to place more (or less) emphasis on recent values. This makes the techniques more responsive to changes, because more recent periods may be more (or less) heavily weighted. Deciding which weights to use requires some experience and a bit of luck. Choice of weights is somewhat arbitrary, because there is no set formula to determine them. If the latest month or period is weighted too heavily, the forecast might reflect a large unusual change in the demand or sales pattern too quickly. A weighted moving average may be expressed mathematically as

$$\text{Weighted moving average} = \frac{\sum (\text{weight for period } i)(\text{demand for period } i)}{\sum \text{weights}} \qquad (15.2)$$

For example, using the demand shown above, Donna's Garden Supply decides to forecast demand for services by weighting the past three months as follows.

Weights Applied	Period
3	Last month
2	2 months ago
1	3 months ago

The results of this weighted average forecast are shown in the following table.

Month	Actual Shed Sales	Three-Month Weighted Moving Average
January	10	
February	12	
March	13	
April	16	$[(3 \times 13) + (2 \times 12) + (10)]/6 = 12\frac{1}{6}$
May	19	$[(3 \times 16) + (2 \times 13) + (12)]/6 = 14\frac{1}{3}$
June	23	$[(3 \times 19) + (2 \times 16) + (13)]/6 = 17$
July	26	$[(3 \times 23) + (2 \times 19) + (16)]/6 = 20\frac{1}{2}$
August	30	$[(3 \times 26) + (2 \times 23) + (19)]/6 = 23\frac{5}{6}$
September	28	$[(3 \times 30) + (2 \times 26) + (23)]/6 = 27\frac{1}{2}$
October	18	$[(3 \times 28) + (2 \times 30) + (26)]/6 = 28\frac{1}{3}$
November	16	$[(3 \times 18) + (2 \times 28) + (30)]/6 = 23\frac{1}{3}$
December	14	$[(3 \times 16) + (2 \times 18) + (28)]/6 = 18\frac{2}{3}$

In this particular forecasting situation, weighting the latest month more heavily provides a slightly more accurate projection.

Both simple and weighted moving averages are effective in smoothing out sudden fluctuations in the demand pattern to provide stable estimates. Moving averages are not without problems, however. Increasing the size of n (the number of periods averaged) does smooth out fluctuations better, but it makes the method less sensitive to *real* changes in the data. In addition, simple moving averages cannot pick up trends well. Because they are averages, they will always stay within past levels and will not predict a change to either a higher or lower level.

Exhibit 15-3, a plot of the data in the preceding examples, illustrates the lag effect of the moving average models.

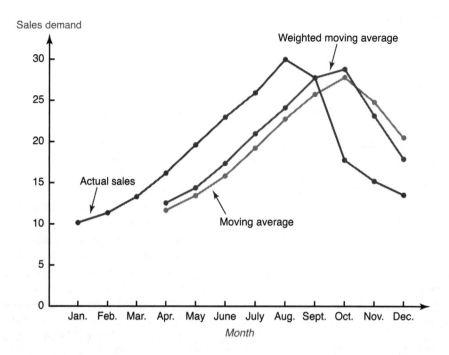

**Exhibit 15-3   Actual Demand Versus Moving Average and
Weighted Moving Average Methods for Donna's Garden Supply**

Source: Jay Heizer and Barry Render, *Operations Management,* 10th Edition, (Upper Saddle River. NJ, Prentice Hall, 2011), p. 112.

Exponential Smoothing

Exponential smoothing is a moving-average forecasting method that is easy to use and efficiently handled by computers. The basic exponential smoothing formula can be shown as follows:

New forecast = last period's forecast

$+\alpha$ (last period's actual demand − last period's forecast)   (15.3) where α is a weight, or **smoothing constant**, that has a value between 0 and 1, inclusive. Equation 15.3 also can be written mathematically as

$$F_t = F_{t-1} + \alpha(A_{t-1} - F_{t-1})$$

where

F_t	= the new forecast
F_{t-1}	= the previous forecast
α	= smoothing constant
A_{t-1}	= previous period's actual demand

(15.4)

The concept is not complex. The latest estimate of demand is equal to the old forecast adjusted by some percentage of forecast error. This error is the difference between the last period's actual demand and the old estimate, $(A_{t-1} - F_{t-1})$.

Here is an example. In January, a car dealer predicted a February demand for 142 Ford Mustangs. The actual February demand was 153 autos. Using a smoothing constant of $\alpha = 0.20$, we can forecast the March demand using the exponential smoothing model. Substituting into the formula, we can obtain

New forecast for March demand = 142 + 0.2(153 − 142) = 144.2

Thus, the demand forecast for Ford Mustangs in March is rounded to 144.

The smoothing constant α can be changed to give more weight to recent data (when it is high) or more weight to past data (when it is low). The closer α is to 0, the closer the forecast will fall to last period's forecast of this period. This contrasts to a regular moving average, in which all data are given equal weight in computing the next period's forecast.

Selecting the smoothing constant—The exponential smoothing approach is easy to use and has been successfully applied by numerous services industries. The appropriate value of the smoothing constant α, however, can make the difference between an accurate forecast and an inaccurate forecast. In picking a value for the smoothing constant, the objective is to obtain the most accurate forecast. The overall accuracy of a forecasting model can be determined by comparing the forecasted values with the actual or observed values.

The **forecast error** is defined as

Forecast error = actual demand − forecast

(15.5)

One measure of the overall forecast error for the model is the **mean absolute deviation (MAD)**. This is computed by taking the sum of the absolute values of the individual forecast errors and dividing by the number of periods of data (n).

$$MAD = \frac{\sum |\text{forecast error}|}{n}$$

(15.6)

Let us now apply this concept with a trial-and-error testing of two values of α.

The Port of Baltimore has unloaded large quantities of grain from ships during the past eight quarters. The port's operations manager wants to test the use of exponential smoothing to see how well the technique works in predicting the tonnage unloaded. He assumes that the forecast of grain unloaded in the first quarter was 175 tons. Two values of α are examined, α = 0.10 and α = 0.50. Exhibit 15-4 shows the actual tonnage, forecasts for both α = 0.10 and α = 0.50 (each rounded to the nearest ton) and the absolute deviations for both forecasts.

Based on this analysis, a smoothing constant of α = 0.10 is preferred to α = 0.50 because it's MAD is smaller. Actually, values for a typically lie in the range of 0.10 to 0.30. A simple computer program can help evaluate potential smoothing constants and find the best value of α.

Exhibit 15-4   Exponential Smoothing MAD Calculations for the Port of Baltimore

Quarter	Actual Tonnage Unloaded	Rounded Forecast with α = 0.10	Absolute Deviations for α = 0.10	Rounded Forecast with α = 0.50	Absolute Deviation for α = 0.50
1	180	175	5	175	5
2	168	176	8	178	10
3	159	175	16	173	14
4	175	173	2	166	9
5	190	173	17	170	20
6	205	175	30	180	25
7	180	178	2	193	13
8	182	178	4	186	4
		Sum of absolute deviations	84		100

$$\text{MAD} = \frac{\Sigma\,|\text{deviations}|}{n} = 10.05$$

MAD = 12.50

Source: Jay Heizer and Barry Render, *Operations Management,* 10th Edition (Upper Saddle River. NJ, Prentice Hall, 2011), p. 114.

Besides the MAD, there are three other measures of the accuracy of historical errors in forecasting that are sometimes used. The first, **mean squared error** (MSE), is the average of the squared differences between the forecasted and the observed values. The second, **mean absolute percent error** (MAPE), is the average of the absolute difference between the forecasted and observed values expressed as a percentage of the observed values. The third, the **bias,** tells whether the forecast is too high or too low, and by how much. In effect, bias provides the average total error and its direction.

Time Series Extrapolation and Seasonal Adjustments

Time series extrapolation is a technique that fits a trend line to a series of historical data points and then projects the line into the future for medium- to long-range forecasts. This section looks at *linear* (straight-line) trends only.

If we decide to develop a linear trend line by a precise statistical method, we can apply the **least-squares method**. This approach, described in detail in every introductory statistics textbook, results in a straight line that minimizes the sum of the squares of the vertical differences from the line to each of the actual observations. We can express the line with the following equation

$$\hat{y} = a + bx \tag{15.7}$$

where $\hat{y} =$ computed value of the demand for services to be predicted
(called the *dependent variable*)

$a =$ y-axis intercept

$b =$ slope of the regression line (or the rate of change in y
for one unit increase in x)

$x =$ the independent variable (which is time in this case)

The slope is found by

$$b = \frac{\sum xy - n\bar{x}\,\bar{y}}{\sum x^2 - n\bar{x}^2} \tag{15.8}$$

The y intercept is computed as follows:

$$a = \bar{y} - b\bar{x} \tag{15.9}$$

The following example shows how to apply these concepts. Shown in the following table are the data for the demand for copies of a popular financial software program from the developer of the program over the period 2006 to 2012. Now let us fit a straight-line trend to these data and forecast 2013 demand.

Year	Copies of the Software Sold
2006	74
2007	79
2008	80
2009	90
2010	105
2011	142
2012	122

With a series of data over time, we can minimize the computations by transforming the values of x (time) to simpler numbers. Thus, in this case, 2006 can be designated as year 1, 2007 as year 2, and so on.

Year	Time Period (x)	Software Demand (y)	x^2	xy
2006	1	74	1	74
2007	2	79	4	158
2008	3	80	9	240
2009	4	90	16	360
2010	5	105	25	525
2011	6	142	36	852
2012	7	122	49	854
	$\Sigma x = 28$	$\Sigma y = 692$	$\Sigma x^2 = 140$	$\Sigma xy = 3{,}063$

$$\bar{x} = \frac{\sum x}{n} = \frac{28}{7} = 4 \qquad\qquad \bar{y} = \frac{\sum y}{n} = \frac{692}{7} = 98.86$$

$$b = \frac{\sum xy - n\bar{x}\,\bar{y}}{\sum x^2 - n\bar{x}^2} = \frac{3{,}063 - (7)(4)(98.86)}{140 - (7)(4^2)} = \frac{295}{28} = 10.54$$

$$a = \bar{y} - b\bar{x} = 98.86 - 10.54(4) = 56.70$$

Hence, the least squares regression line is $\hat{y} = 56.70 + 10.54x$. To project demand in 2013, first determine that $x = 8$ for the year 2013, and substitute this value in the equation:

Forecast for sales in $2013 = \hat{y} = 56.70 + 10.54(8) = 141.02$, or 141 copies of the software

We can estimate demand for other years in a similar fashion. For example, for 2014:

Forecast for sales in $2014 = \hat{y} = 56.70 + 10.54(9) = 151.56$, or 152 copies of the software

To check the validity of the model, plot the historical demand and the trend line in Exhibit 15-5. In this case, we may want to be cautious and try to understand the 2011–2012 swings in demand.

Exhibit 15-5   Demand for Financial Software and the Computed Trend Line

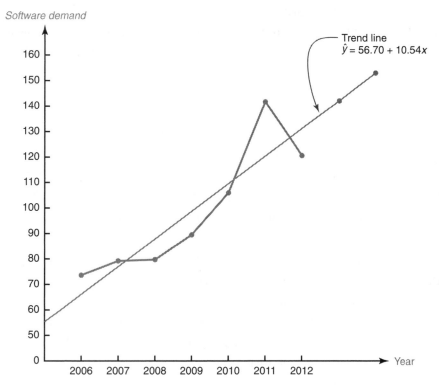

Source: Adapted from Jay Heizer and Barry Render, *Operations Management*, 10th Edition (Upper Saddle River. NJ, Prentice Hall, 2011), p. 121.

Time series forecasting such as that in the preceding example involves looking at the *trend* of data over a series of time observations. Sometimes, however, recurring variations at certain seasons of the year make a *seasonal* adjustment in the trend-line forecast necessary. Demand for coal and fuel oil, for example, usually peaks during cold winter months. Demand for golf clubs or suntan lotion may be highest in summer. Analyzing data in monthly or quarterly terms usually makes it easy to spot seasonal patterns. Seasonal indices can then be developed by several common methods. The next example illustrates one way to compute seasonal factors from historical data. Monthly sales of one brand of tablet computers at Plane Supplies are shown in Exhibit 15-6 for 2011–2012. The exhibit also shows how seasonal indices can be calculated.

Exhibit 15-6   Monthly Sales of Tablet Computers for a 2-Year Period

Month	Sales (units)		Average 2011-2012 Sales	Average Monthly Sales[a]	Seasonal Index[b]
	2011	2012			
Jan	80	100	90	94	0.957
Feb	75	85	80	94	0.851
Mar	80	90	85	94	0.904
Apr	90	110	100	94	1.064
May	115	131	123	94	1.309
Jun	110	120	115	94	1.223
Jul	100	110	105	94	1.117
Aug	90	110	100	94	1.064
Sep	85	95	90	94	0.957
Oct	75	85	80	94	0.851
Nov	75	85	80	94	0.851
Dec	80	80	80	94	0.851
			Total average demand = 1,128		

[a]
$$\text{Average monthly demand} = \frac{1,128}{12 \text{ months}} = 94$$

[b]
$$\text{Seasonal index} = \frac{\text{Average } 2011 - 2012 \text{ demand}}{\text{Average monthly demand}}$$

Suppose we forecasted the 2013 annual demand for tablets to be 1,200 units with a trend equation. Using these seasonal indices, we would forecast the monthly demand as follows:

Jan $\quad \dfrac{1,200}{12} \times 0.957 = 96$ 　　　 Jul $\quad \dfrac{1,200}{12} \times 1.117 = 112$

Feb $\quad \dfrac{1,200}{12} \times 0.851 = 85$ 　　　 Aug $\quad \dfrac{1,200}{12} \times 1.064 = 106$

Mar $\quad \dfrac{1,200}{12} \times 0.904 = 90$ 　　　 Sep $\quad \dfrac{1,200}{12} \times 0.957 = 96$

Apr	$\dfrac{1,200}{12} \times 1.064 = 106$	Oct	$\dfrac{1,200}{12} \times 0.851 = 85$
May	$\dfrac{1,200}{12} \times 1.309 = 131$	Nov	$\dfrac{1,200}{12} \times 0.851 = 85$
Jun	$\dfrac{1,200}{12} \times 1.223 = 122$	Dec	$\dfrac{1,200}{12} \times 0.851 = 85$

For simplicity, trend calculations were ignored in the preceding example. The following example illustrates how indices that have already been prepared can be applied to adjust trend line forecasts.

Hospital forecasting example: As another example of an estimated trend line and seasonality adjustments, we borrow data from a hospital that used 66 months of adult inpatient hospital days to reach the following equation:

$$\hat{y} = 8,091 + 21.5x$$

where y = patient-days

x = time, in months

Based on this model, the hospital forecasts patient-days for the next month (period 67) to be patient-days = 8,091 + 21.5(67) = 9,532.

As well as this model recognized the slight upward trend in the demand for inpatient services, it ignored the seasonality that the administration knew to be present. Exhibit 15-7 provides seasonal indices for inpatient days that are typical of hospitals across the nation. Note that January, March, July, and August seem to exhibit significantly higher patient-days on average, while February, September, November, and December reveal lower patient-days.

To correct the time series extrapolation for seasonality, the hospital should multiply the monthly forecast by the appropriate seasonal index. Thus, for period 67, which was in January,

Patient-days = (9,532) (1.04) = 9,913 (trend and seasonal)

Using this method, patient-days can be forecasted for January through June (periods 67 through 72) as 9,913, 9,266, 9,766, 9,596, 9,618, and 9,639. Taking seasonal effect into consideration can lead to better patient-day forecasts, as well as more accurate budgets.

Exhibit 15-7   Typical Seasonal Indices for Inpatient Days at Hospitals

Month	Seasonal Index
Jan	1.04
Feb	0.97
Mar	1.02
Apr	1.00
May	1.00
June	1.00
July	1.03
Aug	1.04
Sep	0.96
Oct	1.00
Nov	0.96
Dec	0.98

15.6 Causal (Associative) Forecasting; Regression Analysis

Causal or associative forecasting models usually consider several variables that are related to the variable being predicted. After these related variables have been found, a statistical model is built and used to forecast the variable of interest.

Many factors can be considered in a causal analysis. For example, the sales of a product might be influenced by the firm's advertising budget, the price charged, competitors' prices and promotional strategies, or even the economy and unemployment rates. In this case, sales would be called the **dependent variable** and the other variables would be called **independent variables.** The manager's job is to develop the best statistical relationship between sales and the set of independent variables. The most common quantitative causal forecasting model is **linear regression analysis.**

We can use the same mathematical model we employed in the least-squares method of the time series extrapolation to perform a simple linear regression analysis.

The dependent variable that we want to forecast will still be y. But now the independent variable x need no longer be time.[3]

$$\hat{y} = a + bx$$

where y = value of the dependent variable, sales in this case

a = y-axis intercept

b = slope of the regression line

x = the independent variable

To illustrate, consider the case of the Schatz Construction Company, which renovates old homes in Winter Park, Florida. Over time, the company has found that its dollar volume of renovation work is dependent on the Winter Park area payroll. The following table lists Schatz's revenues and the amount of money earned by wage earners in Winter Park during the past six years.

Schatz's Sales ($000,000) y	Local Payroll ($000,000,000) x
2.0	1
3.0	3
2.5	4
2.0	2
2.0	1
3.5	7

Using the least-squares regression approach, we find that

$$\hat{y} = 1.75 + 0.25x$$

or

$$\text{Sales} = 1.75 + 0.25\text{payroll}$$

If the local chamber of commerce predicts that the Winter Park area payroll will be $600 million next year, we can estimate sales for Schatz with the regression equation.

$$\text{Forecast for sales (in \$000,000)} = \hat{y} = 1.75 + 0.25(6) = 1.75 + 1.50 = 3.25$$

or

$$\text{Sales} = \$3,250,000$$

The final part of this example illustrates a central weakness of causal forecasting methods such as regression. Even when we have computed a regression equation, it is necessary to provide a forecast of the independent variable x—in this case payroll—before estimating the dependent variable y for the next time period. Although not a problem for all forecasts, you can imagine the difficulty in determining future values of *some* common independent variables (such as unemployment rates, gross national product, price indices, and so on).

15.7 General Approaches to Forecasting

There are three general approaches to forecasting demand for services that employ the various methods just discussed.

Fundamental System-to-Subsystem Approach

The fundamental method of demand forecasting may employ combinations of techniques described in this chapter. It consists of forecasting the economy, then forecasting industry sales (which are dependent on the economy), and finally forecasting company sales (which are dependent on industry sales).

Economic forecast → Industry demand forecast → Company demand forecast

For example, if the industry demand forecast for next year is $1,222,000,000 and the company's market share is estimated at 2 percent, the demand forecast is $24,440,000.

Most companies cannot afford a staff of economists, so their marketing departments either buy economic and industry forecasts when needed or use forecasts of the economy and industry found in *Business Week*, *The Wall Street Journal*, *Forbes*, government publications, or forecasting service publications.

Industry demand forecasts may be made by using the past year's demand and adjusting this fig-ure up or down according to predictions about the economy for next year. Industry demand forecasts may be found in *U.S. Industrial Outlook*, published annually by the U.S. Department of Commerce, or in trade publications. In addition, most industries have a trade association (see *Encyclopedia of Associations*, published by Gale, a Part of Cengage Learning) that may forecast industry demand. Individual studies of industries are prepared by Predicasts, Inc., in Cleveland, Ohio.

For a new firm, a demand forecast is determined by estimating the market share the company will obtain in its first year of business. This depends on considerations of the value-in-use of the product or service, the degree of differentiation of its product or service, the competitive edge of the new firm, and the marketing program of the new firm. Usually, the initial share of an estab-lished market will be small, and a conservative estimate should be made.

Aggregate-to-Component Forecasts

A restaurant manager may forecast the total number of customers and then estimate the number of dinners, luncheons, and breakfasts. An auto repair shop may estimate the total number of jobs per year and then forecast the number of each type of job. A painting firm may estimate the aggregate of jobs for next month and then forecast the number of residential and the number of commercial jobs. If the total or aggregate number of services can be forecasted, the forecast pro-vides a general bound for the sum of the components and makes component forecasting easier.

Disaggregation into components may be on the following bases:

1. Service disaggregation
   a. Services by classes or types
   b. Services by time of day or week they are supplied

2. Market disaggregation

   a. Geographic disaggregation

   b. Industry, government, and consumer sectors

   c. Industry sectors within the total market

3. Performer disaggregation—a forecast for each person or shop that performs the services

Component-to-Aggregate Forecasts

When an aggregate forecast is desired, it may be more accurate if a forecast of each component of the aggregate is made and then these forecasts added. The preceding section has given the components that make up aggregates.

Using POM for Windows in Forecasting

The Forecasting module of POM for Windows can handle all the forecasting techniques discussed in this chapter. Exhibit 15-8 shows the weighted moving average forecast and relevant statistics for Donna's Garden Supply example. Exhibit 15-9 has the detailed information on errors and forecasts. Exhibits 15-10 and 15-11 illustrate the time series trend line output from POM for Windows for the financial software example with all the relevant statistics.

Exhibit 15-8   POM for Windows Solution of Donna's Garden Supply Example

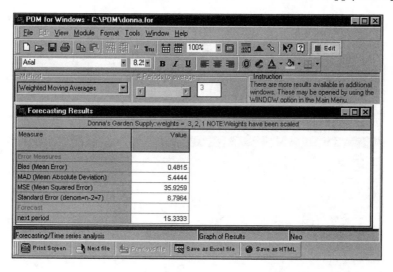

Exhibit 15-9   Details of Weighted Moving Average Forecast
for Donna's Garden Supply Example

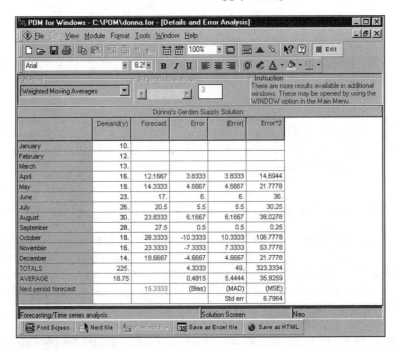

Exhibit 15-10   POM for Windows Solution of Financial Software Example

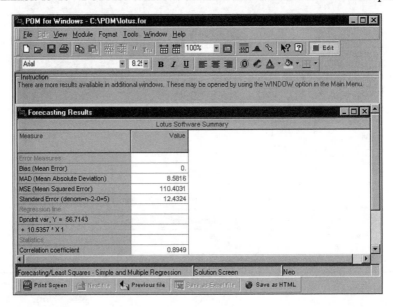

Exhibit 15-11   Details of Time Series Trend Calculation for Financial Software Example

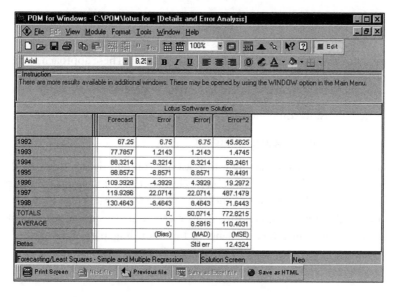

	Forecast	Error	|Error|	Error^2
1992	67.25	6.75	6.75	45.5625
1993	77.7857	1.2143	1.2143	1.4745
1994	88.3214	-8.3214	8.3214	69.2461
1995	98.8572	-8.8571	8.8571	78.4491
1996	109.3929	-4.3929	4.3929	19.2972
1997	119.9286	22.0714	22.0714	487.1479
1998	130.4643	-8.4643	8.4643	71.6443
TOTALS		0.	60.0714	772.8215
AVERAGE		0.	8.5816	110.4031
		(Bias)	(MAD)	(MSE)
Betas			Std err	12.4324

15.8 Summary

Forecasting demand for services is important in most services because fluctuations in demand cannot usually be taken care of by building inventory. When the service is "embedded" in a physical product, forecasting and meeting demand fluctuations are analogous to the manufacturing situation. In either case, the demand forecast is the basis for all planning.

In manufacturing, demand is forecasted in terms of units of physical product. In services, it is not always clear *what* to forecast and what *can be* forecasted. That is, the outputs of some service firms are of almost infinite variety. Basically, however, service demand is in terms of the number of customers and the number of services, and a number of each anticipated service to be demanded.

The selection of a forecasting method depends on four basic factors:

1.   Time requirements

2.   Resource requirements

3.   Input characteristics available or required

4.   Output characteristics required

There are four basic methods of forecasting:

1.   Judgment

2.   Counting

3. Time series

4. Associative or causal

Within these categories there are numerous methods with variations of each. The strategic approaches to forecasting use combinations of these methods. These approaches are

- Economic system to industry system to company system

- Aggregate forecast to component forecast

- Component forecast to aggregate forecast

The technical aspects of actually making a forecast are complex, and a number of books and journals are available that deal with this subject. No forecasting method, as we learned in this chapter, is perfect under all conditions. And even after management has found a satisfactory approach, it must still monitor and control its forecasts to make sure errors do not get out of hand. Forecasting can often be a very challenging, but rewarding, part of managing.

Endnotes

1. For survey articles that address this issue, see Essam Mahmoud, "Accuracy in Forecasting: A Survey," *Journal of Forecasting*, vol. 3, no. 2 (April–June 1984), p. 139; Robin M. Hogarth and Spyros Makridakis, "Forecasting and Planning: An Evaluation," Management Science, vol. 27, no. 2 (February 1981), p. 115; and A. H. Ashton and R. H. Ashton, "Aggregating Subjective Forecasts," Management Science, vol. 31, no. 12 (December 1985), pp. 1499–1508.

2. Leonard Sjoberg, "Aided and Unaided Decision Making Improved Intuitive Judgment," *Journal of Forecasting*, Vol. 1, no. 4 (October–December 1982), p. 349.

3. If there were more than one independent variable introduced, the general form of this multiple regression would be

$$\hat{y} = a + b_1 x_1 + b_2 x_2 + b_3 x_3 + \ldots + b_n x_n$$

where the b_i values represent slope coefficients for the respective x-independent variables.

16

VEHICLE ROUTING AND SCHEDULING

16.1 Introduction

The scheduling of customer service and the routing of service vehicles are at the heart of many service operations. For some services, such as school buses, public health nursing, and many installation or repair businesses, service delivery is critical to the performance of the service. For other services, such as mass transit, taxis, trucking firms, and the U.S. Postal Service, timely delivery *is* the service. In either case, the routing or scheduling of service vehicles has a major impact on the *quality* of the service provided.

This chapter introduces some routing and scheduling terminology, classifies different types of routing and scheduling problems, and presents various solution methodologies. Although every effort has been made to present the topic of vehicle routing and scheduling as simply and as straightforward as possible, it should be noted that this is a technical subject and one of the more mathematical topics in this text. The chapter begins with an example of service delivery to illustrate some of the practical issues in vehicle routing and scheduling.

A Service Delivery Example: Meals-for-ME

A private, nonprofit meal delivery program for the elderly called Meals-for-ME has been operating in the state of Maine since the mid-1970s.[1] The program offers home delivery of hot meals, Monday through Friday, to "home-bound" individuals who are more than 60 years of age. For those individuals who are eligible (and able), the program also supports a "congregate" program that provides daily transportation to group meal sites. On a typical day within a single county, hundreds of individuals receive this service. In addition, individuals may be referred for short-term service because of a temporary illness or recuperation. Thus, on any given day, the demand for the service may be highly unpredictable. Scheduling of volunteer delivery personnel and vehicles as well as construction of routes is done on a week-to-monthly basis by regional site managers. It is the task of these individuals to coordinate the preparation of meals and to determine the sequence in which customers are to be visited. In addition, site managers must arrange for rides to the "group meals" for participating individuals.

Although these tasks may seem straightforward, there are many practical problems in routing and scheduling meal delivery. First, the delivery vehicles (and pickup vehicles) are driven by volunteers, many of whom are students who are not available during some high-demand periods (Christmas, for example). Thus, the variability in available personnel requires that delivery routes be changed frequently. Second, because the program delivers hot meals, a typical route must be less than 90 minutes. Generally, 20 to 25 meals are delivered on a route, depending on the proximity of customers. Third, all must be delivered within a limited time period, between 11:30 A.M. and 1:00 P.M. daily. Similar difficulties exist for personnel who pick up individuals served by the congregate program. Given the existence of these very real problems, the solution no longer seems as simple. It is obvious that solution approaches and techniques are needed that allow the decision maker to consider a multitude of variables and adapt to changes quickly and efficiently.

16.2 Objectives of Routing and Scheduling Problems

The objective of most routing and scheduling problems is to minimize the total cost of providing the service. This includes vehicle capital costs, mileage, and personnel costs. But other objectives also may come into play, particularly in the public sector. For example, in school bus routing and scheduling, a typical objective is to minimize the total number of student-minutes on the bus. This criterion is highly correlated with safety and with parents' approval of the school system.[2] For dial-a-ride services for the handicapped or elderly, an important objective is to minimize the inconvenience for all customers. For the Meals-for-ME program, the meals must be delivered at certain times of the day. For emergency services, such as ambulance, police, and fire, minimizing response time to an incident is of primary importance. Some companies promise package delivery by 10:30 A.M. the next morning. Thus, for both public and private services, an appropriate objective function should consider more than the dollar cost of delivering a service. The "subjective" costs associated with failing to provide adequate service to the customer must be considered as well.

16.3 Characteristics of Routing and Scheduling Problems

Routing and scheduling problems are often presented as graphical **networks.** The use of networks to describe these problems has the advantage of allowing the decision maker to visualize the problem under consideration. Exhibit 16-1 consists of five circles called **nodes.** Four of the nodes (nodes 2 through 5) represent pickup and/or delivery points, and a fifth (node 1) represents a **depot node,** from which the vehicle's trip originates and ends. The depot node is the "home base" for the vehicle or provider.

Exhibit 16-1   Routing Network Example

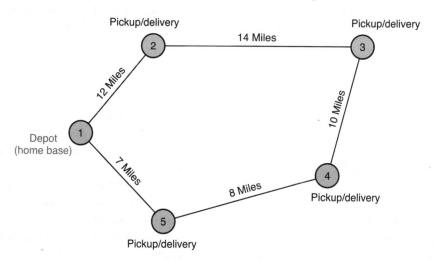

Connecting these nodes are line segments referred to as **arcs.** Arcs describe the time, cost, or distance required to travel from one node to another. The numbers along the arcs in Exhibit 16-1 are distances in miles. Given an average speed of travel or a distribution of travel times, distance can be easily converted to time. However, this conversion ignores physical barriers, such as mountains, lack of access, or traffic congestion. If minimizing time is the primary goal in a routing and scheduling problem, then historical data on travel times are preferable to calculations based on distances.

Arcs may be directed or undirected. **Undirected arcs** are represented by simple line segments. **Directed arcs** are indicated by arrows. These arrows represent the direction of travel in the case of routing problems (for example, one-way streets) or precedence relationships in the case of scheduling problems (where one pickup or delivery task must precede another).

The small network in Exhibit 16-1 can be viewed as a route for a single vehicle. The route for the vehicle, also called a **tour,** is $1 \rightarrow 2 \rightarrow 3 \rightarrow 4 \rightarrow 5 \rightarrow 1$ or because the arcs are undirected $1 \rightarrow 5 \rightarrow 4 \rightarrow 3 \rightarrow 2 \rightarrow 1$. The total distance for either tour is 51 miles.

The tour described in Exhibit 16-1 is a solution to a simple routing problem in which the objective is to find the route that minimizes cost or any other criterion that may be appropriate (such as distance or travel time). The minimum-cost solution, however, is subject to the tour being **feasible.** Feasibility depends on the type of problem, but, in general, implies that

1. A tour must include all nodes.

2. A node must be visited only once.

3. A tour must begin and end at a depot.

The output of all routing and scheduling systems is essentially the same. That is, for each vehicle or provider, a route and/or a schedule is provided. Generally, the **route** specifies the sequence in which the nodes (or arcs) are to be visited, and a **schedule** identifies when each node is to be visited.

Classifying Routing and Scheduling Problems

The classification of routing and scheduling problems depends on certain characteristics of the service delivery system, such as the size of the delivery fleet, where the fleet is housed, capacities of the vehicles, and routing and scheduling objectives. In the simplest case, we begin with a set of nodes to be visited by a single vehicle. The nodes may be visited in any order, there are no precedence relationships, the travel costs between two nodes are the same regardless of the direction traveled, and there are no delivery-time restrictions. In addition, vehicle capacity is not considered. The output for the single-vehicle problem is a route or a tour where each node is visited only once and the route begins and ends at the depot node (see Exhibit 16-1). The tour is formed with the goal of minimizing the total tour cost. This simplest case is referred to as a **traveling salesman problem** (TSP).

An extension of the traveling salesman problem, known as the **multiple traveling salesman problem** (MTSP), occurs when a fleet of vehicles must be routed from a single depot. The goal is to generate a set of routes, one for each vehicle in the fleet. The characteristics of this problem are that a node may be assigned to only one vehicle, but a vehicle will have more than one node assigned to it. There are no restrictions on the size of the load or number of passengers a vehicle may carry. The solution to this problem will give the order in which each vehicle is to visit its assigned nodes. As in the single-vehicle case, the objective is to develop the set of minimum-cost routes, where "cost" may be represented by a dollar amount, distance, or travel time.

If we now restrict the capacity of the multiple vehicles and couple with it the possibility of having varying demands at each node, the problem is classified as a **vehicle routing problem** (VHP).

Alternatively, if the demand for the service occurs on the arcs, rather than at the nodes, or if demand is so high that individual demand nodes become too numerous to specify, we have a **Chinese postman problem** (CPP). Examples of these types of problems include street sweeping, snow removal, refuse collection, postal delivery, and paper delivery. The Chinese postman problem is very difficult to solve, and the solution procedures are beyond the scope of this text.[3] Exhibit 16-2 summarizes the characteristics of these four types of routing problems.

Exhibit 16-2   Characteristics of Four Routing Problems

Type	Demand	Arcs	No. of Depots	No. of Vehicles	Vehicle Capacity
Traveling salesman problem (TSP)	At the nodes	Directed or undirected	1	=1	Unlimited
Multiple traveling salesman problem (MTSP)	At the nodes	Directed or undirected	1	>1	Unlimited
Vehicle routing problem (VRP)	At the nodes	Directed or undirected	1	>1	Limited
Chinese postman problem (CPP)	On the arcs	Directed or undirected	1	≥ 1	Limited or unlimited

Finally, let us distinguish between **routing** problems and **scheduling** problems. If the customers being serviced have no time restrictions and no precedence relationships exist, the problem is a pure routing problem. If there is a specified time for the service to take place, a scheduling problem exists. Otherwise, we are dealing with a combined routing and scheduling problem.

Solving Routing and Scheduling Problems

Another important issue in routing and scheduling involves the practical aspects of solving these types of problems. Consider, for example, the delivery of bundles of newspapers from a printing site to drop-off points in a geographic area. These drop-off points supply papers to newspaper carriers for local deliveries. The drop-off points have different demands, and the vehicles have different capacities. Each vehicle is assigned a route beginning and ending at the printing site (the depot). For a newspaper with only 10 drop-off points, there are 2^{10} or 1,024 possible routings. For 50 drop-off points, there are 2^{50} or more than 1 trillion possible routings. Realistic problems of this type may have over 1,000 drop points! It is evident that problems of any size quickly become too expensive to solve optimally even with supercomputers. Fortunately, some very elegant heuristics or "rule of thumb" solution techniques have been developed that yield "good," if not optimal, solutions to these problems. Some of the more well known of these heuristic approaches are presented in this chapter.

16.4 Routing Service Vehicles

The Traveling Salesman Problem

The traveling salesman problem (TSP) is one of the most studied problems in management science. Optimal approaches to solving traveling salesman problems are based on mathematical programming (see Chapter 18, "Linear and Goal Programming Applications for Services"). But in reality, most TSP problems are not solved optimally. When the problem is so large that an optimal solution is impossible to obtain, or when approximate solutions are good enough, heuristics are applied. Two commonly used heuristics for the traveling salesman problem are the **nearest neighbor procedure** and the **Clark and Wright savings heuristic.**[4]

The nearest neighbor procedure—The nearest neighbor procedure (NNP) builds a tour based only on the cost or distance of traveling from the last-visited node to the closest node in the network. As such, the heuristic is simple, but it has the disadvantage of being rather shortsighted, as we will see in an example. The heuristic does, however, generate an "approximately" optimal solution from a distance matrix. The procedure is outlined as follows:

1. Start with a node at the beginning of the tour (the depot node).

2. Find the node closest to the last node added to the tour.

3. Go back to step 2 until all nodes have been added.

4. Connect the first and the last nodes to form a complete tour.[5]

Example of the nearest neighbor procedure—We begin the nearest neighbor procedure with data on the distance or cost of traveling from every node in the network to every other node in the network. When the arcs are undirected, the distance from i to j will be the same as the distance from j to i. Such a network with undirected arcs is said to be **symmetrical.** Exhibit 16-3 gives the complete distance matrix for the symmetrical six-node network shown in Exhibit 16-4.

Exhibit 16-3   Symmetric Distance Matrix

From Node	To Node (Distances in Miles)					
	1	2	3	4	5	6
1	—	5.4	2.8	10.5	8.2	4.1
2	5.4	—	5.0	9.5	5.0	8.5
3	2.8	5.0	—	7.8	6.0	3.6
4	10.5	9.5	7.8	—	5.0	9.5
5	8.2	5.0	6.0	5.0	—	9.2
6	4.1	8.5	3.6	9.5	9.2	—

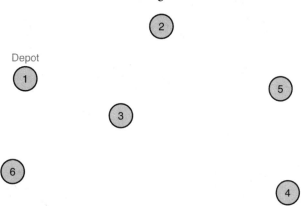

Exhibit 16-4 Traveling Salesman Problem

Referring to Exhibit 16-5, the solution is determined as follows:

1. Start with the depot node (node 1). Examine the distances between node 1 and every other node. The closest node to node 1 is node 3, so designate the **partial tour or path** as 1 → 3. (See Exhibit 16-5(a). Note that the → means that the nodes are connected, not that the arc is directed.)

2. Find the closest node to the last node added (node 3) that is not currently in the path. Node 6 is 3.6 miles from node 3, so connect it to the path. The result is the three-node path 1 → 3 → 6 (see Exhibit 16-5[b]).

3. Find the node closest to node 6 that has not yet been connected. This is node 2, which is 8.5 miles from node 6. Connect it to yield 1 → 3 → 6 → 2 (see Exhibit 16-5[c]).

4. The node closest to node 2 is node 5. The partial tour is now 1 → 3 → 6 → 2→ 5 (see Exhibit 16-5[d]).

5. Connect the last node (node 4) to the path and complete the tour by connecting node 4 to the depot. The complete tour formed is 1 → 3 → 6 → 2 → 5 → 4 → 1. The length of the tour is 35.4 miles (see Exhibit 16-5[e]).

Exhibit 16-5   Nearest Neighbor Procedure

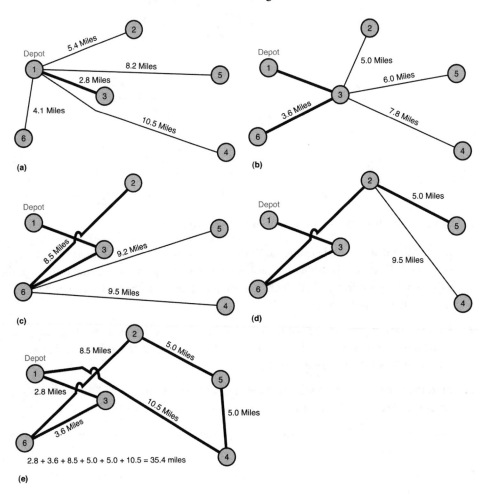

But is this the best-possible route? Examine the network again and try to create a better tour. How about $1 \rightarrow 2 \rightarrow 5 \rightarrow 4 \rightarrow 3 \rightarrow 6 \rightarrow 1$? The total distance of this tour is 30.9 miles versus 34.5 miles for the nearest neighbor-constructed tour. This result points to the limitation of heuristics; they cannot guarantee optimality. For this small a network, it would be possible to enumerate every possible tour. However, for large problems with 100 to 200 nodes, enumerating every combination would be impossible.

Before leaving the nearest neighbor heuristic, it should be noted that, in practice, the heuristic is applied repeatedly by assigning every node to be the depot node, resolving the problem, and then selecting the lowest-cost tour as the final solution. For example, if we repeat the procedure using node 6 as the depot node, the tour that results is $6 \rightarrow 3 \rightarrow 1 \rightarrow 2 \rightarrow 5 \rightarrow 4 \rightarrow 6$ with a total length of 31.3 miles.

Clark and Wright savings heuristic—The Clark and Wright savings heuristic (C&W) is one of the most well-known techniques for solving traveling salesman problems. The heuristic begins by selecting a node as the depot node and labeling it node 1. We then assume, for the moment, that there are $n-1$ vehicles available, where n is the number of nodes. In other words, if we have six nodes in the network, there are five vehicles available. Each vehicle travels from the depot directly to a node and returns to the depot. Exhibit 16-6 shows this for a three-node network where the miles are shown on the arcs. The distance from node 2 to node 3 is 5 miles. The total distance covered by the two vehicles in Exhibit 16-6 is 36 miles: 20 miles for the trip from the depot to node 2 and return, and 16 miles for the trip from the depot to node 3 and return.

But this is not a feasible solution because the objective of a traveling salesman problem is to find a tour in which all nodes are visited by *one* vehicle, rather than by two vehicles (refer to Exhibit 16-6). To reduce the number of vehicles needed, we now need to combine the $n-1$ tours originally specified.

Exhibit 16-6   Initial C&W Network Configuration: Three Node Problem

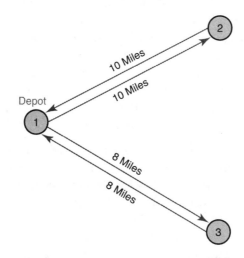

The key to the C&W heuristic is the computation of savings. **Savings** is a measure of how much the trip length or cost can be reduced by "hooking up" a pair of nodes (referring to Exhibit 16-6, nodes 2 and 3) and creating the tour $1 \rightarrow 2 \rightarrow 3 \rightarrow 1$, which can then be assigned to a single vehicle. The savings is computed as follows. By linking nodes 2 and 3, we *add* 5 miles (the distance from node 2 to node 3) but *save* 10 miles for the trip from node 2 to node 1 and 8 miles for the trip from 3 to 1. The total tour length for the complete tour, $1 \rightarrow 2 \rightarrow 3 \rightarrow 1$, is 23 miles. The savings obtained, over the configuration shown in Exhibit 16-6, is 13 miles. For a network with n nodes, we compute the savings for every possible pair of nodes, rank the savings gains from largest to smallest, and construct a tour by linking pairs of nodes until a complete route is obtained.

A statement of the C&W savings heuristic is as follows:

1. Select any node as the depot node (node 1).

2. Compute the savings, S_{ij}, for linking nodes i and j:

$$S_{ij} = c_{1i} + c_{1j} - c_{ij} \quad \text{for } i \text{ and } j = \text{nodes } 2, 3, \ldots, n \qquad (16.1)$$

where

c_{ij} = the cost of traveling from node i to node j

3. Rank the savings from largest to smallest.

4. Starting at the top of the list, form larger **subtours** by linking appropriate nodes i and j. Stop when a complete tour is formed.[6]

Example using the C&W savings heuristic—To demonstrate how the C&W heuristic is used to solve a TSP problem, consider the network shown in Exhibit 16-7. Here, as in Exhibit 16-6, we assume that there is one vehicle for every node (excluding the depot) in the network. The solid lines show arcs that are in use as we begin the C&W procedure. The dashed lines show arcs that *may* be used but are not in use currently. Distances, in miles, are shown on the arcs. The savings obtained from linking nodes 2 and 3 is 13 miles. This is computed as (10 miles + 8 miles) – (5 miles). The 10- and 8-mile distances are the lengths of the return trip from nodes 2 and 3, respectively, to the depot; 5 miles is the distance from node 2 to node 3. Similarly, the savings of linking nodes 2 and 4 is 12 miles: (5 miles +10 miles) – (3 miles). The last pair of nodes to be considered for linking is [4, 3], which yields a savings of 6 miles: (5 miles + 8 miles) – (7 miles).

We next rank the savings for every pair of nodes not yet linked. In order of savings, the pairs are [2, 3], [2, 4], and [3, 4]. The first step in specifying a tour is to link the nodes with the highest savings, nodes 2 and 3. The resulting path is shown in Exhibit 16-8(a). Proceeding to the next highest savings, nodes 2 and 4 are linked as shown in Exhibit 16-8(b). The tour is now complete—the last pair, nodes 3 and 4, cannot be linked without "breaking" the tour. The complete tour is 1 → 4 → 2 → 3 → 1, which has a total tour length of 21 miles. The total savings obtained over the "one vehicle per node" configuration shown in Exhibit 16-7 is 25 miles.

Exhibit 16-7   Initial C&W Network: Four-Node Problem

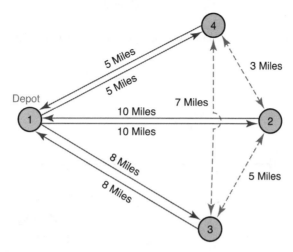

In general, because C&W considers cost when constructing a tour, it yields better quality solutions than the nearest neighbor procedure. Both the Clark and Wright savings heuristic and the nearest neighbor procedure can be easily adjusted to accommodate problems with directed arcs.

Multiple Traveling Salesman Problem

The MTSP is a generalization of the traveling salesman problem where there are multiple vehicles and a single depot. In this problem, instead of determining a route for a single vehicle, we wish to construct tours for all M vehicles. The characteristics of the tours are that they begin and end at the depot node. Solution procedures begin by "copying" the depot node M times. The problem is thus reduced to M single-vehicle TSPs, and it can be solved using either the nearest neighbor or Clark and Wright heuristics.

The Vehicle Routing Problem

The classic VRP expands the multiple traveling salesman problem to include different service requirements at each node and different capacities for vehicles in the fleet. The objective of these problems is to minimize total cost or distance across all routes. Examples of services that show the characteristics of vehicle routing problems include United Parcel Service deliveries, public transportation "pickups" for the handicapped, and the newspaper delivery problem described earlier.

The vehicle routing problem cannot be fully solved with the same procedures as the multiple traveling salesman problem. Consider the simple example illustrated in Exhibit 16-9. Suppose we have a single depot and two buses, 1 and 2. Vehicle 1 has a capacity of 20 people and vehicle 2 a capacity of 10. There are three nodes where travelers are to be picked up. The number of travelers to be picked up is shown in brackets beside each node.

Exhibit 16-8   First and Second Node Hookups: C&W Heuristic

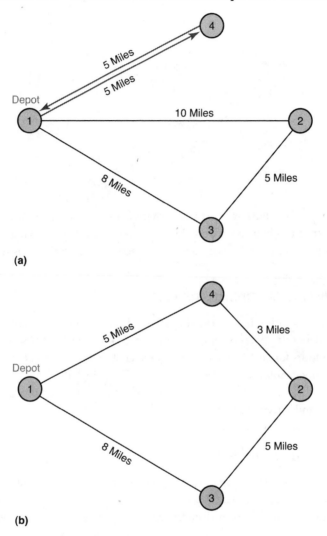

(a)

(b)

Ignoring for the moment the capacity of the buses and the demand at each node, the Clark and Wright heuristic would construct a tour for each vehicle as follows:

- Bus 1's tour: $1 \rightarrow 2 \rightarrow 3 \rightarrow 1$
- Bus 2's tour: $1 \rightarrow 4 \rightarrow 1$

This assignment, however, sends 21 passengers on bus 1, which violates the capacity constraints of bus 1. Thus, this type of problem cannot be solved as a multiple traveling salesman problem. The characteristics of the vehicle routing problem also make it a difficult problem to solve optimally. However, a good heuristic solution can be obtained with the cluster first, route second approach.[7]

Exhibit 16-9   Four-Node Vehicle Routing Problem

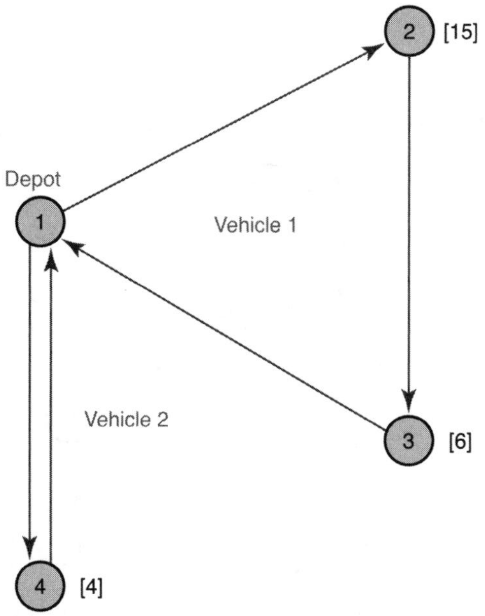

Cluster First, Route Second Approach

The **cluster first, route second approach** is best illustrated by an example. Exhibit 16-10 shows a 12-node problem in which two vehicles must deliver cargo to 11 stations and return to the depot. Cargo demand is bracketed at each node, and distances, in miles, are shown on the arcs. The 12 nodes have been clustered initially into two groups, one for each vehicle. Nodes 2 through 6 are assigned to vehicle 1 and nodes 7 through 12 to vehicle 2. Node 1 is the depot node. In practice, clustering takes into account physical barriers such as rivers, mountains, or interstate highways, as well as geographic areas such as towns and cities that form a natural cluster. Capacity restrictions are also taken into account when developing the clusters. For this example, the capacities of vehicles 1 and 2 are 45 and 35 tons, respectively.

Exhibit 16-10 Vehicle Routing Problem: Initial Solution

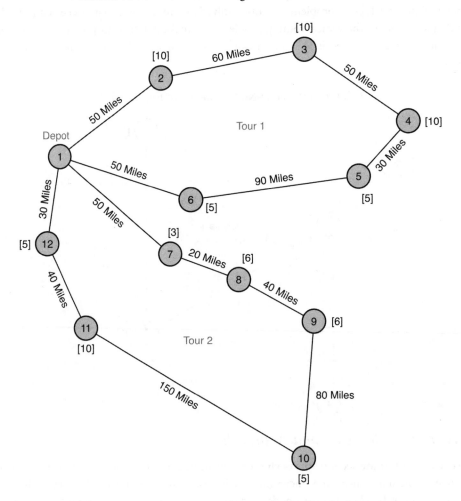

From the initial clustering, vehicle 1 must carry 40 tons, and vehicle 2 must carry 34 tons. Both assignments are feasible. (That is, the demands do not exceed either vehicle's capacity.) Using the C&W heuristic, a tour is constructed for vehicle 1 (tour 1), 1→ 2 → 3 → 4 → 5 → 6 → 1, with a total tour length of 330 miles. Vehicle 2's tour (tour 2) is 1 → 7 → 8 → 9 → 10 → 11 → 12 → 1. Its length is 410 miles.

The next phase of the procedure is to determine whether a node or nodes can be switched from the longest tour (tour 2) to tour 1 such that the capacity of vehicle 1 is not exceeded and the sum of the two tour lengths is reduced. This step is referred to as **tour improvement**. We first identify the nodes in tour 2 that are closest to tour 1. These are nodes 7 and 8. Node 8 has a demand of 6 tons and cannot be switched to tour 1 without exceeding vehicle 1's capacity. Node 7, however, has a demand of 3 tons and is eligible to switch. Given that we wish to consider a switch of node 7, how can we evaluate where the node should be inserted into tour 1 and whether it will reduce the distance traveled? Both these questions can be answered by means of the **minimum cost of insertion technique**.

The minimum cost of insertion is calculated in the same way as the Clark and Wright heuristic. If all distances are symmetrical, the cost of insertion, I_{ij}, can be calculated as follows:

$$I_{ij} = c_{ik} + c_{jk} - c_{ij} \quad \text{for all } i \text{ and } j, i \neq j \tag{16.2}$$

where

$\quad\quad\quad c_{ij}$ = the cost of traveling from node i to node j

Nodes i and j are already in the tour, and node k is the node we are trying to insert. Referring to Exhibit 16-10, node 7 is a candidate for insertion because it is near tour 1. Node 7 could be inserted between nodes 6 and 1 or between nodes 5 and 6. Both alternatives will be evaluated. To calculate the cost of inserting node 7 into tour 1, we require the additional distance information provided in the following table. In practice, this information would be available for all pairs of nodes.

From Node	To Node	Distance
1	7	50 miles
6	7	30 miles
5	7	60 miles
1	5	130 miles
1	8	60 miles

The cost of inserting node 7 between nodes 1 and 6 is 30 miles: (30 + 50 – 50). The cost of inserting the node between nodes 5 and 6 is 0: (60 + 30 – 90). The lowest cost is found by inserting node 7 between nodes 5 and 6, resulting in a completed tour for vehicle 1 of $1 \rightarrow 2 \rightarrow 3 \rightarrow 4 \rightarrow 5 \rightarrow 7 \rightarrow 6 \rightarrow 1$. Exhibit 16-11 shows the revised solution. The total length of tour 1 is now 330 miles, and the length of tour 2 is 400 miles. The distance traveled by the two vehicles has decreased from 740 to 730 miles.

Exhibit 16-11   Vehicle Routing Problem: Revised Solution

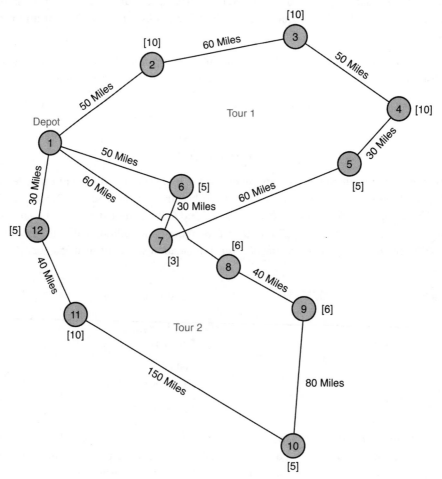

16.5 Scheduling Service Vehicles

Scheduling problems are characterized by delivery-time restrictions. The starting and ending times for a service may be specified in advance. Subway schedules fall into this category in that the arrival times at each stop are known in advance, and the train must meet the schedule. Time windows bracket the service time to within a specified interval. Recall that in the Meals-for-ME program described earlier, meals had to be delivered between 11:30 A.M. and 1:00 P.M. This is an example of a **two-sided window**. A **one-sided time window** either specifies that a service precede a given time or follow a given time. For example, most newspapers attempt to have papers delivered before 7:00 A.M. Furniture delivery is usually scheduled after 9:00 A.M. or before 4:30 P.M. Other characteristics that further complicate these problems include multiple deliveries to the same customer during a week's schedule.

The general input for a scheduling problem consists of a set of tasks, each with a starting and ending time, and a set of directed arcs, each with a starting and ending location. The set of vehicles may be housed at one or more depots.

The network in Exhibit 16-12 shows a five-task scheduling problem with a single depot. The nodes identify the tasks. Each task has a start and an end time associated with it. The directed arcs mean that two tasks are assigned to the same vehicle. The dashed arcs show other feasible connections that were not used in the schedule. An arc may join node i to node j if the start time of task j is greater than the end time of task i. An additional restriction is that the start time of task j must include a user-specified period of time longer than the end time of task i. In this example, the time is 45 minutes. This is referred to as **deadhead time** and is the nonproductive time required for the vehicle to travel from one task location to another or return to the depot empty. Also, the paths are not restricted in length. Finally, each vehicle must start and end at the depot.

Exhibit 16-12   Schedule for a Five-Task Network (S=Start Time, E=End Time)

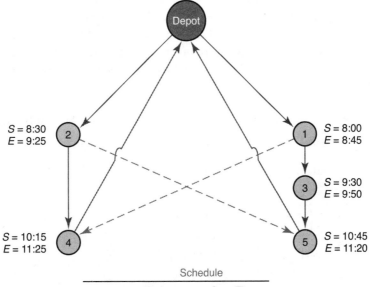

	Schedule	
	Task	Start Time
Vehicle 1	1	8:00
	3	9:30
	5	10:45
Vehicle 2	2	8:30
	4	10:15

To solve this problem, the nodes in the network must be partitioned into a set of paths and a vehicle assigned to each path. If we can identify the minimum number of paths, we can minimize the number of vehicles required and thus the vehicle capital costs. Next, if we can associate a weight to each arc that is proportional or equal to the travel time for each arc (that is, the deadhead time), we can minimize personnel and vehicle operating costs as well as time.

The Concurrent Scheduler Approach

This problem may be formulated as a special type of network problem called a **minimal cost-flow problem**.[8] Alternatively, a heuristic approach may be used. One that is simple to use is the **concurrent scheduler approach**. The concurrent scheduler proceeds as follows:

1. Order all tasks by starting times. Assign the first task to vehicle 1.

2. For the remaining number of tasks, do the following. If it is feasible to assign the next task to an existing vehicle, assign it to the vehicle that has the minimum deadhead time to that task. Otherwise, create a new vehicle and assign the task to the new vehicle.[9]

Exhibit 16-13 presents start and end times for 12 tasks. The deadhead time is 15 minutes. The problem is solved using the concurrent scheduler approach. Initially, vehicle 1 is assigned to task 1. Because task 2 begins before vehicle 1 is available, a second vehicle is assigned to this task. Vehicle 2 finishes task 2 in time to take care of task 3 also. In the meantime, vehicle 1 completes task 1 and is available for task 4. A third vehicle is not required until task 5, when vehicles 1 and 2 are busy with tasks 4 and 3, respectively. Continuing in a similar fashion, the schedule for vehicle 1 is $1 \rightarrow 4 \rightarrow 7 \rightarrow 10 \rightarrow 12$, for vehicle 2 the schedule is $2 \rightarrow 3 \rightarrow 6 \rightarrow 9$, and for vehicle 3 the schedule is $5 \rightarrow 8 \rightarrow 11$.

Exhibit 16-13 Task Times and Schedule for the Concurrent Scheduler Example

Task	Start	End	Assign to Vehicle
1	8:10 A.M.	9:30 A.M.	1
2	8:15 A.M.	9:15 A.M.	2
3	9:30 A.M.	10:40 A.M.	2
4	9:45 A.M.	10:45 A.M.	1
5	10:00 A.M.	11:30 A.M.	3
6	11:00 A.M.	11:45 A.M.	2
7	1:00 P.M.	1:45 P.M.	1
8	1:15 P.M.	2:45 P.M.	3
9	1:45 P.M.	3:00 P.M.	2
10	2:00 P.M.	2:45 P.M.	1
11	3:00 P.M.	3:40 P.M.	3
12	3:30 P.M.	4:00 P.M.	1

	Task	Schedule Start Time
Vehicle 1	1	8:10 A.M.
	4	9:45 A.M.
	7	1:00 P.M.
Vehicle 2	2	8:15 A.M.
	3	9:30 A.M.
	6	11:00 A.M.
Vehicle 3	5	10:00 A.M.
	8	1:15 P.M.

16.6 Other Routing and Scheduling Problems

Scheduling workers is often concerned with staffing desired vehicle movements. The two are of necessity related in that vehicle schedules restrict staffing options, and vice versa. In general, vehicle scheduling is done first, followed by staff scheduling. This approach is appropriate for services such as airlines, where the cost of personnel is small in comparison to the cost of operating an airplane. It is less appropriate, however, for services such as mass transit systems, where personnel costs may account for up to 80 percent of operating costs. For such systems it is more appropriate to either schedule personnel first and then schedule vehicles or to do both at the same time.

Problems that have elements of both routing and scheduling are numerous. Examples include school bus routing and scheduling, dial-a-ride services, municipal bus transportation, and the Meals-for-ME program and other meals-on-wheels programs. Certain routing problems also may take on the characteristics of a combined problem. For example, snow plows must clear busier streets prior to clearing less-traveled streets. In addition, there are usually repeated visits depending on the rate of snowfall. These components introduce a scheduling aspect to the routing problem. Considering that there may be literally thousands of variables involved in the formulation of such problems, it becomes apparent that an optimal solution is impossible to obtain. To solve real-world problems of this type, management scientists have developed some elegant solution procedures. With rare exception, the procedures use heuristic approaches to obtain "good" but not optimal routes and schedules.

The delivery of emergency services, such as ambulance, police, and fire, is not usually considered a routing or scheduling problem.[10] Rather, emergency services are more concerned with resource allocation (how many units are needed) and facility location (where the units should be located).

16.7 Summary

Effective routing and scheduling of service vehicles are two important and difficult problems for managers of services. The consequences of poor planning are costly, and a decision maker must frequently fine-tune the system to ensure that the needs of the customers are met in a timely and cost-effective fashion. The criterion used to measure the effectiveness of service delivery depends on the type of service. Although minimizing total cost is an important criterion, for some services, criteria such as minimizing customer inconvenience and minimizing response time may be equally if not more important.

Solution of routing and scheduling problems begins with a careful description of the characteristics of the service under study. Characteristics, such as whether demand occurs on the nodes or the arcs, whether there are delivery-time constraints, and whether the capacity of the service vehicles is a concern, determine the type of problem considered. The type of problem then determines the solution techniques available to the decision maker.

This chapter discussed the characteristics of routing problems, scheduling problems, and combined routing and scheduling problems. Optimal solution techniques for these types of problems are generally based on mathematical programming. However, in practice, a good but perhaps non-optimal solution is usually sufficient. To obtain a good solution, several heuristic solution approaches have been developed. Two well-known heuristics for solving the traveling salesman problem were presented, the nearest neighbor procedure and the Clark and Wright savings heuristic. Also presented was the minimum cost of the insertion technique for use in solving the vehicle routing problem.

Endnotes

1. Gail Ward of Meals-for-ME provided the information contained in this section. Also see Carol Higgins Taylor, "Meals for ME looks to bring people together," *Bangor Daily News* (December 31, 2008) (accessed 09/28/2012).

2. See Lawrence Bodin, Bruce Golden, Arjang Assad, and Michael Ball, "Routing and Scheduling of Vehicles and Crews: The State of the Art," *Computers and Operations Research*, vol. 10, no. 2 (1983), pp. 70–71.

3. For more information on the Chinese postman problem, see Lawrence Bodin et al., "Routing and Scheduling of Vehicles and Crews: The State of the Art," *Computers and Operations Research*, vol. 10, no. 2 (1983), pp. 111–112. The problem name derives from the fact the original paper was published in the *Chinese Journal of Operations Research*.

4. For a comprehensive survey of solution methods for the traveling salesman problem see David L. Applegate, Robert E. Bixby, Vas[ic]ek Chvátal, William J. Cook, *The Traveling Salesman Problem: A Computational Study*, Princeton University Press, Princeton, NJ (2007).

5. The outline of the nearest neighbor procedure is taken from Lawrence Bodin et al, "Routing and Scheduling of Vehicles and Crews: The State of the Art," p. 87.

6. The outline of the Clark and Wright savings heuristic is taken from Lawrence Bodin et al., "Routing and Scheduling of Vehicles and Crews: The State of the Art," p. 87.

7. The cluster first, route second approach is most appropriate for situations characterized by isolated "clumps" of demand points. However, there is another heuristic called the route first, cluster second approach that is more appropriate for areas in which demand points are evenly dispersed across a region. The procedure begins by constructing a large single tour using, for example, the Clark and Wright heuristic, but this first tour is infeasible because all the vehicles are not in use. The next step is to partition the single tour into smaller feasible tours such that all vehicles are used and the tours are constructed from nodes that are grouped in some natural fashion, if possible. A description of these approaches is given in Lawrence Bodin et al., "Routing and Scheduling of Vehicles and Crews: The State of the Art," p. 98.

8. The minimal-cost-flow problem is a special type of network problem that consists of a depot node, a set of intermediate nodes, and a set of demand nodes. The depot node has a supply of materials to be delivered to the demand nodes, each of which has a known demand. The intermediate nodes do not have demand. For example, an intermediate node could be a train stop where material is not removed from the cars. The network also consists of a set of arcs that may or may not have a limited capacity. For example, an arc may "carry" between 0 and 20 tons of material. In addition, the per-unit cost of transporting material over an arc is known. The objective of the problem is to find the least expensive means (routing) of transporting materials from the depot to the demand nodes. A description of this problem may be found in S. P. Bradley, A. C Hax, and T. L. Magnanti, *Applied Mathematical Programming* (Reading, MA, Addison-Wesley, 1977).

9. This outline of the concurrent scheduler approach is taken from Lawrence Bodin et al., "Routing and Scheduling of Vehicles and Crews: The State of the Art," p. 133.

10. For a complete discussion of emergency service delivery, see R. C. Larson and A. R. Odoni, *Urban Operations Research* (Upper Saddle River, NJ, Prentice Hall, 1981).

17

PROJECT MANAGEMENT

17.1 Introduction

Most service organizations have to take on large, complex projects at one point or another. For example, an airline opening new routes or pulling a jumbo jet out of service for major maintenance faces large expenses if these tasks are delayed for any reason. A department store chain installing a new inventory control system can suffer lost sales and painful ordering costs if time tables are unmet. A government agency installing and debugging an expensive computer spends months preparing details for a smooth conversion to new hardware. A hospital modernizing its operating rooms can endure not only inconvenience, but also a loss of life if the many technical steps involved are not properly controlled.

Large, often one-time projects are difficult challenges to service managers. The stakes are high. Millions of dollars in cost overruns have been wasted due to poor planning on projects. Unnecessary delays have occurred due to poor scheduling. And companies have gone bankrupt due to poor controls.

Special projects that take months or years to complete are usually developed outside the normal operations system. Project organizations within the firm are set up to handle such jobs and are often disbanded when the project is complete. The management of large projects involves three phases (see Exhibit 17-1):

- Planning
- Scheduling
- Controlling

Exhibit 17-1 Project Planning, Scheduling, and Controlling

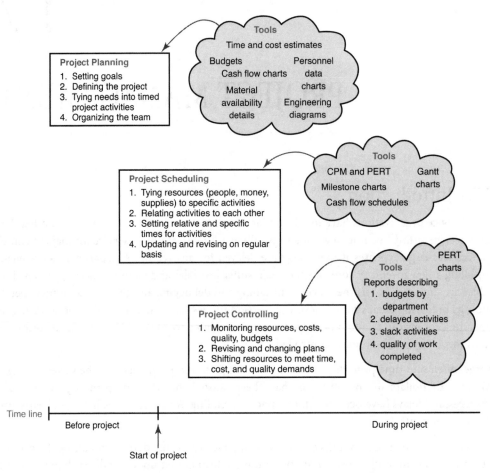

This chapter begins with a brief overview of these functions. Two popular techniques to allow managers to plan, schedule, and control—program evaluation and review technique (PERT) and critical path method (CPM)—are then described in some detail.

17.2 Project Planning

Projects can usually be defined as a series of related tasks directed toward a major output. A new organization form, developed to make sure existing programs continue to run smoothly on a day-to-day basis while new projects are successfully completed, is called **project organization**.

A project organization is an effective way of pooling the people and physical resources needed for a limited time to complete a specific project or goal. It is basically a temporary organizational structure designed to achieve results by using specialists from throughout the firm. For many years, NASA successfully used the project approach to reach its goals. You may recall Project

Gemini and Project Apollo. These terms were used to describe teams NASA organized to reach space exploration objectives.

The project organization works best when

1. Work can be defined with a specific goal and deadline.

2. The job is somewhat unique or unfamiliar to the existing organization.

3. The work contains complex interrelated tasks requiring specialized skills.

4. The project is temporary but critical to the organization.

When a project organization takes on a more permanent form, it is usually called a **matrix organization**. This structure can be used when it is critical for the firm to be highly responsive to external pressures. The firm might find that a matrix structure allows quicker responses to the environment while maintaining continuity and competence in the functional area. Some industries employing matrix project management include chemical, banking, and electronics.

The project management team begins its task well in advance of the project so that a plan can be developed. One of its first steps is to set carefully the project's objectives, and then define the project and break it down into a set of activities and related costs. Gross requirements for people, supplies, and equipment are also estimated in the planning phase.

17.3 Project Scheduling

Project scheduling is determining the project's activities in the time sequence in which they have to be performed. Materials and people needed at each stage of production are computed in this phase, and the time each activity will take is also set.

One popular project scheduling approach is the Gantt chart (named after Henry Gantt). As shown in Exhibit 17-2, **Gantt charts** reflect time estimates and can be easily understood. The horizontal bars are drawn for each project activity along a time line. The letters to the left of each bar tell the planner which other activities have to be completed before that one can begin.

Gantt charts are low-cost means of helping managers make sure that (1) all activities are planned for, (2) their order of performance is accounted for, (3) the activity time estimates are recorded, and (4) the overall project time is developed.

Activity progress is noted, after the actual project is underway, by shading the horizontal bars as an activity is partially or fully completed. For example, as shown in Exhibit 17-2, activities *a, b, c,* and *d* are on schedule because their bars have been shaded up to the vertical status date line. The date line, July 1 in this case, is a status-reporting period that lets participants see which tasks are on time, which are ahead of time, and which have fallen behind schedule. Activities *e, f,* and *g* are all behind schedule; their bars are not shaded in their entirety or up to the status date line.

Exhibit 17-2   Sample Gantt Chart

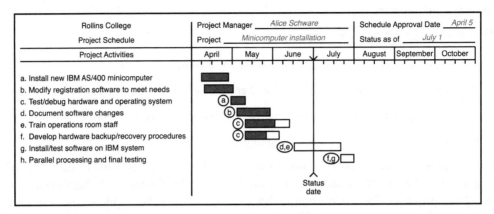

Circled items represent precedence relationships (for example, activity c, test/debug hardware, may not begin until activity a, which is circled, is completed).

Scheduling charts such as this one can be used alone on simple projects. They permit managers to observe the progress of each activity and to spot and tackle problem areas. Gantt charts are not easily updated, though. And more important, they don't adequately illustrate the interrelationships between the activities and the resources.

PERT and CPM, the two widely used network techniques that will be discussed shortly, *do* have the ability to consider precedence relationships and interdependency of activities. On complex projects, the scheduling of which is almost always computerized, PERT and CPM thus hold an edge on the simpler Gantt charts. Even on huge projects, though, Gantt charts can be used as a summary of project status and may complement the other network approaches.

To summarize, whatever the approach taken by a project manager, project scheduling serves several purposes:

1. It shows the relationship of each activity to others and to the whole project.

2. It identifies the precedence relationships among activities.

3. It encourages the setting of realistic time and cost estimates for each activity.

4. It helps make better use of people, money, and material resources by identifying critical bottlenecks in the project.

17.4 Project Controlling

The control of large projects, like the control of any management system, involves close monitoring of resources, costs, quality, and budgets. It also usually means using a feedback loop to revise and update the project plan and schedule and having the ability to shift resources to where they are needed most. Computerized PERT/CPM reports and charts are widely available today on mainframes and personal computers (PCs).

There are a wide variety of reports that can be generated for control purposes by project management software. Here is a summary and brief description of eight that are commonly available in PC software.

1. Detailed cost breakdown for each task.

2. Total program manpower curves showing each department's resource contribution.

3. Cost distribution table listing yearly or quarterly costs by task. (It resembles a project cash flow summary for each activity.)

4. Functional cost and hour summary of how person hours and dollars will be spent by each department.

5. Raw material and expenditure forecast showing a cash flow based on vendor lead times, payment schedules, and commitments.

6. Variance report using a percent complete figure for each activity, including planned versus actual costs to date, estimated costs to date, total cost at completion, earned value of work in progress, and a cost performance index.

7. Time analysis reports related to PERT/CPM schedules, giving estimated completion times, slack and float time, project calendars.

8. Work status report giving weekly task analyses for submission to the project manager for aggregation.

17.5 Project Management Techniques; PERT and CPM

Program evaluation and review technique (PERT) and the **critical path method** (CPM) were both developed in the 1950s to help managers schedule, monitor, and control large and complex projects. CPM arrived first, in 1957, as a tool developed by J. E. Kelly of Remington Rand and M. R. Walker of DuPont to assist in the building and maintenance of chemical plants at DuPont. Independently, the Special Projects Office of the U.S. Navy, working with Booz, Allen, and Hamilton, developed PERT in 1958 to plan and control the Polaris missile program. That project involved the coordination of thousands of contractors, and PERT was credited with cutting 18 months off the project length. Today, PERT is still required in many government contract schedules. If a person were to walk into the offices of a project manager working on a defense department contract, it would not be unusual these days to find a wall covered with a 20-foot-long PERT printout.

The Framework of PERT and CPM

There are six steps common to both PERT and CPM. The procedure is as follows:

1. Define the project and all its significant activities or tasks.

2. Develop the relationships among the activities. Decide which activities must precede and which must follow others.

3. Draw the network connecting all the activities.

4. Assign time and/or cost estimates to each activity.

5. Compute the longest time path through the network; this is called the **critical path**.

6. Use the network to help plan, schedule, monitor, and control the project.

Step 5, finding the critical path, is a major part of controlling a project. The activities on the critical path represent tasks that will delay the entire project if they are delayed. Managers derive flexibility by identifying noncritical activities and replanning, rescheduling, and reallocating resources such as manpower and finances.

Although PERT and CPM differ to some extent in terminology and in the construction of the network, their objectives are the same. Furthermore, the analysis used in both techniques is similar. The major difference is that PERT employs three time estimates for each activity. Each estimate has an associated probability of occurrence, which, in turn, is used in computing expected values and standard deviations for the activity times. CPM makes the assumption that activity times are known with certainty, and hence only one time estimate is given for each activity.

For purposes of illustration, this section concentrates on a discussion of PERT and PERT/Cost. **PERT/Cost** is a technique that combines the benefits of both PERT and CPM. Most of the comments and procedures described, however, apply just as well to CPM.

PERT, PERT/Cost, and CPM are important because they can help answer questions such as the following about projects with thousands of activities.

- When will the entire project be completed?

- What are the critical activities or tasks in the project, that is, the ones that will delay the entire project if they are late?

- Which are the noncritical activities, that is, the ones that can run late without delaying the whole project's completion?

- What is the probability that the project will be completed by a specific date?

- At any particular date, is the project on schedule, behind schedule, or ahead of schedule?

- On any given date, is the money spent equal to, less than, or greater than the budgeted amount?

- Are there enough resources available to finish the project on time?

- If the project is to be finished in a shorter amount of time, what is the best way to accomplish this at the least cost?

Activities, Events, and Networks

The first step in PERT is to divide the entire project into events and activities. An **event** marks the start or completion of a particular task or activity. An **activity,** on the other hand, is a task or sub-project that occurs between two events. Exhibit 17-3 restates these definitions and shows the symbols used to represent events and activities.

Any project that can be described by activities and events may be analyzed by a PERT **network.** Given the following information, for example, the network shown below can be developed.

Activity	Immediate Predecessors
A	—
B	—
C	A
D	B

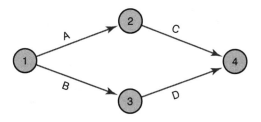

Note that each event was assigned a number. As shown later, it is possible to identify each activity with a beginning and an ending event or node. For example, the preceding activity A is the activity that starts with event 1 and ends at node, or event, 2. In general, nodes are numbered from left to right. The beginning node, or event, of the entire project is number 1, whereas the last node, or event, in the entire project bears the largest number. The last node shows the number 4.

Exhibit 17-3   Events and Activities

Name	Symbol	Description
Event	○ (node)	A point in time, usually a completion date or a starting date
Activity	→ (arrow)	A flow over time, usually a task or subproject

Networks can also be specified by events and the activities that occur between events. The following example shows how to develop a network based on this type of specification scheme. Given the following table, the network illustrated below can be developed.

Beginning Event	Ending Event	Activity
1	2	1–2
1	3	1–3
2	4	2–4
3	4	3–4
3	5	3–5
4	6	4–6
5	6	5–6

Instead of using a letter to signify activities and their predecessor activities, activities can be specified by their starting event and their ending event. Beginning with the activity that starts at event 1 and ends at event 2, the following network can be constructed. All that is required to construct a network is the starting and ending event for each activity.

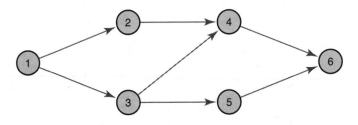

Dummy Activities and Events

A network may be encountered that has two activities with identical starting and ending events. **Dummy activities and events** can be inserted into the network to deal with this problem. The use of dummy activities and events is especially important when computer programs are to be employed in determining the critical path, project completion time, project variance, and so on. Dummy activities and events also can ensure that the network properly reflects the project under consideration. To illustrate, a network is developed based on the following information.

Activity	Immediate Predecessors	Activity	Immediate Predecessors
A	—	E	C, D
B	—	F	D
C	A	G	E
D	B	H	F

Given these data, the following network might result:

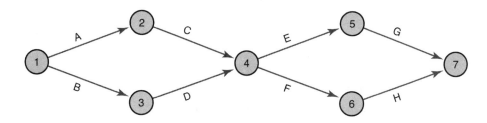

Look at activity F. According to the network, both activities C and D must be completed before we can start F, but in reality, only activity D must be completed (see the table). Thus, the network is not correct. The addition of a dummy activity and a dummy event can overcome this problem, as shown below.

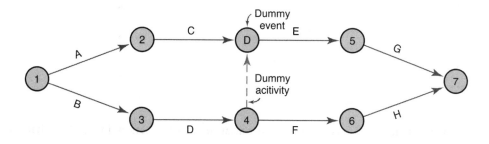

Now the network embodies all the proper relationships and can be analyzed as usual. A dummy activity should have completion time t of zero.

PERT and Activity Time Estimates

As mentioned earlier, one distinguishing difference between PERT and CPM is the use of three **activity time estimates** for each activity in the PERT technique. Only one time factor is given for each activity in CPM.

For each activity in PERT, an **optimistic time, a most probable** (or most likely) **time,** and a **pessimistic time** estimate must be specified. These three time estimates are then used to calculate an expected completion time and variance for each activity. If we assume, as many researchers do, that activity times follow a **beta probability distribution,** we can use the following formulas:[1]

$$t = \frac{a + 4m + b}{6} \quad \text{and} \quad \sigma^2 = \left[\frac{(b-a)}{6} \right]^2 \qquad (17.1)$$

where

t = expected activity completion time

a = optimistic time estimate for activity completion

b = pessimistic time estimate for activity completion

m = most likely time estimate for activity completion

σ^2 = variance of activity completion time

In PERT, after the network has been developed, expected times and variances for each activity are computed. For example, consider the following time estimates:

Activity	a	m	b
1–2	3	4	5
1–3	1	3	5
2–4	5	6	7
3–4	6	7	8

In the following table, expected times and variances of completion for each activity are computed.

Activity	a+4m+b	t	$\frac{b-a}{6}$	σ^2
1–2	24	4	$\frac{2}{6}$	$\frac{4}{36}$
1–3	18	3	$\frac{4}{6}$	$\frac{16}{36}$
2–4	36	6	$\frac{2}{6}$	$\frac{4}{36}$
3–4	42	7	$\frac{2}{6}$	$\frac{4}{36}$

Critical Path Analysis

The objective of **critical path analysis** is to determine the following quantities for each activity:

ES = earliest activity start time. All **predecessor** activities must be completed before an activity can be started. This is the earliest time an activity can be started.

LS = latest activity start time. All **following** activities must be completed without delaying the entire project. This is the latest time an activity can be started without delaying the entire project.

EF = earliest activity finish time.

LF = latest activity finish time.

S = activity slack time, which is equal to (LS – ES) or (LF – EF).

For any activity, if ES and LS can be calculated, the other three quantities can be found as follows:

$$EF = ES + t \qquad\qquad\qquad (17.2)$$

$$LF = LS + t \qquad\qquad\qquad (17.3)$$

$$S = LS - ES \qquad or \qquad S = LF - EF \qquad\qquad (17.4)$$

After these quantities are known for every activity, the overall project can be analyzed.

Typically, this analysis includes

1. The **critical path**—The group of activities in the project that have a slack time of zero. This path is **critical** because a delay in any activity along this path would delay the entire project.

2. *T*—The total project completion time, which is calculated by adding the expected time *t* values of those activities on the critical path.

3. σ^2 —Variance of the critical path, which is computed by adding the variances σ^2 of those individual activities on the critical path.

Critical path analysis normally starts with the determination of ES and EF. The following example illustrates the procedure.

Sample calculations—Given the following illustration, ES and EF will be determined for each activity.

Activity	t
1–2	2
1–3	7
2–3	4
2–4	3
3–4	2

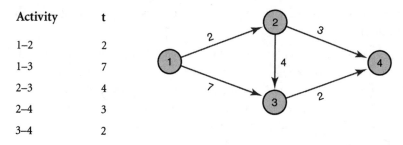

ES is found by moving from the starting activities of the project to the ending activities of the project. For the starting activities, ES is either zero or the actual starting date, say, August 1. For activities 1–2 and 1–3, ES is zero. (By convention, all projects start at time zero.)

There is one basic rule. Before an activity can be started, all its predecessor activities must be completed. In other words, search for the longest path leading to an activity in determining ES. For activity 2–3, ES is 2. Its only predecessor activity is 1–2, for which $t = 2$. By the same reasoning, ES for activity 2–4 also is 2. For activity 3–4 however, ES is 7. It has two predecessor paths: activity 1–3 with $t = 7$ and activities 1–2 and 2–3 with a total expected time of 6 (or 2 + 4). Thus, ES for activity 3–4 is 7 because activity 1–3 must be completed before activity 3–4 can be started. EF is computed next by adding t to ES for each activity. See the following table.

Activity	ES	EF
1–2	0	2
1–3	0	7
2–3	2	6
2–4	2	5
3–4	7	9

The next step is to calculate LS, the latest activity starting time for each activity. Start with the last activities and work backward to the first activities. The procedure is to work backward from the last activities to determine the latest possible starting time (LS) without increasing the earliest finishing time (EF). This task sounds more difficult than it really is.

To illustrate, determine LS, LF, and S (the slack) for each activity based on the following data:

Activity	t	ES	EF
1–2	2	0	2
1–3	7	0	7
2–3	4	2	6
2–4	3	2	5
3–4	2	7	9

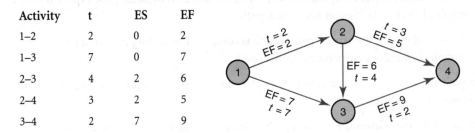

The earliest time by which the entire project can be finished is 9 because activities 2–4 (EF = 5) and 3–4 (EF = 9) *both* must be completed. Using 9 as a basis, work backward by subtracting the appropriate values of t from 9.

The latest time activity 3–4 can be started is at time 7 (or 9 – 2) in order still to complete the project by time period 9. Thus, LS for activity 3–4 is 7. Using the same reasoning, LS for activity 2–4 is 6 (or 9 – 3). If activity 2–4 is started at 6 and it takes 3 time units to complete the activity, it can still be finished in 9 time units. The latest activity 2–3 can be started is 3 (or 9 – 2 – 4). If activity 2–3 is started at 3 and it takes 2 and 4 time units for activities 2–3 and 3–4, respectively, it can still be finished on time.

Thus, LS for activity 2–3 is 3. Using the same reasoning, LS for activity 1–3 is zero (or 9 – 2 – 7). Analyzing activity 1–2 is more difficult because there are two paths. Both must be completed in 9 time units.

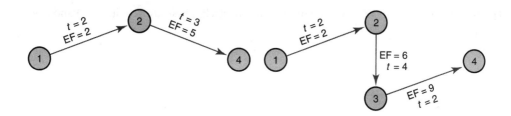

Because both the preceding paths must be completed, LS activity 1–2 is computed from the most binding, or slowest, path. Thus, LS for activity 1–2 *is 1* (or $9 - 2 - 4 - 2$) and *not 4* (or $9 - 3 - 2$). Noting the following relationships, you can construct a table summarizing the results.

$$LF = LS + t$$
$$S = LF - EF \text{ or } S = LS - ES$$

Activity	ES	EF	LS	LF	S
1–2	0	2	1	3	1
1–3	0	7	0	7	0
2–3	2	6	3	7	1
2–4	2	5	6	9	4
3–4	7	9	7	9	0

After ES, EF, LS, LF, and S have been computed, the entire project can be analyzed. Analysis includes determining the critical path, project completion time, and project variance. Consider the following example.

Project analysis—We wish to find the critical path, total completion time T, and project variance σ^2, of the following network.

Activity	t	v	ES	EF	LS	LF	S
1–2	2	$\frac{2}{6}$	0	2	1	3	1
1–3	7	$\frac{3}{6}$	0	7	0	7	0
2–3	4	$\frac{1}{6}$	2	6	3	7	1
2–4	3	$\frac{2}{6}$	2	5	6	9	4
3–4	2	$\frac{4}{6}$	7	9	7	9	0

The critical path consists of those activities with zero slack. These are activities 1–3 and 3–4.

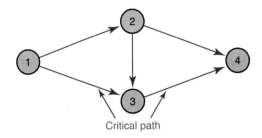

Critical path

The total project completion time is 9 (or 7 + 2). The project variance is the sum of the *activity variances* along the *critical path,* which is 7/6 (or 3/6 + 4/6).

Knowing a network and values for activity times and variances *(t* and σ^2) makes it possible to perform a complete critical path analysis, including the determination of ES, EF, LS, LF, and S for each activity as well as the critical path, T, and *V* for the entire project.

The Probability of Project Completion

Having computed the expected completion time T and completion variance σ^2, we can determine the probability that the project will be completed at a specified date. If we make the assumption that the distribution of completion dates follows a normal curve, we can calculate the probability of completion as in the following example.

Let us say that the expected project completion time T is 20 weeks and the project variance σ^2 is 100. What is the probability that the project will be finished on or before week 25?

$T = 20$

$\sigma^2 = 100$

$\sigma = \text{critical path standard deviation} = \sqrt{\text{critical path variance}} = \sqrt{\sigma^2} = \sqrt{100} = 10$

$C = \text{desired completion date} = 25 \text{ weeks}$

The normal curve would appear as follows:

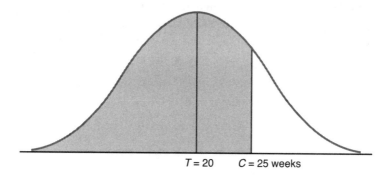

$$Z = \frac{C - T}{\sigma} = \frac{25 - 20}{10} = 0.5$$

(17.5)

where Z equals the number of standard deviations from the mean. The area under the curve, for $Z = 0.5$, is 0.6915. (See the normal curve table in the Appendix, "Areas Under the Standard Normal Curve.") Thus, the probability of completing the project in 25 weeks is approximately 0.69, or 69 percent.[2]

17.6 PERT/Cost

Until now, we have assumed that it is not possible to reduce activity times. This is usually not the case, however. Perhaps additional resources can reduce activity times for certain activities within the project. These resources might be additional labor, more equipment, and so on. Although it can be expensive to shorten activity times, doing so might be worthwhile. If a company faces costly penalties for being late with a project, it might be economical to use additional resources to complete the project on time. There may be fixed costs every day the project is in process. Thus, it might be profitable to use additional resources to shorten the project time and save some of the daily fixed costs. But which activities should be shortened? How much will this action cost? Will a reduction in the activity time in turn reduce the time needed to complete the entire project? Ideally, we would like to find the least expensive method of shortening the entire project. This is the purpose of PERT/Cost.

In addition to time, the service manager is normally concerned with the cost of the project. Usually it is possible to shorten activity times by committing additional resources to the project. Exhibit 17-4 shows cost-time curves for two activities. For activity 5–6, it costs $300 to complete the activity in 8 weeks, $400 for 7 weeks, and $600 for 6 weeks. Activity 2–4 requires $3,000 of additional resources for completion in 12 weeks and $1,000 for 14 weeks. Similar cost-time curves or relationships can usually be developed for all activities in the network.

The objective of PERT/Cost is to reduce the entire project completion time (also called project compression or project crashing), by a certain amount at the least cost. Although there are several good computer programs that perform PERT/Cost, it is useful to understand how to complete this process by hand. To accomplish this objective, a few more variables must be introduced. For each activity, there will be a reduction in activity time and the cost incurred for that time reduction. Let

M_i = maximum reduction of time for activity i

C_i = additional cost associated with reducing activity time for activity i

K_i = cost of reducing activity time by one unit for activity i

$K_i = C_i / M_i$

With this information, it is possible to determine the least cost of reducing the project completion date.

Exhibit 17-4   Cost-Time Curves Used in PERT/Cost Analysis

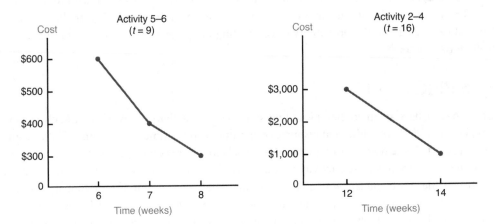

Reducing completion time example—As an illustration, the following information is used to determine the least cost of reducing the project completion time by one week.

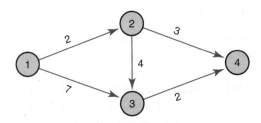

Activity	t (weeks)	M (weeks)	C	Activity	ES	EF	LS	LF	S
1–2	2	1	$ 300	1–2	0	2	1	3	1
1–3	7	4	2000	1–3	0	7	0	7	0
2–3	4	2	2000	2–3	2	6	3	7	1
2–4	3	2	4000	2–4	2	5	6	9	4
3–4	2	1	2000	3–4	7	9	7	9	0

The first step is to compute K for each activity.

Activity	M	C	K	Critical Path
1–2	1	$ 300	$ 300	No
1–3	4	2000	500	Yes
2–3	2	2000	1000	No
2–4	2	4000	2000	No
3–4	1	2000	2000	Yes

The second step is to locate that activity on the critical path with the smallest value of K_i. The critical path consists of activities 1–3 and 3–4. Because activity 1–3 has a lower value of K_i, the project completion time can be reduced by 1 week, to 6 weeks, by incurring an additional cost of $500.

We must be very careful in using this procedure. Any further reduction in activity time along the critical path would cause the critical path also to include activities 1–2, 2–3, and 3–4. In other words, there would be two critical paths and activities on both would need to be "crashed" to reduce project completion time.[3]

17.7 Other Service Applications of PERT

To further illustrate the potential for project management techniques in services, this section provides a larger illustration. This example deals with the relocation of a hospital.

Relocating a Hospital with Project Networks

When St. Vincent's Hospital and Medical Center moved from a 373-bed facility in Portland, Oregon, to a new 403-bed building in the suburbs 5 miles away, a large variety of planning considerations had to be taken into account. Army vehicles and private ambulances had to be used to move patients; police escorts would be needed; local stores would be affected by the move, among many other concerns. To coordinate all the activities, a project network was developed and used as a basic planning tool 8 months before the move. Although the actual network contained dozens of activities, a portion of it is provided in Exhibit 17-5 to illustrate how valuable project management tools can be in planning and carrying out a complex project.

Exhibit 17-5 A Portion of St. Vincent's Hospital Project Network: Critical Activities

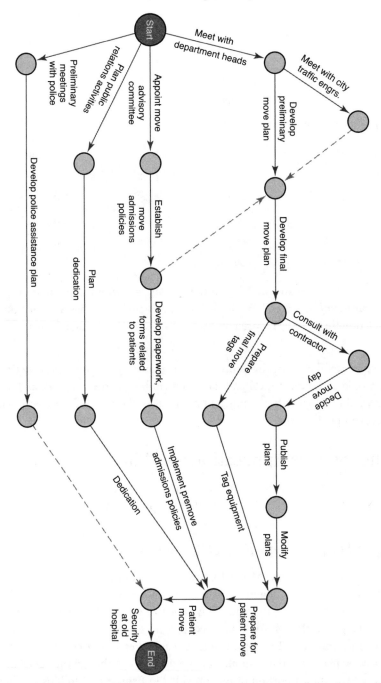

Source: Adapted from R.S. Hanson, "Moving the Hospital to a New Location," *Industrial Engineering* (November 1982). Copyright Institute of Industrial Engineers, 25 Technology Park/Atlanta, Norcross, GA 30092.

17.8 A Critique of PERT and CPM

It has been more than five decades since PERT and CPM were first introduced as project management tools. This is just enough time to step back and examine their strengths and limitations objectively—a process that helps us understand the role of critical path scheduling today.

Because the Department of Defense (DOD) overwhelmingly adopted PERT and made its use a requirement for all defense contractors, PERT's first 10 years were its zenith. Many managers, professors, computer professionals, and magazine and journal editors became converts (and "experts"). With enthusiasm and interest strong, PERT even became a verb, and all good projects were "perted out." This sometimes meant wall-to-wall computer-generated and updated charts and a tendency to trust PERT as a solution to solve all project management problems.

As was probably inevitable, PERT's fashionability dropped off during the 1970s. As some converts became critics, others who had long resented the forced burdens of the PERT and CPM approach became vocal in their scorn of the tool.[4]

Now critical path analysis appears to be leveling out and even increasing once again in popularity. Project managers are more knowledgeable about the pluses and minuses of PERT use and are aided by the spread of powerful but easy-to-use microcomputer-based software packages. As a summary of the discussions of PERT, here are some of its features about which operations managers need to be aware.

Advantages

1. PERT is useful at several stages of project management, especially in the scheduling and control of large projects.

2. It is straightforward in concept and not mathematically complex. Although projects with hundreds or thousands of activities are usually computerized, smaller ones can be tackled easily by hand.

3. The graphical displays using networks help to perceive quickly relationships among project activities.

4. Critical path and slack time analyses help pinpoint activities that need to be closely watched. This provides opportunity for resource reallocation when the project needs to be shortened ("crashed" or "compressed").

5. The networks generated provide valuable project documentation and graphically point out who is responsible for various activities.

6. PERT is applicable to a wide variety of service projects and industries.

7. It is useful in monitoring not only schedules, but costs as well. This helps avoid cost overrun penalties and facilitates "early finish" bonuses.

Limitations

1. Project activities have to be clearly defined, independent, and stable in their relationships. In spite of the focus on the techniques of project management, this step is typically the most difficult.

2. Precedence relationships must be specified and networked together. Sometimes precedences are hard to clarify and are not shown correctly.

3. Time activities in PERT are assumed to follow the beta probability distribution. It is difficult for users to verify whether this actually holds true for each activity. There is now some question about the validity of this assumption.

4. Time estimates tend to be subjective and are subject to fudging by managers who fear the dangers of being overly optimistic or not pessimistic enough.

5. There is the inherent danger of too much emphasis being placed on the longest, or critical, path. Near-critical paths need to be monitored closely as well.

Using POM for Windows for Project Management

POM for Windows Project Scheduling module can be used to determine expected project completion time for a CPM or PERT network with either one or three time estimates. In addition, the software calculates the earliest start, earliest finish, latest start, and latest finish times, as well as the slack for each activity. Exhibit 17-6 shows the output from POM for Windows solution of the following example.

Exhibit 17-6   POM for Windows Solution of the Example

File Edit View Module Format Tools Window Help

Arial

Network type
- Immediate predecessor list
- Start/end node numbers

Method
Triple time estimate

Instruction
There are more results available in

Project Management (PERT/CPM) Results

EXAMPLE Solution

Activity	Start node	End node	Activity time	Early Start	Early Finish	Late Start	Late Finish	Slack	Standard Deviation
Project			36.33						2.29
A	1	4	5.83	0	5.83	7.17	13	7.17	.83
B	1	3	3.67	0	3.67	5.33	9	5.33	.33
C	1	2	2	0	2	0	2	0	.33
D	2	3	7	2	9	2	9	0	.33
E	3	4	4	9	13	9	13	0	.67
F	4	5	10	13	23	13	23	0	1.33
G	4	6	2.17	13	15.17	15.83	18	2.83	.5
H	5	7	6	23	29	23	29	0	1
I	6	7	11	15.17	26.17	18	29	2.83	.33
J	2	8	16.33	2	18.33	20	36.33	18	1
K	7	8	7.33	29	36.33	29	36.33	0	1.33

17.9 Summary

PERT, CPM, and other scheduling techniques have proven to be valuable tools in controlling large and complex projects. With these tools, managers understand the status of each activity and know which activities are critical and which have slack; in addition, they know where crashing makes the most sense. Projects are segmented into discrete activities, precedence relationships among them are determined, and specific resources are identified. This allows project managers to respond to the challenges of managing large and complex projects. Effective project management also allows firms to create products and services for global markets. A wide variety of software packages to help managers handle network modeling problems are available.

PERT and CPM do not, however, solve all the project scheduling and management problems of service organizations. Good management practices, clear responsibilities for tasks, and straightforward and timely reporting systems are also needed. Remember that the models described in this chapter are only tools to help managers make better decisions.

Endnotes

1. Although the beta distribution has been widely used in PERT analysis for many years, its applicability has been called into question. See M. W. Sasieni, "A Note on PERT Times," *Management Science*, vol. 32, no. 12 (December 1986), pp. 1662–1663.

2. Here we are making a simplifying assumption that probability of completing the project in 25 weeks is approximately equal to the probability of completing the critical path in 25 weeks.

3. In this example cost/time curves are assumed to be linear (that is, constant slope). In other words, cost of time reduction per time unit (for example, week and day) is assumed to be the same. However, in many practical applications this may not be true. The cost of the first few reductions may be low, but later ones may cost much more, resulting in nonlinear cost curves. For determining the optimal project compression, see J. Moussourakis and C. Haksever, "Project Compression with Non-linear Cost Functions," *Journal of Construction Engineering and Management*, Vol. 136, No. 2 (February 2010).

4. Two articles describing these attitudes both candidly and humorously are M. Krakowski, "PERT and Parkinson's Law," Interfaces, vol. 5, no. 1 (November 1974); and A. Vazsonyi, "L'Historie de la grandeur et de la decadence de la methode PERT," *Management Science*, vol. 16, no. 8 (April 1970). Both articles make interesting reading (and are both written in English).

18

LINEAR AND GOAL PROGRAMMING APPLICATIONS FOR SERVICES

18.1 Introduction

Many service operations management decisions involve trying to make the most effective use of an organization's resources. Resources typically include labor, money, storage space/capacity, or materials. These resources may be used to produce services such as schedules for shipping and production, advertising policies, investment decisions, or hospital meal plans. **Linear programming (LP)** and **goal programming (GP)** are widely used mathematical techniques designed to help operations managers in planning and decision making relative to the trade-offs necessary to allocate resources.

Examples of problems in which LP and GP have been applied successfully in service management include the following:

- Performance management and evaluation at the American Red Cross[1]

- Allocating police patrol units to high-crime areas[2]

- Capacity Management in Indian Railways[3]

- Long-Range Planning for a West Texas Catholic Diocese[4]

- Revenue Management: Harrah's Cherokee Casino & Hotel[5]

- Scheduling the Chilean Soccer League[6]

This chapter stresses the importance of *formulating* linear programming problems; it leaves the mathematical details of solving such problems to management science texts.[7] Because computer programs are readily available to conduct the mechanics of LP (and are illustrated in this chapter), most operations managers can avoid the complex manual algorithms associated with LP and GP. Most of the chapter looks at the more common linear programming formulations, in which a service organization has but one objective to be attained (such as minimizing labor costs or maximizing profit). Later, the chapter concludes with an extension of LP known as **goal programming** (**GP**). GP is capable of handling decision problems having multiple goals, some of which may be contradictory.

18.2 Overview of Linear Programming

All LP problems have four properties in common:

1. All problems seek to *maximize* or *minimize* some quantity (usually profit or cost). We refer to this property as the **objective function** of an LP problem. The major objective of a typical firm is to maximize dollar profits in the long run. In the case of a trucking or airline distribution system, the objective might be to minimize shipping costs.

2. The presence of restrictions, or **constraints,** limits the degree to which we can pursue our objective. For example, deciding how many units of each product in a firm's warehouse should be stocked in one retail outlet is restricted by space, available labor, and budgets. We want, therefore, to maximize or minimize a quantity (the objective function) subject to limited resources (the constraints).

3. There must be *alternative courses of action* to choose from. For example, if a store stocks three different products, management may use LP to decide how to allocate among them its limited display space and advertising budget. If there were no alternatives to select from, we would not need LP.

4. The objective and constraints in linear programming problems must be expressed in terms of *linear* equations or inequalities.

The best way to illustrate these properties and how to formulate an LP problem is through an example. Now consider the case of a small furniture retailer.

Dixon Furniture Store

Dixon Furniture is planning for its Labor Day weekend special sale. The two items that have been selected for promotion, because of the time of year, are folding tables and chairs; both are ideal for backyard parties. The store has only 100 square feet of space available for displaying and stocking these items. Each table has a wholesale cost of $4, takes up 2 square feet of space, and will retail for $11. The wholesale price of a chair is $3; each requires 1 square foot to stock and will sell for $8. The manager believes that no more than 60 chairs can possibly be sold, but that the demand for the $11 tables is almost unlimited. Finally, Dixon's budget for procuring the tables and chairs is $240. The question facing the store manager is to decide how many tables and chairs to stock so as to maximize profit.

We begin to formulate this situation as an LP problem by introducing some simple notations for use in the objective function and constraints. Let

X_1 = number of tables in stock

X_2 = number of chairs in stock

Now create the LP objective function in terms of X_1 and X_2:

Maximize net profit = retail price – wholesale cost

$$= (\$11\ X_1 + \$8\ X_2) - (\$4\ X_1 + \$3X_2) = 7X_1 + 5\ X_2$$

The next step is to develop mathematical relationships to describe the three constraints in this problem. One general relationship is that the amount of a resource used is to be less than or equal to the amount of resource available.

First constraint: Budget used ≤ budget available

$4\ X_1 + 3\ X_2 \le 240$ dollars available for purchases

Second constraint: Space used ≤ space available

$2\ X_1 + X_2 \le 100$ square feet of floor space

Third constraint: Chairs ordered ≤ anticipated chair demand

$X_2 \le 60$ chairs that can be sold

All three of these constraints represent stocking restrictions and, of course, affect the total profit. For example, Dixon Furniture cannot order 70 tables for the sale because if $X_1 = 70$, the first two constraints will be violated. It also cannot order $X_1 = 50$ tables and $X_2 = 10$ chairs. Hence, we note one more important aspect of linear programming. That is, certain interactions will exist between variables. The more units of one product that the store orders, the less it can order of other products.

18.3 Graphical Solution to a Linear Programming Problem

The easiest way to solve a small LP problem such as that of the Dixon Furniture Store is the graphical solution approach. The graphical procedure is useful only when there are two decision variables (such as number of tables to order, X_1 and number of chairs to order, X_2) in the problem. Where there are more than two variables, it is *not* possible to plot the solution on a two-dimensional graph, and we must turn to more complex approaches or to the use of a computer (which we shall do shortly). But the graphical method is invaluable in providing insights into how other approaches work.

Graphic Representation of Constraints

To find the optimal solution to a linear programming problem, we must first identify a set, or **region,** of feasible solutions. The first step in doing so is to plot each of the problem's constraints on a graph.

The variable X_1 (tables, in the example) is usually plotted as the horizontal axis of the graph, and the variable X_2 (chairs) is plotted as the vertical axis. The complete problem may be restated as

Maximize profit = $\$7X_1 + \$5X_2$

subject to the constraints:

$4X_1 + 3X_2 \leq 240$ (budget constraint)

$2X_1 + X_2 \leq 100$ (space constraint)

$X_2 \leq 60$ (chair demand constraint)

$X_1 \geq 0$ (number of tables ordered is greater than or equal to 0)

$X_2 \geq 0$ (number of chairs ordered is greater than or equal to 0)

To represent graphically the constraints of this problem, the first step is to convert the constraint *inequalities* into *equalities* (or equations); that is,

Constraint 1: $4X_1 + 3X_2 = 240$

Constraint 2: $2X_1 + X_2 = 100$

Constraint 3: $X_2 = 60$

The equation for constraint 1 is plotted in Exhibit 18-1.

Exhibit 18-1   Plotting the Budget Constraint for Dixon

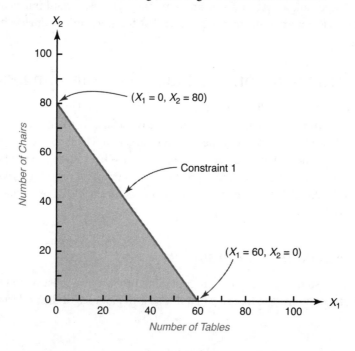

To plot the line in Exhibit 18-1, find the points at which the line $4X_1 + 3X_2 = 240$ intersects the X_1 and X_2 axes. When $X_1 = 0$ (the location where the line touches the X_2 axis), it implies that $3X_2 = 240$ or that $X_2 = 80$. Likewise, when $X_2 = 0$, we see that $4X_1 = 240$ and that $X_1 = 60$. Thus, constraint 1 is bounded by the line running from $(X_1 = 0, X_2 = 80)$ to $(X_1 = 60, X_2 = 0)$. The shaded area represents all points that satisfy the original **inequality**. Constraints 2 and 3 are handled similarly. Exhibit 18-2 shows all three constraints together. Note that the third constraint is just a straight line, which does not depend on the values of X_1.

Exhibit 18-2   **All Constraints Plotted to Produce the Feasible Region for Dixon**

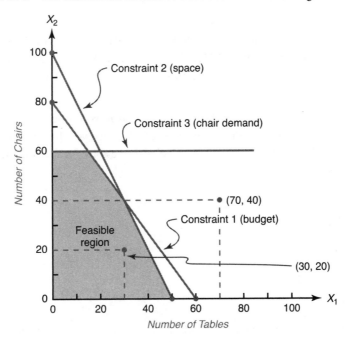

The shaded region in Exhibit 18-2 is the part that satisfies all three restrictions. This region is called the **area of feasible solutions**, or simply the **feasible region.** This region must satisfy *all* conditions specified by the program's constraints and thus is the region in which all constraints overlap. Any point in the region would be a **feasible solution** to the Dixon Furniture Store problem. Any point outside the shaded area would represent an **infeasible solution**. Hence, it would be feasible to order 30 tables and 20 chairs $(X_1 = 30, X_2 = 20)$, but it would violate the constraints to order 70 tables and 40 chairs. This can be seen by plotting these points on the graph of Exhibit 18-2.

Iso-Profit Line Solution Method

Now that the feasible region has been graphed, we may proceed to find the optimal solution to the problem. The mathematical theory behind linear programming states that an optimal solution to any problem (that is, the values of X_1, X_2 that yield the maximum profit) will lie at a **corner point**, or **extreme point**, of the feasible region. The optimal solution is then the corner point lying in the feasible region that produces the highest profit.

There are several approaches that can be taken in solving for the optimal solution after the feasible region has been established graphically. The speediest one to apply is called the **iso-profit line method**.

Start by letting profits equal some arbitrary, but small, dollar amount. For the Dixon Furniture problem, we may choose a profit of $210. This is a profit level that can easily be obtained without violating any of the three constraints. The objective function can be written as $210 = 7X_1 + 5X_2$.

This expression is just the equation of a line; we call it an **iso-profit line**. It represents all combinations of (X_1, X_2) that would yield a total profit of $210. To plot the profit line, we proceed exactly as we did to plot a constraint line. First, let $X_1 = 0$ and solve for the point at which the line crosses the X_2 axis.

$210 = \$7(0) + \$5X_2$

$X_2 = 42$ chairs

Then let $X_2 = 0$ and solve for X_1

$210 = \$7X_1 + \$5(0)$

$X_1 = 30$ tables

These two points can now be connected with a straight line. This profit line is illustrated in Exhibit 18-3. All points on the line represent feasible solutions that produce a profit of $210.

Exhibit 18-3 A Profit Line of $210 Plotted for Dixon

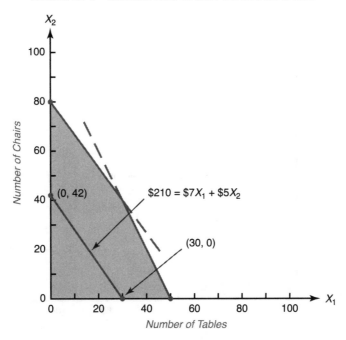

Now, obviously, the iso-profit line for $210 does not produce the highest possible profit to Dixon. In Exhibit 18-4, we try graphing a new line, one yielding a higher profit. Note that the further we move from the origin, the higher the profit will be. Another important point to note is that these iso-profit lines are parallel. There are now two clues as to how to find the optimal solution to the original problem. A series of parallel profit lines can be drawn (by carefully moving the ruler away from the origin parallel to the first profit line). The highest profit line that still touches some point of the feasible region will pinpoint the optimal solution.

Exhibit 18-4   Optimal Solution for the Dixon Furniture Problem

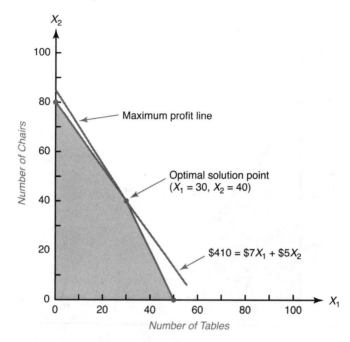

The highest possible iso-profit line touches the tip of the feasible region of Exhibit 18-4 at the corner point $(X_1 = 30, X_2 = 40)$ and yields a profit of $410.

18.4 Computer Solution to a Linear Programming Problem

As mentioned earlier, it is not possible to solve any linear programming problem graphically that has more than two variables. Fortunately, many linear programming software packages are available for larger problems. This section demonstrates how to interpret the output of POM for Windows software. POM for Windows, as well as many other commercial LP software, operates by using an algebraic technique known as the **simplex algorithm**.

The simplex method systematically examines corner points of the feasible region, always searching for the corner point that yields a better value for the objective function. It not only provides the optimal solution to any LP problem, but also provides information in the form of **shadow prices** and **sensitivity analysis** that may be very valuable to managers in their decision-making process. One of the early steps of the simplex method is the conversion of inequality constraints into equalities. It does this by adding a **slack variable** to the left-hand side of each less than or equal to ($\le$) constraint, and subtracting a slack (or surplus) variable from the left-hand side of each greater than or equal to (≥) constraint. Slack and surplus variables represent the difference between the right-hand and left-hand sides of constraints. After this conversion, the constraints of the Dixon Furniture problem would be

$X_1 + 3X_2 + S_1 = 240$ (budget constraint)

$X_1 + X_2 + S_2 = 100$ (floor space constraint)

$X_2 + S_3 = 60$ (chair demand constraint)

For a resource constraint, such as the budget constraint in the Dixon Furniture problem, the slack variable (S_1) represents the **unused** portion of that resource (that is, budget). The slack variable for the floor space constraint S_2 represents unused floor space, and the slack for the third constraint S_3 is the unsatisfied portion of chair demand.

Exhibit 18-5 shows the solution to the Dixon Furniture problem. This is only one of several outputs you can obtain from POM for Windows for linear programming problems. If the problem has two variables, the graphical solution is also available (Exhibit 18-6). The optimal solution in Exhibit 18-5 indicates that slack variables S_1 and S_2 are both zero. This means that both budget and floor space resources will be used to the fullest extent if the optimal solution is implemented, that is, if 30 tables and 40 chairs are purchased. Slack variable $S_3 = 20$ indicates that the chair demand will not be fully satisfied.

Exhibit 18-5 POM for Windows Solution of Dixon Furniture Problem

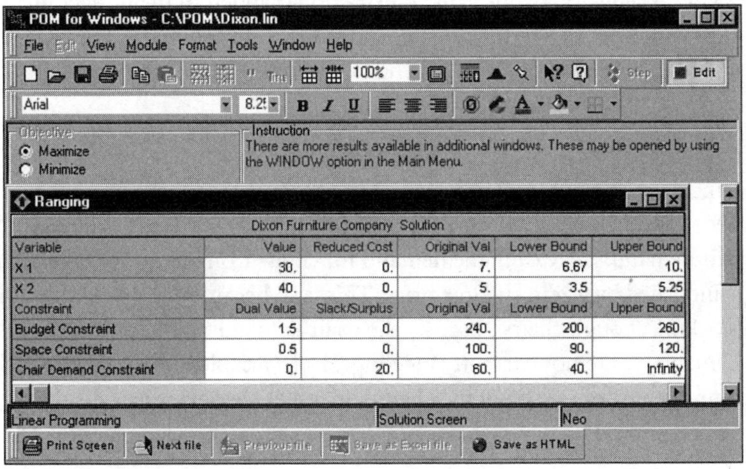

Dixon Furniture Company Solution					
Variable	Value	Reduced Cost	Original Val	Lower Bound	Upper Bound
X 1	30.	0.	7.	6.67	10.
X 2	40.	0.	5.	3.5	5.25
Constraint	Dual Value	Slack/Surplus	Original Val	Lower Bound	Upper Bound
Budget Constraint	1.5	0.	240.	200.	260.
Space Constraint	0.5	0.	100.	90.	120.
Chair Demand Constraint	0.	20.	60.	40.	Infinity

Exhibit 18-6   POM for Windows Graphical Solution of Dixon Furniture Problem

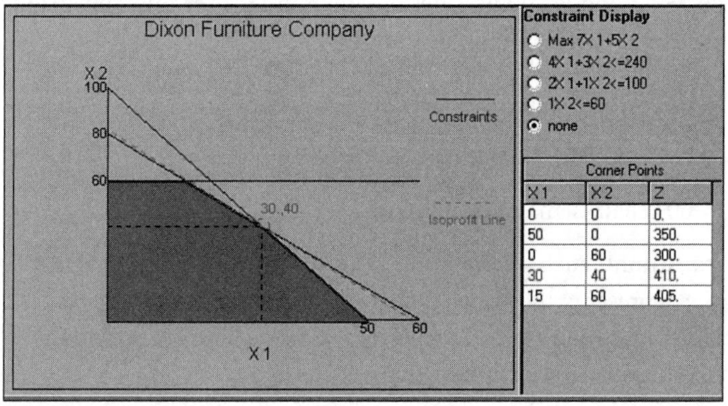

Shadow Prices

Output shown in Exhibit 18-5 also leads to the important subject of shadow prices. Shadow prices are indicated as **dual values** in the computer output. **Shadow price** (or dual value) represents the **change** in the objective function value (that is, profit for Dixon Furniture) for one unit **increase** in the right-hand side of a constraint. For example, how much should Dixon Furniture be willing to pay to obtain an additional unit of each resource (that is, increase the number on the right-hand side of each constraint by one)? Is renting one more square foot of floor space worth $1 or $5 or 25 cents to Dixon? Will an extra dollar added to the budget increase profit by more than $1, or will it not be worthwhile to seek additional funding for the sale? Will an advertising campaign to increase the demand for chairs be a worthwhile effort?

Exhibit 18-5 shows that each additional unit of the first resource (that is, budget dollars) will increase Dixon's overall profit by $1.50. This **shadow price** is valuable information for management. Furthermore, each additional square foot of display area (above the 100 square feet currently fully used) would increase the current $410 profit by $0.50. There is clearly no value to an increase in chair demand. Increasing the demand for chairs from 60 to 61 will not increase profit at all; this is indicated by a zero shadow price. This is so because the optimal solution does not recommend stocking enough chairs to satisfy the chair demand for 60 chairs; there is no point in increasing a demand we are not currently meeting. Slack variable $S_3 = 20$ indicates that the optimal plan is 20 units short of satisfying the chair demand. A shadow price will always be zero if its constraint's corresponding slack variable is not zero.

Sensitivity Analysis

Shadow pricing is actually one form of **sensitivity analysis,** that is, the study of how sensitive the optimal solution would be to errors or changes in inputs to the LP problem. For example, if the store manager at Dixon Furniture had been off by 10 percent in setting the net profit per table at

$7, would that drastically alter the decision to order 30 tables and 40 chairs? What would be the impact of a budget of $265 instead of $240?

Exhibit 18-5 has information available to help a decision maker know whether a solution is relatively insensitive to reasonable changes in one or more of the parameters of the problem. First, consider changes to the right-hand side of a constraint. In doing so, we assume changes are made in only one constraint at a time; the other two remain fixed at their original values. **Lower bound** and **upper bound** values tell us over what range of right-hand side values the shadow prices (dual values) for that constraint will remain valid. In the Dixon example, the $1.50 shadow price for the budget constraint will apply even if the current budget of $240 drops as low as $200 or increases as high as $260.

This concept that the right-hand side range limits the shadow price is important in sensitivity analysis. Suppose Dixon Furniture could obtain additional funding at a cost less than the shadow price. The question of how much to obtain is answered by the upper bound, that is, secure $20 more than the original value $240.

Now let us look at changes in one of the objective function coefficients (unit profits for chairs and tables in the Dixon problem). Sensitivity analysis provides, for each decision variable in the solution, the range of objective function coefficients over which the answer will be the same. For example, the net profit of $7 per table (X_1) in the objective function could range from $6.67 to $10.00 without the optimal solution of $X_1 = 30$, $X_2 = 40$ changing. Of course, if a profit coefficient changed at all, the total profit of $410 would change, even if the optimal quantities of X_1 and X_2 do not.

18.5 Formulating Linear Programming Models

The purpose of this section is to show how a large number of real-life problems can be tackled using LP. We do this by presenting applications in the areas of ingredient blending, transportation/shipping, employee scheduling, labor planning, and media planning. Although some of these problems are relatively small numerically, the principles developed here are definitely applicable to larger problems.

Ingredient Blending Applications: The Diet Problem

The **diet problem**, one of the earliest applications of linear programming, was originally used by hospitals to determine the most economical diet for patients. Known in agricultural applications as the **feed mix problem**, the diet problem involves specifying a food or feed ingredient combination that satisfies stated nutritional requirements at a minimum cost level.

The Whole Food Nutrition Center uses three bulk grains to blend a natural cereal that sells by the pound. The store advertises that each 2-ounce serving of the cereal, when taken with one-half cup of whole milk, meets an average adult's minimum daily requirement for protein, riboflavin, phosphorus, and magnesium. The cost of each bulk grain and the protein, riboflavin, phosphorus, and magnesium units per pound of each are shown in Exhibit 18-7.

Exhibit 18-7   Whole Food's Natural Cereal Requirements

Grain	Cost per Pound	Protein (Units/lb)	Riboflavin (Units/lb)	Phosphorus (Units/lb)	Magnesium (Units/lb)
A	33¢	22	16	8	5
B	47¢	28	14	7	0
C	38¢	21	25	9	6

The minimum adult daily requirement (called the *U.S. Recommended Daily Allowance,* or *USRDA)* for protein is 3 units; for riboflavin, 2 units; for phosphorus, 1 unit; and for magnesium, 0.425 units. Whole Food wants to select the blend of grains that will meet the USRDA at a minimum cost.

Let

X_A = pounds of grain A in one 2-ounce serving of cereal

X_B = pounds of grain B in one 2-ounce serving of cereal

X_C = pounds of grain C in one 2-ounce serving of cereal

Objective function:

Minimize total cost of mixing a 2-ounce serving = $\$0.33X_A + \$0.47X_B + \$0.38X_C$

Constraints:

$22X_A + 28X_B + 21X_C \geq 3$ (protein units)

$16X_A + 14X_B + 25X_C \geq 2$ (riboflavin units)

$8X_A + 7X_B + 9X_C \geq 1$ (phosphorus units)

$5X_A + 0X_B + 6X_C \geq 0.425$ (magnesium units)

$X_A + X_B + Xc = 1/8$ (total mix is 2 ounces or 1/8 pound)

$X_A, X_B, X_C \geq 0$

The solution to this problem requires mixing together 0.025 pounds of grain *A,* 0.050 pounds of grain *B,* and 0.050 pounds of grain *C.* Another way of stating the solution is in terms of the proportion of the 2-ounce serving of each grain, namely, 2/5 ounces of grain *A,* 4/5 ounces of grain *B,* and 4/5 ounces of grain *C* in each serving. The cost per serving is $0.05075, a little over $0.05 per serving.

Transportation Applications: The Shipping Problem

The transportation or shipping problem involves determining the amount of goods or items to be transported from a number of origins to a number of destinations. The objective is usually to minimize total shipping costs or distances. Constraints in this type of problem deal with capacities at each origin and requirements at each destination. The transportation problem is a specific case of linear programming.

The Top Speed Bicycle Company markets a line of 10-speed bicycles nationwide. The firm has warehouses in two cities, New Orleans and Omaha. Its three retail outlets are located near the large market areas of New York, Chicago, and Los Angeles.

The sales requirements for the next year at the New York store are 10,000 bicycles, at the Chicago store 8,000 bicycles, and at the Los Angeles store 15,000 bicycles. The capacity at each warehouse is limited. New Orleans can store and ship 20,000 bicycles, while the Omaha site can warehouse 15,000 bicycles per year.

The cost of shipping one bicycle from each warehouse to each retail outlet differs, and these unit shipping costs are the following:

		To	
From	**New York**	**Chicago**	**Los Angeles**
New Orleans	$2	$3	$5
Omaha	$3	$1	$4

The company wants to determine a shipping schedule that will minimize its total annual transportation costs.

To formulate this problem using LP, we employ the concept of double-subscripted variables. For example, we can let X_{11} = number of bicycles shipped from New Orleans to New York. Let the first subscript represent the origin (warehouse) and the second subscript the destination (retail outlet). Thus, in general, X_{ij} refers to the number of bicycles shipped from origin i to destination j. We could instead denote X_6 as the variable for origin 2 to destination 3, but you will find the double subscripts more descriptive and easier to use. So we also let

X_{12} = number of bicycles shipped from New Orleans to Chicago

X_{13} = number of bicycles shipped from New Orleans to Los Angeles

X_{21} = number of bicycles shipped from Omaha to New York

X_{22} = number of bicycles shipped from Omaha to Chicago

X_{23} = number of bicycles shipped from Omaha to Los Angeles

The objective function and constraints then become

$$\text{Minimize total shipping costs} = 2X_{11} + 3X_{12} + 5X_{13} + 3X_{21} + 1X_{22} + 4X_{23}$$

Subject to:

$$X_{11} + X_{21} = 10{,}000 \text{ (New York demand)}$$

$$X_{12} + X_{22} = 8{,}000 \text{ (Chicago demand)}$$

$$X_{13} + X_{23} = 15{,}000 \text{ (Los Angeles demand)}$$

$$X_{11} + X_{12} + X_{13} \leq 20{,}000 \text{   (New Orleans warehouse supply)}$$

$$X_{21} + X_{22} + X_{23} \leq 15{,}000 \text{   (Omaha warehouse supply)}$$

Why are transportation problems a special class of linear programming problems? The answer is that every coefficient in front of a variable in the constraint equations is always equal to 1. This special trait is also seen in another special category of LP problems, the assignment problem.

The computer-generated solution to Top Speed's problem is shown here. The total shipping cost is $9,600.

	To		
From	New York	Chicago	Los Angeles
New Orleans	10,000	0	8,000
Omaha	0	8,000	7,000

Employee Scheduling Applications: An Assignment Problem

Assignment problems involve determining the most efficient assignment of people to jobs, machines to tasks, police cars to city sectors, salespeople to territories, and so on. The objective might be to minimize travel times or costs, or to maximize assignment effectiveness. Assignment problems are unique because they not only have a coefficient of 1 associated with each variable in the LP constraints, but also because the right-hand side of each constraint is always equal to 1. The use of LP in solving this type of problem yields solutions of either 0 or 1 for each variable in the formulation. The following is an example situation.

The law firm of Ivan and Ivan maintains a large staff of young attorneys who hold the title of junior partner. Ivan, concerned with the effective utilization of his manpower resources, seeks some objective means of making lawyer-to-client assignments. On March 1, four new clients seeking legal assistance come to Ivan. Although the current staff is overloaded, Ivan would like to accommodate the new clients. He reviews current case loads and identifies four junior partners who, although busy, could possibly be assigned to the cases. Each young lawyer can handle at most one new client. Furthermore, each lawyer differs in skills and specialty interests.

Seeking to maximize the overall effectiveness of the new client assignments, Ivan draws up the following table in which he rates the estimated effectiveness (on a 1-to-9 scale) of each lawyer on each new case.

		Client's Case		
Lawyer	Divorce	Corporate Merger	Embezzlement	Insider Trading
Adams	6	2	8	5
Brooks	9	3	5	8
Carter	4	8	3	4
Darwin	6	7	6	4

To solve using LP, we again employ double-scripted variables.

Let $X_{ij} = \{$ 1 if attorney i is assigned to case j
    0 otherwise$\}$

Where $i = 1, 2, 3, 4$ stands for Adams, Brooks, Carter, and Darwin, respectively

$j = 1, 2, 3, 4$ stands for divorce, merger, embezzlement, and insider trading, respectively

The LP formulation follows.

$$\text{Maximize effectiveness} = 6X_{11} + 2X_{12} + 8X_{13} + 5X_{14}$$

$$+ 9X_{21} + 3X_{22} + 5X_{23} + 8X_{24}$$

$$+ 4X_{31} + 8X_{32} + 3X_{33} + 4X_{34}$$

$$+ 6X_{41} + 7X_{42} + 6X_{43} + 4X_{44}$$

Subject to:

$$X_{11} + X_{21} + X_{31} + X_{41} = 1 \text{ (divorce case)}$$

$$X_{12} + X_{22} + X_{32} + X_{42} = 1 \text{ (merger)}$$

$$X_{13} + X_{23} + X_{33} + X_{43} = 1 \text{ (embezzlement)}$$

$$X_{14} + X_{24} + X_{34} + X_{44} = 1 \text{ (insider trading)}$$

$$X_{11} + X_{12} + X_{13} + X_{14} = 1 \text{ (cases assigned to Adams)}$$

$$X_{21} + X_{22} + X_{23} + X_{24} = 1 \text{ (cases assigned to Brooks)}$$

$$X_{31} + X_{32} + X_{33} + X_{34} = 1 \text{ (cases assigned to Carter)}$$

$$X_{41} + X_{42} + X_{43} + X_{44} = 1 \text{ (cases assigned to Darwin)}$$

The law firm's problem is solved with a total effectiveness rating of 30 by letting $X_{13} = 1$, $X_{24} = 1$, $X_{32} = 1$, and $X_{41} = 1$. All other variables are therefore equal to 0.

Labor Planning

Labor planning problems address staffing needs over a specific time period. They are especially useful when managers have some flexibility in assigning workers to jobs that require overlapping or interchangeable talents. Large banks frequently use LP to tackle their labor scheduling.

Arlington Bank of Commerce and Industry is a busy bank that has requirements for between 10 and 18 tellers depending on the time of day. The lunch time, from noon to 2 P.M. is usually heaviest. Exhibit 18-8 indicates the workers needed at various hours that the bank is open.

The bank now employs 12 full-time tellers, but many people are on its roster as available part-time employees. A part-time employee must put in exactly four hours per day, but can start anytime between 9 A.M. and 1 P.M. Part-timers are a fairly inexpensive labor pool because no retirement or lunch benefits are provided to them. Full-timers, on the other hand, work from 9 A.M. to 5 P.M. but are allowed one hour for lunch. (Half the full-timers eat at 11 A.M., the other half at noon.) Full-timers thus provide 35 hours per week of productive labor time.

By corporate policy, the bank limits part-time hours to a maximum of 50 percent of the day's total requirement.

Part-timers earn $4 per hour (or $16 per day) on average, while full-timers earn $50 per day in salary and benefits on average. The bank would like to set a schedule that would minimize its total labor cost. It will release one or more of its full-time tellers if it is profitable to do so.

Exhibit 18-8   Arlington Bank Commerce and Industry

Time Period	Number of Tellers Required
9 A.M.–10 A.M.	10
10 A.M.–11 A.M.	12
11 A.M.–Noon	14
Noon–1 P.M.	16
1 P.M.–2 P.M.	18
2 P.M.–3 P.M.	17
3 P.M.–4 P.M.	15
4 P.M.–5 P.M.	10

We can let

F = number of full-time tellers

P_1 = number of part-timers starting at 9 A.M. (leaving at 1 P.M.)

P_2 = number of part-timers starting at 10 A.M. (leaving at 2 P.M.)

P_3 = number of part-timers starting at 11 A.M. (leaving at 3 P.M.)

P_4 = number of part-timers starting at noon (leaving at 4 P.M.)

P_5 = number of part-timers starting at 1 P.M. (leaving at 5 P.M.)

Objective function:

Minimize total daily labor cost = $50F + $16(P_1 + P_2 + P_3 + P_4 + P_5)$

Constraints: For each hour, the available teller-hours must be at least equal to the required teller-hours.

$$F + P_1 \geq 10 \text{ (9 A.M. to 10 A.M. needs)}$$

$$F + P_1 + P_2 \geq 12 \text{ (10 A.M. to 11 A.M. needs)}$$

$$\tfrac{1}{2}F + P_1 + P_2 + P_3 \geq 14 \text{ (11 A.M. to noon needs)}$$

$$\tfrac{1}{2}F + P_1 + P_2 + P_3 + P_4 \geq 16 \text{ (noon to 1 P.M. needs)}$$

$$F + P_2 + P_3 + P_4 + P_5 \geq 18 \text{ (1 P.M. to 2 P.M. needs)}$$

$$F + P_3 + P_4 + P_5 \geq 17 \text{ (2 P.M. to 3 P.M. needs)}$$

$$F + P_4 + P_5 \geq 15 \text{ (3 P.M. to 4 P.M. needs)}$$

$$F + P_5 \geq 10 \text{ (4 P.M. to 5 P.M. needs)}$$

Only 12 full-time tellers are available, so

$$F \leq 12$$

Part-time worker hours cannot exceed 50 percent of total hours required each day, which is the sum of the tellers needed each hour.

$$4(P_1 + P_2 + P_3 + P_4 + P_5) \leq 0.50(10 + 12 + 14 + 16 + 18 + 17 + 15 + 10)$$

or

$$4P_1 + 4P_2 + 4P_3 + 4P_4 + 4P_5 \leq 0.50(112)$$

$$F, P_1, P_2, P_3, P_4, P_5 \geq 0$$

There are two alternative optimal schedules that Arlington Bank can follow. The first is to employ only 10 full-time tellers ($F = 10$) and to start two part-timers at 10 A.M. ($P_2 = 2$), seven part-timers at 11 A.M. ($P_3 = 7$), and five part-timers at noon ($P_4 = 5$). No part-timers would begin at 9 A.M. or 1 P.M.

The second solution also employs 10 full-time tellers, but starts six part-timers at 9 A.M. ($P_1 = 6$), one part-timer at 10 A.M. ($P_2 = 1$), two part-timers at 11 A.M. and noon ($P_3 = 2$ and $P_4 = 2$), and three part-timers at 1 P.M. ($P_5 = 3$). The cost of either of these two policies is $724 per day.

Marketing Applications: Media Selection

Linear programming models have been used in the advertising field as a decision aid in selecting an effective media mix. Sometimes the technique is employed in allocating a fixed or limited budget across various media, which might include radio or television commercials, newspaper ads, direct mailings, magazine ads, and so on. In other applications, the objective is taken to be the maximization of audience exposure. Restrictions on the allowable media mix might arise through contract requirements, limited media availability, or company policy. An example follows.

The Win Big Gambling Club promotes gambling junkets from a large Midwestern city to casinos in the Bahamas. The club has budgeted up to $8,000 per week for local advertising, the money to be allocated among four promotional media: TV spots, newspaper ads, and two types of radio advertisements. Win Big's goal is to reach the largest possible high-potential audience through the various media. The following table presents the number of potential gamblers reached by making use of an advertisement in each of the four media. It also provides figures regarding the cost per advertisement placed, and the maximum number of ads that can be purchased per week.

Medium	Audience Reached per Ad	Cost per Ad	Maximum Ads per Week
TV spot (1 minute)	5,000	$800	12
Daily newspaper (full-page ad)	8,500	$925	5
Radio spot ($1/2$ minute, prime time)	2,400	$290	25
Radio spot (1 minute, afternoon)	2,800	$380	20

Win Big's contractual arrangements require that at least five radio spots be placed each week. To ensure a broad-scoped promotional campaign, management also insists that no more than $1,800 be spent on all radio advertising every week.

The problem can now be stated mathematically as follows. Let

X_1 = number of 1-minute TV spots taken each week

X_2 = number of full-page daily newspaper ads taken each week

X_3 = number of 30-second prime-time radio spots taken each week

X_4 = number of 1-minute afternoon radio spots taken each week

Objective function:

$$\text{Maximize audience coverage} = 5{,}000X_1 + 8{,}500X_2 + 2{,}400X_3 + 2{,}800X_4$$

Subject to:

$$X_1 \leq 12 \quad \text{(maximum TV spots per week)}$$

$$X_2 \leq 5 \quad \text{(maximum newspaper ads per week)}$$

$$X_3 \leq 25 \quad \text{(maximum 30-second radio spots per week)}$$

$$X_4 \leq 20 \quad \text{(maximum one-minute radio spots per week)}$$

$$800X_1 + 925X_2 + 290X_3 + 380X_4 \leq 8,000 \quad \text{(weekly advertising budget)}$$

$$X_3 + X_4 \geq 5 \quad \text{(minimum radio spots contracted)}$$

$$290X_3 + 380X_4 \leq 1,800 \quad \text{(maximum \$ spent on radio)}$$

The solution to this LP formulation, using our microcomputer software package, was found to be

$$X_1 = 1.9 \quad \text{TV spots}$$

$$X_2 = 5 \quad \text{newspaper ads}$$

$$X_3 = 6.2 \quad \text{30-second radio spots}$$

$$X_4 = 0 \quad \text{1-minute radio spots}$$

This produces an audience exposure of 67,240 contacts. Because X_1 and X_3 are fractional, Win Big would probably round them to 2 and 6, respectively. Problems that demand all-integer solutions are discussed in detail in most management science textbooks.

18.6 Goal Programming

In today's business environment, profit maximization or cost minimization are not always the only objectives that a service organization sets forth. Often, maximizing total profit is just one of several goals, including such contradictory objectives as maximizing market share, maintaining full employment, providing quality ecologic management, minimizing noise level in the neighborhood, and meeting numerous other noneconomic goals.

Linear programming has the shortcoming that its objective function is measured in one dimension only. It is not possible for linear programming to have multiple goals unless they are all measured in the same units (such as dollars), a highly unusual situation. An important technique that has been developed to supplement linear programming is called **goal programming**.

In typical decision-making situations, the goals set by management can be achieved only at the expense of other goals. It is necessary to establish a hierarchy of importance among these goals so that lower-priority goals are tackled only after higher-priority ones are satisfied. Because it is not always possible to achieve every goal to the extent the decision maker desires, goal programming attempts to reach a satisfactory level of multiple objectives. This, of course, differs from linear programming, which tries to find the best possible outcome for a single objective.

How, specifically, does goal programming differ from linear programming? The objective function is the main difference. Instead of trying to maximize or minimize the objective function directly, with goal programming we try to minimize deviations between set goals and what we can actually achieve within the given constraints. In the LP simplex approach, such deviations are called slack variables, and they are used only as dummy variables. In goal programming, these slack terms are either positive or negative, and not only are they real variables, but they are also the only terms in the objective function. The objective is to minimize these deviational variables.

Once the goal programming model is formulated, the computational algorithm is almost the same as for an LP problem solved by the simplex method.

Goal Programming Example: Dixon Furniture Revisited

To illustrate the formulation of a GP problem, let's look back at the Dixon Furniture Store case, presented earlier in this chapter as an LP problem. That formulation, you recall, was

$$\text{Maximize net profit} = \$7X_1 + \$5X_2$$

Subject to:

$$4X_1 + 3X_2 \leq 240 \text{ (\$ of budget constraint)}$$

$$2X_2 + 1X_2 \leq 100 \quad \text{(space constraint)}$$

$$X_2 \leq 60 \quad \text{(chair demand constraint)}$$

$$X_1, X_2 \geq 0$$

where

$$X_1 = \text{number of tables ordered}$$

$$X_2 = \text{number of chairs ordered}$$

We saw that if Dixon management had a single goal, say profit, linear programming could be used to find the optimal solution. But let's assume that the store is breaking in a whole new staff of sales clerks on the Labor Day weekend and feels that maximizing profit is not a realistic goal. The store manager sets a profit level, which would be satisfactory during the training period, of $380. We now have a goal programming problem in which we want to find the mix of tables and chairs that achieves the goal as closely as possible, given the budgetary and space constraints. This simple case will provide a good starting point for handling more complicated goal programs.

We first define two deviational variables:

d_1^- = the underachievement of the profit target

d_1^+ = the overachievement of the profit target

Now we can state the Dixon Furniture problem as a *single-goal* programming model.

Minimize under- or overachievement of target profit $= d_1^- + d_1^+$

Subject to:

$7X_1 + 5X_2 + d_1^- - d_1^+ = 380$ (profit goal constraint)

$4X_1 + 3X_2 \leq 240$ (budget constraint)

$2X_1 + 1X_2 \leq 100$ (space constraint)

$X_2 \leq 60$ (chair demand constraint)

$X_1, X_2, d_1^-, d_1^+ \geq 0$

Note that the first constraint states that the profit made, $\$7X_1 + \$5X_2$, plus any underachievement of profit minus any overachievement of profit has to equal the target of \$380. For example, if $X_1 = 10$ tables and $X_2 = 60$ chairs, then \$370 profit has been made. This misses the \$380 target by \$10, so d_1^- must be equal to 10. Since the profit goal was underachieved, Dixon did not overachieve and d_1^+ will clearly be equal to 0. This problem is now ready for solution by a goal programming algorithm.

If the target profit of \$380 is exactly achieved, we see that both d_1^+ and d_1^- are equal to zero. The objective function will be minimized at 0. If Dixon's manager was only concerned with under-achievement of the target goal, how would the objective function change? It would be

Minimize underachievement $= d_1^-$

This is also a reasonable goal since the store would probably not be upset with an overachieve-ment of its profit target.

In general, after all goals and constraints are identified in a problem, management should ana-lyze each goal to see if under- or overachievement of that goal is an acceptable situation. If over-achievement is acceptable, the appropriate d^+ variable can be eliminated from the objective function. If underachievement is okay, the d^- variable should be dropped. If management seeks to attain a goal exactly, both d^- and d^+ must appear in the objective function.

An Extension to Equally Important Multiple Goals

Now look at the situation in which Dixon's manager wants to achieve several goals, each equal in priority.

Goal 1: To produce as much profit above \$380 as possible during Labor Day sale

Goal 2: To fully utilize the available budget of \$240

Goal 3: To avoid using more than the allotted floor space

Goal 4: To avoid overstocking chairs

The deviational variables can be defined as follows:

d_1^- = underachievement of the profit target

d_1^+ = overachievement of the profit target

d_2^- = underspending of the allotted budget (underutilization)

d_2^+ = overspending of the allotted budget (overutilization)

d_3^- = underuse of the floor space allotted (underutilization)

d_3^+ = overuse of the floor space allotted (overutilization)

d_4^- = underachievement of the chair goal

d_4^+ = overachievement of the chair goal

Dixon is unconcerned about whether there is overachievement of the profit goal, overspending of the allotted budget, underuse of the floor space, or whether less than 60 chairs are ordered; hence, d_1^+, d_2^+, d_3^-, and d_4^- may be omitted from the objective function. The new objective function and constraints are

$$\text{Minimize total deviation} = d_1^- + d_2^- + d_3^+ + d_4^+$$

Subject to:

$$7X_1 + 5X_2 + d_1^- - d_1^+ = 380 \qquad \text{(profit constraint)}$$

$$4X_1 + 3X_2 + d_2^- - d_2^+ = 240 \qquad \text{(budget constraint)}$$

$$2X_1 + 1X_2 + d_3^- - d_3^+ = 100 \qquad \text{(space constraint)}$$

$$X_2 + d_4^- - d_4^+ = 60 \qquad \text{(chair constraint)}$$

All X_i, d_i variables ≥ 0

The setup and solution of this goal programming problem is shown in Exhibit 18-9 and sensitivity analysis output is given in Exhibit 18-10. According to the optimal solution 15 tables and 60 chairs will be stocked. This solution will help Dixon Furniture exceed the minimum profit goal by d_1^+ = \$25, and achieve an underutilization of floor space of d_3^- = 10 square feet. The other two goals will be achieved exactly ($d_2^+ = d_2^- = d_4^+ = d_4^- = 0$).

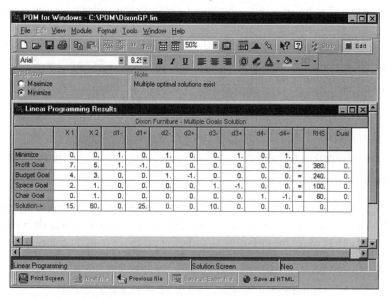

Exhibit 18-9   Setup and Solution of Dixon Furniture
Multiple Goals Problem by POM for Windows

Exhibit 18-10   Sensitivity Analysis Output for Dixon Furniture
Multiple Goals Problem from POM for Windows

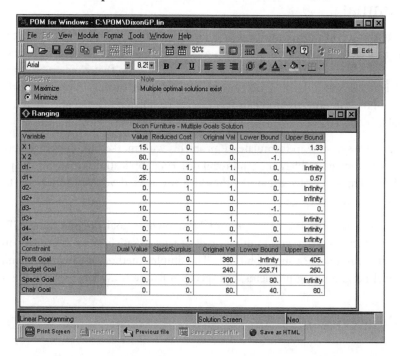

Ranking goals—In most goal programming problems, one goal will be more important than another, which in turn will be more important than a third. The idea is that goals can be ranked with respect to their importance in management's eyes. Lower-order goals are considered only after higher-order goals are met. Priorities (P_is) are assigned to each deviational variable—with the ranking that P_1 is the most important goal, P_2 the next important, then P_3, and so on.

Say Dixon Furniture sets the priorities shown in the accompanying table.

Goal	Priority
Reach a profit as much above $380 as possible	P_1
Fully use budget available	P_2
Avoid using more space than available	P_3
Ordering less than 60 chairs	P_4

This means, in effect, that the priority of meeting the profit goal (P_1) is infinitely more important than the budget goal (P_2), which is, in turn, infinitely more important than the space goal (P_3), which is infinitely more important than ordering no more than 60 chairs (P_4).

With ranking of goals considered, the new objective function becomes

$$\text{Minimize total deviation} = P_1 d_1^- + P_2 d_2^- + P_3 d_3^+ + P_4 d_4^+$$

The constraints remain identical to the previous ones.

18.7 Summary

Linear programming has proven to be a popular tool that can handle a wide variety of service operations management problems. Although a graphical method can be used to actually solve small problems, most organizations have access to LP software that runs on either microcomputers or larger systems and uses a solution procedure known as the **simplex algorithm**. LP not only finds optimal solutions to problems that can be formulated mathematically, but it also provides valuable management information in the form of shadow pricing and sensitivity analysis.

In this chapter we saw how to formulate LP problems with marketing, shipping, labor scheduling, assignment, ingredient blending, and retail ordering applications. Many of the problems at the end of the chapter involve extending the skills you have developed so far and tackling yet more complex service problems.

The final section introduced an extension of LP known as goal programming. GP helps the service manager who is faced with multiple goals. It tries to satisfy goals in priority order rather than maximize or minimize a single objective. The simplex method of LP can be manipulated to also solve goal programming problems, but special software is available specifically for the GP technique.

Endnotes

1. Kalyan S. Pasupathy and Alexandra Medina-Borja, "Integrating Excel, Access, and Visual Basic to Deploy Performance Measurement and Evaluation at the American Red Cross," *Interfaces*, vol. 38, no. 4 (July–August 2008), pp. 324–337.

2. K. Chelst, "An Algorithm for Deploying a Crime Directed Patrol Force," *Management Science*, vol. 24, no. 12 (August 1978), pp. 1314–1327.

3. Raja Gopalakrishnan and Narayan Rangaraj, "Capacity Management on Long-Distance Passenger Trains of Indian Railways," *Interfaces*, Vol. 40, No. 4 (July–August 2010), pp. 291–302.

4. John C. Butler, Leon S. Lasdon, James S. Dyer, and Leslie T. Maiman Jr., "Long-Range Planning for a West Texas Catholic Diocese," *Interfaces*, vol. 39, no. 2 (March–April 2009), pp. 133–144.

5. Richard Metters, Carrie Queenan, Mark Ferguson, Laura Harrison, Jon Higbie, Stan Ward, Bruce Barfield, Tammy Farley, H. Ahmet Kuyumcu, and Amar Duggasani, "The 'Killer Application' of Revenue Management: Harrah's Cherokee Casino & Hotel," *Interfaces*, Vol. 38, No. 3 (May–June 2008), pp. 161–175.

6. Guillermo Duran, Mario Guajardo, Jaime Miranda, Denis Saure, Sebastian Souyris, Andres Weintraub, and Rodrigo Wolf "Scheduling the Chilean Soccer League by Integer Programming," *Interfaces*, Vol. 37, No. 6 (November–December 2007), pp. 539–552.

7. See B. Render, R. M. Stair, and M. E. Hanna, *Quantitative Analysis for Management*, 11th ed. (Upper Saddle River, NJ, Prentice Hall, 2012).

19

SERVICE INVENTORY SYSTEMS

19.1 Introduction

To date, operations managers, both practitioners and academicians, have focused on developing the theory and planning of inventory control systems for manufacturing operations. This chapter extends this theory to the area of service inventory management.

If a service is a deed, performance, or effort, as some writers have defined it, why should we be concerned with inventory problems? There are several reasons for giving considerable consideration to inventories in service businesses.

First, practically all services use some sort of input materials that are kept in inventory. Second, many services supply an output product in addition to some sort of performance. Third, adequate service levels usually mean that performance of service cannot be permitted to be delayed for lack of materials or related products.

Input inventory for services is required for matching service to demand. It is also an operating cost of the system, as in manufacturing. However, the cost of running out of inventory is usually much higher for services because of customer expectations of prompt service. In manufacturing, inventories separate production from customers. In contrast, in services, input materials in inventory are used on customers, provided for customers during the performance of the service, or used up to generate the service.

Many services fall in a classification called the **knowledge industry.** These services usually provide stored rather than oral information. The storage device (book, disk, tape, or report) that contains the information is the unit that is sold. The service is embedded in a low-value container that may be stored. Other services, such as retail, wholesale, and restaurants, must usually retain some output goods in inventory. Exhibit 19-1 shows examples of input materials and output goods for services.

Exhibit 19-1   Input Materials and Output Goods in Services

Type of Service	Input Materials (What Is Processed)	Output Goods (What Is Sold)
Retailers, wholesalers	Consumer goods, repair parts	Consumer goods, repair parts
Restaurant	Raw food, cooked food, beverages	Prepared food, beverages
Publisher	Paper, ink	Books, magazines, newspapers
Bank	Currency, gold	Currency, gold, coins, legal documents
Consulting and advisory	Forms, paper, ink or ribbons	Reports
Legal firm	Forms, paper	Legal documents, reports
Airline, bus, rail line	Gasoline or oil, food and beverages, tickets	Tickets, food and beverages
Movie theater	Tickets, snack foods	Tickets, food
Real estate	Forms, real estate	Legal documents, reports, real estate

19.2 Characteristics of Service Inventories

Input and Output Materials

Manufacturing is concerned with changing the form of input materials. In many services, however, the form of input materials remains unchanged. Retailing and wholesaling, for example, usually involve no change in the form of goods. Real estate services usually accept property as the owner supplies it to sell. Even restaurants serve some foods in exactly the form in which they buy them. Banks, of course, deal in currency, so that input and output are identical.

In services, input materials are often a trivial cost of doing business. That is, many services use only blank paper or forms as process input materials. Inventories of these are usually a small cost of operations.

Output materials may be used on the customer directly, as in the cases of proprietary cosmetics, surgical thread, anesthetics, and prepared food. The customer cannot store such output materials for use at such time as she needs them again. In manufacturing, the customer can always store the goods he needs and continue uninterrupted production. If the service supplier runs out of raw materials, however, the service cannot be performed and customers may be lost.

Perishability

Style goods of retailers, input and output food items of restaurants, and newspapers are examples of perishable inventory items of services. Exhibit 19-2 shows examples of input and output goods with different degrees of **perishability.**

Exhibit 19-2 Perishables in Service Inventories

Life of Items	Items
Very short	Certain transplant organs, tickets for same-day event
Short	Fresh fruit, certain transplant organs, retail items for a commemorative occasion
Medium	Certain retail goods, hospital drugs, seasonal style goods in retailing, credit cards
Long	Postage stamps, books, certain retail and wholesale goods

Sometimes an item in input inventory may have a long life, while the same item in output inventory may have a short life. For example, newspapers keep files on notable living people. Such data are kept for long periods. However, when data from the files are used in a newspaper article, the resale output item (newspaper) has a short inventory life. Conversely, the input information represented by actors playing in a movie is short, but the finished film has a very long inventory life.

These examples of perishability are indications that in services the inventory problem varies tremendously and is often quite different from that of manufacturing. In many services, the amount of inventory purchased is heavily weighted by perishability factors. This implies that the cost of holding perishable items beyond a certain period is high.

Lumpiness of Input Materials

Lumpiness refers to the need to buy in quantities, or "lumps," because of the nature of the input materials, the lead time, and the difficulty or high cost of obtaining small shipments from vendors. It is common in services to have a low-degree of lumpiness and a smoother flow of input materials than in manufacturing. Many small services simply pick up input materials locally as needed. Exhibit 19-3 gives examples of materials for various levels of lumpiness. This aspect of services means that holding costs for input inventory tend to be negligible.

Exhibit 19-3 Lumpiness of Input Materials in Services

Lumpiness	Examples
Smooth	Provision of gas for cooking/heating applications by gas service firms
Minor lumpiness	Office supplies, paint, food supplies, and other locally available items
Moderate lumpiness	Office forms, mail order supplies, textile materials, or lumber cut to order
Major lumpiness	Office forms, clothing, cosmetics, and chemicals requiring months of lead time

19.3 The Input Material Decision Problem

There is a close relationship between the timing of inventory orders and the size of an order. The greater the frequency of orders, the smaller is the order size.

There is also a decision to be made as to whether orders of variable size are to be placed at regular intervals, whether constant-size orders will be placed at irregular intervals, or whether it is possible to place consistent-size orders at regular periods.

Because of random variations in demand for services and in lead time for delivery of input materials, the two variables of order size and timing of purchases may be difficult to specify. The adverse effects of errors in quantity or timing include excessive carrying costs, poor customer service, and excessive order processing or purchase costs.

The input material decision problem must often take into account a series of inventories through which materials move. Exhibit 19-4 shows that the service maintains its own inventory. For replenishment, the service calls on its vendor or supplier. The vendor calls on the factory warehouse, which, in turn, calls on manufacturing for replenishment. If any link in the supply chain runs short, replenishment of the service firm's inventory may be additionally delayed. Such a system, with information loops, has been simulated by distribution requirements planning models.

Exhibit 19-4   Storage Points for Alternative Channels for Materials Supply

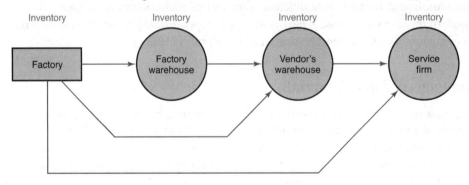

19.4 Service Inventory Control Systems

Managers of service operations can establish control systems for managing inventory. The first step in such a system is to classify inventory items by the ABC method of classification.

ABC analysis divides on-hand inventory into three classifications based on annual dollar volume. ABC analysis is an inventory application of what is known as the **Pareto principle**. The Pareto principle states that there are a critical few and trivial many.[1] The idea is to focus resources on the critical few and not the trivial many.

To determine annual dollar volume for ABC analysis, we measure the *annual* demand of each inventory item times the *cost per unit*. Class A items are those on which the annual dollar volume is high. Such items may represent only approximately 15 percent of total inventory items, but they represent 70 to 80 percent of the total inventory cost.

Class B items are those inventory items of medium annual dollar volume. These items may represent approximately 30 percent of the items and 15 percent of the value. Those with low annual dollar volume are class C, which may represent only 5 percent of the annual dollar volume but approximately 55 percent of the total items.

Graphically, the inventory of many organizations would appear as presented in Exhibit 19-5.

Exhibit 19-5   Graphic Presentation of ABC Classification System

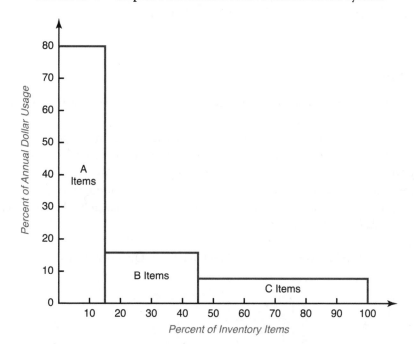

19.5 Inventory Control Systems for Independent Demand Items

The inventory models discussed in this section are based on the assumption that demand for a service/service item is *independent* of the demand for another service/service item. These services (or service items) are directly demanded by the customer, usually as a completed service (or service item), which is also known as an **end service or end item**. For example, the demand for the services of a dentist may be independent of the demand for the services of a heart surgeon. The demand at your drugstore for a *USA Today* newspaper may be independent of the demand for a copy of the *PC World* magazine. This section is concerned with the application of classical inventory models and systems to an independent service demand situation. Section 19.7 discusses models dealing with dependent service demand situations, where the demand for one service will depend on the demand for another. This means that the demand for this service is directly related to or derived from the demand for other end services.

As services subject to independent demand are directly demanded by the customers, they are exposed to demand uncertainty and therefore need to be forecast. Hence, it becomes necessary to forecast the number of patients who will require the services of a dentist, as well as the number of daily newspapers that are to be ordered by a newsstand.

An inventory control system has a set of procedures that indicate the quantity of material that should be added to inventory and the time to do so. Control systems for independent demand service inventory can be broadly divided into two classes: fixed quantity and fixed-period (that is, periodic) systems.

Fixed-Quantity Systems

A fixed-quantity system, also known as a **continuous review system**, adds the same amount to the inventory of an item each time it is reordered. Orders are placed when the inventory on hand is reduced to an amount known as the **reorder point**. Hence, it is event-triggered, with the event of reaching a reorder point occurring any time, depending on the demand for the specific inventory item. Each time the inventory balance is depleted by a sale, the amount of inventory on hand is compared with the reorder point. If the on-hand balance has dropped to this point, a new order (of a prespecified quantity) is placed. If not, no action is taken by the inventory system until the next sale (see Exhibit 19-6).

Exhibit 19-6   Inventory Level in a Fixed-Quantity System

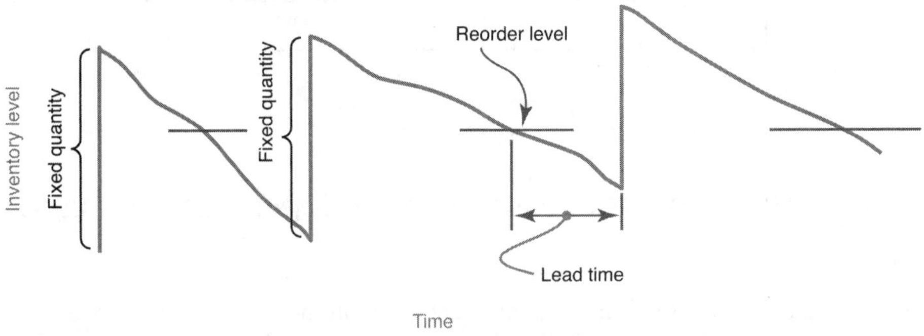

The advantage of a fixed-quantity system is that sometimes a fixed order size is desirable, as in the case of quantity discounts being offered for an order that exceeds a certain size. This method is also appropriate when an order is constrained by certain physical limitations. For example, one may have to order by the truckload, and the capacity of a truck will define the size of the order.

An additional advantage of the fixed-quantity system is that it has lower safety stocks when compared to a fixed-period system. This is because it has to guard against demand uncertainty only during the period between the placement of a new order and the receipt of that order.

Fixed-Period Systems

In a **fixed-period system**, the inventory level is checked at uniform time intervals. It is time-triggered, with the replenishment of inventory occurring by the passage of a given amount of time. Therefore, there is no tally of the on-hand balance of an item when a withdrawal takes place. The stock on hand is counted only when the ordering date occurs. The quantity ordered is the amount necessary to bring the inventory level up to a prespecified target level. Exhibit 19-7 illustrates this concept.

Exhibit 19-7   Inventory Level in a Fixed-Period System

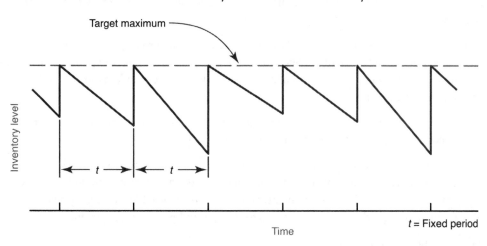

The advantage of the fixed-period system is that there is no physical count of inventory items after an item is withdrawn—this occurs only when the time for the next review comes up. This procedure is also convenient administratively, especially if inventory control is one of several duties of an employee.

This type of inventory control system and the placement of orders on a periodic basis are appropriate when vendors make routine (that is, at a fixed time interval) visits to customers to take fresh orders or when purchasers want to combine orders to save ordering and transportation costs. (Therefore, they will have the same review period for similar inventory items.) Drugstores are an example for this type of system where suppliers make periodic visits (for example, every week, every 2 weeks) to check on the level of items such as toothpaste, shampoo, conditioner, vitamins, pain killers, and so on. If the inventory of an item is below a certain predetermined level, an order will be placed in an amount to bring the level back up to a desired level.

The disadvantage of this system is that because there is no tally of inventory during the review period, there is the possibility of a stockout during this time. This scenario is possible if a large order draws the inventory level down to zero right after an order is placed. Therefore, a higher level of safety stock (as compared to a fixed-quantity system) needs to be maintained to provide protection against stockout both during the review period and during the time required for a fresh order to come in.

19.6 Inventory Planning

Economic Order Quantity (EOQ) Model

Services may buy and store such items as printed forms, various office supplies, cosmetics (in beauty parlors), medical supplies, consumer goods (in retail and wholesale firms), food (in restaurants), and sporting goods (in resort shops). The service firm's inventory control objective will be to minimize the cost of input inventories.

We will develop a fixed-quantity model in which the **economic order quantity** is used to maintain an inventory of business forms. Such forms may be purchased loose, in pads, or in cartons. We must specify the unit whenever calculations are made. In the example, assume that the forms come in a box of 24 pads.

The inventory cost system is made up of two components: holding costs and procurement costs. **Holding costs** are the costs of holding one box for one year.

These costs consist of such items as rent for space, insurance, obsolescence, utilities, and opportunity cost of money tied up in inventory. (The time period is arbitrary and could be days, weeks, or months, for example.) **Procurement costs** are the costs involved in placing a single purchase order, receiving the goods, moving the goods to storage, and processing payment.

To develop the inventory model, let

Q = number of units purchased at one time

D = demand (usage) rate for the printed forms for one year

LT = lead time, that is, the time between placing and receiving an order

ROP = reorder point

The first part of the model is shown in Exhibit 19-8. An order of size Q is used up at rate D. When the inventory reaches zero, a new order arrives. This is so because we placed an order when the inventory reached the ROP to allow for the lead time (LT) that it takes to obtain the goods. Assume that the usage occurs at a constant rate and the lead time is a fixed number of days or weeks.

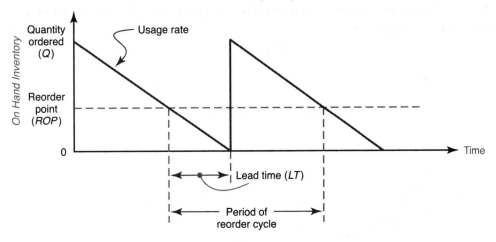

Exhibit 19-8   Inventory Usage Over Time

The second part of the model shows the cost side. In selecting the order size, the larger the order that is placed, the larger is the average inventory for the year. Hence total inventory cost for a year is larger for a large order size Q than for a small order quantity. On the other hand, as Q is increased, fewer orders need to be placed during the year. Therefore, procurement costs decrease as the order size is increased.

Let

H = holding cost for one box of forms for one year

S = cost of placing a single order

Then

$Q/2$ = average inventory (assuming constant demand)

D/Q = the number of purchase cycles per year

The total system cost TC is then

$$TC = S\left(\frac{D}{Q}\right) + H\frac{Q}{2}$$

(19.1)

In Exhibit 19-9, the component costs and total cost are sketched. The economic order size Q^* occurs when the component costs are equal.

$$S\left(\frac{D}{Q}\right) + H\frac{Q}{2}$$

and therefore,

$$Q^* = \sqrt{\frac{2DS}{H}}$$

(19.2)

As an example, suppose that the cost of placing an order for business forms is S = $20, the cost of holding one box in inventory for one year is H = $3.6 per year, and the demand for the forms is D = 36 boxes per year. Then,

$$Q* = \sqrt{\frac{2 \times \$20 \times 36}{\$3.6}} = 20 \text{ boxes}$$

Exhibit 19-9   Cost Components

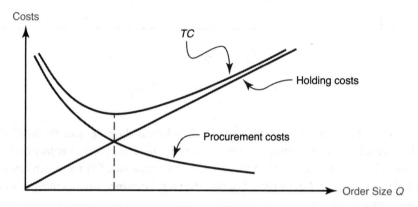

If it takes 2 months from the time that an order is placed until the forms arrive in the stock room, then the reorder level is

ROP = (monthly demand × lead time) = 3 × 2 = 6 boxes   (19.3)

As a safety precaution, a **buffer stock** of two or three extra boxes may be kept in reserve so that if the shipment is delayed, a stockout may be avoided.

Perishable Goods Model

A simple example can illustrate a model for ordering perishable goods. Suppose that a student club has obtained rights to sell brochures for a high school football game. These brochures describe the players of both teams, personalities of the school, and photos of interest. Some local advertising helps pay the publication cost.

The brochures sell for $3 and may be ordered from a local printer for a cost of $1 each. The club faces the problem of how many brochures to order from the printer because those that are not sold are worthless. The cost of the unsold brochures must be deducted from the profits of those that are sold.

As a start, the students

- Estimate alternative possible demands for the brochure.

- Estimate a probability that each demand will occur.

- Compute the conditional profit for stocking an amount equal to each potential demand.

Exhibit 19.10 shows these data. To illustrate the computations, consider a demand of 2,100 brochures and an inventory of 2,300 brochures. Then earn $2 × 2,100 but have an additional cost of $1 on each of the 200 unsold brochures. The net profit of $4,000 is shown in the right column, second row.

Exhibit 19-10   Conditional Profit for Different Combinations
of Demand and Order Quantity

		Order Quantity			
Alternative Demands	Probability	2,000	2,100	2,200	2,300
2,000	0.10	$4,000	$3,900	$3,800	$3,700
2,100	0.30	$4,000	$4,200	$4,100	$4,000[a]
2,200	0.40	$4,000	$4,200	$4,400	$4,300
2,300	0.20	$4,000	$4,200	$4,400	$4,600

a [$2 × 2,100] − [$1 × (2,300 − 2,100)] = $4,000

Exhibit 19-11 shows the computations of expected values for each alternative amount to be ordered. The expected value (or profit) of a particular order quantity is calculated by multiplying each demand probability in Exhibit 19-10 by its respective conditional profit, and then summing over all possible levels of demand. Exhibit 19-11 shows that ordering 2,200 brochures gives the highest expected profit, $4,225. Therefore, the club should order and, hopefully, sell 2,200 copies.

Exhibit 19-11   Expected Values for Ordering Different Quantities

	Order Quantity			
Alternative Demands	2,000	2,100	2,200	2,300
2,000	$ 400	$ 390	$ 380	$ 370
2,100	$1,200	$1,260	$1,230	$1,200
2,200	$1,600	$1,680	$1,760	$1,720
2,300	$ 800	$ 840	$ 880	$ 920
Expected profit	$4,000	$4,170	$4,225	$4,210

19.7 Requirements Planning for Dependent Demand

The demand for many services or service items may be classified as dependent demand, which requires a different type of inventory control system than previously discussed. Service demand is considered **dependent** when it is directly related to or derived from the demand for other services (known as end services or end items). For example, in a restaurant where bread and vegetables are included in every meal ordered, the demand for bread and vegetables is *dependent* on the demand for meals.

The demand for meals may be forecasted. The demand for bread and vegetables is calculated or *derived* from the demand for meals. The meal is an *end* item. The bread and vegetables are *component* items.

A bill of materials (BOM) may be created for end items or services, such as a meal, that *lists* the materials and quantity of materials needed to provide the final service in the *order* they are needed. Exhibit 19-12 shows a bill of materials for Hard Rock Café's Hickory BBQ Bacon Cheeseburger.

Exhibit 19-12   Bill of Materials for BBQ Bacon Cheeseburger

Decription	Quantity
Bun	1
Hamburger patty	8 oz.
Cheddar cheese	2 slices
Bacon	2 strips
BBQ onions	1/2 cup
Hickory BBQ sauce	1 oz.
Burger set	
Lettuce	1 leaf
Tomato	1 slice
Red onion	4 rings
Pickle	5 oz.
French fries	5 oz.
Seasoned salt	1 tsp.
11-inch plate	1
HRC flag	1

Source: Source: Jay Heizer and Barry Render, *Operations Management*, 10th Edition (Upper Saddle River. NJ, Prentice Hall, 2011), p. 172.

Basically, a **requirements planning system** takes a schedule or forecast of end items or services and, using the bill of materials and bill of labor, determines what component items or services are required and when they are required. It also specifies when an operation should be started or item purchased so that it will be completed or arrive when it is required. Thus, a requirements planning system is both an inventory control system (it decides when to order materials and how much to order) and a scheduling system (it decides when an operation should begin).

Requirements planning systems in manufacturing firms initially were called MRP for material requirements planning. As the name implies, these systems were used to plan for the availability of *materials* as required to manufacture a product. Later, as the systems evolved to include the planning and control of resources other than materials, such as labor hours, machine hours, tooling, and cash, they became known as MRP-II systems for manufacturing resource planning. Exhibit 19-13 defines some terms common to MRP systems. As you can see, many of these terms can be used in services as well as manufacturing. The next section describes in more detail the use of MRP-II systems in services.

Exhibit 19-13   Definitions of Terms Used in an MRP Context

Aggregate Production Planning   The planning function of setting the overall level of manufacturing output. Usually stated in broad terms (for example, product groupings and families of products), its main aim is to establish production rates that will achieve management's objectives (for inventory levels, backlogs, work-force levels, and so on).

Bill of Labor (BOL) or Bill of Resources   A statement of the key resources required to produce an item or service. This can be used to predict the impact of the service (or item) scheduled in the master service (or production) schedule.

Bill of Material (BOM)   A listing of all the parts, components, and raw materials and the quantities required of each that go into an end item or parent assembly.

Dependent Demand   The demand for an item or service when it is directly related to or derived from the demand for other items or services. Dependent demand is calculated from the production plans for parent items.

End Item   An item sold as a completed item (that is, finished product) or repair part. Any item subject to a customer order or sales forecast is an end item.

End Service   A service subject to customer orders or sales forecasts. Often, this is the service directly offered to the customer.

Independent Demand   The demand for an item or service when such demand is not related to the demand for other items or services. Independent demand is generated directly by the customers and needs to be forecast.

> **MRP (Material Requirements Planning)**   A set of techniques that uses bills of material, inventory data, and the master production schedule to calculate requirements for materials. It is used to efficiently order and schedule the production of dependent demand inventory items.
>
> **MRP-II (Manufacturing Resource Planning)**   A set of techniques for the effective planning of all the resources (and capacities) of a manufacturing company. It includes and links a variety of functions: business planning, aggregate production planning, master production scheduling, materials requirements planning (MRP), capacity requirements planning, shop-floor and production activity control, and so on. Output from MRP-II systems can be integrated with financial reports, shipping budgets, and inventory projection in dollars.
>
> **Master Production Schedule (MPS)**   A statement of what the firm expects to manufacture of end items and service parts. It provides the specific quantities to be produced and dates for producing them.

MRP-II in the Service Context

Business planning—Both long-term resources (for example, equipment requirements) and short-term resources (for example, working capital requirements, inventory costs, and wages) are considered at this level, together with their corresponding budgets. Units of service are converted to dollars to keep the business plan up to date and are integrated with financial reports. Marketing strategies such as industry variables, competitors' actions, and service mix are also considered in developing the business plan.

Aggregate service planning—The aggregate service plan is a general plan on how the service organization expects to respond to forecasted demand. It is an overall contract between finance, marketing, and operations, answering questions of what services to provide, how much to provide, and when to provide them. This function should be performed monthly or quarterly and should consider current business conditions along with immediate past company performance. It consists of identifying resources and service rates required to support the business plan in a manner consistent with the overall objectives of the company. These overall objectives include how demand variations are to be absorbed. Exhibit 19-14 shows some alternatives for handling demand variations by modifying demand and/or controlling supply.

Exhibit 19-14   Alternatives for Absorbing Variations in Demand

To Modify Demand	To Control Supply
Vary price—seasonal prices	Specialize tasks during peak demand periods
Vary services offered during peaks and troughs	Vary customer participation
Develop alternative services to shift peaks	Vary available work force
Smooth demand via reservations	Under/overtime
	Hire/fire
	Subcontract

Resource requirements planning—Resource requirements planning involves establishing long-term overall levels of capacity. Its purpose is to evaluate the aggregate service plan prior to its implementation. To check its impact on key resources, the aggregate service plan is converted to standard cost dollars, man-hours, and/or equipment hours by using service load profiles and bills of resources. Capacity levels or limits are established, measured, and adjusted so that they are consistent with the aggregate service plan.

Master service scheduling—The master service schedule (MSS) is a realistic, detailed statement of what the service firm expects to accomplish for services delivered to the customer: what, when, and how many. It is more detailed than the aggregate service plan for timing (hours or days) and the type of service (specifically what the customer has requested).

The master service schedule can vary considerably depending on the type of service. The master schedule is based on *customer orders* if the service can be prepared in advance. However, if demand for the service is immediate, it must be *forecast* for inclusion in the master schedule. For example, a physician uses an appointment calendar as a master schedule. This master schedule includes a number of customer orders (appointments made in advance, such as routine check-ups or nonemergency calls), as well as forecast demand (blocks of time reserved for walk-ins and emergency calls). The master schedule for a beautician would also take the form of an appointment calendar. The master schedule for restaurants may be derived solely from customer orders (when reservations are required), solely from forecast demand (when no reservations are taken), or a combination of the two.

Rough-cut capacity planning—Rough-cut capacity planning (RCCP) involves short-term capacity considerations affected by irregularities in demand. It establishes benchmarks for the proper use of personnel, machines, and shifts.

Bills of capacity and bills of labor for *critical* services or resources are the primary inputs to determine rough-cut capacity. From these bills, the capacity requirements for critical work centers are itemized and evaluated. Any work center that cannot produce the desired output within a given time frame because of capacity limitations is highlighted for adjustment. Such adjustments may include increasing capacity, reassigning services to other work centers if possible, and/or rescheduling planned services. If the RCCP shows that the capacity is available, the numbers in the master service schedule become the set of planning numbers that "drive" the service requirements plan.

Service requirements planning—Service requirements planning (SRP) determines the relative importance of services: which services should be performed and when. It uses bills of labor, bills of material, and data on existing orders to convert the master service schedule into requirements for component services. As in MRP, it makes recommendations for service releases and for rescheduling when due dates cannot be met. Specifically, the service requirements plan uses the bill of materials to decide how much of what material is needed to meet the demand contained in the master schedule, and the bill of labor to determine how much of what type of labor is needed to meet the master schedule demand. The SRP will take into account when material is needed and how long it takes to receive the material and generate purchase orders. It will examine when an operation must be completed and how long it takes to complete the operation and generate work schedules for particular service operations.

Capacity requirements planning—The SRP generates purchase orders and work schedules sufficient to meet master schedule demand, but it does not consider whether the firm has enough capacity (for example, workers, space, and money) to execute the schedules. The capacity requirements plan (CRP) determines whether labor and other resources exist to accomplish the service requirements plan. Levels of capacity that are consistent with the service plan are established, measured, and adjusted. For services that use appointment calendars to schedule their work, capacity is predefined as the number of "slots" on the calendar, and no overloads are typically allowed. Emergency cases can be handled with overtime or by rescheduling existing orders.

Lead times play a major role in CRP. Of the five basic elements of lead time in services (preparation, setup, processing, movement, and queue times), it is queue times that are subject to wide variations. Services are typically more sensitive to lengthy queues than are manufacturing concerns. Thus, most services establish a maximum queue length beyond which they perceive queue time to be excessive. Flexible capacity, such as multiskilled workers, allows resources to be shifted and queues reduced.

Shop-floor control—This maintains, evaluates, and communicates data such as work-in-process and actual versus planned service requirements. The foundation for good shop-floor control is realistic planning at higher levels (for example, the master service schedule).

The basis for shop-floor control is a work-in-process file. This file is created when a planned service commences. It states the plan for all existing service orders, operation by operation, as the customer passes through each service. The scheduled completion time is derived from the service requirements planning process. The *appointment calendar* often serves as a dispatch list, showing customer, service(s) to be performed, required setup times, service times, priorities, and expected completion times. Unsatisfactory services can require rework (that is, reservicing). This can create additional capacity problems if rework time has not been considered during the planning process.

Uncertainty and MRP-II

Services must often deal with indefinite lead times and uncertain bills of materials. Although some services can be based on a time standard (such as an hourly rate), the completion time of many services is difficult to predict. One reason is that a service may involve an undefined parent service. The customer describes the symptoms, from which the service provider determines the problem that needs service (that is, the end item). If the symptoms described are incomplete or inaccurate, or if the service provider is not aware of all the possible alternative solutions to the problem, then the wrong bill of labor may be derived and the wrong service performed without the desired end results. For example, if an incorrect diagnosis has been made for a patient or until a diagnosis can be correctly made, the bill of material or labor necessary to support the patient's therapy will be uncertain. In case the patient develops other complications, the BOM/BOL has to change accordingly.

One way to alleviate this problem is to split the desired service into common and optional services. The common services will include those services that are always present in the final service configuration. These can be exploded through the requirements planning process without difficulty. The optional services will vary with the customer needs and must be forecast. For example, an automobile repair shop will offer a tune-up as a service. All the basic tune-up procedures will form the common service.

The replacement of faulty parts (parts and labor) discovered during the tune-up will be an optional service because it is not possible to know beforehand what parts will need to be replaced.

Applications of MRP-II

Regardless of how unstructured a service is, planning for the service requirements enhances efficiency and accountability. Requirements planning systems are used increasingly in many service industries. The list now includes healthcare, educational, and food services.

Using POM for Windows to Solve Inventory Problems

POM for Windows inventory module can solve the ABC and economic order quantity models discussed in this chapter as well as some others that were not discussed. Exhibit 19-15 illustrates the application of this software to the business forms example that was discussed.

Exhibit 19-15   POM for Windows Solution of the Business Forms Example

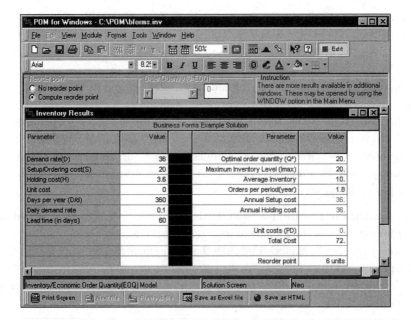

19.8 Summary

Inventory often plays a small role in services because

1. There may be no finished goods inventory.

2. Input inventory such as office supplies may be minimal.

3. Input materials may be immediately obtained from local suppliers so that lead time is short (for example, auto repair parts, food, and gasoline).

In other cases, major input inventories may be required.

Service systems use input and output inventories to meet predetermined service levels. These inventories represent a cost system that must be managed and controlled. Service inventory control systems are classified into two types: independent demand and dependent demand systems.

Two independent demand inventory control systems have been discussed: They are the fixed-period and the fixed-quantity, or continuous review, systems. Other topics addressed include ABC analysis, the EOQ model, and the perishable goods model.

Control of dependent demand inventory items is especially difficult in a service environment, which is characterized by demand variability, on-site production, intermittent processing, low-volume requirements, indefinite lead times, and uncertain bills of labor. Concepts derived from manufacturing resource planning (MRP-II) systems, used for similar situations in manufacturing, can be used to control dependent demand inventory items. Effective implementation of MRP-II logic to service industries can contribute to reduced inventory and improved customer service.

Endnote

1. Vilfredo Pareto (1848-1923), nineteenth-century Italian economist.

APPENDIX A

AREAS UNDER THE STANDARD NORMAL CURVE

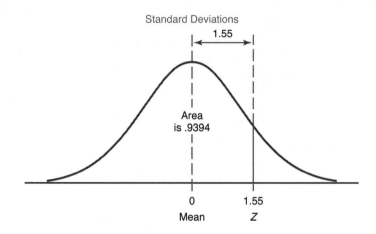

Example of finding an area that extends from minus infinity (∞) to a point to the right of the mean—To find the area under the normal curve, you must know how many standard deviations that point is to the right of the mean. Then the area under the normal curve can be read directly from the normal table. For example, the total area under the normal curve for a point that is 1.55 standard deviations to the right of the mean is 0.9394.

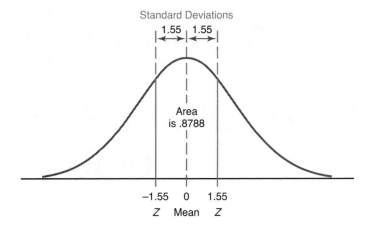

Example of finding an area that extends equal distances on both sides of the mean—For some problems, you may want to find the area under the normal curve between two tails (for example, when the problem states ± a certain number of standard deviations). Then, additional calculations are required. For example, the total area under the normal curve for a point that is 1.55 standard deviations to the right of the mean and − 1.55 standard deviations to the left of the mean is

$$1.0 - [(1.0 - .9394) \times 2] = .8788$$

See the table on the following page.

z	.00	.01	.02	.03	.04	.05	.06	.07	.08	.09
.0	.5000	.5040	.5080	.5120	.5160	.5199	.5239	.5279	.5319	.5359
.1	.5398	.5438	.5478	.5517	.5557	.5596	.5636	.5675	.5714	.5753
.2	.5793	.5832	.5871	.5910	.5948	.5987	.6026	.6064	.6103	.6141
.3	.6179	.6217	.6255	.6293	.6331	.6368	.6406	.6443	.6480	.6517
.4	.6554	.6591	.6628	.6664	.6700	.6736	.6772	.6808	.6844	.6879
.5	.6915	.6950	.6985	.7019	.7054	.7088	.7123	.7157	.7190	.7224
.6	.7257	.7291	.7324	.7357	.7389	.7422	.7454	.7486	.7517	.7549
.7	.7580	.7611	.7642	.7673	.7704	.7734	.7764	.7794	.7823	.7852
.8	.7881	.7910	.7939	.7967	.7995	.8023	.8051	.8078	.8106	.8133
.9	.8159	.8186	.8212	.8238	.8264	.8289	.8315	.8340	.8365	.8389
1.0	.8413	.8438	.8461	.8485	.8508	.8531	.8554	.8577	.8599	.8621
1.1	.8643	.8665	.8686	.8708	.8729	.8749	.8770	.8790	.8810	.8830
1.2	.8849	.8869	.8888	.8907	.8925	.8944	.8962	.8980	.8997	.9015
1.3	.9032	.9049	.9066	.9082	.9099	.9115	.9131	.9147	.9162	.9177
1.4	.9192	.9207	.9222	.9236	.9251	.9265	.9279	.9292	.9306	.9319
1.5	.9332	.9345	.9357	.9370	.9382	.9394	.9406	.9418	.9429	.9441
1.6	.9452	.9463	.9474	.9484	.9495	.9505	.9515	.9525	.9535	.9545
1.7	.9554	.9564	.9573	.9582	.9591	.9599	.9608	.9616	.9625	.9633
1.8	.9641	.9649	.9656	.9664	.9671	.9678	.9686	.9693	.9699	.9706
1.9	.9713	.9719	.9726	.9732	.9738	.9744	.9750	.9756	.9761	.9767
2.0	.9772	.9778	.9783	.9788	.9793	.9798	.9803	.9808	.9812	.9817
2.1	.9821	.9826	.9830	.9834	.9838	.9842	9846	.9850	.9854	.9857
2.2	.9861	.9864	.9868	.9871	.9875	.9878	.9881	.9884	.9887	.9890
2.3	.9893	.9896	.9898	.9901	.9904	.9906	.9909	.9911	.9913	.9916
2.4	.9918	.9920	.9922	.9925	.9927	.9929	.9931	.9932	.9934	.9936
2.5	.9938	.9940	.9941	.9943	.9945	.9946	.9948	.9949	.9951	.9952
2.6	.9953	.9955	.9956	.9957	.9959	.9960	.9961	.9962	.9963	.9964
2.7	.9965	.9966	.9967	.9968	.9969	.9970	.9971	.9972	.9973	.9974
2.8	.9974	.9975	.9976	.9977	.9977	.9978	.9979	.9979	.9980	.9981
2.9	.9981	.9982	.9982	.9983	.9984	.9984	.9985	.9985	.9986	.9986
3.0	.9987	.9987	.9987	.9988	.9988	.9989	.9989	.9989	.9990	.9990
3.1	.9990	.9991	.9991	.9991	.9992	.9992	.9992	.9992	.9993	.9993
3.2	.9993	.9993	.9994	.9994	.9994	.9994	.9994	.9995	.9995	.9995
3.3	.9995	.9995	.9995	.9996	.9996	.9996	.9996	.9996	.9996	.9997
3.4	.9997	.9997	.9997	.9997	.9997	.9997	.9997	.9997	.9997	.9998

Source: Adapted from John Neter, William Wasserman, and G. A. Whitmore, *Applied Statistics*, 3rd ed.
Copyright © 1988 by Allyn and Bacon.

Appendix A Areas Under the Standard Normal Curve   457

INDEX

funding
  private nonprofit organizations, 334
  public nonprofit organizations, 329
future trends
  customers
    age distribution, 51-52
    education, 52
    household, 52
    income, 52
    occupation, 52
  technology and, 124-125

G

Gantt charts, 389
gaps model of service quality, 252-254
Garvin, David, 249
GDP (gross domestic product) by industry, 6-7
General Electric, 141
generating ideas, 150
global channels, 61
global customers, 61
global economies of scale, 61
global enterprises, 60
globalization of services
  alliances, 65
  classification of firms from international
    perspective, 60
  foreign direct investments, 65
  global channels, 61
  global economies of scale, 61
  global enterprises, 60
  global environment for service businesses,
    63-64
  growth of, 55-56
  history of, 55
  influence on design of new services, 132
  international trade, 56-57, 64
    increased demand for services, 57-58
    increased trade of goods, 58-59
    U.S. trade balance, 8-9

reasons for, 59-60
    advances in technology, 62
    common customer needs, 60-61
    favorable logistics, 62
    global channels, 61
    global customers, 61
    global economies of scale, 61
    government policies and regulations, 62
    transferable competitive advance, 62
  trends, 66-67
goal programming. See GP
goals
  GP (goal programming)
    Dixon Furniture Store case study, 428-432
    overview, 409-410, 427-428
  of private nonprofit organizations, 336
  of public nonprofit organizations, 329
goods
  compared to services, 3-4
  definition of, 3
  design, 134-135
  international trade, increase in, 58-59
  public goods, 326
government regulation, 62, 81, 295
GP (goal programming)
  Dixon Furniture Store case study, 428-432
  overview, 409-410, 427-428
GPSS, 243
graphical representation of constraints,
  411-413
gravity model of site selection, 192-194
"greatest happiness" principle, 103
gross domestic product (GDP) by industry, 6-7
group versus solo waits, 224
growth
  of international trade, 55-56
  of services, 9, 57
    industrial society, 10
    postindustrial society, 11-13
    preindustrial society, 10
guarantees, 264-266
guidelines for ethical business behavior,
  104-105

linear regression analysis, 358

Location module (POM for Windows), 210-211

location selection
  business profiles, 182
  center of gravity method, 188-190
  common mistakes, 185-186
  definition of, 181
  dominant location factors, 183-184
  explained, 182
  factor weighting, 187-188
  general criteria, 184-185
  multilocations, 186-187
  POM for Windows, 210-211
  warehouse multisite locations and sizes, 190-191

location set-covering problem, 195

locational transformation, 164

logistics, 62, 167-168

long-term perspectives, 256

love needs, 41

lower bound values, 419

loyalty, 147

LP (linear programming)
  assignment problems, 422-423
  diet (feed mix) problem, 419-420
  Dixon Furniture Store case study, 410-411
  graphical representation of constraints, 411-413
  iso-profit line solution method, 414-416
  labor planning problems, 424-425
  media selection, 426-427
  overview, 409-410
  sensitivity analysis, 416-419
  shadow prices, 416-418
  shipping problem, 421-422
  simplex algorithm, 416

lumpiness, 437

M

MAD (mean absolute deviation), 351

major innovations, 130

Malcolm Baldrige National Quality Award (MBNQA), 40, 260-261

Malone, John C., 124

management
  demand management, 222
  management contracting, 64
  private nonprofit organizations, 334
  supply and demand. *See* supply and demand
  supply chain management, 167
    challenges, 168-170
    logistics, 167-168

management information systems (MIS), 121

Managing in the Service Economy (Heskett), 85

manufacturing, service sector contributions to, 9

manufacturing-based quality definitions, 249

manufacturing supply chains
  explained, 165-166
  management
    challenges, 168-170
    logistics, 167-168

MAPE (mean absolute percent error), 352

market failure, 327

marketing activities, influence on consumer behavior, 44

marketing program design and testing, 155

marketing sources, 48

marketing systems, 24

Marle, David J. De, 73

Marriott International Inc., 25, 141

Marriott, J. W. "Bill," 25, 146

Marshall, Alfred, 72

Maslow, Abraham, 41

master production schedule (MPS), 448

master service schedule (MSS), 449

matching supply and demand. *See* supply and demand

public sector organizations
    management challenges, 328-330
    purpose, 326-328
  significance, 325-326
  tax exemption, 324-325
normal curve, finding area under, 455-457
North Slope Hospital, 202-204
not-for-profit organizations. *See*
  nonprofit organizations
number of business starts, 8

O

objective function, 410
objectives, 79
occupations of consumers, 52
occupied versus unoccupied wait time, 223
office automation, 116
office layout
  design checklist, 206-207
  workstations, 207
One World, 113
one-sided time windows, 380
operating strategy, 85
operational-level systems, 120
operations planning, demand forecast as basis
  for, 342
operations systems, 24
OPQRST key, 198
optimistic time estimate, 395
order-taking, 143
organization
  matrix organization, 389
  project organization, 388
output materials, 436
overbooking, 220
ownership
  private nonprofit organizations, 334
  of services, 21

P

p charts, 283-285
Pareto diagrams, 274-275
Pareto principle, 438
Pareto, Vilfredo, 453
part-time employees, 227
partial employment, 32
partial productivity, 292
partial tour, 371
passengers. *See* consumers
patients. *See* consumers
pattern of demand, studying, 219
PDSA (plan-do-study-act) cycle, 269-270
perceived quality, 74, 250
perceived risks, 49
perception, influence on consumer
  behavior, 45
performance, 250
  defining, 302-303
  performance measurement of queues, 234
perishability, 22, 437
perishable goods model, 444-445
personal services
  asymptotically stagnant personal
    services, 300
  progressive personal services, 300
  stagnant personal services, 299
personal sources, 48
personality, influence on consumer
  behavior, 45
PERT (program evaluation and
  review technique)
  activities, 393-394
  activity time estimates, 395-396
  advantages, 405
  critical path analysis, 396-400
  dummy activities/events, 394-395
  events, 393-394
  framework, 391-392
  limitations, 406

X-Y-Z